HRADER
F.B.

REISE
F.B.

BORZA
F.B.

V. DEFINE
H.B.

PRICE
Q.B.

J. DEFINE
H.B.

POTTS
E

QUIGLEY
(Sub-End)

LE ROY
(Sub-H.B)

HALKO
(Sub-G)

MOLLET
(Student-Mgr)

DAVID STEWA
(COACH)

ALL THE WAY TO #1

The Story of the Greatest High School Football
National Championship Teams of the 20th Century

Timothy L. Hudak

with John R. Pflug Jr.

DEDICATION BY TIMOTHY L. HUDAK

Timothy L. Hudak

To my dear wife and best friend, Patti, who has encouraged me in all of my writing projects and has racked up more miles going to high school football games in more places than she ever dreamed possible and never once complained as long as we found every used bookstore in the area.

DEDICATION BY JOHN R. PFLUG JR

J. Robert Pflug

Gene Boerner and John R. Pflug Jr.

To my dad, J. Robert Pflug, captain of the 1923 Massilion Tigers and coach at Bradford (Pa.) High School from 1932-1950. After his first season as Bradford's coach, he engineered a streak where his teams won 31 games, lost 2, then won the next 25. Bradford's record during his career there was W-122, L-26, T-5, .814. In his elder years, he restored the family farm known as "Headquarters" in Browns Cove, Albemarle County, VA, in the Charlottesville area.

And to my friend, Gene Boerner, *"The Tigers Greatest Booster"* and the keeper of all the flames he lit.

Publishing Information
Library of Congress Control Number: 2014918308
ISBN: 978-0-9652659-7-3

Published by Pflug, LLC.
5057 Headquarters Farm Lane
Crozet, VA 22932

Book Design by Convoy
weareconvoy.com

Printed by Versa Press, Inc.
1465 Spring Bay Road
East Peoria, IL 61611

ALSO BY TIMOTHY L. HUDAK

The Charity Game,
The Story of Cleveland's
Thanksgiving Day High School
Football Classic

Wildcats!
The History of St. Ignatius
High School Football, Vol. I, To 1945

Wildcats!
The History of St. Ignatius
High School Football, Vol. II, 1946-1996

Wildcats!
The History of St. Ignatius
High School Football, Vol. III, 1997-2008

When the Lions Roared,
The Story of Cathedral Latin
School Football

Storming the Erie Shores,
The Story of Villa Angela-St. Joseph Athletics

The Game of the Year,
The Complete History of the Intense Rivalry that is
St. Ignatius-St. Edward Rivalry

*These books are available now at **www.SportsHeritagePublications.net***

Acknowledgements

No book is ever the result of the efforts of just one person, or in this case, two people. A book whose subject "stars" covered the length and breadth of the country required us to seek assistance from people at high schools and libraries in almost a dozen states and cities. When the opportunity presented itself, we even visited a few of these places. In every instance we were met with enthusiastic support from those from whom we were seeking assistance. They often went above and beyond in their efforts to help us to tell this story. It is here that we would like to take a moment, in no particular order of importance, to express our thanks.

Typical of the help we received was that provided by the staff at the Lowndes County Historical Society and Museum in Valdosta, Georgia. When first contacted by phone, Executive Director Donald Davis enthusiastically agreed to generously provide whatever materials he might have. About a year later, author Tim Hudak and his wife Patti Graziano traveled to Valdosta and visited the Historical Society in person. Executive Director Davis and Harry Evans, in the Special Collections and Research departments, were "southern hospitality" personified as they opened the Museum's vast collection to us. Without them the chapters about the Valdosta Wildcats would not be nearly as complete.

The same could be said about the other people who so generously gave of both their time and various collections to help with this project, and that is who we thank here now. On the West Coast, David Dilgard and Kathy Dinwiddie of the Everett (Wash.) Public Library were most helpful, as was local Everett historian Larry O'Donnell. Elaine Seed, librarian at De La Salle High School in Concord, Calif., provided material from that school and Librarian Judi Weaver at Corvallis (Ore.) High School also supplied material about the team representing her school.

Heading east across the country, the assistance of Librarian Renate Bernstein of Washington High School in Cedar Rapids, Iowa, was generously given, as was that of Jordan Grams, the Librarian at Reagan High School in Austin, Texas. The assistance of Robert Pruter, among his other talents a Chicago area high school football historian, was invaluable in telling that part of our story.

In Toledo, Ohio, the staff at the Toledo Public Library, especially Librarian Irene Martin, and Scott High School Librarians Elaine Luster and Anne Matney were most generous in providing assistance to us, as was Librarian Ellen Barnhizer at Waite High School. In Massillon, Ohio, the late Gene Boerner, as well as Gary Vogt and Ron Prunty, all of the Massillon Tigers Football Booster Club, went out of their way to make their extensive archival collection available to us whenever we needed to stop by, as did Bill Dorman at the Paul Brown Museum. At Archbishop Moeller High School in Cincinnati the help of Gavin Gray and Dick Beerman was most appreciated.

In Pennsylvania, Ken Frew, Research Librarian at the Historical Society of Dauphin County in Harrisburg (Harrisburg Tech) and Heather Henry, librarian at Berwick High School, provided great assistance for the story about the championship schools from their respective area. As we reach the East Coast, Patricia Ells, library coordinator at the Everett High School Library and Mark Parisi, Reference Librarian at the Parlin Memorial Library in Everett, Mass., provided invaluable assistance. In Miami, Librarian Angel Hernandez at Miami High School provided some much needed assistance about the Stingarees and Reference Librarian John Shipley in the Florida Room of the Miami-Dade County Library was most helpful the day we stopped by his facility to do research. At Coral Gables High School all the people we met in our two visits to the school were most helpful, especially Librarian Ana Zuniga and her student helpers from the yearbook staff, as well as Dan Finora, a transplanted Ohioan in the school's athletic department who has been a fixture at Coral Gables High School for more than 50 years.

In addition to these fine people from the variously mentioned schools and libraries there are several others whose help and assistance has proven to be uniquely invaluable. Tex Noel of the Intercollegiate Football Research Association provided some timely and unique tidbits of information about the high school game. Jay Hudak of North Richland Hills, Texas, did some essential newspaper microfilm work to acquire material about the Reagan Raiders, as did Bob McKenney of Cincinnati who similarly acquired much needed information about Archbishop Moeller High School. Peter Toomey's editing has only made this a clearer and more interesting book for the reader. The work of Matt Thomas in taking the raw material of the photos and other pictures assembled for this project and turning them into something truly pleasing to the eye cannot be under estimated—as the reader will soon find out.

As is true with any book of this nature, the authors alone are responsible for any conclusions drawn, charts/lists made, etc. And as such, they are solely responsible for any errors contained herein.

Coral Gables High School halfback Dick Whittington takes off around the right side against Southwest High on Nov. 23, 1967. (Coral Gables High School Yearbook)

TABLE OF CONTENTS

Preface

No team has ever dominated high school football on the national level for anything approaching 100 years—not even close. However, there is a small handful of schools that have had more of an impact on the game at the high school level than the other 15,000+ schools that have fielded football teams during the 20th century. This is the story of those select teams.

Before delving into our story, however, we should look at the parameters of this book. First of all, why the 20th century? Purely an arbitrary time frame, but it makes sense. For one thing, it represents a classic timeline: 100 years with a definite beginning, 1900, and a definite ending, 1999. It also corresponds to the years that saw high school football, following the example of the college game, evolve into a mature, modern sport. The period before 1900 saw the game of football still in its infancy with a minimum number of both high schools and colleges participating, although more schools were taking up the sport yearly. There were still some growing pains to be endured during the first decade of the 20th century, but with the rules changes that went into effect by 1912 the game of football was basically set as the one we now see every weekend during the fall.

The period after 1999 belongs to a new century with a whole new set of champions—so far. Surprisingly enough, with one significant exception, none of the national champions named since the year 1999 were ever named national champion before that year.

Secondly, let us define what we mean by the term "team". In one context "team" can refer to something like the "West High School *team* of 1950", i.e., the football aggregation representing a school for a single season. There will be some instances in this book when "team" is used in that manner.

However, for the overwhelming majority of this book, "team" will be used in a manner more closely resembling the term "program", as in "the West High School football team from 1947 to 1954". In this context "team" refers to how the aggregation representing a school performed over a number of years and thus established its legitimacy as one of the greatest high school football national champions of the 20th century.

Finally, there are years when two and even three schools have been named national champion, based on the choices of more than one national championship selector. However, since it is our purpose to highlight a particular team during its time of national success, co-champions may not always be mentioned each time they occur. A complete list of all national champions for the years 1900-1999 will be found in Appendix II.

Introduction

The game of American football first began at the college level in 1869 when Rutgers defeated Princeton, six goals to four, and the game has been with us ever since. The high schoolers in New England took to the game shortly thereafter and, like the college game, it spread to high schools around the country.

Almost from the beginning, those playing football wanted to know who was the best. For example, back in October of 1890 the very first high school football game ever played in Cleveland, Ohio, was for "the championship". The determination of a city champion was relatively easy even in those earliest days. A state champion was a little more difficult to select. With no polls or even state high school athletic associations to make a determination, it often came down to one team or school challenging another, or all of the other teams, to a game for the state championship. Often, too, the sportswriters at big city newspapers would make a selection and declare a team the state champion based on its accomplishments throughout the season. Over the succeeding years these selected champions have become accepted as the true or actual champion.

If picking a state champion was difficult, how then could a national champion be chosen? Again, there were no polls in those earliest days and, like today, no playoff system. However, there were two means by which national high school football champions were selected.

The first was, believe it or not, via a playoff game, or more correctly an arranged challenge game between two schools from different parts of the country, similar to the challenge "system" often used to determine state champions in those earliest days.

Newspapers in the respective cities, and in the nation's biggest cities if the game so warranted the attention, were often "helpful" in publicizing that a particular intersectional game was being played for the national championship. Sports historian Robert Pruter explains the "system" thusly:

"At an early point in the history of high school intersectional football the concept of the 'mythical' championship game came into being. The participating teams never engaged in any sort of playoffs nor were they chosen from an independently produced regional or sectional ranking. Usually these games were arranged by the participating schools within a couple of weeks of the game date. The only criteria for these so-called intersectional title games were that both schools were impressively unbeaten in their local area (although there were exceptions to this), and that there were promoters at two such schools who were quickly willing to make the necessary arrangements, travel and financial considerations."

▲ A scene from the Dec. 6, 1902 national championship game between Hyde Park (in solid jerseys to the right) and Brooklyn Polytechnic Prep. The ice covered field is evident from the player in the middle of the photo who has slipped and fallen. (Robert Pruter Collection)

There have been as many as 30 of these national championship games, but none since 1939. On December 30, 1939, Pine Bluff (Ark.) High School played Baton Rouge High School and won 26-0. That championship game will probably be the last national championship high school football game ever to be played. The reason for this is that under current conditions virtually all states prohibit their high schools from playing any games after their respective state playoffs have been concluded. Recent attempts to arrange such national championship games have been emphatically rejected by the state associations involved.

The second method of determining a national high school football champion is one with which we are more familiar—polls and rankings. Back in 1927 an enterprising and enthusiastic high school coach and official from Minnesota by the name of Art Johlfs developed the first national high school football poll system under the name of the National Sports News Service. After some further research Johlfs retroactively took the national championship list back to 1910. The NSNS pretty much had the field to itself until 1982 when the new national newspaper, *USA Today*, started issuing its own national high school football rankings. Since then there have probably been upwards of two dozen organizations putting out various human and computer generated polls and rankings (at the college level there have been two to three times that many over the years).

Is one system any better than another, it depends on who you ask. If Poll A picks your school to be #1, then that poll is likely the most accurate in your eyes. And more than likely the people putting out Poll A feel that theirs is superior to Polls B, C and D. The reality is that no one poll or ranking system is any better or more accurate than any other. These polls seldom ever agree on the No.1 team in the country; if they did there would not be years with as many as four schools named the national champion.

So what purpose do the national polls and rankings serve? As high school sportswriters like Doug Huff and Mark Tennis so aptly state it, "It's simple: they add public interest to the sport and serve as a barometer for team performance much like all-star games for individuals. Debates about who's No. 1 nationally will never be settled, but the wide-ranging recognition for the athletes and coaches involved, no matter where their teams are placed in the rankings, are well-deserved."

The earliest recognized national championship high school football game, and thus the naming of the first national champion, took place between Madison

High School of Madison, Wisconsin, and North Tonawanda High School of North Tonawanda, New York, in 1897.

Like most schools at this time, Madison High School was relatively new to football, but the school's football team had gotten off to a flying start. The first team had been formed in 1893, and through the 1897 season they had put up a splendid record of 28-1-0 against high school opponents from Wisconsin, Minnesota and Illinois. In 1897 the team was 7-0-0 and had yet to give up a point. The Madison people issued a challenge to all comers to play for the U.S. championship. The team from North Tonawanda High School, the recognized champions of the northeast, accepted the challenge and the game was played that Christmas Day in Detroit, with the Madison team coming away with a 14-0 victory.

For the next several years the center of high school football, at least as far as a national champion might be concerned, moved a little bit south to Illinois. Several Illinois high schools would make a claim to the national championship during those years, but none of these has ever been confirmed. Then in 1902 the powerful Hyde Park team of Chicago outscored four high school opponents by 231-0. Like Madison High School a few years before, Hyde Park wanted to see how it stood up against an eastern team. This West vs. East mentality was actually a carry over from the college game. The eastern schools played a slower, more mass momentum type of game, while the western schools tended to play a faster, more wide open brand of football which featured a lot of ball movement. Remember, this is still the pre-forward pass era. Of course, each camp felt that its brand of football was superior. Since there was not yet a lot of intersectional play at the college level, a game like this at the high school level, if arranged, would attract a lot of attention.

Hyde Park was able to secure a game with Brooklyn Polytechnic Prep of New York City on December 6, 1902, at the University of Chicago's Marshall Field. As an indication of how important the westerners felt this game to be, none other than University of Chicago head coach Amos Alonzo Stagg tutored the Hyde Park boys for the big game. (Like most high schools at that time Hyde Park did not have a formal football coach.) And University of Michigan coach Fielding Yost even dropped in with some pointers a few days before the game.

To say the game was one-sided would be a major understatement. At the half Hyde Park held a 40-0 advantage on the way to a 105-0 victory. And if there was any doubt as to what this game meant in the greater scheme of football,

▾ *The 1902 Hyde Park national championship team. Future all time great at the U. of Chicago, Hall of Famer QB Walter Eckersall, is holding the football in the center of the photo. (Robert Pruter Collection)*

one local Chicago paper ran the following headline after the game, "West Defeats the East by 105-0."

It would be more of the same the following season. This time it was another Chicago area team, Cook County champion North Division High School, which received an invitation to play Boys' High of Brooklyn, New York. The game was set for November 28, 1903, at Washington Park in Brooklyn. Newspapers in both parts of the country saw this as another West vs. East battle for the national high school championship. Like the previous season, this game was another blowout for the Chicagoans who came away with a 75-0 victory.

In 1904 the championship picture left Chicago for a short time, but it would stay in the Midwest. That season the championship would be decided in a game between Detroit Central High School and Toledo (Oh.) Central High School. Toledo took the lead on a touchdown, 5-0 (the worth of a touchdown back then), but failed to kick the goal after touchdown. The Detroiters later recovered a Toledo fumble and returned it 55 yards for a touchdown, adding the goal to take a 6-5 lead, which proved to be the final score.

There is no known national champion for the 1905 season. In 1906 Chicago was back in the championship picture. That season North Division High School won the Cook County title. This time a West Coast team came calling and a game for the scholastic football championship was arranged with Seattle High School, to be played in Seattle, Washington, on January 1, 1907. It took two and a half days

▼ *1903 game action between a couple of Chicago area teams, soon to be national champion North Division High and future titlist Englewood High School, played at the U. of Chicago's Marshall Field. (Robert Pruter Collection)*

▲ *The 1903 national championship team from Chicago's North Division High School. (Robert Pruter Collection)*

for the North Division boys to reach the Emerald City by train, arriving there on December 28.

A large crowd of more than 6,000 fans packed Seattle's Madison Park for the game, played in ankle-deep mud as the result of snowmelt that left the playing field looking more like a small lake than a gridiron. Both teams scored touchdowns in the first half, which ended in a 5-5 tie. Late in the game Seattle recovered a North Division fumble at the 40-yard line. The Seattle team marched steadily toward the end zone in the mud and muck and, with just 40 seconds left in the game, Seattle's Jay Smith scored a touchdown. Seattle High's 11-5 victory gave it the national championship.

There is no recognized national champion for 1907. In 1908 Chicago's Englewood High School won the Cook County championship with a record of 8-1-1. The team then accepted the challenge of Butte High School in Butte, Montana, to play for the national championship. Butte had not lost a game during the previous two seasons.

The 15 member Englewood team left Chicago by train on Monday night, December 14, 1908, arriving in Butte on the 17th. Like the North Division High School team had done on its trip to Seattle in 1906, the Chicago *Tribune* reported that the Englewood team "will take its own water in five gallon bottles and no member of the squad will be allowed to risk his condition by drinking water which is not of the pure Lake Michigan variety." This was a practice no doubt suggested by University of Chicago head coach Amos Alonzo Stagg, who also took along water for his team on its extended trips.

As the *Tribune* noted, the game, played on Sunday, December 19, was "one of the most interesting and sensational games ever played in the far west." In the first quarter, Butte took a 4-0 lead on a 30-yard field goal (which at this time was worth four points). But before the half had expired, Englewood scored a touchdown and added the extra point for a 6-4 lead. The purple and white Englewood team dominated play in the second half. The boys used plays provided by Coach Stagg, including a triple pass that was "considered a piece of art." A lone Englewood touchdown provided the only points of the second half to give the "easterners" an 11-4 victory and the national title.

Following this game, the Englewood team continued its western excursion by boarding a train for Denver and a game with Longmont High School of that

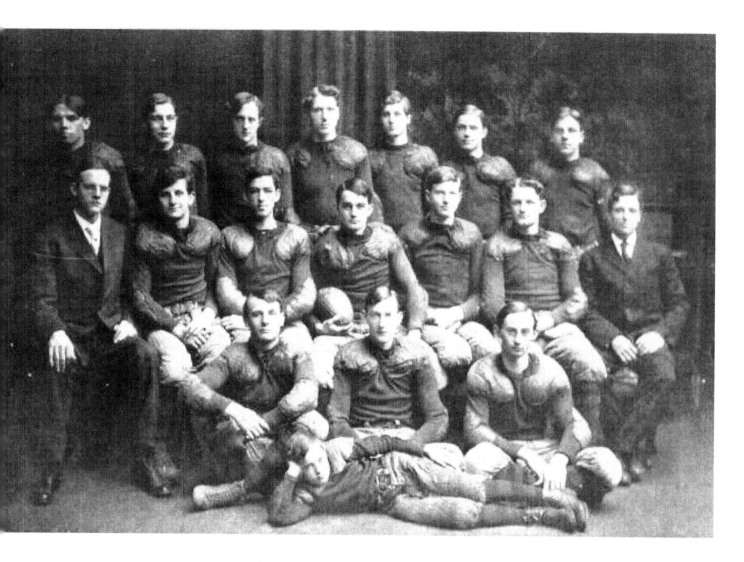

▲ *A picture of the 1906*
national champion team from
Seattle High School, taken
from the school's yearbook.

city. That game, played on Christmas Day, suffered under terrible conditions and resulted in what was described by the Chicago *Tribune* as "a miserable excuse for a football game." After winning what is considered the national championship game against Butte High School, the Englewood lads lost to Longmont, 13-0. However, this game is looked upon as something akin to an exhibition game since Longmont High School was not yet a member of the State Interscholastic League of Colorado.

Englewood High School would come back with an even better team in 1909. The purple and white rolled through its Cook County opponents, winning all eleven games. Nine of those victories came by shutout as Englewood outscored its opponents by a margin of 163 to 12. The team also placed four boys on the All-City first and second squads.

Following the regular season, the Englewood team was planning another western trip that would have included games with schools in Butte, Mont., Seattle, Wash., and Lincoln, Neb., over the Christmas holiday. However, due to opposition by members of the Englewood and Seattle faculties, the trip was cancelled.

Be that as it may, Englewood's 1909 aggregation was far superior to its 1908 national championship squad, which is sufficient for the purple and white to retain the national championship for a second consecutive season in 1909.

Thus ends the first decade of the 20th century as far as high school football national champions are concerned. There was no one dominant team, but one city that was squarely in the middle of most of the action. As the second decade gets underway that city would provide the first truly superior team, led by the first great high school football coach.

▾ A picture of the starting line-up of the 1908 national champion team from Englewood High School. (Chicago Sunday Tribune)

## CHAPTER 1

THE FIRST GREAT TEAM

Oak Park High School
Oak Park, Illinois

Robert Carl Zuppke was born in Berlin, Germany, on July 2, 1879; his father moved the family to Milwaukee, Wisconsin, two years later. Zuppke attended Milwaukee's West Division High School where he played on the football team in 1895. That season the school's principal banned the game for being too rough, which was just as well for Zuppke since he had broken his collarbone in a 69-0 defeat against Fond du Lac High School.

In September of 1903, Zuppke entered the University of Wisconsin as a junior after teaching in grade school for a couple of years to earn his tuition money. Zuppke loved football and went out for the Badgers team, but he never played on the Wisconsin varsity because he was too small. He did, however, play on the "scrub" team as well as the varsity basketball squad. While at Wisconsin, Zuppke took in many of the Badgers' football games and had an opportunity to see at work some of the great coaches of the day and of all time, men like Amos Alonzo Stagg of Chicago, Fielding "Hurry Up" Yost of Michigan, and Dr. Henry Williams of Minnesota. He even did a little coaching at this time, instructing the team from Mount Horeb High School two or three times a week at the request of a fraternity friend.

Always a very good artist, Zuppke left Milwaukee in 1905 to pursue a career as a commercial artist in New York City. He remained in the Big Apple for a year, returning to the Midwest in 1906 to take a job as a furniture illustrator for a company in Grand Rapids, Michigan. Bob's love of athletics would cost him his job in Grand Rapids when he and a few other employees turned the company's shop into a gymnasium where they would hold late afternoon boxing matches. The owner came by one day, saw what was going on, and fired everyone except the photo retoucher, who was the hardest to replace. At this time the folks at the University of Wisconsin told Zuppke about an opening for a football coach and gymnasium director at the Muskegon High and Hackley Manual Training School. Zuppke went for the interview, getting the job and a $1,000 yearly salary. The legendary Harold "Red" Grange played for Bob Zuppke at the University of Illinois and notes in his biography of the great coach, "In those early days, 1906, Zuppke began to develop the open type of game for which he was later to become famous and which was a major factor in the evolution of football from massed movement to the modern, exciting style of mixed aerial and running assault."

▲ *Robert "Bob" Zuppke, Oak Park's head coach from 1910-1912. (Oak Park High School Yearbook)*

Note: *The official and complete name of the high school in Oak Park is "Oak Park and River Forest Township High School", but we will refer as it is more commonly known, Oak Park High School. Also, the* Chicago Tribune *and the other Chicago newspapers often referred to Oak Park as "the suburbanites" because the school was, strictly speaking, not within the Chicago city limits, but slightly to the west.*

When the forward pass became legal in January of 1906, it only added to Zuppke's growing arsenal of plays, which also included laterals, split bucks, spinner plays, reverses, and fake reverses. In the earliest days of the forward pass, many coaches used it only as a threat or as a desperation play to gain big yardage late in a game. However, to again quote from "Red" Grange's book, "Zup's Muskegon and Oak Park teams used the pass for strictly business purposes, to gain ground." In other words, Bob Zuppke, even as a high school football coach, was one of the first to employ the forward pass as a regular part of his offensive attack.

Bob Zuppke coached football at Muskegon High from 1906 thru 1909. During those seasons his team won 29 games, lost only four, and tied two. Zuppke's fame spread with his success and soon other schools were vying for his services. In early 1910 he announced that he was taking the position of athletic director at a school in Cleveland. However, as the 1909-10 school year was wrapping up, a fellow teacher at Muskegon, Joe Tallman, contacted his brother, a teacher at Oak Park High School just outside of Chicago and told him about Zuppke. The Oak Park principal, John Hanna, then visited Muskegon to see Zuppke and wasted no time in hiring him. In his book, "Red" Grange notes that "to earn his $2,000 (salary), he taught five history and three gymnasium classes; coached and managed the football, basketball, baseball, swimming, and track teams; managed the tennis team; and offered to help Mrs. Zuppke with the dishes but was never allowed to do so."

Oak Park's football fortunes had not been very good in the years before Zuppke reported to the school. In 1909, the team had finished dead last in its division of the Cook County football league. However, Zuppke's new plays and innovations quickly changed all of that. His open style of play added a dimension of speed previously unknown at Oak Park, or at other area schools as well. He extensively used the forward pass—a play still coming into its own, though quite frankly spurned by many football enthusiasts and "experts", especially in the East where they still overwhelmingly favored the mass momentum plays of the recent past.

Unlike today where a football team at a good sized high school might have 50 to 70 and possibly as many as 100 boys turn out for the first practice, Zuppke had 14 boys show up that first day, which was probably close to average for a team at that time. After several weeks of intense practice, it was time to put Coach Zuppke's program to the test.

The season opened with the traditional first game against a team of Oak Park alumni. Zuppke's boys were obviously still breaking in their coach's system, but despite that they managed to defeat the older boys by a score of 5 to 0. In the team's first game against a regular opponent, the boys suffered a 6-2 defeat at the hands of the Maywood Young Men's Club. Before starting Cook County play they took on a team from Wisconsin, St. John's Academy of Delafield. Showing the form that they would only continue to perfect, the Oak Park boys came away with a convincing 25-0 victory.

Oak Park's first game with a county rival took place on Saturday, October 15, against North Division High School. Zuppke emptied just about his whole bag of tricks as the team scored 10 touchdowns, added seven extra points (all kicked by future U. of Illinois star and College Football Hall of Famer Bart Macomber) and even added a safety in humbling North Division by a score of 59-0. In describing how Oak Park had attained such a one-sided victory, the *Chicago Tribune* stated that "forward passes, trick formations, and almost everything known to the new game were tried with success."

Oak Park took on Morgan Park the following Saturday. It was a tight game throughout and with less than a minute to play Oak Park was clinging to a 6-3 lead. "Red" Grange relates what happened next, "Near the close of the contest, the opponents took a time out and the Oak Parkers, believing that the game was over, left the field. Morgan Park quickly lined up and scored a touchdown, which the officials had to allow."

A huge Oak Park miscue had allowed Morgan Park to win the game, 9-6. It would prove to be the last game that Oak Park would lose while Bob Zuppke was the team's head coach.

Oak Park won its next three games by a combined score of 74-0, including a 21-0 victory over the Maywood Young Men's Club, avenging the team's earlier 6-2 defeat at their hands. On Saturday, November 19, Oak Park battled Hyde Park High School for the Cook County championship. Oak Park managed to score the only points of the first half to take a 6-0 lead at the intermission. Playing its usual strong defensive game and adding single tallies in each of the last two quarters, Oak Park came away with a 22-0 victory and the Cook County championship.

Describing the team's play in that game, the *Chicago Tribune* noted that "Oak Park won by superior speed. The team displayed a brilliant attack varied by frequent use of the forward pass, double passes, a couple of triple passes and [onside] kicks."

On Saturday, November 26, Oak Park played neighboring Austin High in what was their traditional annual game, with Oak Park handing Austin its worst defeat of the season, a 45-0 thrashing. While this ended football in the Chicago area, Zuppke's Oak Park team still had a couple of games to deal with. On December 1, it was announced that the team would be traveling to the Pacific Northwest for a game in Seattle, Washington, on December 26 and another in Portland, Oregon, on the 31st. The 15- member team, along with Coach Zuppke, a student manager, and a business manager left Chicago by train on Tuesday, December 20, arriving in Seattle on December 23.

Since the schools in Seattle had been prohibited at this time from playing out-of-state schools, Oak Park would actually be playing the team from nearby Wenatchee High School. After taking a 9 to 0 lead at the half, the Chicagoans would add two more touchdowns and two PATs in the third quarter to go up 22-0. That is when things got really interesting.

During the timeout between the third and fourth quarters, as the *Chicago Tribune* reported, "The Wenatchee boosters opened up half a carload of their prize apples. The crowd in its eagerness to get the [free] fruit surged on the field, and it was some time before the gridiron was cleared. Once cleared for action, the Oak Park boys formed to complete their slaughter. Before they reached the goal line, however, the crowd again burst into the field in quest of choice apples and began rioting among themselves, the police unable to control the situation. ... The rioting had become so general and beyond the power of the police that ... [the referee] with the common consent of both sides called the game eight minutes before the end of the last quarter.... Although the Seattle people tried to stop the fighting in the crowd, it was impossible, and the only way out was to call the game."

Thus ended Oak Park's first contest on the West Coast, a 22-0 victory with a most unusual conclusion.

Two days later, Coach Zuppke and his team boarded the train and headed to Portland, Oregon, for their next game, billed by the *Portland Record-Herald* as being for "the interscholastic football championship of the United States." The Oak Park boys would be playing the team from Portland's Washington High School, the undefeated city and state champions, on New Year's Eve.

More than 4,000 fans turned out for the game on a day in which the weather was ideal. Unfortunately, especially for the Oak Park team, game day had been preceded by several days of rain that turned the field muddy, putting the normally fast paced Oak Park offense at something of a disadvantage. The muddy and wet gridiron also made the ball slick and hard to handle for both teams.

The game was scoreless through the first two quarters. Washington High finally dented the scoreboard with a 30-yard field goal in the third quarter. Later in the same quarter, Washington High fumbled the ball at its own 30-yard line, with the Oak Park team coming up with the loose pigskin. As the *Tribune* reported, "... on the next play Oak Park scored a touchdown through the perfect execution of a triple pass from Macomber to Armstrong to Russell. Russell made a great run, shook off three tacklers, and finally planted the ball behind the posts. Macomber kicked the goal."

Those would be the final points of the game as Oak Park came away with a very hard fought 6-3 victory, a victory that gave the team its first national championship.

▸ *Though a little grainy after more than 100 years, this is the team picture of the 1910 Oak Park national championship team as it appeared in the 1910 edition of* Spalding's Official Football Guide.

OAK PARK AND RIVER FOREST TOWNSHIP HIGH SCHOOL TEAM

EDWIN KONOLD (1)
(Captain) Right Tackle

RONALD FAIRFIELD (2)
Left Guard

ROBERT C. ZUPPKE (3)
Coach

ROSCOE COTTER (4)
Left Tackle

PAUL TRIER (5)   PAUL RUSSELL (6)
Left End   Right Half-back

FRED RICE (7)
Full-back

LENNOX ARMSTRONG (8)
Right End

FRANK MEAD (9)   RALPH SHILEY (10)
Guard (Sub.)   Left Half-back

JAS. WANZER (11)   OTIS RANDALL (12)
Center   End (Sub.)

BARTLETT MACOMBER (13)
Right Guard

K. M. PATTERSON (14)
Manager of Western Trip

MILTON GHEE (15)
Quarter-back

FARRINGTON TIMME (16)
Tackle (Sub.)

BARTLETT HACKLEY
Manager

RAYMOND BERRY
Half-back (Sub.)

Oak Park's 1911 passing tandem of Barton Macomber (above) and "Eckie" Russell (following page). (Inter Ocean newspaper)

The train ride back to Chicago was a real adventure with the boys enduring temperatures as low as -35° F, a blizzard, and a broken down engine that had to be replaced while the team was still many miles west of Minneapolis. The team finally arrived back in Chicago on January 5, 1911.

For the 1911 season, Zuppke had seven of his players back from the 1910 team, which gave some veteran experience to the squad that had now swelled to 35 prospective players. One of the leading returnees was Bart Macomber, who Zuppke switched from the line to quarterback.

The defending Cook County and national champions opened their season with a 9 to 0 win in the annual game with the Alumni. In its first regular game of the season, Oak Park easily defeated the Maywood Athletic Club, 31-0, and came back the following Saturday to humble the Maywood Young Men's Club, 29-0.

On Saturday, October 7, Oak Park played its first game against a strictly high school opponent when the team traveled to Culver, Indiana, to play the Culver Military Academy. It was a close game throughout, but the Chicagoans were able to keep their goal line from being crossed for the fourth consecutive game and came away with a hard-fought 12-0 win. The victory itself was something of an accomplishment for, as the *Tribune* reported, it marked the first time in seven years that a Chicago team had defeated the Military Academy. The star of the game for Oak Park was quarterback Bart Macomber who scored all of his team's points on field goals from the 20 and 30-yard lines, a 25-yard touchdown run, and by adding the placement after the touchdown.

Zuppke's team next played Lake Forest Academy the following Saturday. Lake Forest was outweighed by the Oak Park team, but as the *Tribune* noted, Lake Forest "played a fast and hard game and repeatedly broke through the opponent's line." However, the one thing Oak Park did better than Lake Forest was put points on the scoreboard. Led by Bart Macomber's two field goals and one placement, Oak Park prevailed by a score of 17-6.

On Saturday, October 21, Oak Park opened its Cook County High School Football League play by thumping University High, 39-0. The following Saturday, Oak Park took on Englewood High School. Englewood had been named national champion in both 1908 and 1909, but just two years later the team was but a shadow of its former self. As the *Tribune* began its story of the game, "Russell went over with the initial touchdown in the first minute of play, and thereafter it was a procession, eighteen touchdowns following." Paul Russell led the team with six TDs and Macomber added two, along with making an incredible 16 of 18 placements in Oak Park's 111-0 victory. It was the highest score ever rung up by a Chicago area team,

the second highest point total at the time in Illinois history. Macomber's 16 PATs is still the third highest single game total for an Illinois high school football game.

Oak Park easily won its next two games over Lane Tech, 23-0, and Wendell Phillips High, 28-0. Oak Park had now outscored its opponents by 290-6 in running up a record of 8-0-0. As luck would have it, Oak Park's next game on Saturday, November 18, was the season finale against undefeated Hyde Park High School, a game that would decide the Cook County championship.

Like the other games that Oak Park had played that season, this one was a bit one-sided. The *Tribune* described it this way, "(Oak Park's defensive) line was as invulnerable as its attack was bewildering. ... All the intricate formations Coach Zuppke ever evolved were used with effect. The famous 'flea flicker', 'whoa-back', and other uncanny formations worked with much success."

The final score of 24-0 gave Oak Park not only the Cook County title, but also the Illinois state championship.

The local season was now complete, but Oak Park was again looking to play an out of town opponent. The team had already arranged to play a game in Cleveland against one of that city's best teams on Thanksgiving Day, but on November 14 the Oak Park School Board passed a resolution forbidding teams from playing any games outside of the county, citing their concern over long trips and bad weather such as Oak Park had encountered the previous year. That being the case, and since the Cleveland team was also unable to travel, the Oak Park Athletic Association sent a delegation of representatives to Boston in an attempt to sign that city's best team to a game to be played in Chicago for the national championship. Four or five Boston area teams were battling it out for that area's top honors, and after all was said and done the team chosen for the championship trip was St. John's Prep of Danvers, Massachusetts. Former Oak Park player Milton Ghee, who was then a

 *Oak Park's 1911 National Championship team. (Chicago Tribune)*

OAK PARK ELEVEN DEFEATS ST. JOHN'S FOR NATIONAL TITLE

Interscholastic Football Champions of the East Fall Before the Whirlwind Attack of Local Suburban Team—Score Is 17 to 0.

RUSSELL IS THE HERO OF SENSATIONAL GAME

Star Half Back Eludes Opposing Players With Ease for Long Open Field Runs—Macomber's Punting Is a Feature.

▲ *Headline in Chicago's* Inter Ocean *newspaper of Dec. 3, 1911 announcing Oak Park's victory over St. John's of Boston for the 1911 national championship.*

student at Dartmouth, told his hometown newspapers that St. John's Prep was one of the best teams on the East Coast.

The game was scheduled for the afternoon of Saturday, December 2, at the University of Chicago's Marshall Field, which would make for a truly busy week for St. John's Prep. The team would leave Boston on Thursday afternoon, November 30, (Thanksgiving Day that year) after playing a football game against Boston College High at 10:00AM that morning. The St. John's team of 15, along with its coach Roy W. Jones and Athletic Director Fr. Thomas, arrived in Chicago on Friday afternoon, December 1.

More than 8,000 high school football fans were on hand for this much anticipated game. The *Chicago Daily News* exhorted the home team to "Win the national championship!" The playing field was wet and slippery, a condition that at times hindered both teams.

The game started off slowly, with the two teams exchanging punts. After one of the St. John's kicks Oak Park had the ball at its 35-yard line. Bart Macomber fired a pass to his left end John Barrett, with Barrett taking the ball all the way to the end zone for a 65-yard Oak Park touchdown. Macomber added the placement to give the home team a 6-0 lead. Paul Russell added a touchdown in the second quarter to give Oak Park an 11-0 advantage at the half.

The second half opened with St. John's kicking off. It was the practice in those earliest days of the game to punt much more often than teams do now, the strategy being to gain field position by holding your opponent after the kick. That was somewhat the situation when, on second down and with the ball at his own 30-yard line, Bart Macomber promptly punted the ball back to St. John's. The strategy worked better than anticipated when the St. John's punt returner fumbled the ball. Oak Park's Paul Russell picked up the loose pigskin "and with the aid of excellent interference" took the ball all the way to the end zone for his second touchdown of the game. Macomber added the placement to give Oak Park a 17-0 lead just two plays into the second half.

Neither team scored after that, though Oak Pak seemed to have the better of it. In describing the home team's 17-0 victory the next day, the *Tribune* noted that

> *"Western football scored another victory over the east yesterday ... by open play in which the forward pass was the deciding factor. The varied attack of the local team, its cunning in following the ball, and its hard, aggressive defensive play were features which swung the tide of victory to the suburbanites. There was little variation of attack to the visitor's play. The backs generally lined up so close to the line that they lacked the necessary drive and momentum to gain ground when they met resistance.*

"On the other hand, Oak Park sprung plays which were so bewildering to St. John's that large and substantial gains resulted. The open formations could not be solved and the hard, aggressive driving of the local backs always were good for the desired results.

"... Oak Park ... played a better brand of football, it was more aggressive and its offense was so varied and effective that gains could not help but result."

Oak Park had won its second consecutive national championship, and in even more convincing fashion than the first. Local postseason honors went to eight of the Oak Park players, with five being named to the *Tribune*'s High School All-Star first team and three to the second team. Bart Macomber and Paul Russell led this contingent, with Russell garnering the additional honor of being named the All-Star team's captain.

Even more honors came the team's way from no less an authority on football than *Spalding's Official Football Guide*, at the time the country's premier publication about the sport and edited by the esteemed Walter Camp. Not only did Spalding's concur that Oak Park had won the national championship, but its Cook County High School All-Star Eleven named six Oak Park players. Singled out for special praise was right halfback Paul Russell, of whom the Guide noted "Russell is unquestionably the greatest player that has been developed in the league since Eckersall and Steffen." (Walter Eckersall and Walter Steffen were both early University of Chicago quarterbacks and both are in the College Football Hall of Fame.)

The year 1912 was a landmark year for football. If you saw a game before that season, and then did not see one until today, you might not recognize it as being the same game of football. All of that changed with the rules changes adopted between the 1911 and 1912 campaigns. What you would have seen in 1912 is basically what you still see today, more than a century later. Among the changes that went into effect are:

- *A team now had four downs to go 10 yards to make a first down, instead of three downs to go five yards as had been the old rule.*

- *The field was shortened from 110 yards to 100 yards, with 10 yard end zones added; these were known as forward pass zones in which a forward pass could now be legally caught.*

- *Kickoffs were now moved back to the 40-yard line, instead of the old 55-yard line midfield stripe.*

- *The 20-yard limit on forward passes was lifted, as was the previous 20-yard limit on calling pass interference.*

- *The point value for a touchdown was increased from five points to six.*

There have been hundreds of rule changes and tweaks since 1912, but the game is essentially unchanged since that season.

For the 1912 season, head coach Bob Zuppke had a team loaded with veterans, perhaps none more important than HB/FB John Barrett and quarterback Bart Macomber, who was playing in his third season on the team, his second at quarterback. Oak Park entered the season as the two-time defending national champion, the defending state champion and riding a 16-game winning streak.

The season opened with the annual game against the alumni. In an attempt to get used to the new rules, both teams stayed pretty much with basic running plays between the tackles, Oak Park winning the contest 8-0 on a pair of Bart Macomber field goals and a safety. Against the Maywood Young Men's Club the following week, Zuppke still had his team running a pretty conservative book of plays, in part because a couple of his regular players were out nursing injuries. As the *Tribune* noted, "Straight football mixed with only two forward passes and without the use of a single trick play" resulted in a 20-0 win for Oak Park.

By the time of the third game everyone was healthy and it showed as Oak Park rolled over each new opponent. Elgin High School lost to Zuppke's team by a 42 to 0 score. Culver Military Academy, which had stubbornly fallen to Oak Park the previous year by 12-0, was blown away this time; led by John Barrett's four touchdowns Oak Park blasted the cadets, 54-0. Lane Tech was the next victim of the Oak Park juggernaut, taking it on the chin by a 42-0 score.

After the Lane Tech game Walter Eckersall, now a sportswriter for the *Tribune*, said about Zuppke's team: "The strategic attack and almost impenetrable defense of the suburbanites will make the team a hard one to beat this season. The team has formations of the deceptive variety which are executed in a manner that would be a credit to a college team." However, Eckersall did notice one problem with the Oak Park team, "Fumbling at critical times was the glaring fault of Oak Park." No doubt Coach Zuppke would address that "fault" at practice.

On October 19, Englewood "held" Oak Park to 50 points less than the suburbanites had scored against them the previous season, but Englewood still suffered a 61-0 defeat; Barrett and Macomber combined to score seven touchdowns in the game. The following week Oak Park took on Evanston Academy in a game that had local prep school championship implications. Oak Park was already 6-0-0, Evanston Academy was 2-0-1. The

▾ *The 1912 Oak Park National Championship team. (Robert Pruter Collection)*

first sentence of the *Tribune*'s report of the game says it all, "Uncorking some of the most startling football that has ever been displayed on a local gridiron, Oak Park High school's national champions fairly swamped Evanston Academy in what was supposed to be the deciding match of the western prep championship yesterday." The score was only 7-0 after the first quarter, but behind four touchdowns each by John Barrett and Bart Macomber, Oak Park rolled to a 101-0 victory.

It was more of the same the following week against Hyde Park as John Barrett, Bart Macomber, and Penn Carolan combined for 53 points in Oak Park's 59-0 victory. The victory was the 14th consecutive shutout and 25th straight win for Zuppke's team.

Oak Park's next game was against Wendell Phillips High School on November 9. Taking the initial kickoff, the Phillips team advanced to the Oak Park 40-yard line, from where right tackle Essig drop kicked a field goal to give Wendell Phillips a 3-0 lead. Not only were those the first points scored against Oak Park that season, but it was the first time the team had trailed in a game since the national championship game in Portland, Oregon, 22 months earlier. Wendell Phillips maintained its slim 3-0 lead through the first quarter, but by halftime Oak Park had regained its form to go up 13-3. The second half belonged completely to Oak Park as the team came away with a 33-3 victory. While it looked like an easy win for Oak Park, the *Tribune* noted that "it was only by the hardest kind of battling and by uncorking many plays heretofore never known in the Oak Park repertoire that Coach Zuppke's champions were able to gain the victory."

The next game against University High was billed as being for the Cook County League championship because both teams were undefeated in league play. But, it proved to be another easy win for Oak Park as the boys came away with a 64-0 victory and their third straight league title.

Oak Park had now completed the season's regular schedule. However, Lake Forest Academy, also undefeated, had challenged Oak Park to a game to decide the Illinois championship. The game was played on Friday, November 22, at the Wendell Phillips High School field.

▸ *This photo from the Chicago Tribune of Dec. 1, 1912 shows the starting backfield for Oak Park: Barrett, Macomber, Shiley and Carolan, as well as Everett High School's team captain, George Brickley.*

FROM 15,000 TO 20,000 WILL SEE OAK PARK-EVERETT GAME TODAY

Greatest Crowd That Ever Saw School Football Contest in New England Expected at Fenway Park---Massachusetts Team Favorite With Many---Prize at Stake Is National Supremacy.

Standing, Left to Right—Cannell, Quarterback; Sweetland, Right Halfback; Howard, Fullback; Capt George Brickley, Left Halfback; Geo O'Donnell, Coach Front Row—R. Bond, Right End; Wehrner, Right Tackle; Morrison, Right Guard; Pieroth, Center; McDonald, Left Guard; Bold, Left Tackle; Reed, Left End.
EVERETT HIGH SCHOOL FOOTBALL TEAM.

▲ *The headline in the Boston Globe of Nov. 30, 1912 announcing that day's high school national championship game and picturing the Everett High School team.*

The *Tribune* reported that "with a line which has held at bay every team it has met throughout the season, Lake Forest came to Phillips field feeling confident that if its team lost it would not be the fault of the forwards." Initially it was Lake Forest's passing game that let it down, but eventually Oak Park's superior running game and offensive line would tear apart and through the Lake Forest "forwards".

John Barrett would be a one-man wrecking crew for Bob Zuppke's team this day. Intercepting two passes and scoring three touchdowns in the first half, Barrett added a fourth touchdown after the intermission in leading Oak Park to a convincing 40-0 victory and the 1912 Illinois state championship.

An interesting side note to this game is what happened to Bart Macomber during the contest, especially in light of today's huge concern with concussions. Bart was hit in the head early in the game, and as the *Tribune* reported "he appeared dazed and often called for time before announcing his signals. … Coach Zuppke had no one available to replace his star quarter and he went through the second half ordered to take things more easily." As is well known, it would take almost a century before concussions and similar football injuries would be properly addressed.

On Monday, November 25, the *Tribune* announced its All-High School Eleven and not too surprisingly Oak Park dominated with six of the eleven selections. All four backfield positions were awarded to Oak Park players: quarterback Bart Macomber, left halfback Penn Carolan, right halfback Ralph Shiley, and fullback John Barrett. In addition, Paul Trier was named to the right tackle position and left tackle honors went to Harry Goelitz.

Having already tucked away the Cook County and Illinois championships, Oak Park had one more game to play. The team's representatives had contacted the people at Everett High School in Everett, Mass., about playing a game for the national "prep" championship. After a couple of meetings to iron out the details of the game, on November 20 the Everett folks accepted Oak Park's challenge. The game was scheduled to be played on Saturday, November 30, at 2:00P.M. in Boston's Fenway Park. Unlike the situation of the previous year, apparently the Oak Park School Board was in agreement with this trip as even school principal John Hanna traveled to Boston for the game.

This cartoon of highlights of the 1912 national championship game between Oak Park and Everett was typical for that era. (Boston Daily Globe)

Everett High School owned a splendid record of 10-1-0, outscoring its opponents 437-21. The team's lone defeat was by a single point, 21-20, to Malden High School. As the *Tribune* related about Malden's win, "According to reports from the east the victory was a fluke, two of the touchdowns being scored on fumbles. Boston critics concede that Everett is the better school..."

Oak Park entered the game at 11-0-0, having outscored its opponents 524-3.

MOMENTOUS MOMENTS IN THAT HEAD-SPINNING, WHIRLIGIG GAME THOSE WESTERNERS CALL FOOTBALL

By WALLACE GOLDSMITH.

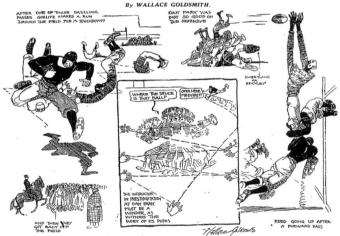

Reproduced with permission of the copyright owner. Further reproduction prohibited without permission.

Game day conditions were deemed ideal for the contest, with only a brisk north wind affecting the play on the gridiron. The *Boston Daily Globe* reported "the largest crowd that ever watched a school football game in this city" was in attendance, estimates ranging up to more than 12,500 people.

Oak Park was on the receiving end of the opening kickoff. After an exchange of possessions Oak Park had the ball for a second time, now at the Everett 40-yard line. A first down pass from Macomber to Harry Goelitz was good for a 40-yard touchdown, but Macomber missed the extra point kick. After again holding Everett on its ensuing possession, Oak Park quickly marched 90 yards to a second touchdown to take a 12-0 lead after one quarter of play. Early in the

This was the headline in the Chicago Tribune of Dec. 1, 1912 for its story about Oak Park's national championship game with Everett High School in Boston.

OAK PARK ELEVEN CRUSHES EVERETT IN CLASH FOR TITLE

Eastern Team No Match for Chicagoans, Who Triumph 32 to 14 in Boston Game.

MACOMBER A BRILLIANT STAR

Barrett and Goelitz Run Quarterback Close Race for Premier Honors of Contest.

MONSTER CROWD SEES STRUGGLE

Boston, Mass., Nov. 30.—[Special.]—In one of the most exciting games ever seen in Boston the Oak Park High school, champion of the west, defeated Everett High school in the intersectional championship game at the Fenway park, the home of the Boston Red Sox, today, 32 to 14.

Never was the open game more successfully played. The triple passing of the visitors was worked to perfection.

Goelitz, the Oak Park left tackle, carried the ball on this play for long gains time and

"OAK PARK OPENED THE EYES OF EASTERN FOOTBALL FOLLOWERS TO THE POSSIBILITIES OF THE GAME UNDER THE NEW RULES. THEIR STYLE WAS A COMPLETE REVELATION."

second quarter, Everett High recovered an Oak Park fumble in the Everett end zone for a touchback. The Everett squad then went 80 yards in just four plays to pull within five points of the visitors, 12-7 at the half.

Midway through the third quarter Bart Macomber added to Oak Park's total when he crashed across the Everett goal line from one yard out, pushing Oak Park's advantage to 18-7. Early in the fourth quarter Everett, halfback Fred "Buck" Sweetland closed out a drive with a one-yard plunge for a touchdown, the extra point cutting the Oak Park lead to 18-14.

Oak Park came right back after the ensuing kickoff with another scoring drive, this one of 52 yards. John Barrett went the final two yards for the touchdown, and when Bart Macomber added the placement Oak Park had increased its lead to 25-14. The Chicagoans got the ball right back on the first play after the ensuing kickoff when Penn Carolan recovered a fumble at the Everett 40-yard line. It took Oak Park only six plays to score another touchdown and increase its lead to 32-14.

The game ended a short while later. The 32-14 victory gave Bob Zuppke's Oak Park team its third consecutive national championship.

On December 2, 1912, the *Boston Evening Transcript* said this about the Oak Park team and its performance against Everett:

> *"Oak Park opened the eyes of Eastern football followers to the possibilities of the game under the new rules. Their style was a complete revelation. Triple passes in the backfield were the simplest that the visitors had in their repertoire, frequently the ball changed hands four times and sometimes five. These plays went off like clockwork. Each boy had a special part assigned to him and seldom did anyone miscue. When the ball was passed from one boy to another there was not the slightest slackening in speed and that was the remarkable feature of the whole performance. Each boy in the Oak Park line knew who was to carry the ball finally and which side of the line he was going to make his run; his path generally was cleared of Everett tacklers by the finest kind of interference. When it came to straight football, charging through the line the Oak Park boys were almost as strong as they were on the trick plays."*

Oak Park was not the only great high school football team in 1912. Over in Ohio, the high school in little Fostoria had started playing football in 1895, but from 1902 until 1915 there was not a better team in the Buckeye State. Fostoria was named state champion in 1902, 1906, 1907, 1910, 1911, 1912, 1914, and 1915—eight state championships out of the 11 that were named during those years.

The 1912 Fostoria High School football team, the first team (varsity) on the left and the second team on the right.

Lawrence C. Boles was the coach of the Fostoria team from 1907-1912, putting together a record of 48-4-2 and four state championships. However, 1912 was easily the greatest of all of those seasons for the Fostoria High School Redmen. The team that year was a scoring machine. In its opening game it defeated Tiffin High School by an 84-0 count and never let up during the rest of the season. In its third game, Fostoria slaughtered Crestline High School by 131-0 and in Week Six the team again went over the century mark with a 103-0 victory over Prairie Depot High School.

With its record for the season a perfect 7-0-0, all by shutout, Fostoria then accepted the challenge of Buffalo Central High School, the champions of New York State, to play for the national championship (there have been several seasons in which there were more than one recognized national championship game, as well as multiple recognized national champions). The New Yorkers proved to be no greater an obstacle for the Redmen than any other team they had faced during the season. During the game, played in Fostoria, when the Buffalo team was reduced to just nine players due to injuries Coach Boles lent them some of the Fostoria reserves so that the game could continue. Fostoria handily defeated Buffalo Central by a 74-0 count, Fostoria's 14th consecutive shutout over two seasons.

During the 1912 campaign Fostoria had outscored its opponents 596-0, at the time a national scoring record, averaging 74.5 points per game. George Little, then the head football coach at the University of Cincinnati, had officiated at some of Fostoria's games. He stated that the Fostoria team had the forward pass nearer to perfection than any team he had ever seen, and that the Redmen could defeat any college team in the state with the possible exception of Ohio State.

Fostoria High School is recognized as national co-champion along with Oak Park for 1912. That Fostoria squad was the first great team from Ohio - the state that would eventually dominate the ranks of the high school football national champions.

———

In his four seasons at Muskegon High School, Bob Zuppke's team compiled a record of 29-4-2 and, according to the *Chicago Tribune* (Dec. 15, 1912), his teams won three Michigan state championships. Before Zuppke arrived at Oak Park, that school's total football record was a less than impressive 54-57-11. In three seasons at Oak Park, Zuppke led the team to a 34-2-0 mark and won three Cook County, two Illinois, and three national championships. Zuppke's combined high school record was 63-6-2, .904.

When a coach wins like that at the high school level the local colleges tend to take notice, especially when your high school is located in the greater Chicago area and in the heart of Western Conference (now Big 10) country. Schools such as Northwestern and Purdue dangled lucrative offers in front of him, and Lafayette University offered to double his current salary to $4,000. However, Zuppke accepted the $2,700 offer from the University of Illinois and he never regretted it. He remained the head coach of the Fighting Illini from 1913 until 1941, posting a record of 131-81-12 and winning four national championships.

Bob Zuppke was one of the true innovators in the early days of football. He took to the newly legalized forward pass like a duck to water, being one of the earliest proponents of its use as an integral part of an offense's attack strategy. His many innovations included the spiral pass from center, the flea-flicker, the screen pass, the offensive huddle and the onside kick. (Not the same play that we are familiar with today, back in this era the onside kick was a play used by the offense. When lining up in punt formation, any player on the offense who lined up even with or behind the kicker was eligible to catch or recover the kick and retain it for his team, as long as the kick first went 10 yards. The teams that truly perfected this play were able to have one of the eligible players catch the ball in midflight, making the onside kick, in essence, a precursor to the forward pass.)

Zuppke also came up with plays with quite innovative names like the "whoa-back", "Flying Dutchman", "gee-haw", and "Razzle Dazzle." Of Bob Zuppke, the 1912 edition of *Spalding's Football Guide* said "he undoubtedly stands as one of the best coaches in the Middle West" and that no college coach in the Midwest or the East has been "able to adapt themselves to the open game as readily and with such brilliancy..."

Bob Zuppke is one of only two coaches to ever win a national championship at both the high school and the college levels—you will read about the other coach later in this book.

Bob Zuppke may have left Oak Park High School, but the football team would continue to roll right along, piling up more victories and more championships. Replacing Zuppke as the Oak Park head coach was Glenn Thistlethwaite. Thistlethwaite was a young man of 28, but he was already an experienced coach. From 1909 to 1912 he led the football team at Earlham College, a small Quaker school in Richmond, Indiana, to a respectable record of 18-9-0.

Thistlethwaite's task at Oak Park would not be an easy one, replacing as he was the most successful high school football coach in the country at that time; not surprisingly, there were those who felt that Oak Park's best days were now behind it. Gone, too, were some of the stalwarts of Oak Park's championship teams

▲ *Oak Park ball carrier picks up big yardage in this 1920 game action. (1921 Oak Park High School Yearbook)*

like Penn Carolan and the great Bart Macomber. However, for the 1913 campaign, Thistlethwaite had returning veterans including team captain Ralph Shiley, John Barrett and a half-dozen more around whom to build his team.

There was another change to the high school football scene in Chicago for the 1913 season. The former Cook County League was now divided into two leagues, the Chicago Public High School Athletic League (Wendell Phillips, Hyde Park, Lane Tech, Englewood, Crane, and Schurz high schools) and the Chicago-Suburban High School Athletic Conference (Oak Park, Evanston, University High, New Trier, and Thornton high schools).

Oak Park got off to a somewhat inauspicious start when the varsity was defeated by the Alumni team, 10-0, in their traditional season opener. However, any fears of a drop off in the team's fortunes were soon laid to rest. In Oak Park's first game against a high school opponent, the boys humbled Kankakee High School by a 64-0 count and came right back the following Saturday to down Elgin High by almost the same score, 66-0. In the fourth week of the season, Rockford High School managed to cross the Oak Park goal line and even registered a safety, but they paid a stiff price for those points in a 58-8 defeat.

One of the main reasons for the team's continued success was the play of halfback John Barrett, who was piling up touchdowns and points almost faster than the scorer could count them. Barrett's performance against Thornton High the next week was typical of what he would do all season. On the first play from scrimmage he took the handoff and raced 85 yards for an Oak Park touchdown. He would go on to add five more TDs during the game and kick seven placements in Oak Park's 73-0 victory.

On Saturday, October 18, Oak Park took on the defending Iowa state champions from Clinton High School. Unlike the team's previous four games that were won by a 261-8 margin, this game would put Oak Park to a real test. Midway through the third quarter, Clinton held a 14-6 lead, but then Oak Park and John Barrett came to life. Over the last quarter and a half, Barrett scored three touchdowns and two extra points. This, along with a touchdown from Ralph Shiley, carried the Chicagoans to a 32-14 triumph.

Oak Park would get another scare the following week, but this time it was from a Chicago team. In its game against Suburban Conference rival University High, Oak Park fell behind early when University scored on a field goal just three minutes into the game. Oak Park came back to take a 12-6 lead at the half, but the game was hardly "in the bag." Once again it would be the play of John Barrett, combined with some heads-up play by the Oak Park defense, that helped to secure the triumph. Barrett scored three touchdowns and a placement over the game's final two quarters while the defense came up with several fumble recoveries and interceptions, all of which helped to propel Oak Park to a 31-13 win.

▲ *The blocking forms as an Oak Park runner starts around the left side in this 1920 game action. (1921 Oak Park High School Yearbook)*

Glenn Thistlethwaite's team then cruised past New Trier, 84-0, in a league contest and Evanston Academy, 43-3, in a non-league tussle.

On Saturday, November 15, Oak Park took on Evanston High School in the game to decide the Suburban Conference title. Evanston played tough in holding Oak Park to its lowest point total of the season, but like every team before it, Evanston could not stop John Barrett. After a scoreless first quarter, Barrett punched across two touchdowns in the second and another in the third period. Evanston finally got on the scoreboard in the final frame, but it was a case of too-little-too-late as Oak Park came away with a hard fought 19-7 victory and its fourth consecutive league championship, it's first in the new Suburban Conference.

Oak Park had finished the season 9-1-0, but the team did have one more contest to play. A game had been arranged with Scott High School of Toledo, Ohio, to be played on Saturday, November 22. The outcome would decide the national championship.

A light rain throughout the contest kept the gridiron and the ball wet and slippery. Oak Park struck for two touchdowns in the first quarter, but the Scott team quickly regrouped and Oak Park led by only 13-7 at the half. However, the Oak Park offense kept the Toledoans off balance throughout the game; its passing attack being especially effective. The second half belonged to the Chicagoans as they added three more touchdowns while shutting out Scott en route to a 32-7 victory.

Glenn Thistlethwaite's first season at Oak Park had proved a rousing success as the team won its fourth consecutive national championship—no other high school team ever matched that accomplishment over the balance of the century. Four Oak Park players made the All-Cook County team, led by the All-County team captain, John Barrett. Barrett scored 223 points (44% of the team's total of 503) on 35 touchdowns and 13 placements during the 1913 campaign.

Over the next several seasons, Glenn Thistlethwaite continued to have some pretty good teams at Oak Park. In 1914, Oak Park fielded another good team that finished with a record of 9-3-1. The team's season finale against Everett (Mass.) High School is listed by the *National High School Football Record Book* (2002) as a national championship game. However, as will be explained in the following chapter, this was not a national championship game and it had nothing to do with the fact that Everett won the game by an 80-0 margin.

From 1914 through 1917, Oak Park won 31 and lost 10, with no ties. Then, in 1918, the team got hot again. That season Oak Park was undefeated in nine games, 8-0-1. The next year they were a perfect 10-0-0 and Cook County champions for the second straight year. Not much national recognition came its way during those two seasons, but all of that would change in 1920.

▲ *The pursuit follows this Oak Park ball carrier down the field in game action from 1920. (1921 Oak Park High School Yearbook)*

▲ *Somewhere in that mass of humanity to the right of the picture is an Oak Park ball carrier picking up some tough yardage in 1920. (1921 Oak Park High School Yearbook)*

▲ *The Oak Park defense in action during the 1920 championship season. (1921 Oak Park High School Yearbook)*

The 1920 edition of Glenn Thistlethwaite's Oak Park eleven was not a high scoring team like some in past years, but they were very good on defense. However, that overall assessment of the team's offense was belied by the results of Oak Park's first game of the season, a 40-0 victory over Harrison High School. That game accounted for almost a quarter of all of the points that Oak Park would score during the entire season.

Oak Park's next encounter was a more typical example of its games throughout the season, a 7-0 win over Elgin High School, followed by a 28-14 victory over Bloom High School. On October 16, the Suburban Conference's two best teams met in a showdown for first place when Oak Park took on New Trier in front of 2,500 fans. After a scoreless first half, New Trier broke on top 3-0 in the third quarter. In the first minute of the fourth quarter, Oak Park team captain Herbert Steger booted a game-tying field goal from about 40 yards away. Neither team would score again and the game ended in a 3-3 tie.

Oak Park won its next three games, but none of the victories came easily. Before more than 3,000 fans on its home field, Oak Park scored two touchdowns in the first half against Proviso High and made them stand up for a 13-0 win. The next week Oak Park trailed Evanston High 3 to 0 at the half before, as the *Tribune* noted, "The Western suburb boys sprung a lot of new and shifty stuff in the second half and swamped the north shore lads by a final count of 27 to 3." On November 13, at its own one-yard line, Oak Park held Deerfield for four downs early in the first quarter; that would prove to be Deerfield's only good scoring opportunity as Oak Park came back for a 21-0 victory.

Oak Park and New Trier were now tied for first place in the Suburban Conference, both teams undefeated, their tie game as the only blemish on their respective records. On November 18, at the league's regular monthly meeting it was arranged for the two teams to have a playoff to decide the league title, the playoff game to be held on Friday, November 26. In that game, the only scoring of the first half came when Oak Park team captain Herbert Steger returned a blocked field goal attempt by New Trier 85 yards for a touchdown and then added the extra point. Thistlethwaite's lads then "exploded" for 17 unanswered points in the second half as Oak Park came away with a 24-0 victory and the league title.

Oak Park had now gone 27 straight games over the last three seasons without a defeat, posting a record of 25-0-2. There was another team that was on something of a similar streak; the team from Steele High School in Dayton, Ohio, had not lost a game over the previous two seasons. A game between Oak Park and Steele High was arranged to be played in Dayton on Saturday, December 4.

The two teams were met that Saturday by a steady downpour and ankle deep mud. In the first quarter, Steele had the ball inside the Oak Park one-yard line and

1920 Oak Park national championship team. (1921 Oak Park High School Yearbook)

again at the Chicagoans' five, but both times they failed to score. Finally, in the second quarter the home team scored a touchdown to take a 6-0 lead at the half.

On Oak Park's first possession of the third quarter, Herbert Steger scored a touchdown on a 32-yard run to tie the game at 6-6. However, the Oak Park captain was injured on the play and had to leave the game. That loss may have slowed down the Chicagoans, but it did not stop them. In the fourth quarter, Oak Park struck for two quick touchdowns in the span of just four plays to give the Chicagoans a 19-6 victory.

Oak Park's yearbook stated that the "football squad ended the season with as good a claim as anybody to the National Prep title." And indeed the team was named national champion, giving the suburban Chicago team its fifth national championship of the last 11 seasons.

Oak Park would win its first four games of the 1921 season to run its winning streak to 32, but finished the year with a 6-2-1 record. After that season Glenn Thistlethwaite left the school and returned to the college ranks, coaching at Northwestern and Wisconsin for five years each before spending some time at a couple of smaller colleges.

## CHAPTER 2

COAST TO COAST

Everett High School

Everett, Massachusetts / Everett, Washington

W hat are the odds that two high schools with the same name, from cities with the same name, located on opposite coasts of the country, would both win multiple national championships within a span of just seven seasons? If you are talking about Everett High School from Everett, Mass., and Everett High School from Everett, Wash., and the years are 1914-1920—then the odds of that happening are excellent.

Let us begin this part of our story on the East Coast at Everett High School in the town of Everett, Mass. Everett High School has one of the oldest and most successful school boy football programs anywhere in the country. They have been fielding a team there since at least 1892 and started winning state championships almost from the very start with pre-20th century titles in 1896, 1897, and 1899. During the first decade of the 20th century the team, continued to play a decent brand of football but only added one more state title, that coming in 1903.

The school's first known football coach was Harry A. Dame, who mentored the team from 1905 thru 1908. In 1909 the school hired Cleo O'Donnell to take over the program. By the time he left to join the college ranks seven years later, O'Donnell would leave behind a legacy that would be hard to match.

Cleo O'Donnell was a native of Charlestown, Mass. After high school at Boston Latin he enrolled at Holy Cross College in Worcester, Mass., in 1904. O'Donnell played football at Holy Cross all four years and was named the team captain in 1907. Upon graduation he coached football at Somerville High School in Somerville, Mass., for one year before accepting the job at Everett.

O'Donnell's first two seasons at Everett High were fairly successful as his team compiled a record of 15-5-4. In 1911 the Crimson Tide was 8-2-0 and named state champions. The 1911 season would prove to be the launching pad from which would spring the greatest era of Everett High School Crimson Tide football.

The 1912 Crimson Tide blew through its first seven opponents, not allowing a single point while scoring 327 of its own. Only Cambridge Latin had given the Everett team anything to worry about, but Latin still met the fate of the others in a 12-0 defeat.

Then, on November 9, came the big game with Everett's traditional rival Malden High School. The game began like all of Everett's previous games and by halftime the Crimson had jumped to a 20-0 lead. But things began to change after the intermission. In the third quarter Malden got its running game going and

Cleo O'Donnell was the head coach at Everett (Mass.) High School from 1909-1915. (Everett High School Yearbook)

advanced to the Everett one-yard line, where it had a first and goal. The Everett boys put up a tremendous goal line stand and forced Malden to relinquish the ball on downs, the ball still resting at the one. On first down Everett team captain George Brickley, standing deep in his end zone, attempted to punt the ball away, but Malden's Joe Heaney came in from the right side, leapt into the air, and blocked Brickley's kick. Heaney then quickly got up and fell on the loose ball for a Malden touchdown. The extra point cut Everett's lead to 20-7.

The game was now being played in a driving rain. Throughout the third and fourth quarters, Malden continued to surge toward the Everett goal line, but each time the Everett defense was able to stop them short. With just a minute and a half left in the game, Malden was forced to punt from the midfield stripe. Trying to field the kick, Everett's Jack Cannell bobbled and then dropped the ball; Malden left tackle "Red" Welch scooped up the loose ball and fell over the goal line for a Malden touchdown. The extra point tightened the score at 20-14.

▲ *This drawing from* The Boston Globe *of Tuesday, Oct. 13, 1914, shows highlights of Everett's big win over Rindge High.*

Following the ensuing kickoff, Everett's lead still appeared to be secure as the Crimson Tide had the ball at the Malden 30-yard line with less than a minute re-maining. Standing in punt formation, quarterback Jack Cannell had the snap from center go sailing over his head. As *The Boston Globe* reported, "Before Cannell could recover the leather he was pushed out of the way by Hill, one of the Malden ends, while Redmond Walsh, Malden's right tackle, seized the ball and by clever dodging landed it behind the goal posts." Walsh's return of the blocked punt more than 60 yards for a touchdown tied the score, while the critical extra point kick was good to give Malden a stunning 21-20 victory.

Everett rebounded to win its last three games, all by shutout. This late season surge by the Crimson Tide was enough to convince the Boston area sportswriters that the loss to Malden was a "fluke" and they awarded the state championship to Everett High School.

Based on being declared the state champion, and in some corners the best team in New England, the Crimson Tide received a challenge from Oak Park High School of Chicago to play for the national championship on Saturday, November

30. The Everett team was not too excited about playing in this game, coming as it would just two days after its final game on Thanksgiving Day. It would also be the Crimson Tide's third game in seven days. However, since the game was to be played in Boston's Fenway Park they accepted the challenge.

As we have learned in the previous chapter, Oak Park's "western" style of play led to a 32-14 defeat for Everett—but this would not be the last we would hear of Everett-Oak Park. Everett's 1912 season ended with a very fine record of 10-2-0.

Cleo O'Donnell's 1913 squad, as it had the previous year, opened with a string of seven shutouts, outscoring the opposition by 251-0. Unfortunately, one of Everett's opponents, Haverhill, also shut out the Crimson Tide, resulting in a 0-0 tie. On November 8, Everett had its annual game with Malden High. This time there would be no miracle finish for Malden, the Crimson making sure of it with a 54-6 win. Malden would have to take solace in the fact that it would be the only team to score on Everett the entire season.

Three more shutouts followed, Cambridge Latin giving the Tide a scare before falling 13-0.

On Saturday, November 29, Everett played a big intersectional postseason game with Lafayette High School of Buffalo, N.Y. Lafayette had gone through the season unscathed against other high school opponents, its only defeat a 6-0 loss at the hands of the Syracuse University freshman team. They were the champions of Buffalo and one of the best teams in the Empire State. The Lafayette team was also a reputed master of the "open" style of play, but it was unable to perform up to its normal standards against the Crimson Tide. The wet and muddy game day conditions may have adversely affected the team's performance, but as *The Boston Globe* reporter noted, "Lafayette showed little or no offense. What they could have accomplished on a dry field is a matter of conjecture, but it is doubtful if under the most favorable conditions that they would have threatened the Everett goal by their method of attack."

Everett broke the scoring deadlock by pushing across a touchdown in the first quarter for a 7-0 lead. The Tide made it 13-0 at the intermission. After a scoreless third period, Everett exploded for three tallies in the fourth quarter to put away the "westerners" by a 33-0 count.

The people at Everett High School had tried to arrange a rematch with undefeated Oak Park in an effort to even the ledger after the previous season's defeat. However, the Oak Park team, which was named national champion in 1913 for the fourth consecutive season, declined the offer saying that they had already shut down for the year. The Crimson Tide was naturally disappointed, but took the opportunity to schedule a game with Oak Park for the following season to be played on November 28, 1914.

Halfback Jackson Cannell was a star of the 1914 Everett (Mass.) High national champion team. (Everett High School Yearbook)

Cleo O'Donnell's team finished the 1913 campaign with a near-perfect mark of 11-0-1 and was again named Massachusetts state champion.

Since 1911, head coach Cleo O'Donnell's Crimson Tide had put together three very good seasons. In 1914 they were about to embark on a season the likes of which few teams have ever come close to enjoying.

The Crimson Tide opened on September 26 with a 60-0 thrashing of Marlboro High School, and came back the following Saturday to humble Revere, 70-0. Saturday, October 10, began a stretch where the team played three games in a span of just eight days.

The first was another one-sided blowout as the Crimson Tide rolled to a 54-0 victory over Chelsea High. Two days later, on Monday the 12th, the Everett team suited up against Rindge Tech. (Starting at right guard for Rindge Tech was future Hollywood star Walter Brennan.) This Columbus Day game was played in the morning with 2,000 fans in attendance. After a scoreless first quarter, Everett scored a touchdown in each of the next three periods. Rindge Tech never really put up a scoring threat until late in the game, but time expired before they could complete the drive. The 21-0 final would prove to be the closest game of the season for Coach O'Donnell's team.

The third game of the week came on Saturday, October 17, when Everett played Wellesley High at Everett Field. "The field was a sea of mud", which led directly to the Crimson Tide's first points. Early in the second quarter Wellesley held Everett for downs deep in Wellesley's end of the field. When Wellesley tried to punt the ball out of danger, its punter fumbled the slippery

BOSTON SUNDAY GLOBE—DECEMBER 6. 1914

IT'S A 62-0 RUNAWAY FOR EVERETT.

Stamford High No Match For Home Team at Any Stage —4500 Persons See Closing Game.

▲ *Drawings from* The Boston Sunday Globe *of Dec. 6, 1914, depict action from the national championship game between Everett (Mass.) and Stamford (Conn.) high schools.*

ball and an Everett player fell on it in the end zone for a touchdown. Everett later added a field goal and a pair of touchdowns en route to a 23-0 victory, its tenth consecutive shutout.

With the season nearing its midpoint, one newspaper reporter noted that "Everett High, with many veterans and a few new players, has developed into a great all-around football machine which seems likely to go through its season without a defeat." The same reporter also noted that Everett, Boston Latin, and Fitchburg High were the only teams left in Massachusetts that were both undefeated and unscored upon. He also pointed out that Manchester High of nearby New Hampshire "is also in this class." What he failed to note was that Everett High and Manchester would face off against each other in less than two weeks.

On Saturday, October 24, Everett rolled over Melrose High School by a score of 48-0. This victory kept Everett's record unscathed and set up the mid-season "showdown" with Manchester High to be played at the Everett Athletic Grounds the following Saturday, October 31—Halloween day.

The Everett-Manchester match-up received a lot of pregame publicity in the local newspapers. An article in *The Boston Globe* noted that the game "probably will be attended by a record-breaking crowd. Both teams are stronger than a year ago and one of the best school games of the season is assured."

In fact, both teams entered their first meeting ever undefeated. The newspaper noted that this game "will, in the opinion of many, determine the scholastic championship of two States." As for the Crimson Tide's preparation for this game, the *Globe* noted that the team "spent more time than usual to trick plays and forward passes, which they figure may help against the Manchester team ..."

The *Globe* reported that "over 3,500 persons witnessed this struggle between the two premier schoolboy elevens of this section of New England." As predicted, the game was a dandy. Everett kicked off to open the game. After an exchange of possessions, Manchester was on the move. The New Hampshire team advanced to the Everett 12-yard line, but a fourth down fake field goal try failed when Manchester's pass fell incomplete.

The *Globe* then noted that "from this time on things changed, for Everett took the aggressive..."

Everett came right back down the field, moving the ball entirely on the ground. The drive came to a successful conclusion when halfback George Green carried the ball into the end zone from the one-yard line for the game's first points. That would prove to be the only scoring of the first half, with Everett leading 7-0 after two quarters of play.

Everett increased its lead in the third quarter with a touchdown and a long field goal. The Crimson Tide added a fourth quarter touchdown to close out the scoring in Everett's 22-0 victory.

One of the features of the game was the play of Everett tackle Karl Johnson, *The Boston Globe* noting that "he opened up holes big enough to drive a horse and wagon through" (this was 1914 after all).

▾ *The 1914 Everett (Mass.) High School national champion team, considered by many to be the single best high school football team of all time.* (The Boston Globe)

All the Way to #1

With its record now a sterling 7-0-0 and the odds-on favorite to be named the best team in Massachusetts, if not all of New England, the Crimson Tide cruised through the next four games on its schedule, averaging 39 points per game while still yielding none.

Now came the game that everyone in Everett, and many in New England, had been waiting almost two years for—the rematch with Oak Park. Oak Park came east with a good team, but not a great one, having won eight games against two losses. Coach Glenn Thistlethwaite was also a little shorthanded for this game, having to leave behind in Chicago one of his starting guards who was nursing a few injuries. That guard, a young man whose name you may recognize, was Ernest Hemingway.

"HE OPENED UP HOLES BIG ENOUGH TO DRIVE A HORSE AND WAGON THROUGH"

The game was played at the South End Grounds, the home of the National League's Boston Braves. A crowd variously estimated at from 8,000 to 15,000 turned out on Saturday, November 28, for the 2:00P.M. kickoff. This game, it should be noted, was being played just two days after Everett's tough encounter with Cambridge Latin on Thanksgiving Day, Thursday, November 26.

Once the game got underway, it sure did not look as if the Crimson Tide was playing on only one day's rest. The team started right in on the Chicagoans and never let up. They scored five touchdowns in the first quarter alone, and by the time the final whistle had sounded the Everett squad had rolled to an 80-0 victory—its most lopsided win of the season.

This game is considered in many circles to have been played for the national championship, but it most definitely was not. While the Everett team was of national championship caliber, the Oak Park team of 1914 was far from it, not even having won its own league title. And, as we have also seen, this game had been scheduled a year in advance, further negating its "national championship" credentials.

However, Everett's next game was for the national championship. Following its victory over Oak Park, Everett High School was contacted by Stamford High School of Stamford, Connecticut. Stamford was recognized as the "undisputed champions of Connecticut and New York" and wanted to play Everett for the national championship. The Everett folks agreed to the game, which was played at 2:00P.M. on Saturday, December 5, at the Everett field.

More than 4,500 fans were on hand for this game, completely cramming the spectator area of Everett field. The game was hard fought from the start, but Everett enjoyed a clear advantage, as evidenced by Stamford making only two first downs the entire game. Everett fought its way to a 21-0 lead by halftime. The Crim-

An action sequence from the game between Everett (Mass.) and Rindge high schools on Oct. 12, 1915. (The Boston Globe)

son Tide pushed across two more touchdowns in the third quarter and closed out the game with a four-TD fourth quarter. Final score: Everett 62, Stamford 0.

This most convincing victory earned for the Everett High Crimson Tide its ninth state championship, the title of New England champions as well as the championship of the United States.

What a season 1914 was for the Crimson Tide. 13-0-0 and setting a new national record for points in a season by outscoring the opposition 600-0. In reviewing the 1914 interscholastic football season, the 1915 edition of *Spalding's Football Guide* said that the Everett team "was recognized as the greatest contingent of schoolboys ever developed in the long history of the gridiron sport in New England... Everett High's style of play comprised a frequent use of the forward pass and a running attack that was propelled by a swift quartet of backs, reinforced by a line that was able to tear open holes through an opposing front that was more like a finished varsity [i.e.: college] eleven than that of a schoolboy team."

In February of 1960, *Sport Magazine* published an article about the greatest high school football team of all time. Its choice—the 1914 Everett High School Crimson Tide. Again in August of 1984, *Sports Illustrated* published a similar article, and again the choice as the best team of all time was Everett High, 1914.

Now, a century after they took the field, the legacy of the 1914 Crimson Tide of Everett High School remains intact as the best team in high school football history.

For the 1915 campaign, Coach Cleo O'Donnell had a solid corps of returning veterans, many of whom would make the various All-Scholastic teams at season's end. As it had done for the past couple of seasons, the Crimson Tide sailed right through most of the first seven games on its schedule. After easily defeating Fitchburg, 44-0, and Mechanic Arts School, 55-0, the Tide had a bit of a struggle with Rindge Tech on Columbus Day. The game was mostly a punting duel, but Everett managed to find the end zone near the end of both the second and fourth quarters as the Crimson Tide came away with a 13-0 victory.

The Everett team then regained its dominating form and won the next four games by an average score of 48-0. These games included victories over a couple of teams that in the past had given Everett fits: a 48-0 decision over Manchester (N.H.) High and a 47-0 thumping of Malden.

Next up was Medford High School in a game played on November 13. Everett won the game to raise its season record to 8-0-0, but the date proved to be unlucky for the Crimson Tide in one respect. Medford managed to put three points on the scoreboard via a field goal to avoid a shutout in Everett's 27-3 win. Those three points were the first points scored against the Crimson Tide in two years, not since November 8, 1913, the team having posted 25 consecutive shutouts.

Against Somerville on November 20, Cleo O'Donnell used several substitutes, in part because of injuries to key players, but also to rest a few players because the team had two more games coming up in the next seven days. With some of the regulars not playing, the team struggled a bit but managed to come away with a 13-0 win over Somerville. The Crimson then showed its usual form with a 48-0 walloping of Melrose High on Thanksgiving Day. Cleo O'Donnell's lads now had to prepare for the two biggest games on their schedule, against the two toughest opponents they would face all season.

A CENTURY AFTER THEY TOOK THE FIELD, THE LEGACY OF THE 1914 CRIMSON TIDE OF EVERETT HIGH SCHOOL REMAINS INTACT AS THE BEST TEAM IN HIGH SCHOOL FOOTBALL HISTORY.

The first of these games took place on Saturday, November 27. Everett would be taking on Waltham High School in a game to decide the state championship. Both teams entered the contest undefeated although Waltham, despite outscoring its opponents by 528-6, did have one smudge on its record, a 0-0 tie with Newton High School to go with its 12 victories. The game was played at Boston's Fenway Park with a crowd reported at more than 20,000 - double the previous Massachusetts schoolboy record.

This was a closely played and hotly-contested game throughout, with defense being front and center. Most of the first quarter was spent on the Everett side of the field. Waltham made it to the two-yard line on one occasion, but lost the ball on downs. The "Watch City" boys also had a field goal try blocked late in the quarter.

‣ *Everett (Mass.) halfback Fred Marshall, one of the stars of the Maroons' 1915 national champion team.* (The Boston Globe)

Early in the second quarter, Everett took over the ball at its 20-yard line and then went on the best drive of the game by either team—80 yards in 20 plays, all on the ground. Halfback Fred Marshall went the final six yards for a touchdown. The extra point try was missed, leaving the Crimson with a 6-0 lead.

Waltham had its best chance to score in the third quarter as the team marched to the Everett one-yard line. At that point a fumble at the goal line was recovered by an Everett player in the end zone for a touchback. That would prove to be Waltham's last scoring opportunity as Everett held on for a 6-0 victory and its fifth consecutive Massachusetts state championship.

This victory set up a game for the national championship between Everett High and the reigning Michigan champions from Detroit Central High School. Detroit Central had won the national championship back in 1904. From 1910 to 1914, the Motor City boys had gone undefeated three times in posting a mark of 42-3-2. Central was again undefeated in 1915, currently 11-0-0 and having outscored the opposition by 523 to 14. After defeating Oak Park in a game billed as having been for the championship of the Midwest, the Central people had sent out letters to the top teams in New York and Ohio, as well as to the reigning national champions from Everett, in an attempt to schedule a game for the national title. Central head coach Edbert C. Buss was reported by one of the Boston newspapers as having attended the Everett-Waltham game. After defeating Waltham, Coach O'Donnell decided to accept the Detroit challenge. The game would be played in Detroit on Saturday, December 4, at Navin Field, the home of the Detroit Tigers.

▸ *The 1915 Everett (Mass.) national co-champion team 25 years later. (The Boston Globe)*

The 1915 Detroit Central High School co-national champion team.

The Detroiters were favored to win this game, if for no other reason than they outweighed the Crimson by 17 lbs. per man, living up to their nickname of "Monsters of the Midway".

When upwards of 15,000 fans filed into Navin Field that Saturday afternoon they found the field conditions to be decidedly less than perfect. Depending on what part of the gridiron one was standing on, it was either covered in a couple inches of mud and water or frozen over with ice and snow.

In the game's opening minutes, the Crimson recovered a Detroit fumble at the Central 20-yard line, but could advance it no further than the 10-yard line before giving it up on downs. That would prove to be Everett's only real scoring opportunity of the game. Although Detroit Central had a huge advantage in total yardage, 355-125, and first downs, 19-6, the hometown team faired no better when it came to scoring points. Despite having the ball inside the Everett 10-yard line on three different occasions, the Detroiters were unable to punch the ball into the end zone.

With neither team able to dent the other's goal line the game ended in a 0-0 tie. Neither team tried a field goal, though the Detroiters had the much better opportunity. Everett maintained its national championship for a second consecutive year, but this time it had to share the title with Detroit Central.

With the end of the 1915 season came the end of Cleo O'Donnell's tenure as the Everett football coach. From 1911 thru 1915, his teams had won 53 of 59 games, while losing just four and tying two. Defense was a big part of O'Donnell's winning strategy and in their last 49 games his teams had posted 46 shutouts. His offense was a bit ahead of its time in using the pass extensively, especially after suffering the 32-14 defeat at the hands of Bob Zuppke's Oak Park team in 1912. O'Donnell was known to be a strict disciplinarian with a tongue to match. Under Cleo O'Donnell the Crimson Tide had won five consecutive Massachusetts state championships from 1911 to 1915 and national titles in 1914 and 1915. A century later, his 1914 Everett High School Crimson Tide is still looked upon by many as the greatest high school football team in history.

Upon leaving Everett High School, Cleo O'Donnell joined the ranks of college coaches. He served as the head coach at Purdue for two seasons. Then after World War I, he returned to his alma mater, Holy Cross, to coach the football team for 11 years and achieved a very good 69-27-6 record. He left coaching after the 1929 season and became the Athletic Director at Holy Cross until 1933. He took his last collegiate coaching job at St. Anselm College in Manchester, New Hampshire, where he had a record of 28-11-2 from 1935-1940. O'Donnell died suddenly in 1953.

Almost 3,100 miles west, and then slightly north, of Everett, Massachusetts, is the other Everett High School, located in its namesake city of Everett, Washington. Strangely enough, there are some interesting parallels between the two Everett football teams other than their names and cities. Both were coached by outstanding football men, both of whom had become the captain of their college team in 1907 and who both went on to coach successfully at the college level. Both teams saw success begin in 1911, an era that would see each team win continuous state titles over a number of years—topped off by a pair of national championships.

Everett (Wash.) High School as it looked upon its opening in 1910. (Everett Yearbook)

The first football game at Washington's Everett High School is said to have been played in 1894; however, the historical record of the team remains a bit sporadic through 1907, although the team appears to have won more games than it lost. In 1908, Mr. G. J. Sweetland was hired as the school's full-time football coach and the team's fortunes immediately picked up. That season the Everett team rolled through its first seven games averaging more than 24 points per contest while allowing a total of only six points to be scored against it in posting six consecutive shutouts. This included a 19-0 victory over Bellingham Normal College; the playing of college teams would become a not insignificant

▲ *This drawing from the Everett (Wash.) High School yearbook celebrates the football team's 1912 championship of the Northwest.*

▼ *Action from an Everett (Wash.) home game in 1914. (Everett High School Yearbook)*

part of the Everett schedule over the coming years. In the final game of the 1908 season, the team lost to Wenatchee High School, 12-9, its only defeat that year.

Sweetland had been signed to just a one-year contract. He moved on after the season and the school then hired Enoch Bagshaw, who reported for duty in the fall of '09 as a history teacher and the football coach. Bagshaw did not fare as well as Sweetland, his team finishing with a 5-3-0 mark. Since he was also on a one-year contract, the school authorities opted not to renew Bagshaw's contract, instead replacing him with Ralph Cole. Unfortunately for Mr. Cole, almost immediately after taking his assignment at Everett, he became so ill that he could not continue at the school. Somewhat in desperation, the school authorities rehired Bagshaw at $25 per week and he resumed his teaching and coaching duties on September 16, 1910. The Everett team finished that season with another mediocre record of 5-4-0. There was some thought of again replacing Bagshaw, but his one-year deal was renewed—a move that would prove to be one of the best that the Everett High School authorities ever made.

Enoch "Baggy" Bagshaw, who was eventually known as "Mr. Coach" in the Pacific Northwest, was born on January 31, 1884, in the city of Flint in Wales. One of 12 siblings, Bagshaw's father moved the family to Washington State in 1892. Bagshaw attended Seattle High School where he played football. He was not a big lad, but fast and competitive. He graduated from Seattle High in 1903 and entered the University of Washington to study mining engineering. While at the university, Bagshaw also played football, earning the honor of being named team captain for the 1907 season. He graduated with his engineering degree in 1908.

After his on-again, off-again start at Everett High School, Bagshaw settled into the position as head football coach for the 1911 season, a season that would see the first of what were later called Bagshaw's "Wonder Teams". One thing that Bagshaw did for this season in an effort to enhance the football schedule was to play the better teams in the area, an idea that also appealed to the school's administration. After a close game with the alumni to start the season, Everett breezed through its next three games. The team then played Bagshaw's alma mater, now known as Broadway High School, a team that had handed Everett a string of defeats in recent years. This

The o-line opens a big hole for this Everett (Wash.) ball carrier during this 1915 game action in front of a large home crowd. (Everett High School Yearbook)

Enoch Bagshaw was the head football coach at Everett (Wash.) High School from 1909-1920 (Everett High School Yearbook)

time the tables were turned and Everett came away with a 19-0 win, a victory that the yearbook noted "at once put Everett in the limelight."

The victories continued to pile up, with only a tough Lincoln High team able to score on Everett, although Bagshaw's team still came away with a hard-fought 12-6 win. The next game, against Tacoma High School, was equally tough. In fact, for the first time in recent memory, Everett failed to score, but neither did Tacoma as the game ended in a 0-0 tie. In the final game of the season Bagshaw's team played Olympia High School, the champions of southwestern Washington. It was another blowout as Everett won by 56-0, a victory that the yearbook noted "marked the close of the best football season in the history of Everett High School, and stamped her as the leader in the state."

The 1912 season saw two new items added to the Everett football program. First and foremost was that the school authorities authorized a new football field and grandstand to be built for their championship team—the boys finally getting their own home field.

Secondly, Bagshaw added some college teams to the schedule and would include them every season, the thought being that playing these bigger teams would only help his team against the tougher high schools now on the schedule. There were probably those who doubted this strategy when Everett was defeated by the University of Washington varsity, 55-0, in the first game of the season, but overall the boys would go 1-1-1 against collegiate competition that year.

The season ended with Everett posting a 6-1-2 record, but going undefeated against high school opponents, 5-0-1. That lone tie, 3-3 against a strong team from Queen Anne High School, resulted in some controversy as far as the state championship was concerned. Queen Anne was undefeated and claimed the state championship, in part by virtue of its tie with Everett. Everett, in like manner, claimed the state title since as the reigning champion they had still not been defeated. The state school authorities ruled in Everett's favor; but, to avoid further controversy they decided to no longer name an "official" state champion, at least for a few years.

The continued success of Bagshaw's team led to some unforeseen consequences. In the 1913 season the team went 8-0-1 (including a 174-0 win over Bellingham High School) and captured another state championship ("official" or not). However, the cities of Seattle, Spokane, and Tacoma banned the playing of intercity games, in effect banning their schools from playing games against the Everett football team. This forced the Everett school authorities to get somewhat creative in filling the team's schedule. The games against collegiate foes were now almost a must to fill the schedule, as were out-of-state games with teams from cities such as Portland, Oregon.

Despite this handicap, Everett continued to roll up the victories—and state championships. Bagshaw's 1914 squad was a perfect 7-0-0. The 1915 team finished 7-2-0, but only one of those defeats was to a high school opponent, Hoquiam High, and that by just a single point, 13-12. It would prove to be the team's only loss to a high school opponent from 1909 thru the 1921 season. Despite that loss the Everett team still retained its state championship.

Everett was 9-3-0 in 1916 and 10-0-1 in 1917—and the team added two more state championships. The war year of 1917 saw Everett play an even greater variety of opponents, which now included military teams from nearby bases. Bagshaw's team even played, and won, a doubleheader that season, defeating Bremerton High School and Sedro-Wooley High School on the same day! Everett High finished the 1917 season with seven shutouts and outscored its opponents 569-19.

Bagshaw's football team had now won seven consecutive state championships, but the close of the 1917 season would see a temporary end to the Bagshaw era at Everett High School. This was brought about by two events not directly connected to football. The first was World War I and the U.S. entry into that conflict. In the spring of 1918, Enoch Bagshaw enlisted in the U.S. Army, becoming a first lieutenant in the Engineer Corps. The second event was the Spanish flu epi-

▾ *Running back George "The Wildcat" Wilson (with ball) was the first superstar at Everett (Wash.) High School and played on both of the school's national championship trams. (Everett High School Yearbook)*

Toledo, Ohio-
December 15th- 1919-

This contract entered into between the Everett High School
Everett, Wash- and the Scott High School, Toledo, O- for a
foot ball game to be played at Everett Washington January
First 1920-
The Everett High School Managment agrees to pay the
Toledo Scott High School managment a net sum of $5000.00-
Said money to be payed as follows-
$3000.00 to be deposited with Mr- A.R.Manson 2310 Yale
Ave- N- Seattle Washington on or before Tuesday December 16th-
6 P.M. Pacific time- Or said sum may be deposited with the
American Express Railway Co- as may be prefered- Said money to
be to our credit and order-
The balance of $2000.00 to be paid at the conclusion of
game on Jan- first 1920 to Mr- F.L.Siebert.Jr- manager of the
Toledo Scott High School-
Players on both teams to be eligible under the rules gov-
erning athletics in the schoolsof their respective states-
No player on either team can be used in this contest who
has not been a member of the foot ball squad the entire season
of 1919-
Either team not fullfilling their part of this contract
to pay a forfeit of $2000.00 within 10 days of date of game
said date being Jan- 11th- 1920-
Weather conditions interfering with this game the Scott
Team agrees to remain in Everett and play game on Jan- 3rd-1920
The Everett High School managment to pay an additional
sum equal to the lodging and meals for 20 men for two days-
The foot ball used in this contest to become the property
of the team winning the game-Game ending in a tie the Scott
team to retain the foot ball-

Signed-

For- Everett,Wash- High School as per
telegram-

‒‒‒‒‒‒‒‒‒‒‒‒‒‒‒‒‒‒‒‒‒‒‒‒‒‒‒‒‒‒Prin-
For- Scott High School, Toledo, O-

‒‒‒‒‒‒‒‒‒‒‒‒‒‒‒‒‒‒‒‒‒‒‒‒‒‒‒‒‒‒Ath- Mgr-
For- Scott High School, Toledo, O-

▸ *The contract between Everett (Wash.) and Toledo Scott high schools that made possible the 1919 national championship game.*

demic of 1918 that killed millions of people around the world. The United States was not spared from the ravages of the flu, which forced the closing of many institutions, including schools and churches, and the cancellation of many events, not the least of which were college and high school football games. A former Everett gridder by the name of "Wad" Sundstrom was named to take Bagshaw's place in 1918 while he was in the Army, but there were no games played that season because of the influenza outbreak.

It must have seemed like a cool breath of fresh air when the football season of 1919 rolled around. Memories of the scourge of both the World War and the Spanish influenza were quickly becoming sad memories and it was time to move on to more pleasant endeavors. For Everett High School this meant the return of Enoch Bagshaw as the football team's head coach. Despite the year off, "Baggy" would have another great team led by some outstanding veteran players. The team would excel at running the ball both up the middle and around the ends, but it was also one of the best passing teams that Bagshaw had yet put on the field. The yearbook described the line as "from end to end … there was not one weak spot in the whole line. It was a stone wall on defense while on offense it had tremendous charging power." That line was also described as devastating.

While the team no longer counted military units among its opponents, Everett still played college teams and a few out-of-state teams. As it had for the last several years, Everett's 1919 football season opened against a college team, the College of Puget Sound from Tacoma. Using what was then known as "straight football", which meant that the team primarily kept the ball on the ground, Everett easily defeated the collegians by a score of 44 to 7. They then dispatched the team from Bremerton's Union High School by a score of 77-0.

Next up was a game with another college team, the freshman squad from the University of Washington. Early in the first quarter, the college team had a first and goal at the Everett one-yard line. Four plays later, after a great goal line stand the high schoolers took possession with the ball still at the one-yard line. It was a bruising battle, with the Everett team leading 7-0 at the half after scoring in the second quarter. Everett had much the better of it in the second half, but an intercepted pass returned for a touchdown by the college freshmen prevented an Everett victory, the game ending in a 7-7 tie.

"FROM END TO END ... THERE WAS NOT ONE WEAK SPOT IN THE WHOLE LINE. IT WAS A STONE WALL ON DEFENSE WHILE ON OFFENSE IT HAD TREMENDOUS CHARGING POWER."

Bagshaw's team cruised through its next three games outscoring the opposition 163-0, a fourth game was won by forfeit. The team had an open date on Saturday, November 22, until Bagshaw arranged a game with Vancouver High School. Despite having something of a reputation as a very good football team, the Vancouver team was no match for the Everett lads and fell by a score of 59 to 7; they could, however, take solace in the fact that they were the first high school eleven to score against Everett that season.

With its record now 7-0-1, Everett arranged a game on Thanksgiving Day with Lincoln High of Portland, Ore., which like Everett was undefeated and reputed to be one of the best in Oregon. The mud at Everett's Athletic Field could not slow down Bagshaw's team, and neither could Lincoln. Final score: Everett 125, Lincoln 7.

The team now thought that its season was over, but when Scott High School of Toledo, Ohio, offered to play them for the championship of the United States, Everett accepted the challenge. As we will see in the next chapter, Scott High School, which only opened its doors in 1913, fielded one of the best teams in the country from 1916 thru 1923, posting a record of 61-5-1. Scott played in no fewer than four national championship games, the second of which was played on January 1, 1920, on Everett's Athletic Field.

Diagram Shows Progress of Ball in Game with Toledo's Scott High School Eleven

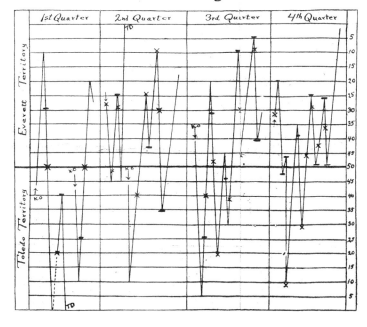

A play-by-play chart of the national championship game between Everett (Wash.) and Toledo Scott high schools on Jan. 1, 1920. (Everett Daily Herald)

The 1919 Everett (Wash.) High School national championship team.

▲ *1920 Everett (Wash.)*
backfield ace, Les Sherman.
(Everett High School Newspaper)

A copy of the game contract between Everett and Scott high schools still exists. Unlike today, when such a document might take multiple pages of legal mumbo-jumbo, this contract was a one-page affair. The basic clauses were as follows:

1. Everett High School would pay Scott High School $5,000 for playing the game; $3,000 up front and $2,000 at the conclusion of the game.
2. Players on both teams had to be eligible per the rules of their respective state.
3. Should weather force the postponement of the January 1 play date then the Scott High School team agrees to stay in Everett to play the game on Jan. 3.
4. The game ball becomes the property of the winning team; in the event of a tie the Scott team gets the ball.

The national championship contest was a hard-fought game played, as described by the *Everett Daily Herald*, "on a sloppy field that was covered by a mist of slippery mud." The newspaper went on to note that "the biggest crowd that ever witnessed an athletic event in Everett sat in the grand stand and bleachers wildly cheering Everett's progress in the great intersectional football match." Among those in attendance was Washington's Governor Louis F. Hart and his wife.

After the kickoff, reported as being at 12:18, Everett halfback Vern Hickey gave his team a 7-0 lead with a two-yard run for a touchdown. Early in the second quarter, on fourth and goal from the Everett six-yard line, Scott halfback Tommy Andrews scored on a play that was described by *The Daily Herald* thusly:

"...the Toledo boys scored a touchdown on a play that they dug out of the mothballs before starting from the East. It was an old-fashioned criss-cross with a touch of modern camouflage which made it effective. The Everett end was drawn in, and the Toledo man with the ball was run in on the reverse of the play, took it around the Everett end and over the goal line, as easily as if he were on a Sunday afternoon promenade."

The extra point pulled the game even at 7-7. The balance of the game would be a great defensive struggle. Scott had the ball six inches from the Everett end zone, and the police "making efforts to keep the crowd back," when the final whistle blew ending the game in a 7-7 tie.

Both teams ended the season undefeated with eight victories, Everett having two ties and Scott one. Everett and Scott and Harrisburg Tech of Pennsylvania (more on that team later) all shared the national championship for 1919.

The next fall Enoch Bagshaw had a solid corps of returning players upon whom to build his team. Included in this group was fullback Lester Sherman, like quite a few older high school students a returning World War I veteran who had served in the U.S. Navy.

▸ *The 1920 Everett (Wash.) backfield: Glen "Scoops" Carlson, Walter Morgan, George "The Wildcat" Wilson, Les Sherman, Carl Michel, Ed Manning.*

▸ *This Everett (Wash.) ball carrier races for a touchdown during this 1920 home game. (Everett High School Yearbook)*

Coach Bagshaw had put together another good team with which to face the 1920 season, but who were these guys going to play? The intercity restrictions of Seattle, Spokane, and Tacoma were still being enforced and good teams to play were getting harder and harder to find. Bagshaw managed to line up six games for his team, but only one of which was a legitimate high school eleven, Stanwood High. The other five opponents included the Everett Alumni, two military teams, and a couple of college teams in the University of Washington freshmen and St. Martin's College. Those games only took the team's schedule up to Halloween, with the whole month of November devoid of games. Bagshaw would have to do some real scrambling during October if he hoped to fill out his team's schedule.

The season opened on Monday, September 13, with the game against the alumni. As the school's yearbook noted, "The Alumni team that opposed the high school boys was composed of some of the best players ever turned out in Everett High School." Although the hard-fought game ended in a 13-13 tie, the yearbook

▸ *An Everett (Wash.) ball carrier eludes the opposition defense during the 1920 season while the official (far right in bulky sweater) tries to keep up. (Everett High School Yearbook)*

▸ *A short plunge at the goal line produces another Everett (Wash.) touchdown in 1920. (Everett High School Yearbook)*

noted that "it was a fair indication that the Everett 1920 team was headed towards another championship."

The next game was supposed to have been with Stanwood High School, but at the last minute they backed out. Fortunately, Bagshaw was able to get Sedro-Wooley High School to play Everett in Stanwood's place, the game being played on Saturday, September 25. Knowing that his boys were far superior to the Sedro-Wooley contingent, Bagshaw played the second team backfield and several second team linemen for the entire first half. He then let the first team get its work in during the second half "and they managed to run up the score at leisure" in Everett's 67-0 win.

Next came the two military teams on the schedule. The first of these was the team representing the Bremerton Navy Yard. This team would seem to have had quite an advantage against a team of 16- to 18-year old high school lads, all of the sailors being at least 21 years old and outweighing Bagshaw's boys by a healthy margin. According to the Everett yearbook the Navy team's commanding officer "told them to remember it was a high school team they were playing and not to pull any 'rough stuff'." The sailors and their CO had to be a bit surprised when the game ended and they found themselves on the short end of a 27-9 score.

~ THE EMBLEM OF VICTORY ~

▲ *The logo for the Everett (Wash.) Soaring Seagulls. (Everett High School Yearbook)*

▾ *Cleveland's East Tech High School football team traveled to Washington State to play Everett High School for the 1920 national championship. (Everett High School Newspaper)*

The Naval Base Hospital team came to Everett's Athletic Field the following Saturday. These sailors no doubt had heard about the game the week before, but it did not help them. Bagshaw's eleven walked all over this bunch of sailors, 84-0, scoring four touchdowns in the final six minutes.

With no game scheduled for Saturday, October 16, Bagshaw took his team to Seattle to watch the University of Washington take on the University of Montana. This was actually something of a scouting trip for the Everett lads; before the Washington-Montana contest (won by Montana, 18-14) there was a game played between the Washington freshman and the team representing St. Martin's College, both of whom the Everett team would be playing over the next two weekends.

The Washington freshmen were the first to face Everett. This team had played Bagshaw's squad to a 7-7 tie the year before, but this time Everett came away with a 20-0 victory. Eight days later, on Halloween Sunday, it was St. Martin's College that paid a visit to Everett's Athletic Field. This was another hard fought game, but Everett High School got all of the Halloween treats and St. Martin's the tricks as Bagshaw's team collected a 19-0 victory.

With no game scheduled for the weekend of November 5-6, Bagshaw again took his team to Seattle to watch the University of Washington team play another game, this time in a 3-0 loss against Stanford. Meanwhile Bagshaw had been busy arranging a couple of games for the boys. The first of these took place on Saturday, Nov. 13, against the team from The Dales High School, the champions of Oregon. Apparently this was an off year for Oregon high school football, or the Everett team was truly that good, as Everett rolled to a 90-7 win over the Oregon titlists.

The second game was arranged for Thanksgiving Day against East High School of Salt Lake City, Utah. The East High Leopards had won the championship of Utah and "the mountain section" for the last three seasons and their 1920 team was said to be the best of the three. The Turkey Day game would show that Utah football did not quite stack up to the game played on the coast. Final score: Everett 67, East High 0.

Having now defeated a couple of teams believed to be the best in their respective state, Bagshaw was looking for other challenges for his team. He found one at Long Beach High School, reputedly the best team in Southern California. This time Bagshaw's team would be playing on the road. On game day, the city of Long Beach shut down as if for a holiday and some 15,000 supporters of the local team turned out for the game. This

EVERETT WINS U.S. CHAMPIONSHIP

proved to be a much tougher contest than Everett's previous two games, but they still managed to emerge victorious 28-0.

Having defeated the best of the West, Bagshaw now wanted his team to play the best eastern team in a game for the national championship. Their choice was East Technical High School of Cleveland, Ohio, coached by Sam Willaman (who would coach the Ohio State Buckeyes from 1929-1933). East Tech was 9-0-0 and had outscored its opponents 462-7 while winning the championships of both Cleveland and Ohio. Among the team's nine victories was a 14-7 decision over 1919 national co-champion Toledo Scott, a loss that was Scott's only defeat of the season and its first since 1918. Scott had tied Everett in a national championship game in 1919, so playing the conqueror of the Toledoans was a natural for Everett.

Arrangements for the game were finalized on December 22, with the game to be played on New Year's Day, 1921, in Everett, Wash. Reserved seats for the game went on sale in Everett on December 27 and reportedly sold out within three hours—all 20,000 of them.

There would be 20 people in the East Tech contingent heading to the great Northwest, 18 players along with head coach Willaman and Athletic Director Gordon Frost. The Clevelanders left by train for the West Coast on Christmas Eve and arrived in Seattle on December 30. Coach Willaman decided that his team would stay in Seattle until the day of the game; his reasoning being that Everett was only a 1½ hour bus ride away and that by staying in Seattle his team would be able to use the facilities at the University of Washington for their practice sessions.

This game would be one that emphasized different styles of play. While East Tech ran the ball as much as anyone, the team excelled at the passing game and used it often. On the other hand, Everett relied heavily on "straight football" for the bulk of its offense. Besides the obvious home field advantage, the Everett squad also enjoyed a size advantage by outweighing the Clevelanders by an average 23 pounds per man.

Kickoff was scheduled for noon of January 1. The gridiron was in great shape and, although overcast, the weather was co-operating as well, *The Daily Herald* reporting that "There is just the right kind of zip and snap in the air that puts pep into the players and spectators alike."

After a scoreless first quarter, Everett took a 16-0 lead in the second, in part due to a couple of East Tech miscues. Neither team was able to score in the third quarter, although East Tech seemed to dominate the play continuing into the fourth quarter. East Tech's persistence finally paid off with a 30-yard touchdown pass. The placement was good, cutting the Everett lead to 16-7.

There would be no more scoring over the balance of the game, Everett High School coming away with a hard fought 16-7 victory, having scored all of its points in the second quarter. In a postgame story that he wrote for one of the Cleveland newspapers, East Tech head coach Sam Willaman blamed the loss on his team's fumbles, but he also noted that "the treatment we received at Everett from fans, players and officials was of the highest order."

The victory secured for Everett its ninth consecutive state title and a second consecutive national championship, albeit one the team again had to share, this time with Oak Park High School.

This would prove to be the last year for Enoch Bagshaw as the head coach at Everett High School. His outstanding success had attracted the attention of the University of Washington, which hired him as its new head coach shortly after the 1920 season had ended.

▲ *The 1920 national champion football team from Everett (Wash.) High School. (Everett High School Yearbook)*

Enoch Bagshaw led his team to a truly remarkable record of success. Overall his record at Everett High School was 84-13-8. In his last nine seasons as the Everett head coach (with a year out for military service during World War I), Bagshaw's team compiled a record of 74-6-8. Only one of those defeats was at the hands of another high school, and that by a single point. In Bagshaw's last three seasons, the Everett Seagulls won 27 games and had four ties, but not a single defeat against a schedule that included college teams, military teams, and some of the best schoolboy teams from around the country. Bagshaw's teams won the state championship nine consecutive seasons (1911-1920—no champion declared for 1918) and a national championship in his last two.

At the University of Washington, Bagshaw would coach the Huskies for nine seasons with a record of 63-22-6. He is the first coach to ever take Washington to the

▲ *This 1919 national championship team from Harrisburg Tech outscored its opponents by 701-0.* (Harrisburg Sunday Patriot-News)

Rose Bowl, doing it in 1923 and again in 1925. Bagshaw left the Huskies after the 1929 season and was appointed the state Supervisor of Roads by the governor. He died suddenly of a heart attack in 1930 while attending a meeting at the state house.

In 1921 under new head coach Earl "Click" Clark, the Seagulls won another state championship, the tenth in a row, with a record of 6-0-1. From 1917-1921 the team's record was 33-0-5. Not too surprisingly, they continued to have a hard time scheduling games and seldom played more than six or seven games a season until almost 1930.

————————

The story of the greatest national champions would not be complete without at least a short mention of another outstanding team from these earliest years. Harrisburg (Pa.) Tech, had the shortest, but one of the most successful, football "careers" of any of the schools in our story. Opened in the fall of 1904, the school fielded its first football team the following season. The team won the first game it ever played in 1905, defeating Marysville, 5-0, a game played before "twenty rooters (that) accompanied the Tech team", but they lost the other five games played that season.

Like many high school programs, the Tech team got off to a slow start—in 1907 the boys did not score a single point in going 0-5-0. Gradual improvement led to the team's first undefeated campaign in 1913 and the next season they went 7-1-1, with the highlight being Tech's first victory over arch-rival Harrisburg Central.

The 1916 season would mark the start of Tech's football supremacy, one that would last until the school closed 10 years later. As the Tech yearbook, *The Tatler*, put it, "The change in Tech football history was marked by the year 1916. Up until that time Tech had only been able to gain the city championship once. It now changed gradually from a small, unimportant team to one of the four leading teams in the U.S."

The team's won-lost record bears this out. From 1905-1915 Tech was a modest 45-34-12, .560. But from 1916-1925 a splendid 83-17-0, .830. Harrisburg Tech hit its high water mark during the period from 1917 thru 1920. In 1917 Tech won its first two games before suffering a 31-0 loss at the hands of Easton High School. Tech rebounded from that loss by defeating Altoona High School the following week, 117-0, the most points that Tech ever scored in a single game. Beginning with that stunning win over Altoona, Tech closed out the season with six consecutive victories, setting up the remarkable and record breaking seasons of 1918 and 1919.

Despite the world war and the Spanish flu epidemic, the Tech team, now referred to as the Maroons from their uniform color, managed to play a nine game schedule plus two postseason games in 1918. Coached by Paul Smith, the Maroons got off to a flying start with a 63-0 victory over Wilkes-Barre High School and never looked back. Tech's closest game came in the fourth week of the season against Lebanon High School, but the Maroons managed to pull out a 13-0 win. Tech went on to finish the season a perfect 9-0-0, allowing only 10 points to be scored against it.

After the season had been completed the Lebanon team asked for a rematch since the Cedars had had a good season and wanted to even the account with Tech. The Maroons agreed to the game and promptly dismantled the Lebanon eleven by a whopping 73-0 score.

Tech was then challenged to a game for the state championship by Johnstown High School, a team that had been scored upon only once in the previous two seasons. It was another dismantling by the Maroons as they crushed the "Johnnies" 76-7, Johnstown scoring its lone touchdown on a recovered fumble.

Harrisburg Tech finished the 1918 campaign a perfect 11-0-0, having outscored the opposition 724-10. They won the Pennsylvania championship and

▲ *The starting backfield*
for the 1919 Harrisburg Tech
football national champions:
FB Tony Wilbach, HB Carl
Beck, HB Paul Garrett, QB
Charles Lingle, (Harrisburg
Sunday Patriot-News)

are recognized as the 1918 national champions. The Maroons were the first high school team to ever score more than 700 points in a season and their total of 724 is still the second highest total for any team playing 11-12 games in a season.

While there was the normal amount of loss due to graduation, the 1919 Harrisburg Tech team had a nucleus of six returning seniors around whom to build for the coming season. Coach Smith would need every good player he could lay his hands on because Tech's schedule included many of the best teams in Pennsylvania. Leading the way for the Maroons would be halfback Carl Beck, one of the greatest high school athletes period. Beck would lead the team with 34 touchdowns and on the last day of the season have a game that most players can only dream of.

The Maroons opened the 1919 season just where they had left off the previous year, blowing away the opposition. In winning its first three games, Tech scored 233 points without giving up any. Week Four, the Maroons lined up opposite the team from Baltimore Polytechnic, one of the best teams in Maryland. But Maryland football was apparently not on a par with that of the Keystone State as Tech came away with an 89-0 win.

Tech then played three straight games with prep schools from around the state because none of the local teams would put Tech on their schedule. Tighter games, but three more wins and three more shutouts. Then it was Greensburg High, always a thorn in the Maroons' side and the 1918 champion of Western Pennsylvania; but, this was Tech's year and Greensburg fell, 39-0.

Tech posted shutouts in its next two games to set up a last-game showdown with the undefeated team from Erie High School, with the state championship on the line. Played in Erie, this game would prove to be the Maroons' toughest contest of the season, but they prevailed by a 20 to 0 count.

Having finished the season a perfect 11-0-0 and having secured another Pennsylvania title, Coach Smith's team was looking for a team to play for the national championship. They found just the opponent in Portland (Maine) High School, the champion of the New England states. The game was played in Harrisburg and, as previously mentioned, Tech halfback Carl Beck had the game of the season. He scored five touchdowns against Portland, including two on runs of 60 yards and a pair of 50-yard jaunts. Harrisburg Tech won the game 56-0 and was named national champion for a second consecutive season by none other than Walter Camp—the most respected football authority in the country and known as the "Father of American Football."

Harrisburg Tech would win the first five games in 1920 to extend its win streak to 34 straight, but the 1918 and 1919 seasons are those by which the Maroons are forever remembered. In 1919 they again topped the 700 point mark, outscoring their opponents by 701-0. Harrisburg Tech was the first and is still one of only two schools to ever score 700 or more points in consecutive seasons. It has been estimated that during those two seasons, the Maroons averaged a point every 46 seconds that they were on the gridiron.

In 1926, upon the completion of two new high schools, both Harrisburg Tech and Harrisburg Central were closed. Tech may be gone, but memories of the Maroons will last forever and their 1919 team is often listed with those considered to be among the all-time best.

## CHAPTER 3

GLASS CITY CHAMPIONS

Scott High School & Waite High School
Toledo, Ohio

Nestled in the northwest corner of Ohio is the city of Toledo. It is known even today as the Glass City based on its decades-long reputation as a center of the glass-making industry in this country. More recently Toledo has gained some additional fame thanks to its numerous mentions on the television show M*A*S*H by favorite son Jamie Farr, playing Cpl. Max Klinger.

However, in the early days of the 20th century it was the high school athletes of Toledo, more specifically the high school football teams, who put Toledo on the map. As we will relate, Toledo was the only city of its size to be the home to multiple schools that were proclaimed high school football national champions and one of only two cities to earn that distinction during the entire 20th century.

The first Toledo school to get mentioned in connection with the national high school football championship was the city's Central High School. As we already related, Central played Detroit's Central High School back in 1904 in one of the earliest recognized games for the national championship. But for a missed extra point by the Toledoans, along with a fumble that the Detroiters returned for a late touchdown and then converted the game winning extra point, the Glass City might have had its first national champion in 1904. However, Toledo would not have to wait too long to claim its first national high school football title, and it would come thanks to the city's newest high schools.

James Wakeman Scott High School opened on the west side of Toledo in 1913 and just a year later Morrison R. Waite High School opened on the city's east side. In 1914 the city fathers decided that Toledo did not need three high schools, so the much older Central High School was closed.

With the two remaining schools serving/representing opposite sides of town, rivalries between the two were as natural as snow in the winter. One of the first places in which this cross-town competition appeared was the gridiron. Scott and Waite high schools would enjoy one of the most intense football rivalries in Ohio, made even more intense because their annual battle took place on Thanksgiving morning, the traditional day on which such rivalries were then held and still are in many places. The first of these games took place in 1914, and before long the Scott-Waite football game had become a Turkey Day game of interest, not just in Toledo, but throughout much of the Midwest.

▲ *This Waite ball carrier "carries the mail" in 1914 in one of the first games ever played at Waite High School, the new school building in the background. (Toledo Blade)*

The results of the annual Scott-Waite football game would soon have implications far beyond the Toledo city limits - but we are getting a little ahead of our story.

Scott High School fielded its first football team that very first year of 1913. For a fledgling team the boys were not bad, finishing the season with a record of 6-2-0. One of the teams that Scott is supposed to have scrimmaged that year was the team from the University of Notre Dame. The same Notre Dame team that had Gus Dorais at quarterback and a chemistry major by the name of Knute Rockne at end. The same Notre Dame team that surprised and crushed Army 35-13 later that season in one of the most significant games in football history. The high school team only lost to the Ramblers by 10-0, but then it was just a scrimmage.

The Scott team only won two of nine games the following season, but rebounded to 5-2-1 in 1915. In 1916 the football team was coached by a young Tom Merrell, of whom the school yearbook noted "it is largely due to him that Scott has developed her great fighting spirit which has spread from football to all branches of Athletics." In anticipation of what they hoped would be a great season, the student body made it known that they wanted more seating around their football field. With the students raising all of the money themselves, new stands were erected at Scott Field that accommodated 4,200, bringing the field's total capacity to around 6,000.

Somewhat in anticipation of things to come, but also reflecting its position on the Ohio-Michigan border, the Scott team's 1916 schedule would be split between opponents in Ohio and Michigan, with a few "extras" tossed in. Tom Merrell's gridders opened the season on September 30 with a 64-0 thrashing of Ross High School from Fremont, Ohio. The boys continued to roll the following week with a 59-7 win over the team from Monroe (Mich.) High. This victory, as the yearbook noted, set up "the big game of the year with our old rivals, Detroit Central." More than 5,000 fans, the biggest crowd ever in Scott Field's short history, turned out to see the big game with the Detroiters, a team that had shared the 1915 national championship with Everett (Mass.) High School. After a scoreless first quarter the Toledoans picked up a head of steam and rolled to a 37-2 triumph over the defending national champions—a huge victory for such a young program.

Due to inclement weather the following week, a crowd only about a tenth the size of the previous week's showed up at Scott Field for the game against the team representing the Mt. Pleasant (Mich.) Indian School. It was another one-sided affair with the home team coming away with a 57-0 victory.

With its record now 4-0-0 after crushing the Indian School, Tom Merrell's team was getting something of a reputation, one that was eliciting game invitations from around the country. The team's convincing win over Detroit Central was no doubt also a major factor behind this interest. Among others, Washington's Everett High School and teams from Beverly, Mass., Dunkirk, N.Y., and Chicago were inquiring about possible postseason games. As the *Toledo Blade* noted, "It is probable that Scott will play a post-season game if it defeats Waite in the Thanksgiving Day battle, but which team will be selected depends upon that team's record at the time."

Scott scored its biggest triumph of the season, point wise, on October 28 when the team throttled Findlay High, 90-0. Next up was a game that was billed as a true test of Scott's abilities. Coming west to Toledo for a game on November 4 was the team from Erie (Pa.) High School, described by one veteran observer as "a powerful, hard-fighting combination." It was the consensus that this would be a crucial hurdle for the Scott team to overcome if it had any postseason ambitions.

After two hard-fought periods, Scott enjoyed a 13-0 lead over the Pennsylvanians at the half. The Toledoans added three more touchdowns in the second half; the Erie team avoided a shutout with a field goal in the fourth quarter as Scott came away with an impressive 32-3 victory.

On November 11, Scott took to the road for the first time all season to play in Muskegon, Mich., against that city's high school. Avenging the defeat that it was handed the previous year, Tom Merrell's team kept its record clean with a 33-0 victory. The team's next opponent was Freeport (Ill.) High School, a team that claimed to be the undisputed champion of Illinois. The Scott team was not intimidated and came away with a one-sided 54-6 victory.

Next up was the big Thanksgiving morning battle with Waite High School, the third meeting of this young rivalry. Waite had won the first game in 1914 by a 34-13 margin, but Scott had come back in 1915 to win 21-0. Waite entered this game with a 4-3-1 record.

There were some 6,000 fans on hand at Scott Field that Thursday morning for this much anticipated game. Waite played tough throughout the first half, holding Scott to one touchdown in each of the first two quarters. Leading by only 13-0, a thoroughly awakened Scott team took the field after the intermission and buried

▲ *Head Coach Tom Merrell led Scott High School to the 1916 national championship. (Scott Yearbook)*

The Scott team practicing in Los Angeles during its West Coast trip in 1919. (Scott Yearbook)

the east siders under a torrent of seven touchdowns en route to a 57-0 triumph.

With the season now over, Scott was boasting a splendid record of nine victories and no defeats, having outscored all comers by a 483-18 margin. Newly named as the Ohio high school champion, it was now time for the team to look to a postseason opponent in an effort to add the national championship to its trophy case. The team from Haverhill (Mass.) High School, deemed to be the best team in the east, was chosen as Scott's opponent and would host the Ohioans in a game for the national championship to be played on Saturday, December 9. Even in Boston, the Scott team was picked as the favorite in this game, the feeling being that the Toledo team was stronger than the Detroit Central contingent that tied Everett (Mass.) High School in the game for the 1915 national championship, and that Haverhill was not as good as that Everett team had been. All this despite the fact that Haverhill had the advantage of playing on its home field and possessed a weight advantage over Tom Merrell's boys.

The Scott High gridders left Toledo by train on Thursday, December 7. They traveled in a private car added to the regular New York Central train, the car then being picked up in Albany, N.Y., by a train of the Albany & Boston Railroad and arriving in Boston late on the morning of Friday, December 9.

More than 10,000 people were on hand for the game at the Haverhill stadium. The weather conditions were fine despite a prediction of rain, but the early morning frost melted as the day grew warmer, causing the gridiron to become somewhat slick.

The game got underway shortly after 2 P.M. After recovering a Haverhill fumble at the home team's 23-yard line, Scott went in for a touchdown and a 7-0 lead halfway through the first quarter. Defense would dominate the balance of the first quarter and both the second and third periods as well. As the game entered the final stanza Scott was still holding onto its 7-0 advantage. Early in the fourth quarter Scott halted a drive by the home team and Haverhill was forced to relinquish the ball on downs at the Scott 36-yard line. Mixing passes with runs, it took the Toledoans only nine plays to get to the Haverhill one-yard line. Facing fourth and goal at that point, halfback George Urschel flipped a pass to Waldorf Kirk in the end zone for a Toledo touchdown. The extra point try was missed, but Scott had now extended its lead to 13-0.

Neither team scored during what remained of the fourth quarter, Scott High School coming away with a 13-0 victory and the national championship.

The people of the Boston area knew and appreciated good high school football when they saw it, even when that good football came at the expense of their local teams. Typical comments of the Scott performance were these written in the *Boston Post* after the game, "The Scott high school eleven ... gained the strongest claim to the national high school football championship with its 13 to 0 victory over the unbeaten Haverhill high school eleven ... the team uncovered a fine repertoire of plays, using shift formations in the majority of its offensive plays, and making its offense still more bewildering to its opponents by delayed and fake passes from the quarter-back."

In 1917 Scott had another good season in winning eight of nine games. They dropped a 20-12 decision to Detroit Central, but won the big Thanksgiving Day game with Waite, 19-0. In the Spanish influenza-shortened season of 1918 and now coached by J.K. "Pat" Dwyer, Scott played but six games and posted a record of 4-2-0. However, one of those losses was a 17-0 defeat at the hands of Heidelberg University. Although Scott lost the Thanksgiving Day game to Waite by a score of 12-7, they are still recognized as the 1918 Ohio scholastic champion.

As was mentioned in the previous chapter, it was a totally different and much more pleasant atmosphere that greeted everyone with the coming of the 1919 football season. The Scott football team was no exception as Coach Pat Dwyer had his charges ready and honed to a fine edge from the very first game.

The Scotters defeated West High of Columbus, Ohio, in the season opener, 27-0. The team's next game was against Xenia High School, billed as the champions of southwestern Ohio. Scott's 114-0 victory prompted the *Toledo Blade* to note that "no thought need be given to southwestern Ohio high school football by Toledo teams."

On Saturday, October 25, the team from Massillon's Washington High School paid a visit to Scott Field. As the *Toledo Blade* later noted, "Right here in Toledo something not down upon the books was sprung by Massillon high's eleven. Little advance information prepared no one for the surprise pulled by the yellow and black team, which proved to be as heavy as Scott and a blamed sight better at times."

Massillon, coached by John Snavely, already had a couple of state championships under its belt and like everyone else was rebounding from 1918. The Tigers had gotten off to a good 4-0-0 start in the current season, but since Scott had defeated them the previous year by 35-7, it appears that the Toledo team may have

▲   *The Scott team photo taken in Los Angeles during its West Coast trip in 1919. (Scott Yearbook)*

taken Massillon a little lightly—almost too lightly. The Tigers were led by half-back Harry Stuhldreher, who would soon be toting the football for Knute Rockne as one of the legendary Four Horsemen. Of Stuhldreher's play in this game the *Toledo Blade* stated that "during the time Stuhldreher was in the game the team outclassed Scott."

Stuhldreher gave Massillon a 7-0 lead on its first possession with a pair of runs that netted 65 yards and a touchdown, but Scott came back to take a 14-7 advantage at the half. The third period was a punting duel until late in the quarter when Massillon tied the score at 14-14 with a long touchdown aerial.

At this point of the game, it had become evident to Coach Dwyer that Massillon was doing most of its damage over the left side of Scott's defensive line, so Dwyer made a change to his defensive personnel. The strategy worked; the hole in the Scott defense was plugged for the balance of the game and all Scott had to do was find a way to score the winning points. Those came on a 40-yard run by Gene Flues early in the fourth quarter, giving Scott a 21-14 advantage.

That would prove to be the final score. Coach Dwyer's team had been given a big scare, but it had prevailed.

The following week Scott had another tough game, this time with Detroit Central. A first quarter Scott touchdown provided the only points scored during the first three periods. Scott added a couple of late TDs in the fourth quarter to make the 19-0 victory look a little easier than it really had been.

After finally getting something of a breather with a 48-6 victory over East Cleveland's Shaw High School, it was back into the fire against Scott's third substantial opponent in four weeks. On Saturday, November 15, the Scotters lined up on their home field against Marietta High School, the reputed champion of southern Ohio, having not lost a game in two years. Like the Detroit Central game, Scott scored early in the first quarter, and then neither team scored through the third. Scott sealed the victory in the final frame with a pair of touchdowns that gave the Toledo team a 20-0 victory.

The victory over Marietta all but sewed up the Ohio championship for Scott, even though they still had one more Ohio team to play—cross-town rival Waite on Thanksgiving morning. A victory by Scott in this game would ensure a postseason game with the Boston area champion, a big stepping stone toward a national championship. Waite, only 3-3-0 entering the Thanksgiving game, was not supposed to pose much of a threat and Scott was as much as a 20-point favorite; but, as the Scott yearbook put it, "the keen spirit of rivalry" would have something to say about the outcome of this game. The Scott yearbook also noted that Thanksgiving morning dawned "anything but favorable, the cold, the drizzle of rain, and the snow and sleet contributing much to the general discomfort of players and spectators alike." Despite the weather conditions "the crowd that witnessed the struggle was fully as large as any that ever assembled at Scott Field."

On the muddy gridiron the game quickly turned into a punting duel. The game was still scoreless late in the fourth quarter when Scott gained possession of the ball after yet another Waite punt. Then, in just three plays, Scott moved the ball 50 yards and into the end zone for the game's only points, giving the Scotters a 6-0 victory.

After what were called a series of elimination games in the Boston area, the team from Somerville High School won the right to play Scott in a postseason contest, the game to be played in Toledo at Scott Field. Somerville, the acknowledged "champion of the New England District", entered the game with a record of 5-0-2 and had yet to give up a point.

The game was played on Saturday, December 6, the conditions very similar to those in which the Scott team had to play on Thanksgiving Day—snow, rain, and sleet.

All of the scoring in this game came courtesy of Scott halfback Herb Skinner. Early in the first quarter he put his team into the lead with a short touchdown plunge, then added a seven yard touchdown run in the third quarter.

The 13-0 victory improved Scott's record to 8-0-0.

With the championship of the eastern half of the country now theirs, the Toledoans were looking to the other side of the country to find a suitable team to play for the national championship. At that time former Scott head coach Tom Merrell was working for a shipbuilding company in Long Beach, California, and he helped to arrange for Scott to play the winner of the California High School Federation

WHO WOULD HAVE THOUGHT THAT A HIGH SCHOOL FOOTBALL GAME COULD HAVE DRAWN MORE ATTENTION THAN A ROSE BOWL GAME?

championship. Long Beach High School, by virtue of its 48-0 championship win over Fullerton High, was set to play Scott on New Year's Day, 1920, as part of the Tournament of Roses celebration.

Scott left Toledo and arrived in Los Angeles a couple of days before the game and had even run through a couple of practice sessions in anticipation of the big game. However, the game was canceled, in part because it was felt that the Long Beach-Scott game would detract from the Rose Bowl game between Harvard and the University of Oregon, also scheduled to be played on New Year's Day as part of the Tournament of Roses festivities. (Who would have thought that a high school football game could have drawn more attention than a Rose Bowl game?)

This unanticipated turn of events left Scott available to accept an invitation from Everett High School in Washington to play for the national championship—an offer that also included a very generous guarantee of $5,000 for the Toledoans.

The outcome of the Scott-Everett game, a 7-7 tie, was related in the previous chapter. The headline the next day in the *Toledo News-Bee* read,

"BREAKS OF GAME DENY SCOTT VICTORY IN THRILLING STRUGGLE"

with the emphasis on "breaks". The Toledoans obviously felt that a "break" or two went against them. This referred in particular to the final seconds of the game, during which Scott's Richard Vick completed a 20-yard pass to quarterback Eddie Scharer. Two of the Everett defenders tackled Scharer at the goal line, but Scharer was able to drag himself into the end zone. As the *Toledo Blade* reported, "Referee Strong, however, declared the ball dead six inches from the line."

▲ *Head Coach J.K. Dwyer led the Scott High School football team to a share of the 1919 national championship. (Scott Yearbook)*

With the crowd encroaching on the playing field, the two teams lined up for another play. Scharer went up the middle and into the end zone. This time referee Strong was about to rule a Scott touchdown, but the umpire ruled that both teams were offside on the play. Despite police efforts to hold them back, the crowd was now swarming over the field; Scott had no other alternative but to try a run up the middle, an attempt that was stopped by the Everett defense.

It was a tough way to not win a game, but afterward both teams praised the clean play and sportsmanship of the other. As a result of the tie game the two teams shared the national championship that season.

In both 1920 and 1921, Scott High School again had very good football teams, but not excellent teams. The 1920 contingent opened the season with a 125-0 thrashing of Norwalk High School and through the first five games was 5-0-0 and had outscored the opposition by 277-3. However, Scott lost its bid to play for another national championship when Cleveland's East Tech came to town and handed Pat Dwyer's team a 14-7 defeat. Based in large part on this victory, it was the East Tech team that played for the national championship, losing to Everett (Wash.)

The Scott football team enjoyed a grand and well-deserved banquet after the 1919 season. (Scott Yearbook)

High School, 16-7. The Scott team had to console itself by defeating Waite High in their annual Thanksgiving Day tussle by a score of 35-0.

Scott also had a good season going in 1921, but another 14-7 loss to East Tech again threw a wrench into its championship hopes, and a 42-0 loss to Waite finished them off in a 7-2-0 season.

The next three seasons would produce one of the most amazing battles for national high school football supremacy that the country has ever seen.

It is relatively common for two teams to go up against each other for the bragging rights of their city; a little less common for those same two teams to battle for state laurels. But it is unheard of for two high school teams from the same city to face each other in their annual game, played no less in the high profile venue of Thanksgiving morning, with the national title hanging in the balance. But that very situation did occur between two high schools from the same moderately-sized Midwestern city, and it happened not once, but in three consecutive seasons—something that has never happened before or since. During those three seasons, 1922, 1923, and 1924, the football teams from Scott and Waite high schools in Toledo, Ohio, would combine to post a near perfect record of 50-1-1. That is the enviable record they took into their annual Thanksgiving Day game. That game, while not specifically a national championship game, for all intents and purposes decided the national championship for those three seasons.

The Scott football team was coached in 1922 by Dr. William A. Neill, in his second year as the team's head coach after serving as an assistant coach at the school

▲ *Dr. William A. Neill was the Scott head football coach from 1921-24 and led the team to a pair of national championships. (Scott Yearbook)*

for several seasons. Dr. Neill and his coaching staff of three would have to find replacements for the many good players who had graduated after the 1921 season, but they had plenty to choose from as more than 200 boys turned out for the first practices in September. Eventually this group would be whittled down to the two dozen lads who made the team.

Most of the preseason talk around Toledo that year, however, seemed to focus on the city's east side and the Waite High School Indians. From its first season in 1914 thru the 1920 campaign, Waite had only enjoyed moderate success on the gridiron while posting a record of 33-27-1. In 1921, under the direction of new head coach Larry Bevan, the team really came into its own. Despite being held to just seven points in their lone defeat at the hands of Steele High School of Dayton, the Indians had still managed to average almost 61 points per game, thanks in no small part to a 114-0 win over Tiffin High School and a 162-0 whipping of Ada High School. Late season victories - over powerful teams like Lakewood (Ohio), Stivers High of Dayton, Boston area power Malden High and, of course, Waite's big win over Scott - had the locals looking forward to Waite's next campaign in 1922.

As the 1922 season got underway Coach Neill's Scott High squad went methodically about its business by disposing of Tiffin High by a score of 57-0 in its first game. However, as if to downplay the team's ability the *Toledo Blade* had this to say about Dr. Neill's boys, "Scott had no first-class punter in the game, and the kickoffs lacked distance. The lack of weight in the back field handicaps the line plunging game, but taken as a whole the youngsters are keeping their heads up and apparently are capable of assimilating the instructions of the coaching staff." If that is the press they received after a 57-point win, what would be said of them if they lost a game?

Nonetheless, the Scotters seemed to ignore the press clippings and won their next three games by an average score of 54-0. Undefeated after four games, Scott now had to face its nemesis of the last two seasons, Cleveland's East Tech, which had won both of the previous games between the two teams, ruining promising seasons for the Scotters in the process. The East Tech game was one of two contests that the Scott coaches had been gearing their team up for, the other being the annual set to with Waite.

The East Tech game was played at Scott Field before a huge crowd, one that included about 800 Tech fans who had come to Toledo from Cleveland on a special New York Central train. As expected it was a hotly contested game. Scott took advantage of a botched East Tech punt to gain possession of the ball at the East Tech 20-yard line early in the first quarter, scoring the game's first touchdown shortly thereafter. Scott added another touchdown in the second quarter, but those were the only points that either team would score during the first three periods of a still very tight game. Then, in the fourth quarter, the Scott offense really came to life

and put the game away with three touchdowns for a resounding and emphatic 33-0 victory.

Scott again kept its goal line uncrossed in its next game, a 39-0 victory over the team from Marietta High School. On Saturday, November 18, the Scotters took to a muddy Scott Field against the team from Marinette (Wis.) High School. Marinette was rated among the best teams in Wisconsin and its three state championships since 1917 were the proof. Nonetheless, Dr. Neill's team treated the visitors like all of the other teams on its schedule, jumping out to a 45-0 lead after three quarters before letting up a bit in a 45-19 victory.

Scott's record was now a perfect 7-0-0 and it was just a week and a half until the annual Thanksgiving Day game, quickly becoming a classic, against Waite.

Coach Larry Bevan's Waite team in 1922 was also continuing the success that it had the previous season. The Indians opened their season with a 76-0 victory over Cleveland's West Tech High School. The amazing thing about that game was not the score, but the fact that in Waite's 10-game schedule West Tech was one of only three Ohio teams that it would play, the other two being cross-town rival Scott and Doane Academy of Granville. Waite would play teams from seven other states stretching from Iowa in the west to Kentucky and West Virginia in the south to Pennsylvania in the east. All of that traveling, whether it was by the Waite team going out of town or the other teams coming to Toledo, was pretty remarkable for that era.

Waite followed up its win over West Tech with a 71-0 thumping of Doane Academy. When the team from Male High School in Louisville, Ky., showed up at the Waite bowl the following Saturday they were treated in a similar manner and sent on their way on the short end of a 34-0 count.

Harrisburg Tech was one of the best teams in Pennsylvania at this time, as well as being former national champion, when the team arrived in Toledo the next weekend to play Waite. It was not just the Tech football team that came west, however, but an entourage that included the school's 75-piece band and about 500 loyal rooters. Probably not as joyful a trip back home to Harrisburg after suffering a 52-7 defeat at the hands of Larry Bevan's team.

The Waite onslaught continued over the next two Saturdays. When Lane Tech visited from the Chicago area, Coach Bevan did not even use his first line players, instead starting the entire second team. Not a problem as Waite came away with a

▲   *Scott Halfback Grim (far left in striped jersey) looking for an opening against the Waite defense in their 1922 meeting. (Scott Yearbook)*

66-0 victory. Parkersburg (W.Va.) High School came to Toledo as the champion of its area, but went home on the short end of a 55-7 score.

The Washington High School Tigers of Cedar Rapids, Iowa, were next on the Waite schedule. After a heavy rain, the Waite bowl was covered in water and mud, making the footing treacherous, fumbling frequent, and passing difficult. In spite of these handicaps, Waite took the lead in the first quarter on a 30-yard pass completion; as the Cedar Rapids school paper later noted, "a creditable achievement, considering the playing conditions." Later in the first half, Waite added a second touchdown after a long drive. Cedar Rapids later dented the scoreboard when it dropped Waite fullback Carl Stamman in the end zone for a safety, but those would be the only points that the Iowans could muster.

Waite had played its toughest game of the season and had managed to emerge victorious, 13-2.

On the Saturday before Thanksgiving the team from Indiana's South Bend High School visited Toledo and the Waite bowl. It was another game in which Waite's bench players had a chance to show their stuff. Waite 67, South Bend 6.

Like Scott High School, Waite's 8-0-0 record was also perfect as the two teams headed into their Thanksgiving Day showdown. The Indians had scored 434 points in their first eight games, allowing only 22. In winning its seven contests Scott had outscored the opposition by 335-19. Both teams featured explosive offenses and stingy defenses—it would be an interesting game.

Two days before Thanksgiving, the *Toledo Blade* estimated that upwards of 26,000 fans would attend the big game at Scott Field, a game not only for local bragging rights, but also to give the victor the opportunity to play an appropriate opponent for the national championship. The newspaper also reported that while the Waite team appeared to be in perfect health, several key Scott players were in less than prime physical condition. As to the outcome of the game, the *Toledo Blade* predicted, "Waite will enter the game favored to win.... A Scott victory while not impossible, of course, would be an upset in every sense of the word." To which the *Toledo Blade* added, "Whichever team emerges from the battle as winner will be widely recognized as having a legitimate claim to the scholastic title, the team that any contending aggregation must play to lay claim to the mythical [national] high school championship."

Waite kicked off to open the game. The Scotters immediately moved the ball to the Waite 20-yard line, but they were held on downs and Waite went on offense for the first time. The Indians promptly marched 80 yards in the opposite direction; on fourth and goal from less than two yards away, Indians' fullback and team captain Carl "Dutch" Stamman plunged into the end zone for the game's first points. The extra point gave Waite an early 7-0 lead.

Early in the second quarter Scott finally got some production out of its offense as the team marched down the field for a touchdown to pull within a point at the half, 7-6. The team's momentum continued early in the third quarter when Scott scored a touchdown on its first possession to take a 13-7 lead. The score remained unchanged until the first play of the fourth quarter when the Scott defense came up with a

▲ *Waite tacklers (solid jerseys) halt the progress of a Scott running back in the 1922 Waite-Scott game. (Scott Yearbook)*

safety on a blocked Waite punt to increase its lead to 15-7. Late in the quarter, Waite found the end zone with its second touchdown of the game, the extra point cutting the Scott lead to a single point. Scott then took the ball and ran out the last few minutes to preserve its big upset victory, 15-14.

The day after the game, the Scott faculty manager told the *Toledo Blade*, "As it is we will claim the national schoolboy championship and are ready to defend it." The Scott officials sent a challenge to schools on the west coast and within a week the team from Corvallis High School in Corvallis, Ore., accepted. It took a couple of weeks to finalize the details before a game for the national title was scheduled to be played in Oregon on New Year's Day, 1923.

In the meantime, Waite had also played an inter-sectional game. Ensuring that Toledo high school football was well represented on the east coast, the Indians defeated Boston area power Malden High by a 13 to 0 count to finish the season at 9-1-0.

The Corvallis High team entered the game with Scott with a perfect 8-0-0 record, easily the best season thus far in the team's 13-year history. It had rained heavily for several days before the game and the Corvallis team was hoping that the "heavy field" would slow down the Ohioans.

While the field was still soggy, January 1 dawned with perfect weather for a football game. A record crowd of more than 7,000 was on hand to view the national championship game. That crowd included practically the entire town of Toledo, Ore., located some 20 miles from Corvallis, which came out to cheer for the namesake Ohioans.

The first quarter was scoreless, the smaller Corvallis team gamely holding its own. Scott finally broke through to score a touchdown in the second quarter; but the extra point failed and the half ended with Scott in the lead, 6-0. The Scott offense finally got rolling in the third quarter as the Ohioans scored a pair of touchdowns to push their lead to 18-0. In the fourth quarter the Ohioans added two more touchdowns, the first set up by the recovery of a Corvallis fumble.

The final score was Toledo Scott 32, Corvallis 0—the national championship for 1922 was back in Ohio.

In 1923 both the Waite and Scott teams picked up right where they had left off the previous season.

Larry Bevan's Waite Indians again faced a schedule heavy with non-Ohio teams, teams that were often considered among the best in their parts of the country. The season got off on the right foot when the Indians defeated Morenci (Mich.) High School, 33-3.

Waite, however, got a real scare in its second game, played against Cleveland's Glenville High School. Glenville had earned a share of the Cleveland city championship the previous year and was again a strong team; however, "fate" just did not seem to be on the Tarblooders' side in 1923. Rules changes by the Ohio High School Athletic Association just before the season began made about a half-dozen returning Glenville players ineligible for 1923, while an auto accident injured five more. Nonetheless, the Glenville squad traveled west to face Waite. Despite this "handicap", the Tarblooders played tough and the game remained scoreless into the fourth quarter. Finally, with just 39 seconds remaining on the game clock, Waite found the end zone on a touchdown pass that produced the game's only points to give Waite a 7-0 victory.

Waite then went on a scoring binge and averaged 55 points per game while defeating teams from five different states: South Park High of Buffalo, N.Y., 73-0; Pine Bluff (Ark.) High School, 19-7; Male High School of Louisville, Ky., 40-0; Toledo's Woodward Tech, 68-0; Terre Haute (Ind.) High School, 74-7.

With their record now 7-0-0, the Indians next had to face the team, other than Scott, that had given them the most trouble in 1922—Washington High from Cedar Rapids, Iowa. The Washington Tigers were having another great season in 1923 and a national championship for the Iowans was a definite possibility.

The box score in the Toledo *Blade on Jan. 2, 1923, after the Scotters defeated the team from Corvallis (Ore.) High School to win the national championship.*

World's Champs!

CORVALLIS (0)		SCOTT (32)
Daniels	L.E	Metzger
Schwiening	L.T	Allen
Taylor	L.G	Zweigle
Mosier	C	Marlhugh
Epperly	R.G	Overmeyer
P. Montgomery	R.T	Farison
Olson	R.E	Hartman
Denman	Q.B	Evans
R. Montgomery	L.H	Grim
Edwards	R.H	Lauffier
Avrit (C)	F.B	Hunt (C)

Scott . . . . 0 6 12 14—32
Corvallis . . . . 0 0 0 0— 0
Touchdowns — Grim, Lauffier, Evans, Hunt, Farison. Goal from touchdown—Evans 2.

Officials—Sam Dolan, Oregon Agricultural College, referee; Vincent Borleske, Whitman College, umpire; R. B. Rurok, Wisconsin,

The game was played on November 10 in Toledo. The Tigers great running back, Elmer Marek, gave his team an early first quarter lead by kicking a field goal from the 25-yard line. The score remained 3-0 late into the third quarter, at which time the Tigers recovered a fumble at the Waite 10-yard line, with Marek smashing into the end zone three plays later for a 10-0 Cedar Rapids lead. Waite finally got on the scoreboard in the fourth quarter to cut the lead to 10-6, but that would be as close as the Indians would get.

▸   *The 1923 Toledo Scott National Champions.* (Scott Yearbook)

The 10-6 defeat crushed Waite's championship hopes, but not those of Cedar Rapids Washington—and this was not to be the last that Toledoans would see of the Washington High Tigers in 1923.

The following week Waite took out its frustrations on Columbus West High School, trouncing the team from Ohio's capital by a 115-0 score and setting up the annual Thanksgiving Day clash with Scott High.

Coach Neill met with the prospects for his Scott team in early September of 1923 and within a few weeks the roughly two dozen boys to make the varsity were selected. Frequent scrimmages with the University of Toledo and a team made up of local policemen followed. However, the Scott team suffered a big blow a week before the first game when it was learned that seven key members of the squad were ineligible to play because of the new eight semester rule that had been adopted by the Ohio High School Athletic Association earlier in the month, the same rule that had thrown a monkey wrench into Glenville's hopes. The new rule stated that no student could participate in athletics after he had been enrolled in school for more than eight semesters. Coach Neill had no choice but to replace the ineligible boys as the team continued to prepare for the season.

Scott opened the season with three shutout victories, averaging 31 points per game. It was supposed to be more of the same when twice-defeated Findlay High visited the Scotters for the fourth game, but only a late touchdown saved the Scotters from an embarrassing result, Scott escaping with a 7-0 victory.

Next up for Scott was the undefeated team from Watertown (Mass.) High School, rated as one of the leading teams in the east and as the *Toledo Blade* noted, "heralded as a team with a wicked offense and a stonewall defense." Coach Neill's team was not impressed, as its 85-0 victory attests. The boys then traveled to Cleveland for another interesting battle with East Tech, this time played at Dunn Field, the home of the Cleveland Indians. The game was scoreless at the half, in no small part due to Scott's many lost fumbles, four alone in the first quarter. The Toledoans finally settled down in the second half long enough to record a 20-0 victory.

After this close call due to the sloppiness of play by his team, plus the near miss against a considerably inferior Findlay team, Coach Neill had to be wondering on the train ride back to Toledo how his team would handle the remaining games on its schedule—the team's toughest games of the season. He would soon find out.

Back in Toledo, the Scotters first took on the visiting team from Spokane (Wash.) High School, rated as the Pacific Coast champions. It was a back and forth game, but in the end the home team doubled up the visitors from the "left coast", 20-10.

Having further enhanced its nationwide reputation with a victory over the Pacific Coast title holders, Scott now had about a week and a half to prepare for

▲ *More than 26,000 fans were in the seats at Waite stadium in 1923 when Waite and Scott met in the 10th meeting between the two teams. (Toledo Blade)*

▸ *Following page, top: Getting a key block from offensive lineman Gentner, Scott halfback Fritz Lauffler dashes through a big hole during the Scott-Waite game in 1923. (Scott Yearbook)*

▸ *Following page, bottom: Scott quarterback Eddie Evans breaks to the outside on an end run against Waite in their 1923 meeting. (Scott Yearbook)*

its annual Thanksgiving morning game with Waite. That game to many in Toledo and the surrounding Midwest, had now become *the* game of the year. Scott entered the game with its slate clean at 7-0-0, while Waite had just that one loss to Cedar Rapids Washington to go with its seven victories.

The Scott-Waite game in 1923 was the 10th game of this series and one of the biggest. It was reported by the *Toledo Blade* that some 26,000 fans packed the Waite bowl for the game, filling the seating area, with the overflow standees 10 to 20 deep around the playing field. At that time it was an unheard-of attendance total and a figure still seldom seen at a high school game. It was also reported that a total of 40,000 tickets had been sold and that the refunds ran upwards of $20,000.

Everyone came to see what they hoped would be a great high school football game—and they were not disappointed. The action started early when, on Waite's second play from scrimmage, halfback Buddy Kinker slipped through a hole in the middle of the line and raced 68 yards for a touchdown to give the Indians an early 6-0 lead. Later in the first quarter, with the ball deep in the Waite end of the field, the Scott defense blocked a Waite punt attempt and then recovered the loose ball in the end zone for a Scott touchdown. The extra point kick gave the Scotters a 7-6 lead.

After a scoreless second quarter, Scott added to its lead with a touchdown pass off a fake field goal try, the extra point increasing the Scott lead to 14-6. With just six minutes left in the fourth quarter, Waite scored its second touchdown of the game, the extra point cutting the Scott lead to just a single point at 14-13. After an exchange of possessions Waite was driving for the potential winning points when, with just seconds remaining, the interception of a Waite aerial preserved Scott's triumph, 14-13.

Waite would not be playing for a national title, but its season was not yet over. As a reward for a fine season, Coach Bevan had arranged a game for his team with Lake Charles High School of Louisiana—to be played in the Pelican State. It was a tough game, especially being played so far from home, but the Indians upheld Toledo's gridiron reputation by holding Lake Charles to just 36 yards of total offense and two first downs in a 14-0 victory.

▲ *Scott halfback Fritz Lauffler rushes ahead for a few yards in the game with Washington High of Cedar Rapids, Iowa, that would decide the 1923 national title. (Scott Yearbook)*

Two huge games played and won, but now Coach Neill's Scott team had another big game, the biggest of the season, coming up. On Sunday, December 2, the *Toledo Blade* announced that the officials at Washington High in Cedar Rapids had "voted to accept Scott's challenge for a post-season game here for the interscholastic championship of the United States."

The sports editor of the *Toledo Blade* felt that Scott "will be mighty lucky to come out on top" against the Cedar Rapids team, making Scott a decided underdog. The Washington High Tigers, coached by Leo Novak, were 10-0-0, having already defeated Waite and a very strong Harrisburg Tech team, giving Tech its only loss in eleven outings. To defeat Cedar Rapids it was felt that Scott would have to control Washington High's star halfback Elmer Marek, a true triple threat man.

The game was sold out a day in advance as more than 20,000 fans were expected to fill Scott Field. Among the spectators were many high school and college football people, most notably Fielding H. Yost, the legendary head coach at Michigan.

Near the end of the first quarter the Scott team took advantage of a Washington miscue when it recovered a Tigers fumble. The Toledoans turned it into a touchdown on the second play of the second quarter, the extra point kick giving them a 7-0 lead.

On the ensuing kickoff Cedar Rapids again fumbled the ball, the loose pigskin being recovered by Scott at the Washington four-yard line. Three plays later Scott had increased its lead to 14-0, a lead it maintained until the halftime intermission.

Scott kicked off to open the second half. On its second play from scrimmage Washington High fumbled the ball, which was again recovered by Scott at the Cedar Rapids 20-yard line. A few plays later, another Scott touchdown and extra point had increased the Toledoans lead to 21-0.

The Tigers of Washington High were down, but not out, not as long as they had Elmer Marek running with the ball. In lightning-like fashion, before the third quarter was half over Marek single-handedly brought his team back into the game with touchdown runs of 55, 9, and 70 yards, plus three successful extra point kicks, all of which pulled Cedar Rapids into a 21-21 tie.

All the Way to #1

Both teams now battled up and down the field, neither yielding much to the other. There was just a minute and a half left on the game clock when Scott got the ball for what would probably be its last chance. The Scotters quickly advanced the ball to the Washington seven-yard line, from where they won the game with a field goal from the 21-yard line with just 36 seconds remaining.

Coach Neill's team had successfully defended its national championship.

Scott High was the national champion for 1923, but its season, strangely enough, was not over. As a "reward" for winning the game with Cedar Rapids, the Scott team was given permission to travel to Portland, Ore., to play a game with the team representing Columbia University Prep. In essence this was an exhibition game because, as the *Toledo News-Bee* noted, it was a game "which had no bearing on Scott's national championship title." The game was probably more exciting than Coach Neill and his team would have liked, but they prevailed nonetheless, 20-17.

▾ *One of the few times during the Scott-Cedar Rapids game when Cedar Rapids' star running back Elmer Marek is held for no gain by the Scott defense. (Scott Yearbook)*

▲ *This drawing from the Scott High School yearbook, the Scottonian, depicts how the Scotters "tied up" the 1923 national championship against a wide variety of opponents.*

While Waite's loss to Scott eliminated the Indians from the 1923 national championship picture, another Ohio team was still in the running. The Shaw High School team of East Cleveland, annually a strong Cleveland area squad, was also having an outstanding football season. Led by All-Scholastic quarterback Barton Momberger, called by the Cleveland *Plain Dealer* "one of the greatest high school players ever produced here," Shaw was playing and defeating some of the best teams in the area. Shaw knocked off local powers like Cleveland East, 14-9, and East Tech, 10-0, along with Canton McKinley, 21-7, and Detroit's Northern High School, 29-6.

Shaw finished the 1923 season with a record of 8-1-0, but that one loss comes with an asterisk. That game was played against Elyria High School, in Elyria, Ohio. After Shaw had two touchdowns disallowed by the game officials, the Shaw coach took his team off the field in protest of what he considered the biased nature of the officiating. Shaw was declared the loser, 1-0, by forfeit. This unusual loss did not seem to affect Shaw's reputation in the least, either in Ohio or nationally, and the team received calls from around the country for postseason match-ups. The school accepted the challenge of Salem (Mass.) High School for a game to be played at Shaw's new stadium on December 1. Salem High was a state power in the Bay State, the last remaining undefeated team in Massachusetts and coached by William Broderick, who had previously worked wonders at Haverhill High School. However, Shaw easily won the game, 26-0, behind the fine play of Barton Momberger who accounted for all of his team's points by throwing for two touchdowns, running for two more, and kicking two extra points.

Despite finishing the season with that one tainted loss to go along with its nine victories, Shaw is recognized as sharing both the 1923 Ohio and national championships with Toledo's Scott High School.

Scott High School opened the 1924 season with a brand new concrete stadium, Siebert Stadium, which replaced the school's former wooden stands. The football team then "christened" its new gridiron with an 18-8 victory over the Alumni team.

Because there were scouts from several high schools in attendance the following week against Woodward High, Coach Neill stuck to a relatively conservative game plan, mixing in a few passes with the running game. The result was not nearly as close as the 19-13 Scott victory might indicate.

Victories over Toledo's Libbey High School, 26-0, and Streator (Ill.) High, 33-0, followed in quick order. Stivers High of Dayton, Ohio, however, proved to be a much more stubborn foe. Scott High took a 7-0 lead early in the game, then held that lead until Stivers tied the score in the third quarter. Missed field goal tries by both teams in the fourth quarter resulted in a 7-7 final. The tie ended Scott's winning streak at 22, but the boys still had not suffered a defeat in 23 straight games.

Coach Neill's team next faced its old rival from Cleveland East Tech in another tough game played before some 8,000 fans; the hometown fans were not disappointed as Scott prevailed, 20-7.

For the second straight season the team from Findlay High School threw a real scare into the Scotters; but by the margin of a missed extra point Dr. Neill's team prevailed, 7-6. A 40-0 win over Carl Schurz High School of Chicago left Coach Neill's team with a record of 7-0-1 as they prepared to meet Waite in their annual Thanksgiving morning tussle.

After having their 1923 championship aspirations short circuited by close losses to Cedar Rapids Washington and Scott high schools, the Waite Indians of head coach Larry Bevan entered the 1924 campaign with another multi-state schedule designed to take the team to national prominence if they were successful. That schedule featured schools from six states plus Ohio and again included teams ranked among the best in their respective neck of the woods.

Of course, Bevan would need the players with which to take on this tough schedule; unfortunately, after the 1923 season he had lost about a dozen players to graduation and the eight-semester rule. However, with only one starter returning for the '24 season, Bevan was still able to put together a team that would do the Waite faithful proud. That became most evident in the season's first game on Saturday, September 27. As the *Toledo Blade* later noted, "The ability of the Waite High coaches to put a big and apparently well seasoned team on the field for the opening game was amply demonstrated Saturday." A 90-0 victory over Morenci High of Michigan showed that the Waite team was seasoned indeed.

It was more of the same the following Saturday when Waite took on another Michigan team, representing Detroit Northern High School. Shutting out the visitors 32-0, Waite's defense limited the Detroiters to just one first down.

With the team now referred to as the Purple Hurricane because of its purple and gold school colors, Coach Bevan's squad next played two local Ohio teams. Waite had an easy time of it as the Purple Hurricane blew aside Toledo's Woodward Tech, 59-0. Next up was the team from Carey High School, 4-0-0 thus far in the '24 season. Nonetheless, Waite again had little difficulty in downing the visitors, 49-7.

Waite would now play four intersectional games that had the potential to make or break its national championship aspirations. On October 25, the team from Louisiana's Lake Charles High School came north and paid a visit to the Waite bowl. More than 7,000 fans saw a dandy of a game. After a sustained march in the first quarter, Waite took a 7 to 0 lead. Later in the first half Waite added to its total when a Lake Charles punt was blocked and returned 55 yards for a Waite touchdown. After a scoreless third quarter, both teams tallied in the final stanza as Waite came away with a very convincing 20-6 victory.

▾ Larry Bevan coached the Waite High School football team from 1921-24, winning the national championship in his last season. (Waite Yearbook)

All the Way to #1

▲ *Another sold-out Scott stadium for the Waite-Scott game in 1924.* (Toledo Blade)

On the first day of November, the Waite squad met the undefeated team from Memphis (Tenn.) Central High School in another game played at the Waite bowl. The game was close through the first three quarters, but a four-touchdown explosion by Waite in the fourth quarter swept the Hurricanes to a 44-7 victory.

The Bloomington (Ind.) High School Indians came to Toledo on November 8. In a game that pitted Bloomington's vaunted aerial attack against Waite's ground assault, Coach Bevan's Toledoans managed to stay just ahead of the visitors throughout the contest. The 38-35 final, in Waite's favor, showed just how close the game had been.

The following Saturday, Waite played another Indiana team, representing Peru High School. From the opening kickoff, when the Peru return man fumbled the ball, the rout was on as Waite breezed to a 74-0 victory.

That point in the season had now been reached that all of Toledo and much of the Midwest had been eagerly anticipating, the annual Thanksgiving morning clash between Waite and Scott. Scott had won eight of the previous 10 games in this series, including the last two by the narrowest of margins, one point. Those two victories had helped secure for Coach Neill's Scott team the national championship.

Once again, for the third consecutive season, that national title was pretty much on the line in this game between the two Toledo and Ohio powers. Scott had now gone 27 consecutive games without a loss, its last defeat coming in this same game back in 1921. Scott's tie earlier in the season with the powerful team from Dayton Stivers would probably not hurt its chances at a third consecutive national title should the Scotters defeat Waite.

For the past three seasons, 1921 to 1923, Waite had been very close to gaining national honors each season only to suffer that one key loss—and twice it had been at the hands of Scott. Once again the Purple Hurricane was undefeated as the Thanksgiving Day game approached. And this time Coach Bevan and his team,

▲ *Scott left end Tom Ramsey (striped jersey) out battles this Waite defender for a pass during the 1924 Scott-Waite game. (Scott Yearbook)*

FOR THE THIRD CONSECUTIVE SEASON, THAT NATIONAL TITLE WAS PRETTY MUCH ON THE LINE IN THIS GAME BETWEEN THE TWO TOLEDO AND OHIO POWERS.

recognized as the best Waite squad to have ever represented the school in its short history, were determined to see a different outcome.

At least from a personnel standpoint, the advantage seemed to rest with Waite; Coach Bevan's team was said to be in tip-top shape to the last man—even after having gone through three tough scrimmages earlier in the week with the team from Dayton's Steele High School. Such was not the case over on the west side of town at Scott High School. Coach Neill lost three players on eligibility issues and three more to injuries; because of these missing players the make up of his starting backfield was still up in the air as the big game approached.

The *Toledo Blade* said of the Scott-Waite game, "As far as the unbiased observer can see, the result of the game is a tossup."

A sellout of upwards of 21,000 people filled Scott's Siebert Stadium for the 10:30 A.M. kickoff on Thanksgiving morning. The game would be played in 15 minute quarters, instead of the normal 12 minute periods.

Late in the opening quarter Waite took a 6-0 lead. The teams then battled mightily throughout the balance of the first quarter and the second as well, but neither side could manage any points. The third period also failed to yield any points for either team.

The fourth quarter opened with Scott tying the score on a 20-yard pass play. With about two minutes left in the game, Waite intercepted a Scott pass deep in the Scott end of the field and a few plays later turned the turnover into a touch-

down that gave the Indians a 13-6 lead. Two minutes later the final whistle blew ending the game and Waite came away with a 13-6 victory.

Stories soon began to pop up as to who would now play Waite for the national championship. There were even stories about other teams' claims to the national title, mainly Dayton Stivers and Cedar Rapids Washington. In response to those claims on Monday, December 1, the *Toledo Blade* noted: "... the Associated Press affords a pretty fair idea of what constitutes a national championship and Friday morning the A.P. received requests from Washington, D.C., Philadelphia, Buffalo, Chicago, Cincinnati, and Spokane for a story on the Waite-Scott game. The display of interest from so wide a territory would indicate that in the cities mentioned at least, the opinion prevailed that the game at Siebert stadium was for the national scholastic football title."

The Toledo Blade of Dec. 8, 1924, highlights the running of Waite halfback Pete Pencheff in the national championship game against Everett (Mass.) High School.

That opinion not withstanding, a game was arranged with Everett High of Massachusetts to play for the national championship on Saturday afternoon, December 6, in the Waite bowl. As has already been noted, Everett High had won national championships in 1914 and 1915; this would be the fourth time that Everett found itself playing in a game for the national title. Thus far in 1924, Everett High had a record of 6-1-3; however, the team had failed to score a single point in its last three games, a 28-0 loss to Malden High and a pair of 0-0 ties.

The suspense in this game lasted all of two minutes, because that is how long it took Waite to cross the Everett goal line for the first time. Scoring a pair of touchdowns in each quarter but the third, and one in that period, Waite crushed the easterners in ringing up a 46-0 victory before some 12,000 loyal followers. Waite's domination was complete; Everett did not register a single first down, did not complete a single forward pass, and never started a play on the Waite side of the midfield stripe.

The Waite Indians had finally succeeded after three near misses. The team had won its first state and national championships. And for the third consecutive season the high school football national champion resided in Toledo, Ohio.

Following the 1924 season, both the Waite and Scott programs would come back to earth, as it were. From 1925 through the 1931 season both teams would

▲   *Waite halfback Claire Dunn gains some tough yardage up the middle against Toledo DeVilbiss in 1932. (Waite Yearbook)*

play good, but not spectacular, football and post almost identical records, Scott at 42-15-7 and Waite 43-16-8. Not until 1932 would either of the two teams again reach national prominence.

Despite the deepening economic depression that gripped the nation, in 1932 Waite still managed to play teams from around the country, though not in the same numbers as they had back in the pre-Depression days. The team was now coached by Don McCallister, who had taken over leadership of the team the previous season. After winning just twice in 1930, in McCallister's first season of 1931 his team finished at 9-2-0. The Waite team had a full 10-game schedule assembled for the '32 campaign and fully half of the opponents were new to the Waite schedule.

The season opened on Friday night, September 16. A football game played under electric lights being a relatively new addition to the high school game, this was a brand new experience at the Waite bowl. It would be the first of seven consecutive Friday night home games for the Indians. The opponent that first evening was Bucyrus High School, a game that Waite won easily, 71-0. The following Friday night, Waite entertained the team from Flint (Mich.) Central High. Flint Central would end the season as Michigan's co-champion, but this night it was no match for Waite, which came away with a 25-0 victory.

On Friday night, September 30, more than 8,000 fans came out to see the Indians take on Washington High School of Cedar Rapids, the first meeting between the two teams since 1923. Led by Francis Lengel's three touchdowns in the first quarter and a total of four for the game, Waite won easily by a 35 to 0 score.

McCallister's team next hosted Newport (Ky.) High School, another undefeated out-of-state power. That night Francis Lengel scored four touchdowns for the third time in the young season and Waite held Newport to just two first downs in registering a 55-0 shutout. Against Dayton Roosevelt the following week, Waite raised its record to 5-0-0 with a convincing 47-2 thumping of the Dayton eleven.

Four of Waite's next five games were against local Toledo schools and all ended with almost identical scores. A previously undefeated Woodward High was bounced, 19-0, on October 21. The following Friday night, Toledo Central Catholic fell victim to another of Francis Lengel's touchdown onslaughts as Waite's great running back tallied three times in the second half to give Waite an 18-0 win.

The string of local games was briefly interrupted by a contest with Cincinnati's Roger Bacon High School, won by Waite, 38-0.

Most of the Toledo teams were having fine seasons and that was again evident on Saturday, November 12, when Waite traveled across town to play Libbey High School, both teams still undefeated. Waite would take advantage of a couple of Libbey turnovers to pull out a 19-0 victory. Despite only having won two games all season, Scott High battled Waite all the way in their traditional Thanksgiving game, but in the end Waite prevailed by an 18 to 0 count.

Waite's season appeared to be over until De Vilbiss High School, Toledo's other remaining undefeated team, challenged Waite to a postseason game to decide the city championship, a challenge that Waite head coach Don McCallister eagerly accepted. Before some 12,000 fans, De Vilbiss managed to score more points against Waite than any previous opponent in 1932, but seven points was hardly enough when playing against the Indians. And that was especially so when one of those Indians was Francis Lengel, who led the Waite attack by scoring three touchdowns and passing for two more in Waite's 41-7 triumph.

The Waite victory clinched not only the city title for the Indians, but also the Ohio championship. But the season still had one more game in it for the Waite footballers and their fans.

Before coming to Waite High School, Don McCallister had been the head coach at Miami (Fla.) Senior High School from 1928 thru 1930 where his teams had amassed a record of 25-3-3. McCallister arranged a game to be played in Miami between Waite and Miami Senior High School to decide the national championship. The Miami Stingarees under first-year Coach Jesse Yarbrough were 8-2-0 and had already defeated Palmetto High School for the Florida championship. This game would be significant for Waite for another reason. A recent ruling by the Ohio High School Athletic Association had banned postseason games beginning with the 1933 football season. This game, therefore, would be the last permitted postseason game for an Ohio team unless or until, as the *Toledo Blade* noted, "the Ohio association some day rescinds its new rule prohibiting such contests."

More than 8,000 fans were on hand at Moore Park in Miami for this game, played at 3 P.M., Monday, December 26. The first break of the game went Waite's way when early in the first quarter the Indians punted to the Stingarees, who fumbled the ball deep in their own end of the field. It was recovered in the end zone by Waite for a touchdown and a 6-0 lead. Later in the quarter, Miami scored on a 68-yard touchdown pass play, the extra point giving the home team a 7-6 lead that it carried into the intermission.

In the third quarter Waite struck again, a 13-yard aerial from Francis Lengel to Russ Morse turning the trick as the Indians took a 13-7 lead. There would be no more scoring over the balance of the second half. The Waite defense was key in this game as it held the Stingarees to just 29 yards of total offense in the second half and came up with a game total of nine takeaways, six interceptions and three fumble recoveries.

Waite's 13-7 victory had secured for the Indians the national championship for 1932.

For a town of its size, Toledo had a truly remarkable run of high school football success during the first quarter of the 20th century. Of the 21 National champion-

▲ *Waite's Glen Myers tackles a Miami High ball carrier in the 1932 national championship game. Waite's Melvin Cramer (without helmet) and Russ Morse run up to assist. (Waite High School Yearbook)*

ship games played between 1900 and 1925, Toledo schools played in seven of them (33%), with a record of 4-2-1. The city added a fifth championship game victory with Waite's win in Miami in 1932. The city's teams won or shared the national title six times during that 25-year span, adding a seventh title with Waite's win in Miami.

While Waite and Scott high schools would have some very good seasons in subsequent years and even be named state champion again, they would never reclaim the pinnacle of national acclaim that they enjoyed during the first quarter of the century.

## CHAPTER 4

PB AND THE TIGERS

Massillon High School
Massillon, Ohio

"In the beginning when The Great Creator was drawing plans for this world of ours, He decided there should be something for everyone. He gave us mountains that reach to the sky, deep blue seas, green forests, dry deserts, gorgeous flowers and gigantic trees. Then he decided there should be football and he gave us Massillon. He created only one Massillon. He knew that would be enough."

— *Ron Maly, Des Moines (Iowa) Sunday Register*

For more than three quarters of a century the name "Massillon" has been synonymous with high school football greatness, at times in almost legendary proportions. What follows is the story of how Massillon became "Massillon".

Massillon High School opened in 1879. The school played its first football game in 1891, losing to the Beta Theta Pi fraternity of Wooster College by a score of 38-0. Teams representing Massillon High were intermittent over the balance of the 19th century. The school never played more than three games (if any at all) in any one season until 1899, when the team representing the school went 3-3-1 against an assortment of high school, junior high and business college teams. Finally, in 1903 a regular school team was established under the direction of Prof. James Collier.

From 1903 until 1908 the Massillon football team had a combined record of 13-30-3, but in 1909, under the direction of Coach Ralph "Hap" Fugate, the team posted a record of 9-0-1 and was named Ohio's state champion. Six more years of mediocre results followed, but in 1916 under John Snavely the team had its first perfect season, going 10-0-0 and being named the state champion for a second time. (The school had been renamed Washington High School in 1914.)

The team's fortunes continued to press ahead and Massillon had its first true "golden era" under the direction of Coach Dave Stewart. After Stewart's first team went 5-4-0 in 1921, Massillon would win 33 and lose only five over the next four seasons, including another perfect 10-0-0 season and the team's third state crown in 1922.

Coach Stewart left Massillon following the 1925 campaign and for a time the team's play was less than spectacular. Massillon's record bottomed out in 1931 at 2-6-2; however, the Tigers did manage to defeat arch-rival Canton McKinley by a 20-6 count, so all was not lost. The win over McKinley, however, was not enough

The 1899 Massillon High School football team, the first team at the school to play a relatively full schedule of seven games.

to save Coach Elmer McGrew's job and his four year stint at Massillon came to an end with the final whistle of that McKinley game.

An intense search for a new head coach was begun immediately. Massillon school board president H. W. Bell, who had kept in touch with Dave Stewart after he left Massillon, asked the former Tigers coach for some recommendations. Stewart did not hesitate in recommending Massillon alumnus Paul Brown for the job. After interviewing Brown, then only 24 years old, Bell hired him as the Massillon head coach.

If men like Walter Camp, Amos Alonzo Stagg, Bob Zuppke, "Pop" Warner, and Knute Rockne comprised the first generation of football's great coaches and innovators, then Paul Brown was among the greatest of the second generation.

Paul Brown was born in Norwalk, Ohio, on September 7, 1908. The family moved to Massillon when he was nine years old because his father, a railroad dispatcher, was transferred to the city. Brown entered Massillon's Washington High School (henceforth referred to as "Massillon" or "Massillon High School") in 1922. At first his athletic energy was expended on the track team as a pole vaulter, but after football coach Dave Stewart noticed his determination to excel he brought the 150-pound youngster onto the football team. Harry Stuhldreher, soon to earn fame as one of Notre Dame's legendary Four Horsemen, was then the Tigers quarterback, but upon his graduation Brown took over as the team's signal caller for the 1924 and 1925 seasons. He led the Tigers to a 15-3-0 record those two years, defeating Canton McKinley, 6-0, in 1924, but dropping a 6-3 decision to the Bulldogs the following season.

After graduating from Massillon, Brown enrolled at Ohio State, but stayed there only a year before transferring to Miami University in Oxford, Ohio. He joined the football team, but had to wait his turn at quarterback until the current signal caller, Weeb Ewbank, graduated. In his two seasons as the starter at Miami, Brown led the team to a record of 14-3-0 and was named to the All-Ohio small college second team.

Paul Brown had considered studying history on a Rhodes scholarship upon graduating from Miami, but instead he turned to coaching. On the recommendation of his old high school coach, Dave Stewart, Brown was hired in 1930 as the head coach at Severn Prep, a preparatory school in Maryland for the U.S. Naval Academy at Annapolis. Brown posted a record of 16-1-1 in two years at Severn and won the Maryland state championship in his very first season.

▲ *Harry Stuhldreher played for Massillon High and went on to play for Knute Rockne at Notre Dame, earning fame as one of that school's legendary Four Horsemen.*

Although Paul Brown had grown up in Massillon and always considered it his hometown even after moving away later in life, coming from the relative refinement and exclusivity of preppy Severn to blue collar Massillon had to be an "adjustment" to say the least. The nation was in the throes of the Great Depression and Massillon was no exception. Like many districts around the country, the school board was broke, the football equipment was all hand-me-downs and many of the players went hungry at least part of the time. Football was not exactly at the top of everyone's priority list, especially after a season in which the team had won only twice in 10 outings. This was a time when football at Massillon was still just a "sport", but Paul Brown was about to change that.

The 1932 season, Brown's first at Massillon, got off to a flying start as the Tigers won their first five games. They then played Barberton High School to a scoreless tie before dropping the final four games of the season, the last three by shutout including a 19-0 loss to McKinley in the traditional final game of the season.

There was some grumbling around town about those four losses, especially the loss to McKinley. Paul Brown would be the Massillon coach for eight more seasons and, although nobody knew it at the time, the Tigers would lose only four more games over those remaining eight seasons.

The 1932 Tigers team had scored a total of only 79 points. In 1933, with the team having had a full year to learn Brown's system, things began to pop. The Tigers won their first four games by a total of 175-0, but in Week Five they were again shut out by Barberton, losing the game 6 to 0. Four more victories followed in as many weeks, setting up the season finale with McKinley. Both teams entered the game with

▲   *Paul Brown as he looked
in his early days at Massillon's
Washington High School. Student
Sports magazine would name
Brown as the football "Coach of the
Century" for the 20th century as
the result of his accomplishments
at the high school, college, and
professional levels. (Massillon Tiger
Football Booster Club Collection)*

identical 8-1-0 records, but for the second straight season the Bulldogs shut out the Tigers, this time 21-0.

In 1934, Paul Brown added the duties of Athletic Director to his responsibilities at Massillon. He was also the main influence behind forming the Massillon Booster Club that same year. In addition to this Brown was named Director of Recreation for the whole city. While the Booster Club was initially formed for such basic reasons as to make sure the football players were getting proper meals and had a ride home from practices, eventually it would take a broader role in supporting all athletics in the school system. Through his duties as Athletic Director, Brown could now organize football at all levels of the educational system, appoint all of the various coaches and make sure that every coach was teaching the Brown's system.

The year 1934 would be another year of improvement for the Tigers, but not totally. They opened with a 37-0 win over Tiffin, then defeated East Cleveland Shaw by 46-0. Week Three saw the Tigers traveling to Sharon, Pa., to play that city's high school, still coached by Brown's old mentor Dave Stewart. It would prove to be one of the toughest games of the season for the Tigers, but Brown's team prevailed, 27-0.

The Tigers would win their next six games by 311-0; even their old nemesis Barberton could not survive the onslaught and fell 54-0. With a record of 9-0-0 it was again time for the season finale with Canton McKinley.

As it was for the Massillon Tigers, 1934 was also a banner year for the Canton McKinley Bulldogs of head coach Jimmy Aiken. Aiken had come to Canton in 1932, the same year that Paul Brown had taken over at Massillon. Before taking the reins at McKinley, Aiken had been a very successful coach at Findlay High School, posting a record of 60-13-9 and winning the 1925 state championship. After going 6-3-0 in 1932 and 9-1-0 in 1933, Aiken's Bulldogs were a perfect 10-0-0 thus far in 1934, having defeated teams from across the state and Pennsylvania.

The Massillon-McKinley game was always a special occasion and getting more special each year, but the 1934 edition of the rivalry was especially intense and significant. Not only was neighborhood pride at stake, but the state and possibly the national championship were also up for grabs.

In a stadium designed to hold a third as many people, more than 20,000 attended the game in Massillon—the largest crowd till then to see a Massillon-McKinley football game, or any sporting event in Stark County. Overhead the Goodyear blimp, hangared in Akron, flew with a huge banner that read, "YEA TIGERS, YEA BULLDOGS".

McKinley was on the receiving end of the opening kickoff and promptly marched right down the field for a touchdown and an early 7-0 lead—the first points that the Tigers had allowed the entire season. Following the ensuing kickoff Massillon responded by marching right back down the field 64 yards for a touch-

down of its own. The Tigers failed on the extra point try.

After each team's quick score within the first five minutes of the game neither team scored over the balance of the first half, McKinley taking a 7-6 lead into the locker room at the intermission.

McKinley was on the receiving end of the second half kickoff. This time the Bulldogs marched 62 yards to pay dirt, adding the extra point to increase their lead to 14-6. Late in the same quarter, the Bulldogs closed out a 46-yard drive for another touchdown and again added the point. There would be no more scoring in the game as McKinley came away with a 21-6 victory.

Not only did the victory give the Bulldogs the 1934 Ohio championship (with the Tigers finishing second) but McKinley was also declared the national champion that season.

It was bad enough that the Tigers had lost to McKinley on their home field, but people in Massillon were starting to think that maybe Paul Brown could not win the big game after having

▲   *From the Massillon Independent* before the annual battle with Canton McKinley in 1935. (Massillon Tiger Football Booster Club Collection)

lost all three of his games with McKinley and being outscored 61 to 6 in the process. Rumor had it that if the Tigers lost a fourth straight time to the Bulldogs there would be some changes made in the Massillon coaching ranks. If Paul Brown heard those rumors—and there was not much that happened in Massillon as regards the football team that he did not know about—he never let on.

After a preseason of intense practice, the Tigers opened the 1935 football campaign on Friday night, September 20, with a 70-0 thrashing of Akron East—almost the same number of points that Brown's first team in 1932 had scored for the entire season. The Tigers then breezed through their next three games averaging almost 59 points per game. Portsmouth gave Massillon a scare in Week Three when they held the Tigers to just seven points during the first half, but Brown's team rebounded with a 39-point spurt in the second half of a 46-0 victory.

After another easy victory, 64-0, over Youngstown South, Barberton gave the Tigers a tough battle by shutting out Massillon in the first quarter, but a 21-point second quarter outburst by the Tigers settled the issue in a 34-0 win. The Alliance Aviators were ready for the Tigers the following week, and one of the Aviators' assistant coaches even predicted that Brown's team would only score 25 points. That

EVENING INDEPENDENT, MASSILLON, OHIO

HAIL TO THE CHAMPIONS!

OHIO
SCHOLASTIC
CHAMPIONS
1935

COACH
PAUL E BROWN

Massillon

WASHINGTON
HIGH

GANGWAY FELLOW!
LET SOMEBODY
RUN, THAT CAN RUN.

CANTON
McKINLEY

LEHMAN
STADIUM

DRAWN BY
A D SMALL

▲ *Tribute to the newly-crowned 1935 Ohio and national champions from Massillon appeared in the* Massillon Independent *on Nov. 25, 1935. (Massillon Tiger Football Booster Club Collection)*

coach was right on the money as Alliance held the Tigers to their lowest point total thus far. Unfortunately for Alliance, like every other team that had already faced the Tigers, the Aviators failed to score and lost the game, 27-0.

Lopsided victories over the following three weeks pushed the Tigers' record to 9-0-0 just in time for the annual showdown with McKinley.

As it had the year before, the 1935 season came down to the annual Massillon-McKinley game. The Bulldogs, the defending Ohio and national champion, came into the game with a 6-2-1 mark. To the casual observer this probably looked to be a one-sided game in Massillon's favor, and indeed the Tigers were favored by two or three touchdowns; but, as is well known, all too often these rivalry games take on a life of their own. And for Paul Brown, there was the added pressure of finally defeating McKinley—or else!

Somewhat out of character, Brown told the media early that week, "We expect to win. This is the first time in the four years my teams have played Canton that I have said that. I think we have the better team... The kids are ready and eager to go."

Paul Brown knew that these words would be used by McKinley coach Jimmy Aiken to fire up the Bulldogs, but Brown was more interested in how his words would affect his own team. After three straight losses to the Bulldogs he was trying to build their confidence. Not only did his players have something of a defeatist attitude toward the Bulldogs, but even the people in Massillon were openly talking about the "McKinley jinx".

It had snowed the day before and game day dawned bitterly cold, yet 12,000 fans (short for "fanatics") crammed Canton's Lehman Stadium for the big game. It was a defensive struggle throughout the first half and at the intermission the score was still as it had begun, 0-0.

Early in the third quarter, Massillon recovered a McKinley fumble at the Bulldogs' 21-yard line. Seven plays later Tigers fullback Bob Glass followed his line into the end zone, clearing the goal line by barely a foot. Massillon failed on the extra point try, leaving the Tigers with a 6-0 lead.

Late in the same quarter, McKinley blocked a Massillon punt attempt, the Bulldogs recovering the loose ball at the Massillon 25-yard line. Several plays later McKinley had a first and goal at the Tigers' six. With a tie game or actually falling behind staring the Tigers in the face, Paul Brown changed his defense. He went to an eight-man defensive line, something he had done only once before during the season. McKinley tried three running plays and netted minus-one yard. On fourth and goal the Bulldogs went to the air, but a pair of Massillon defenders batted the ball to the ground in the end zone.

▾ *The 1935 Massillon Tigers, Ohio and national champions. (Massillon High Yearbook)*

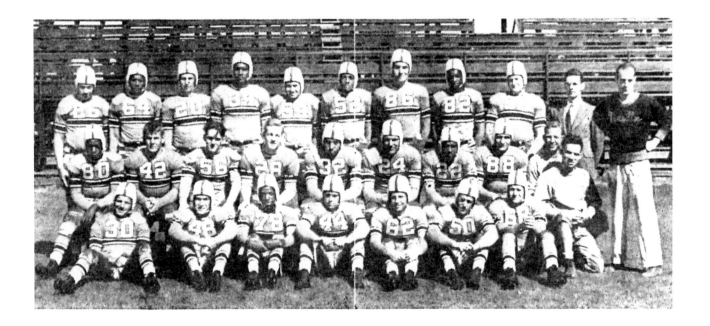

That would prove to be McKinley's last real scoring opportunity. When the final whistle sounded, it not only signaled the end of the game, but also that a Paul Brown Massillon team had finally defeated the McKinley Bulldogs, 6-0.

The 1934 Massillon-McKinley game had ended with McKinley winning the game and both the Ohio and national championships. The 1935 game between the Tigers and the Bulldogs ended in a victory for the Tigers, a victory that similarly gave Massillon its fourth Ohio championship and first national title. That would pretty much be the scenario for the next half dozen years, and more than a few beyond that, as Stark County would dominate the high school football scene both in Ohio and the country at large for the next couple of decades.

THERE WAS NO COLOR BAR AT MASSILLON. THE BEST PLAYERS PLAYED. AT A TIME WHEN MANY NORTHERN SCHOOLS WERE SEGREGATED OR DID NOT CHOOSE TO PLAY BLACK ATHLETES, BROWN CONSISTENTLY STARTED AFRICAN AMERICANS.

By now Paul Brown's system had become well ingrained into the fabric of Massillon life, especially as far as athletics was concerned. Before each season Paul held a dinner that was attended by the Massillon football players and their parents. It was at this preseason dinner that Brown "laid down the law", clearly setting out the rules that he expected his players to follow during the season, and which he expected their parents to enforce.

As George Cantor points out in his biography of Paul Brown, the Massillon coach had another rule that would remain unchanged: "What was also made clear at these introductory meetings was that there was no color bar at Massillon. The best players played. End of story. Buut Anderson, Edgar Herring, the Gillom brothers Odell and Horace—at a time when many northern schools were segregated or did not choose to play black athletes, Brown consistently started African Americans."

As they had done the previous two seasons, the 1936 Massillon Tigers opened their season with four lopsided victories. They then went on the road to play New Castle (Pa.) High School, a team that had not lost a home game in three years. The game was played in what the newspapers described as a "deluge of rain," somewhat apt for the New Castle team known as the Red Hurricane.

The wet and muddy field conditions did not help either team and punting was key; Massillon's Charley Anderson got his team out of one big hole early in the game with a tremendous 82-yard boot. Massillon took a 6-0 lead in the second quarter and added another touchdown in the third quarter. Those would prove to be the only points of the game as the Tigers held on for a tough 13-0 victory.

Four more lopsided wins over teams from Alliance, Akron North, Columbus East and Barberton high schools followed in quick order. And then it was Saturday,

The cover of the program for the 1936 Massillon-McKinley football game. (Massillon Tiger Football Booster Club Collection)

November 21, and some 21,000 fans somehow managed to cram themselves into the 7,000 seats of Massillon Stadium for the McKinley game.

The McKinley Bulldogs, now coached by John Reed, like the Tigers entered the game a perfect 9-0-0 and having defeated teams from around Ohio as well as Pennsylvania and Illinois. Despite the evenness of their respective won-lost records, this game went heavily in favor of the Tigers. Massillon outgained the Bulldogs 349 yards to 68 yards and held the McKinley offense to just three first downs. Nonetheless, points were hard to come by for the Tigers, but they managed a touchdown in the second quarter and then secured the win with a pair of fourth quarter scores.

The 21-0 victory ensured that the Tigers had successfully defended both their state and national championships

Having won 20 straight games, and 29 of their last 30, the Massillon Tigers were gaining quite a reputation. They were also attracting a lot of people to their home games and it was obvious to Paul Brown that the current Massillon Stadium was woefully inadequate to accommodate the crowds that were now expected at every game. Brown first convinced school board president Dr. H. W. Bell that a new stadium was needed, then he went out and convinced the Works Progress Administration (WPA—one of President Franklin Roosevelt's Depression era "alphabet soup" relief programs) to provide the money for the purchase of the land necessary to build a 20,000 seat stadium. Old Massillon Stadium was torn down after the final game of the 1938 season and the new Tiger Stadium was ready for business in time for the first game of the '39 campaign.

During the 1937 football campaign, Paul Brown's Tigers faced some of the stiffest competition of his nine years at Massillon. During those years Brown's teams averaged 357 points per season, but in 1937 they would score only 228, the lowest total except for Brown's first year in 1932. Not only was the competition getting stiffer, but local teams were now somewhat wary of playing the Tigers and Brown was having to go farther afield to find opponents. Fortunately, there were teams from around the Midwest that wanted to see just how good Massillon was and were willing to schedule them at least once.

Massillon fullback Bob Glass crashes through the line and into the end zone for a touchdown against McKinley in 1936. (Massillon Tiger Football Booster Club Collection— Massillon Independent)

One of those Midwestern teams that added the Tigers to its schedule in 1937 was Horace Mann High School of Gary, Ind. The defending Indiana champions opened their season at Massillon Stadium before a packed house of some 10,000. The visitors scored 13 points against the Tigers, the most by any team since 1934.

But those points came in the final quarter and after the Tigers had built up a 33-point lead, the game ending with Massillon on the long end of a 33-13 score.

On September 24 the team from Mansfield High School came to Massillon Stadium. It would be a game of the Tigers of Massillon vs. the Tygers of Mansfield. It was a tough defensive struggle all the way, with Massillon making only eight first downs and Mansfield held to just three. Massillon's Tigers scored on their first possession of the game to take an early 6-0 lead. That score looked to be just the first of many for Massillon, but such was not to be the case. Mansfield came back in the second quarter with a touchdown of its own to tie the game at 6-6. The score then remained unchanged through the final whistle. Massillon's win streak had been stopped at 21, but they were still undefeated in 22 straight games.

The Tigers would win their next four games, including a 39-0 victory over previously undefeated and unscored-upon Franklin High School of Cedar Rapids, Iowa.

On October 29 the Tigers played host to the Red Hurricanes of New Castle High School. New Castle had given the Tigers a real battle before losing the previous year in Pennsylvania, but now the Red Hurricane was hoping to return the favor on the Tigers' home turf. The game was another defensive struggle, with New Castle netting just 112 yards of total offense and Massillon limited to only 91 yards. The turning point of the contest came in the second quarter when the Hurricanes intercepted a Massillon aerial deep in the Massillon end of the field and turned it into a touchdown two plays later. The extra point gave the visitors a 7-0 lead.

Those would prove to be the only points of the game as the Tigers saw their unbeaten streak ended at 26 in a row. The whole right side of the Massillon starting line never played in the game due to injury or illness, but Coach Brown refused to use that as an excuse.

Over the next two weeks Youngstown's Chaney High School, 28-6, and Barberton, 28-0, fell before the Tigers, raising Massillon's record to 7-1-1 and setting up the annual showdown with Canton McKinley on Saturday, November 20. The undefeated Bulldogs had not played the week before, a fortuitous break in their schedule after three tough games with Dover, Alliance, and Steubenville. As it had the previous season, this game would decide Ohio's football championship.

Massillon opened the scoring when Bob Glass scored on an eight-yard scamper on the Tigers' first possession of the game. McKinley came right back to tie the score on a 70-yard touchdown pass. Neither team connected on its extra point try and the half ended in a 6-6 deadlock. Bob Glass put the Tigers back into the lead with a two-yard run around his right end in the third quarter. An interception by the Tigers on McKinley's ensuing possession set up the game's final score by the Tigers.

The new Massillon Tiger Stadium as it looked on Sept. 15, 1939, just before the first game was played. (Massillon Tiger Football Booster Club Collection - Massillon Independent)

The 19-6 victory gave Paul Brown's team its third consecutive state title, with the Bulldogs again finishing second.

The end of the 1937 campaign saw the curtain come down on the career of one of Massillon's greatest players. Fullback Bob Glass was a member of the Tigers varsity for three seasons, earning All-Ohio honors each time. In those three seasons, Glass scored 331 points on 47 touchdowns and 25 PATs; Glass's career point total and career touchdowns are still school records more than 75 years later. After graduating from Massillon, Bob went on to Tulane University, but his schooling and football career were interrupted by World War II. Bob joined the Marine Corps and was sent to the South Pacific. In February of 1945, Bob Glass was killed in action during the intense fighting on the island of Iwo Jima.

Like the previous season, the 1938 Massillon football schedule would feature three opponents from out of state. The season would also mark another milestone in Tigers history as the team would play before 116,000 fans both home and away, the first time their attendance had topped the 100,000 mark—the Tigers were quickly becoming *the* attraction in high school football.

The season opened on September 16 against the first of the non-Ohio teams when McKeesport (Pa.) High School visited Massillon Stadium. McKeesport had been undefeated the past two seasons, and the *Independent* later noted, "It was a ding-dong battle from start to finish, marked by hard tackling and sparkling passes."

The Tigers jumped off to a good start with an early first quarter touchdown, but the extra point try failed. While Massillon was traditionally a very good team running the ball, this season they would go to their aerial game with more frequency and that started right with this very first game. In the second quarter, a pair of touchdown aerials increased the Tigers' lead to 19-0 at the intermission. McKeesport broke through and avoided a shutout with a fourth quarter score, but the day belonged to Massillon with a 19-7 triumph.

Victories over Mansfield and Warren Harding followed, leading into the second game against a Pennsylvania foe. This time the Tigers would be taking to the road to play Sharon High School. Sharon was still coached by former Massillon and Paul Brown mentor Dave Stewart. Stewart had been the football coach at Sharon High School since 1928 and would remain there until he retired in 1947. His

▲ *Massillon's Ray Getz makes a catch for a sizable gain against Youngstown East during the 1939 season. (Massillon Tiger Football Booster Club Collection)*

team entered this game as the defending Pennsylvania state champion and riding an 18-game win streak. The Tigers had won six in a row since losing to New Castle, the only defeat in their last 33 contests, so something had to give.

Some 2,000 Massillon fans made the trip to New Castle by car and special train. They were expecting to see an outstanding game and they were not disappointed as the *Independent* reported that this was "...one of the finest football games anyone could ever hope to witness. There have been none like it in Washington high school history and you may never see another. There have been sensational finishes ...but never have four quarters been packed with more offensive football and thrills than the 48 minutes of last night's game."

Turnovers would play a huge part in this game, especially in the first half. Using a fumble recovery and an 80-yard punt return by Vince Snyder, the Tigers jumped to a 13-0 lead in the first quarter. The Sharon team came right back in the second quarter, taking advantage of two recovered Massillon fumbles to tie the score at 13-13. In the final two minutes of the half, the Tigers bounced back to add another touchdown and take a 19-13 lead at the intermission.

Each team scored a touchdown in the third quarter as the game remained tight, but a 12-0 run by the Tigers in the final stanza sealed the deal for Massillon as the Tigers survived an exciting game to bring home a 37-20 victory. A key difference in the game had been the Massillon passing attack, which accounted for 123 yards, to zero yards through the air for the Sharon team.

The Tigers quickly added victories in their next five games. Among those wins was a 52-7 thrashing of New Castle before 12,000 fans, the largest crowd ever to see a football game in that city. The Tigers scored two touchdowns in each quarter and limited the Red Hurricane to just 14 net yards, minus-25 on the ground.

For the third consecutive season, Massillon and Canton McKinley would meet as a pair of undefeated teams to decide the Ohio championship. It was McKinley's turn to host the event and it would be viewed by 18,000 fans in the brand new Fawcett Stadium, built for the then-princely sum of $250,000. (It cost four times that amount just to remodel the stadium's press box in 2011.)

With the game still scoreless the first quarter ended with the Tigers on the march toward the Bulldogs' goal line. As the second quarter got underway, Massillon was at the McKinley 27-yard line, but it took 10 more plays before the Tigers could fight their way through the Bulldogs defense and into the end zone for a

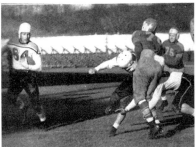

▲ Top: Massillon's Bill
Zimmerman is off on an end
sweep against Mansfield
in this 1939 game action.
(Massillon Yearbook)

▲ Bottom: Massillon's
George Slusser goes for good
yardage against Mansfield
High during the 1939 season.
(Massillon Yearbook)

▲ Massillon's outstanding success
earned for the Tigers a coveted spot
on the cover of "LIFE" magazine in
November of 1939. (Massillon Tiger
Football Booster Club Collection)

Massillon runningback Fred Blunt dives into the end zone for a touchdown against Youngstown East in 1939. (Massillon Tiger Football Booster Club Collection)

touchdown. The extra point try was no good, leaving the Tigers with a 6-0 lead. Two possessions later, McKinley fumbled deep in its own end of the field, the loose pigskin being recovered by the Tigers at the Bulldogs' 27-yard line. Seven plays later the Tigers were back in the McKinley end zone. The extra point try again failed, but the Tigers had pushed their lead to 12-0.

Those would be all of the points scored by either team for the balance of the game. In a second half heavy on defense, the Bulldogs three times got within the shadow of the Massillon goal posts—or even closer—but each time the Tiger defenders successfully protected their end zone using Paul Brown's eight-man line.

For the third consecutive season the Tigers and the Bulldogs had finished 1-2 in Ohio.

The 1939 season opened for Massillon with a game in the brand new Tiger Stadium before more than 15,000 fans. The opponent that day was Cleveland stalwart Cathedral Latin. The Lions would have some classic battles with Massillon within just a few years, but this day it would be the Tigers and not the Lions who would rule the jungle. Massillon halfback Tommy James scored the first touchdown in the new stadium on a 39-yard run and the Tigers kept right on scoring after that. The game ended with Massillon on the long end of a 40-13 score.

The next week Massillon crushed Mansfield, 73-0, to set up an early-season showdown with Warren Harding. Harding played the Tigers tough for the first two and a half quarters. Massillon led by only 6 to 0 at the intermission, but halfway through the third quarter the team finally found its scoring punch. A pair of touchdowns in the last few minutes of the third quarter and two more in the final period carried the Tigers to a 33-0 victory.

The Tigers pushed their record to 9-0-0 by rolling over their next six opponents, outscoring them 294 to 6.

And then came the traditional season finale with Canton McKinley on Saturday, November 17, at Fawcett Stadium. This was not one of the strongest Bulldogs teams of recent years, having scored just 95 points over their first nine games, but the McKinley defense had allowed only 33 points in posting a still respectable 6-2-1 record. However, this was Canton McKinley vs. Massillon—past records do not count.

The *Independent* described the scene at Fawcett Stadium thusly:

> *"While 22,000 fans filled every inch of the stadium and sat on the slope at the northwest end, the Tiger and Bulldog elevens waged their hottest duel since the terrific game of 1935 ... It's tradition that the underdog plays over his head and the favorite tightens up in a Massillon-Canton game and that was what took place Saturday. The Bulldogs were over their heads compared with past performances this season, but perhaps they were only playing the brand of ball of which they were really capable of producing. They adopted a first half strategy of consuming as much time in the huddle as possible to purposely delay the game with the hope of keeping down the score and possibly capitalizing on a break."*

The first quarter ended without either team denting the scoreboard. It marked only the second time during the entire season that the Tigers had failed to score during a quarter. The Tigers scoring "drought" ended in the second period with a pair of touchdowns that gave Massillon a 13-0 lead. McKinley came back with a 41-yard touchdown pass play that tightened the score at 13-6 at the half.

Early in the third quarter, Massillon stopped McKinley on downs at the Tigers 15-yard line. The Tigers then went back down the field on an 85-yard touchdown march, the extra point ending the game's scoring as the Tigers closed out their season with a 20-6 victory.

For the second consecutive season the Tigers had gone undefeated, 10-0-0, extending their winning streak to 23 in a row while bringing home another Ohio championship and adding a third national title to their trophy case. The team had

▸ *Newspaper
headlines tell the story
of Massillon's 1939
championship season.
(Massillon Tiger Football
Booster Club Collection)*

▲ *By 1940 Paul Brown's coaching reputation had reached such a point that he was giving clinics for other coaches, including his old high school coach, Dave Stewart (far right). (Massillon Tiger Football Booster Club Collection)*

▸ *Massillon halfback Tom James gets a nice block from fellow halfback Ray Getz (22) against Toledo Waite in 1940. (Massillon Tiger Football Booster Club Collection)*

now become so popular nationwide that the Tigers even made the cover of "LIFE" magazine that year.

In a very real sense, Paul Brown's coaching career at Massillon High School had been leading up to the 1940 season. Observers of high school football around the country got a small preview of what Massillon would be like that year when the Tigers had a spring game against the varsity team from Kent State University on Monday, April 15. The Tigers scored seven touchdowns in building a 47-0 lead; the Kent State coach had seen enough as he took his players off the field before the game was completed.

The season began in earnest on Friday, September 13, when Cleveland's Cathedral Latin paid a visit to Tiger Stadium. The Lions would end the season by dominating Cleveland's Senate League (one of the toughest school boy leagues in the country) and winning the Cleveland city championship, but on this day they were no match for the Tigers. Paul Brown's team rolled up 517 yards of total offense and held the Lions to just 32. The Tigers led 32-0 at the half and shortly after the start of the third quarter Brown pulled his starters. It did not seem to matter as the Tigers added another 32 points after the intermission on their way to a 64-0 victory.

Massillon's run through the 1940 season had officially begun.

Next up was the team from Weirton High School, one of the top teams in West Virginia. The game with the Red Raiders was played on September 20 and attracted a record 18,300 fans to Tiger Stadium. It did not take long for the Raiders of Coach Carl Hamill to find out what Latin had learned the previous week—on offense the Tigers could score at will and it was nearly impossible to move the ball against the Massillon defense. The Tigers built a 41-0 lead after two quarters and Brown's starting eleven was done for the day. In the 48-0 victory, the Tigers amassed 447 net yards and held the Red Raiders to just 67.

MASSILLON 28, WAITE 0
DEVILBISS BEATS SANDUSKY

In a congratulatory letter that he later wrote to Paul Brown, Weirton Coach Hamill said that the Tigers were the best high school team that he had ever seen and suggested that Brown might want to add the University of West Virginia team to his schedule.

Week Three brought Warren Harding to Tiger Stadium. As the Massillon *Independent* noted, "Warren fans were warned ahead of time that the present Massillon club is rated as the best ever turned out by Coach Paul Brown—today they believe all of the stories and can even add a few for good measure."

When the Massillon first team was on the field, it seemed that they could, and did, score whenever they wanted to. A perfect example occurred during the Tigers' first offensive series. On that possession halfback Tommy James scored on a 46-yard run, but the play was called back when both teams were ruled to be offside. On the very next play James did it again, racing 46 yards to pay dirt and this time there were no flags.

The Tigers led 20-0 after the first quarter and early in the second period end Horace Gillom put the game on ice, as the *Independent* related,

> "...but the straw that broke the camel's back was a 75-yard dash by Horace Gillom. Running from punt formation, he was practically on his own after he got by the line of scrimmage. Tacklers bounced off him. He shook others from his legs and body and with a lithe twist, sent another whirling through the air, to get himself in the open. Then with only the safety-man between him and the goal posts, he turned on that extra speed he always seems to have and outlegged his opponent to the goal. It was one of the finest runs ever seen here, a great performance by a great football player."

Brown again pulled the starters after just two quarters with his team enjoying a 40-0 lead. The 59-0 final was the worst beating that a Harding team had ever suffered. Once again the final stats were lopsided, 434 net yards for the Tigers and just 43 for Harding.

◄ *Left: Halfback Tom James follows his interference around the right side for some big yardage during the 1940 campaign. (Massillon Yearbook)*

◄ *Right: A nice flying block allows Massillon halfback Tom James to go for big yardage during the 1940 season. (Massillon Yearbook)*

WEIRTON COACH HAMILL SAID THAT THE TIGERS WERE THE BEST HIGH SCHOOL TEAM THAT HE HAD EVER SEEN AND SUGGESTED THAT BROWN MIGHT WANT TO ADD THE UNIVERSITY OF WEST VIRGINIA TEAM TO HIS SCHEDULE.

On Friday, October 4, the Tigers took to the road and traveled to Erie, Pa., to take on that city's East High School team. The record Erie crowd of almost 22,000 had to be pretty excited when their East High Warriors held the Tigers to a three and out on their first offensive possession of the game—but that would prove to be an aberration rather than the rule. Only two other times during the entire game would the Tigers fail to score when on offense, and both of those failures were the result of pass interceptions. Speaking of the Tigers' passing game, it proved to be most productive this day; the Tigers only completed nine of 20 aerials, but five went for touchdowns.

Like the previous week against Harding, the Tigers handed East High its worst defeat in 20 years of football, 74-0. Stats for this game are not available, except to note that East High managed just one first down the entire game. One is left to wonder what the yardage totals for each team had been.

On Friday, October 11, the Tigers traveled to Akron's Rubber Bowl to play the Alliance Aviators. The game was arranged by the Akron Junior League as a charity event. In that regard it was a total success as more than 33,000 people attended the game, the largest crowd before which either the Tigers or the Aviators had ever played.

While the score might indicate otherwise, this was not the blowout that Massillon's earlier games had been. As the *Independent* noted,

"Alliance had Massillon so completely scouted that the Aviators made the going anything but a breeze for Paul Brown's grand aggregation. It was the first time this year that the Tigers had seen an enemy on the wrong side of the Massillon 30 when Alliance recovered a fumble in the first period, and the Aviators are the only team that forced Brown to keep his first string in action for four quarters ... The statistics favored Massillon by a heavy margin but the Aviators' brave-hearted defense in the clutch kept the score down."

The Tigers scored the first time they had the ball on a 39-yard Horace Gillom end around play. When Alliance was forced to punt on its ensuing possession, Tommy James fumbled the ball and Alliance recovered the loose pigskin at the Tigers' six-yard line; it marked the first time all season that a team had gotten beyond the Massillon 30-yard line. The Aviators pushed the ball to the one, but on fourth and goal the center of the Massillon defensive line halted the Alliance ball carrier at the line of scrimmage and the ball went over to Massillon on downs.

Although the statistical story was again heavily in Massillon's favor with 501 net yards to Alliance's 33 and the Aviator's only making one first down, the Alliance defense kept its team in the game. The *Canton Repository* noted "the spirited defensive play of the Aviators that threw back the famed Massillon running attack," even though the Tigers managed 341 yards rushing.

The Tigers added a pair of second quarter touchdowns to take a 20-0 lead at halftime. Alliance shut out Massillon in the third quarter, but a 20-point outburst by the Tigers in the final period sealed Alliance's fate. Final score: Massillon 40, Alliance 0.

Paul Brown's efforts in Massillon were not solely concerned with the football team. He was involved in many aspects of both school and city life, and used the football team's success to aid other projects. One of those was the Massillon High School marching band. Although the school's marching band dated back to 1917, Brown brought in George Bird, a veteran of several high school and college bands as well as the Cincinnati Conservatory of Music, to turn the marching band into a real showpiece for those attending Tigers football games.

Like the Tigers themselves, the marching band was given an opportunity to "strut its stuff" at the Akron Rubber Bowl at halftime and after the game with Alliance; and they did not disappoint as this description from the *Independent* heartily demonstrates:

"At their best for this show, the Tiger bandettes quickly reviewed all their regular stuff—and then wowed the spectators with a flag formation done with lights after the big stadium lamps had been extinguished. Almost without hesitation, the band offered a salute to Alliance, roared down the field with "Hold that Tiger," came back with "Rampart St. Parade," and then of-

fered imitations of a Dixieland band with a brass section playing and the rest of the band doing a dance step.

"In the post-game performance the band played "Take Down the Flag," and then concluded a brilliant performance with a novelty number that included a military march, a Dutch dance, a swing tune and a hillbilly hop—and this called "Mutiny in the Band," just about stole the show.

"A tribute to the band's performance is the fact that few persons moved from their seats until the bandettes rolled off down the field. But that was the senior band. The Massillon junior high crew, a 100-piece organization, was sensational. Few college bands would have attempted the routine offered by the juniors."

The Tigers continued to roll in their next two games, humbling Steubenville by 66-0 and thumping Mansfield, 38-0. The Mansfield Tygers were a stubborn lot as they held Massillon scoreless in the first quarter, but Massillon tallied twice in each of the last three periods to capture their 30th consecutive victory by a 38-0 count.

With the team's record now 7-0-0 came perhaps the most anticipated game in several years. Not everyone in Ohio was of the opinion that the Tigers were the greatest high school team in the state—and some of those people lived in Toledo. In 1939 the folks at Waite High School, coached by future Purdue mentor Jack Mollenkopf, had challenged the Tigers to a postseason game to decide which was the best team in the state, but Paul Brown was not interested in playing any postseason games. Waite instead played Portsmouth High School, another undefeated team, in what was billed as a game for the state championship. Waite defeated Portsmouth, 9-7, and along with Massillon and Hamilton High School is recognized as Ohio's champion for 1939.

During the off-season there was an almost continuous clamoring from people in both cities to arrange a game between Massillon and Waite, but neither team had the same open weekend. Finally, the Massillon people paid Canton Lehman's guarantee of $1,200 to get out of the Tigers scheduled game with that team, thus opening up the first weekend of November for a game with Waite. The game was scheduled for Friday night, November 1, at Tiger Stadium. The Waite Indi-

▼ *This coffin was meant for the Massillon Tigers, but it was used by the McKinley Bulldogs after Massillon's 34-6 victory in 1940. (Massillon Tiger Football Booster Club Collection - Canton Repository)*

▲ *Before a sellout crowd, Massillon running back Fred Blunt picked up five yards on this run against Canton McKinley in 1940. (Massillon Tiger Football Booster Club Collection)*

ans came to town with a 19-game winning streak claiming to be the sole champion of Ohio. Despite being played in a driving rain, a capacity crowd of more than 22,000 was on hand for this game—while another 2,500 had to be turned away at the gate.

The inclement weather held down the score, but little else, as the Tigers rolled to their 31st consecutive victory. A blocked punt by the Tigers in the first quarter led to Massillon's first touchdown. The only points of the second quarter came off another blocked Waite punt, the ball rolling out of the end zone for a safety. Leading 8-0 at the half, the Tigers added a TD in the third quarter and two more in the fourth for a 28-0 victory. As they had in all of their other victories, the Tigers totally dominated the game's statistics, holding the Indians to just one first down, seven yards rushing, and 14 yards passing.

There was now no longer any doubt, at least in Toledo, who the best team in Ohio was.

Maybe there was a let down after the big game with Waite. Or maybe the Tigers were looking ahead to their annual clash with another undefeated, 8-0-1, McKinley Bulldogs team. Or maybe Coach Brown was just being cautious. Perhaps all of the above. Whatever it was, when the Tigers traveled to Youngstown to play that city's East High on Friday, November 8, the Tigers built up a 26-0 half time lead and then Paul Brown pulled all of his starters for the entire second half. There would be no scoring in the last two quarters by either team, the first time in recent memory that the Tigers had been shut out in consecutive quarters. The 26-0 final was the Tigers' closest game of the season.

More than 20,000 people were on hand for the season finale against the Canton McKinley Bulldogs. The game, played at Tiger Stadium on a bitterly cold Saturday, November 16, had been sold out for at least the previous two weeks.

After a scoreless first quarter, the Bulldogs broke into the scoring column with a touchdown in the second. Not only were those the first points scored against the Tigers all season, it also marked the first time that the Tigers had trailed in a game.

Later in the second quarter, the Tigers finally got on the scoreboard on a play that the *Independent* called "... the thriller of all thrillers. ... Fading back to his 35, James fired a tremendous forward to his right. Gillom, leaping over the head of (McKinley defender) Brown on the Canton 25, tipped the ball with one hand,

▲ *The 1940 Massillon Tigers,*
Paul Brown's last state and
national championship team
at Massillon Washington High
School—and one of the country's
all-time great high school
teams. (Massillon Yearbook)

caught it with the other, stiff-armed Brown, broke loose from Ed Snyder and hot-footed down the sidelines for the score."

The extra point then gave the Tigers a 7-6 lead, one they took into the locker room at the half.

The Tigers would totally shut down the McKinley offense in the second half, while shifting theirs into high gear. Early in the third quarter the Tigers increased their lead to 14-6. A short while later they added to their advantage with a play that by itself could be the definition of razzle-dazzle. The *Independent* described the play "(With the ball on the McKinley 17-yard line) Getz lateralled to James, who

All the Way to #1

▲ The 1940 Massillon Washington starting line-up achieved something unique in the annals of high school football, something that may never be repeated—all 11 players were named to the All-Ohio team. (Massillon Tiger Football Booster Club Collection— Massillon Independent)

lateralled to Blunt, who lateralled to Robinson, who fired a forward pass to Gillom, standing alone in the end zone." Touchdown!

Massillon had increased its lead to 21-7. The Tigers would add two more touchdowns in the fourth quarter to put away the Bulldogs, 34-6.

The 1940 season was now completed—perhaps the greatest season in Massillon Washington High School football history. Paul Brown's Tigers had gone 10-0-0 for the third consecutive year and pushed their winning streak to 33 in a row while again winning state and national titles. Over the past six seasons, Paul Brown's team had posted a record of 58-1-1 and won a record six consecutive state championships and four national championships.

In 1940 the Tigers had played before 180,500 people, an average of more than 18,000 per game. How big a deal was that—the only team in the state to play before more people was the Ohio State Buckeyes.

How good were the 1940 Tigers? If All-State selections are any indication then they are the all-time best team in Ohio. For the only time in state history, all 11 starters from the same team made the United Press International All-Ohio First Team, and those 11 were the starting eleven of the 1940 Massillon Tigers: ends Horace Gillom and Herman Robinson; tackles Eli Broglio and Gene Henderson; guards James Russell and William Wallace; center Gordon Appleby; quarterback Richard Kingham; halfbacks Ray Getz and Tommy James; fullback Fred Blunt. Horace Gillom was also selected as the most outstanding scholastic player in Ohio.

When people talk about the all-time great high school football teams they mention teams like the 1914 Everett (Mass.) team and the 1919 Harrisburg Tech squad—and now they have to add the 1940 Massillon Tigers to the mix.

And the Massillon Tigers legend was just beginning.

Paul Brown had now been at Massillon High School for nine years. He has often been quoted as saying that the only two jobs that he ever really wanted was coaching at Massillon High School and coaching at Ohio State University. After the 1940 season, Ohio State was looking for a new head football coach. Paul was definitely interested—and many of his rival high school coaches were definitely interested in seeing that Brown was selected to become the new coach of the Buckeyes. It was something like self-preservation: they could not beat him, so the next best thing was to get him shipped off to Columbus. Brown applied for the job and was selected as the Buckeyes new head coach, taking over for the 1941 season.

In his nine seasons at Massillon, Paul Brown posted a record of 80-8-2, .900, and won six state championships and four national titles. At Ohio State, Brown would win the school's first national championship in 1942. Later with the Cleveland Browns, his teams would play in 10 consecutive professional championship games, winning seven of them.

Paul Brown and Bob Zuppke are the only coaches to ever win a national championship at both the high school and college level, but Paul Brown stands alone as the only coach to win national titles at all three levels of football: high school, college, and professional.

▾   Massillon Washington football fans showed their patriotism in a most unique way during World War II. With the money raised through the sale of war bonds a B-17 bomber was purchased for the Army Air Corps and christened "Spirit of Ohio's Massillon High School." (Massillon Tiger Football Booster Club Collection— Massillon Independent)

## CHAPTER 5

THE TIGERS—PART II

Massillon High School
Massillon, Ohio

I t often happens in sports that the man coaching a team immediately after a coach of legendary stature is thrust into a somewhat unenviable position through no fault of his own. No matter how well he does, if the new man does not continue to have the extraordinarily good results that his predecessor had, then he will be considered to be unsuccessful—or worse.

Perhaps the ultimate example of this situation occurred when Heartley "Hunk" Anderson replaced Knute Rockne after Rockne's unexpected death in a plane crash in March of 1931. A former player for Rockne from 1918-1921, Anderson was selected after two years as the head coach at St. Louis University. Anderson had decent, though not spectacular, results as Notre Dame's head coach in posting a 16-9-2 mark from 1931 to 1933. But he was always compared to what Rockne had done, especially Knute's four national championships, and it certainly did not help Anderson that just prior to his death Rockne had won back-to-back national titles. When Anderson's team finished 3-5-1 in 1933, Notre Dame's first losing season since 1888, it was time for a change.

Paul Brown's leaving Massillon Washington High School was hardly as dramatic, but the situation for his successor was certainly similar to that of Hunk Anderson at Notre Dame. Over the previous six seasons, Brown's Massillon Washington teams had finished 58-1-1, were currently riding a streak of 33 games without a defeat, had six consecutive state championships under their belt, had won four national titles, and had just won back-to-back national titles.

The post-Paul Brown era at Massillon began with a succession of Massillon High School alumni taking over the coaching reins. Into the breach for the 1941 season stepped William "Bud" Houghton, a 1928 Massillon grad and an assistant varsity coach under Paul Brown from 1933-1940. Only a 6-6 tie with the powerful Mansfield High Tygers prevented Houghton's team from having a perfect season. However, the 9-0-1 Tigers did capture a seventh consecutive state championship, albeit one they had to share with both Mansfield and Martin's Ferry high schools.

The Tigers had played their last game of 1941 on November 22 when just 15 days later literally everything changed again. The United States was thrust into the midst of the Second World War when Japanese naval forces attacked the U.S. Navy base at Pearl Harbor, Hawaii. As the saying goes, "the best laid plans" of hundreds of thousands of Americans were altered that fateful day and among them was Bud Houghton. Answering his country's call in early 1942, Houghton enlisted in the U.S. Navy as a physical fitness instructor, a position taken by many of the country's coaches, Paul Brown among them.

Replacing Houghton as "interim head coach" would be another Massillon grad, Elwood "Kam" Kammer, Class of 1926. Kammer would lead the Tigers for the next three years. Like Bud Houghton before him, Kammer continued the winning ways established by Paul Brown as the Tigers cruised through the first nine games of the 1942 season. In a dramatic reversal of fortune in the season finale, however, the Bulldogs of Canton McKinley completely turned the tables on the Tigers with a stunning 35-0 defeat, a loss later called the most famous football defeat in Ohio history. The Bulldogs had ended Massillon's unbeaten streak at 52 in a row and when McKinley was named the Ohio champions, they had also ended Massillon's seven-year hold on the state's top spot.

The Massillon Tigers rebounded in 1943 to post a perfect 10-0-0 record—the team's sixth perfect season out of the last nine. They even managed to avenge their 1942 loss to the McKinley Bulldogs, 21-0, preventing the Bulldogs from winning a second consecutive state title, which landed back in Massillon.

The 1944 season, Kammer's last at Massillon, saw the Tigers finish a mediocre 7-3-0, those three defeats equaling the Tigers' losses for the previous 10 seasons combined.

Elwood Kammer retired from coaching in January of 1945. With Bud Houghton still serving in the Navy, another interim head coach was named to lead the Tigers, 1936 grad Augie Morningstar, captain of Massillon's first national championship team back in 1935. Morningstar would pilot Massillon through one of its more unusual seasons; the Tigers would not lose a single game in 1945, but they would play five ties, ending the season with a record of 5-0-5. One of those tie games took place in Cleveland at that city's lakefront Municipal Stadium against defending state champion Cathedral Latin. A huge throng of 51,049 people took in the game, the largest crowd ever to see a regular season high school football game in Ohio, possibly in the country.

With his naval service completed, Bud Houghton returned to Massillon Washington High School in 1946 to resume his pre-war duties as the head football coach. Houghton had limited success this time around and posted a combined record of 12-6-2 for the 1946 and 1947 seasons. After the 1947 season, Bud Houghton left Washington High School and accepted the head coaching job at the University of Akron.

▲   *In six years as the Tigers'*
head coach, 1948-1953, Chuck
Mather led the team to six
consecutive state titles and
three national championships.
(Massillon Yearbook)

The search to find the next Massillon coach began immediately and was quite an extensive one, totaling more than 50 candidates. Finally, on May 5, 1948, the Tigers' new coach, Charles V. Mather, was introduced to the Massillon public.

Chuck Mather, as he was more popularly known, was the first non-Massillon High graduate appointed to coach the team since Paul Brown's first season in 1932. Mather graduated from Ohio Northern University in 1937 and that fall took over as the head football coach at the high school in Brilliant, Ohio, a small town near Steubenville along the southeastern edge of the state. Brilliant High School was what was then known as a Class B school due to its small size. The school did not even have a football team during the two years prior to Mather being named to coach the sport there. Not too surprisingly, the team lost all seven of the games it played in 1937, but improved to 4-3-1 in 1938 and to 6-2-0 in 1939.

Following the 1939 season, Mather took over as the head football coach at Leetonia (Oh.) High School. Leetonia was another Class B school, but here Mather had much greater success. His team lost the first game he coached in 1940, tied the second game, and won the next seven. In 1941 the Bears kept that streak alive by winning all 10 games on their schedule, pushing the run to 18 in a row while also being the highest scoring team in Ohio.

With the coming of World War II, Chuck Mather did his duty by joining the Coast Guard in 1942. Mustered out during the first half of 1945, he returned to coach the Leetonia Bears that fall. The team went 9-0-1, extending Mather's personal unbeaten streak to 28 in a row; the Bears were also named the mythical Class B state champion that season.

Chuck Mather loved coaching at Leetonia, but he wanted to move up to a bigger Class A program. When the coaching position at Hamilton High School near Cincinnati came open, he applied and was hired. In his two years at Hamilton, his teams posted a record of 17-3-0.

When Chuck Mather took the reins at Washington High School, there was understandably a little confusion and uncertainty among the Massillon players. Massillon had traditionally used a T-formation based offense; however, after the 6-4-0 season in 1947, Bud Houghton had decided to change to the single wing. He had already started instructing his team in the single wing when he moved on as the Akron coach. Chuck Mather was an advocate of the T-formation with a balanced line, so when he came on board it was back to the T.

If there was any doubt as to how this flip-flopping on offense would affect the team, Massillon's fans needed to look no further than Chuck Mather's very first game as head coach. On September 17, the Tigers played the Lions of Cleveland's Cathedral Latin School. The Lions had been the best team in Ohio over the previous four seasons, winning or sharing the state championship in 1944, 1945, and

1946 and finishing fourth in 1947. Massillon had last defeated Latin in 1941, seven years previously.

In what just may be the most amazing first quarter of any Massillon Tigers football game, the action started before many of the estimated 16,000 fans at Tiger Stadium had settled into their seats. On the second play of the game, Massillon sophomore halfback Irv Crable raced 49 yards to pay dirt. On the Tigers' second possession, fullback Al Brown took the ball on second down and raced 61 yards for another touchdown. On the Tigers' third possession, it was back to Crable, who on first down raced 55 yards for a third Massillon TD. On the ensuing kickoff the Lions return man fumbled the ball; it was picked up by Massillon end Jack Houston and returned 22 yards for yet another Massillon touchdown.

The Tigers had leaped out to a 25-0 lead after one quarter and had run just five plays on offense. Within the first couple of minutes of the second quarter the score ballooned to 38-0. Massillon's scoring pace slowed down a bit as Mather cleared the bench, but the Tigers still came away with an impressive 44-13 victory.

The victories continued to roll in thru Week Four, when the Tigers had to play the Aviators of Alliance High School, in Alliance, Ohio, on Friday night, October 15. The Aviators had not defeated the Tigers in 15 consecutive games dating back to 1933, so why should this one be any different. But it was. The Tigers actually out-gained the Aviators, 225-217, but the only payoff comes with the points on the scoreboard and there Alliance had the edge, 14-0.

THE TIGERS HAD LEAPED OUT TO A 25-0 LEAD AFTER ONE QUARTER AND HAD RUN JUST FIVE PLAYS ON OFFENSE.

Rebounding from that setback, the Tigers won their next four games, setting up another final-game showdown with Canton McKinley. While the Tigers' loss to Alliance had eliminated any chance of a national championship, the Tigers were still very much in the thick of the race for the state title. Until 1947, the state championship had been determined by popular acclaim. However, beginning with the 1947 season, the Associated Press (AP) poll was recognized by the Ohio High School Athletic Association as the official designator of the state football champion (at this time every school in the state was lumped into the same poll).

Despite the loss to Alliance, Massillon was still ranked high in the AP poll. So was undefeated Canton McKinley, which had played and defeated many of the same teams that Massillon had played, including a 46-7 thrashing of the Tiger tamers from Alliance.

The game with McKinley was played in Tiger Stadium on Saturday, November 20. The Tigers had not defeated the Bulldogs since 1943, suffering two losses and playing a couple of ties since then. However, the 22,000 spectators on hand for the

▲ *A Massillon ball carrier*
tries to turn the corner in
this 1950 game action.
(Massillon Yearbook)

game knew it would be a real battle, with the top-ranked Bulldogs hoping to hold off the #2 Tigers, the state title going to the victor.

The Tigers took a 7-0 lead in the first quarter, but a McKinley touchdown in the second cut the Massillon lead to 7-6 at the half. In the third quarter the Tigers added another seven points, but early in the fourth quarter the Bulldogs struck again, making the score 14-12 with about eight and a half minutes left on the game clock. When the Tigers went back on offense after the ensuing McKinley kickoff, Coach Mather got exactly what he needed from his team, a time consuming touchdown drive that ate up almost seven minutes of the clock and gave the Tigers a 21-12 lead with a minute and a half to play.

That would prove to be the final score. The victory propelled Massillon to the top of the final AP poll as the Tigers won their first state championship in five years. McKinley finished second in the poll and Hamilton High School, which Chuck Mather had coached the year before, came in third.

The 1949 season would prove to be almost identical to the one just completed. The Tigers would play the exact same ten teams, though in a slightly different order. After nine games, the Tigers record again showed just a single defeat, this time Mansfield being the culprit. In that game, witnessed by more than 19,000 fans, the Tigers had held a 12-7 lead at the half; but after neither team scored in the third quarter, the Mansfield passing attack produced a fourth quarter touchdown and a 14-12 lead. Late in that final frame, a safety provided the final points in Mansfield's 16-12 victory. Ironically, the Mansfield coach was Augie Morningstar, former Massillon standout and the Tigers' coach in 1945.

Once again the season finale would have a state title on the line when the Tigers faced off against another undefeated team of Canton McKinley Bulldogs. A high-scoring contest was anticipated by the 23,000 who witnessed the game at Canton's Fawcett Stadium as both teams were averaging about 43 points per contest, but such was not to be the case. After a scoreless first half, a touchdown by the Tigers' Irv Crable in the second half would prove to be the only points of the game as the Tigers held on for a 6-0 victory. The Massillon victory was enough to propel the Tigers back to #1 in the final AP poll, with Mansfield coming in second and Canton McKinley third.

The 1950 campaign would prove to be the best thus far for a Chuck Mather coached Massillon football team. The Tigers scored 407 points in winning their ten games, while giving up just 37. Although there were a few anxious moments, not once during the entire season did the Tigers ever trail an opponent. Even against one of Ohio's most taxing schedules—three of the Tigers' opponents that season finished in the final AP Top 10 (#3 Barberton, #8 Canton McKinley, and #9 Steu-

▲   *Massillon fullback Homer Floyd flies by the camera on his way to a 79-
yard touchdown run as the Tigers defeated arch-rival Canton McKinley, 48-7,
in 1953. (Massillon Tiger Football Booster Club Collection—Plain Dealer)*

benville), but the Tigers defeated that trio by a combined score of 103-18. The usually climactic finale with Canton McKinley was anti-climactic in 1950. The Tigers easily disposed of the Bulldogs, 33-0, the largest margin of victory for Massillon over a McKinley team in their 55 meetings to that time.

After that season-ending game with McKinley, the Tigers handily won the 1950 AP poll race to finish with their third consecutive state championship under head coach Chuck Mather. The Tigers were also named national champion for 1950. It was Massillon's fifth national title, giving the school more national championships than any other school in the country.

While winning both the state and national championship was indeed big news, another news item would have topped even that for Massillon football fans—had it come to fruition. After the 1950 football season, the Ohio State University was looking for a new coach to replace the newly departed Wes Fesler. Chuck Mather applied for the job with the Buckeyes. The initial voting by the OSU selection committee actually leaned in Mather's favor, but the votes of Ohio's Governor Frank Lausche and Senator John Bricker decided the issue in favor of another candidate—Wayne Woodrow "Woody" Hayes.

With 20 seniors from the 1950 squad having graduated, many felt that 1951 would be a rebuilding year for Chuck Mather and his Massillon Tigers. However, the results of the first two games seemed to indicate that the Tigers were not rebuilding, simply reloading. The Tigers opened the season against two new entries on their schedule, and these newbies received the same "warm" welcome that many of their predecessors had. On September 14, the Tigers handed Toledo Libbey a 39-0 defeat and the following week Elder High School of Cincinnati fell by a 42-6 score.

On Friday night, September 28, the Tigers went on the road to Steubenville, Ohio, to take on the Big Red of Steubenville High School. It was always tough playing along the banks of the Ohio River and this game would be no exception. The game was scoreless until the Tigers scored a touchdown on the second play of the second quarter to take a 6-0 lead. The score stayed that way until the third period when the Big Red tied the game, the touchdown set up by a pass interception at the Massillon 35-yard line. Late in the fourth quarter and with the score still deadlocked, the Tigers started what would be their last possession from their own 12-yard line. Mather's team marched steadily down the field, overcoming a couple of penalties along the way. Finally, with just 10 ticks of the game clock remaining, the Tigers found the end zone. The successful extra point kick sent the 2,000 Massillon fans in attendance home with a thrilling 13-6 victory to talk about.

The Tigers easily defeated Akron South the following week, setting up a game with the Alliance Aviators at Tiger Stadium on October 12. The Aviators were led by a junior quarterback named of Len Dawson, and on this night young Mr. Dawson gave the Tigers a real scare. The Tigers were well aware of Dawson's talents, yet they were almost unable to stop him. He completed 17 of 30 passes for 195 yards and twice scored touchdowns from the one-yard line after his passing had moved the team into scoring position. The Tigers' defense, however, countered Len Dawson's passing with three interceptions and three recovered Alliance fumbles. The Massillon ground attack chipped in with 371 yards. The combined effort of the Tigers' offense and defense added up to a 34-21 Massillon victory.

Mansfield was easily dispatched by the Tigers, 54-0, but next came always-stubborn Warren Harding. More than 12,000 fans packed Warren Stadium for this game and the locals were not disappointed as the Panthers scored the only touchdown of the first quarter and tallied again in the second period to take a 13-0 lead; Massillon turnovers had initiated each Panther scoring drive. But the Tigers came right back with a pair of touchdowns late in the second quarter to send the game into the halftime break deadlocked at 13 apiece. A third Massillon turnover just after the second half kickoff gave the Panthers ideal field position at the Massillon 35-yard line. It took the Panthers only four plays to find the end zone and take a 19-13 lead less than three minutes into the third quarter.

That would prove to be all of the scoring in the game as Warren Harding's 19-13 victory halted the Massillon win streak at 20 in a row. This was no fluke win by the Panthers as they dominated every offensive category—and Massillon's six turnovers certainly did not help the Tigers, either.

The Tigers bounced back the following week by defeating a stubborn Toledo Waite team, 21-0. On Friday night, November 9, the 8-0-0 Barberton Magics paid a visit to Tiger Stadium for what proved to be one of the Tigers' toughest games, in a season filled with difficult encounters. The Tigers only crossed the midfield line twice during the game, but it would be the Tigers second trip that would prove to be the difference. A Barberton pass was intercepted at midfield and returned to the Magics' 22-yard line. Six plays later, the Tigers put the ball into the end zone to give Massillon a 6-0 lead.

The Tigers would protect that slim lead for the balance of the game, but it would take no fewer than five tremendous goal line stands to do it. Barberton dominated the Tigers in every offensive category that day, except on the scoreboard, as Massillon held on for a 6-0 victory.

The following week was the annual tussle with Canton McKinley, but like the previous season there would be no dramatics as to the outcome of this particular game. McKinley came into the game having won just twice in nine previous games and the Tigers easily dismantled the Bulldogs by a 40-0 tally. That victory finally gave the Tigers the edge in this series, 26-25-5.

When the final Ohio AP poll for 1951 came out, the Tigers were at #1 for the fourth consecutive season, with Steubenville (#2), Barberton (#6), and Warren

Head Coach Chuck Mather celebrates his team's sixth consecutive state championship in 1953 with co-captains John Traylor and Bruce Schram. (Massillon Tiger Football Booster Club Collection)

Harding (#7) also in the Top 10. Once again the Tigers had survived the state's toughest schedule.

The next two seasons would see head coach Chuck Mather's Massillon Tigers totally dominate Ohio high school football and, by extension, the entire country as well.

The 1952 campaign kicked off on Friday night, September 12, when the Tigers treated about 12,000 loyal fans to a 54-0 victory over Akron South at Tiger Stadium. The Tigers would alternate home and road games over the first half of the season, but the results never varied. For its second game, the team traveled to Cincinnati to play Elder High School, the Tigers returning home with a 33-0 win. The Big Red of Steubenville came to Tiger Stadium the following week only to suffer a 43-13 defeat. Barberton visited Massillon for the fourth game of the season; this time the Tigers would not need five goal line stands to preserve their victory as they swept by the Magics, 40-19.

On Friday night, October 10, the state's top ranked Tigers traveled to Alliance to take on the Aviators, then ranked at #7 in the weekly AP poll. The 11,000 fans who crammed into Mount Union College Stadium were in for a real treat as they witnessed one of the most exciting games of the season. Future pro football Hall of Famer Len Dawson was in his senior year as the Alliance quarterback and once again he put on a spectacular show as he completed 16 of 32 aerials for 220 yards, 2 TDs, and no interceptions. Dawson also scored a touchdown and all three of Alliance's PATs.

Alliance got on the scoreboard first, recovering a Massillon fumble at the Tigers' 29-yard line and then scoring on a 24-yard pass from Dawson to end Ray Olds. Massillon came back and answered that score with two of its own to take a 14-7 lead at the half.

The third quarter opened in spectacular fashion. Alliance kicked off and the ball bounced over Massillon's John Francisco at the 15-yard line. Francisco chased after the ball and picked it up four yards deep in the end zone where he hesitated just a moment before starting up field. Picking up some tremendous blocking from his teammates, coupled with his own great broken field running, Francisco stunned the crowd as he went 104 yards for a Massillon touchdown—still the fourth longest kickoff return in Ohio high school history. Alliance immediately answered that touchdown with one of its own on another Dawson-to-Olds aerial to

A typical Massillon Tigers home crowd during the Tigers' phenomenal 30-year championship era. A sellout— as virtually every game since then. (Massillon Tiger Football Booster Club Collection)

cut the Massillon lead to 20-14. On the ensuing kickoff, Massillon's Lee Nussbaum caught the ball at his 23-yard line and, like Francisco on the previous kickoff, returned the ball all the way for another Massillon touchdown.

Alliance would add a final touchdown in the fourth quarter, but it would not be enough as the Tigers held on for an exiting 27-21 victory. Talking about this game many years later, Massillon head coach Chuck Mather said, "Two things I remember about that game: we scored (two) touchdowns on kickoff returns and Len Dawson came over to our bus and congratulated us. I couldn't believe a high school boy would have such maturity to make a high class gesture like that."

Over the balance of the season, things got a lot less hectic for Massillon and its fans. The Tigers cruised through their next four games, outscoring the opposition by 199-32 while averaging 440 yards of offense per game.

Entering the season finale with Canton McKinley, the Tigers were 9-0-0. McKinley had rebounded from the disastrous 1951 campaign and came into this one with a more respectable record of 6-2-1. However, like the previous two games of this rivalry, this one would also be a one-sided Tigers' victory. Massillon held a 34-0 lead early in the fourth quarter before McKinley finally dented the scoreboard with a safety and a touchdown. The Tigers countered with a late touchdown to make the final score 41-8.

The next day, the Cleveland, Canton, and Akron newspapers all declared the Tigers the state champion and the AP poll made it official a couple of days later as the Tigers claimed their fifth consecutive state title. Massillon was also named by the National Sports News Service as the country's #1 team for 1962, the Tigers' sixth national title.

Riding a 13-game winning streak, Chuck Mather's Tigers rolled right into the 1953 season and did not miss a beat. They would again play a schedule that featured some of the top-rated teams in Ohio and make it look easy. The Tigers started right in on that schedule by defeating Akron Garfield at Tiger Stadium by a 39-0 score. The following week right back at the stadium, Canton Lincoln marched 86 yards to take a 6-0 lead on the first offensive possession of the game; but, the Tigers came roaring back and scored the game's next 55 points en route to a 55-13 victory.

Lima Central, 40-0, and Steubenville, 35-6, were the next to fall. Alliance High School was without the services of the now-graduated Len Dawson this season and it showed in a lack of offensive production - the Tigers came away with a 33-6 win. Against the normally tough Mansfield Tygers, Chuck Mather's offense totaled 583 yards in putting together a 41-7 triumph.

An overflow crowd of more than 22,000, the largest of the season, was on hand when Warren Harding came calling at Tiger Stadium for the season's seventh game. Among the crowd were 7,000 Harding loyalists who had made the trip from Warren to witness this battle for first place in Ohio.

As expected, it was a tough game from the very start and with less than a minute remaining in the second quarter there was still no score. The Tigers then broke the deadlock with a 41-yard touchdown pass that gave Massillon a 7-0 lead at the intermission.

While the first half was pretty even statistically, the Tigers dominated the numbers in the second half as they rolled up 230 yards of offense to just 59 for Harding. The only points of the third quarter came with just 30 seconds remaining in the period as Massillon doubled its lead to 14-0. Midway through the fourth quarter, the Tigers pushed across another touchdown, but this time missed the extra point to leave their lead at 20-0. Harding finally broke into the scoring column following an interception at the Massillon eight-yard line, the TD coming a couple of plays later with 1:20 left to play. However, the Tigers eliminated any doubt as to the outcome with a touchdown in the game's closing seconds.

The hard-fought 27-6 victory further entrenched the Tigers in the #1 spot in the latest AP Ohio poll.

After a 41-2 shellacking of Toledo Waite, the Tigers faced off against the 8-0-0 team from Fremont Ross High School, at the time the fifth ranked team in the state. The Ross team saw three promising drives in the first quarter end with lost fumbles, but even at that they managed to take a 7-0 lead. Those lost scoring opportunities hurt the Little Giants dearly as the game progressed, the Tigers coming back to score the game's next 40 points and go on to a 40-7 victory.

Canton McKinley was having another down year and entered the traditional season finale with the Tigers with a record of 3-5-1. The Bulldogs' fans among the 16,500 at Fawcett Stadium that day were hoping for the big upset; what they saw instead was an unbelievable first half offensive explosion by the Tigers. In their first four plays from scrimmage the Tigers scored three touchdowns. Over their next nine plays they added three more six-pointers—six touchdowns on only 13 snaps of the ball!

The score was already 42-0 in the second quarter when the Bulldogs finally found the end zone, but by then the game had been decided as the Tigers went on to record another lopsided victory over McKinley, 48-7.

The 1953 season ended with the Tigers sporting a record of 10-0-0 for the second consecutive season and running their undefeated string to 23 in a row. Massillon was again ranked #1 in the final AP Ohio poll and for the second straight year Massillon was also named by the National Sports News Service as the nation's best team, the school's seventh national title.

Following the 1953 season, Chuck Mather decided to move on to the college ranks and was hired as the head coach of the University of Kansas Jayhawks. The legacy that Mather left behind at Massillon is almost unsurpassed, rivaling the record of the great Paul Brown himself. In his six seasons at Washington High School, Chuck Mather's teams won 57 and lost only three, with no ties, for a winning percentage of .950. His teams were state champion all six seasons that he coached at Massillon and national champion three times; Mather is the only coach in Ohio history to win six consecutive AP poll championships. Only Paul Brown's six year run from 1935-1940—58 wins, one loss, and one tie, six state championships (by popular acclaim), and four national championships—surpasses Mather's accomplishments at Massillon.

IF A BOY WANTED TO PLAY FOOTBALL FOR MASSILLON AND WENT OUT FOR THE TEAM, THEN HE WAS ON THE TEAM—CHUCK MATHER WAS THE FIRST COACH OF THE MASSILLON TIGERS WHO NEVER CUT A BOY WHO CAME OUT FOR THE TEAM.

Mather used many of the tried and true methods of other successful coaches, but he was not afraid to add a modern touch now and then if he thought it might help. He built a reputation as an offense-minded coach and his use of the T-formation with a balanced line proved to be an immediate success. He also liked to open things up a bit with the passing game, as well as the use of the pitchout, backfield fakes, audibles, and wide sweeps behind pulling linemen. Mather pioneered the use of IBM computers coupled with movies to grade players and he even tried using closed-circuit TV to give the bench a better view of the game action. When his coaches went out to scout an upcoming opponent, they were instructed to not only scout the team as a whole, but also the players at each position. Finally, if a boy wanted to play football for Massillon and went out for the team, then he was on the team—Chuck Mather was the first coach of the Massillon Tigers who never cut a boy who came out for the team.

The job of finding Chuck Mather's successor began immediately upon his resignation and involved more than 100 candidates. The selection committee finally settled on Tom Harp, who at the age of 27 became the second-youngest coach of the Tigers. Harp's previous coaching position had been at Carrollton (Oh.) High School where his teams compiled a record of 20-6-1 in three seasons.

Harp inherited a 23-game winning streak when he took over the reins of the Tigers in 1954. His first two games saw that streak hit 25 with lopsided victories over Struthers High School, 68-0, and Canton Lincoln, 47-0. Week Three had the Tigers traveling to Alliance to take on the Aviators. Always one of the tougher games on the Massillon schedule, this year it proved to be too tough as the Aviators halted the Massillon win streak by defeating the Tigers, 19-7.

The Tigers rebounded to win their next six games, setting up the annual tussle with Canton McKinley. This season the Bulldogs had a very good team and entered the big game with a record of 8-1-0, including a 26-6 victory over Alliance. It was the closest Massillon-McKinley game of the last five years, but the Tigers prevailed by a score of 26-6. The victory enabled Massillon to again finish first in the final AP state poll for a record seventh consecutive year, followed by #2 Alliance, #3 Canton McKinley, and #4 Mansfield, all teams that had been on the Tigers' schedule.

For most schools, the Tigers' results over the next three seasons would have been considered to be very good; however, the previous 20 seasons had seen the bar set awfully high at Massillon and anything but a first place finish did not seem to cut it. In 1955 the Tigers finished 8-1-1; their season-finale loss to Canton McKinley made the undefeated Bulldogs state champion while the Tigers finished at #2.

When Tom Harp left Massillon after the '55 season to join the staff of Earl "Red" Blaik at West Point his successor at Massillon was Lee Tressel. Tressel's first season in 1956 saw the Tigers finish 8-2-0, losing to another undefeated Canton McKinley team that claimed its second consecutive state championship. Massillon finished eighth in the AP poll that season, the team's lowest finish since 1947. In 1957 the Tigers won eight of nine games and finished second in the final AP poll to Benedictine High School of Cleveland, the one team to defeat the Tigers.

After the '57 season, Lee Tressel left Massillon to take over as the head coach at Baldwin-Wallace College, located a little southwest of Cleveland in Berea, Ohio. Tressel would coach the Yellow Jackets thru the 1980 season, posting an excellent record of 155-52-6 and winning the Division III national championship in 1978.

Tressel was succeeded at Massillon by Leo Strang, a truly colorful coach—both literally and figuratively—who would usher in the next great era of Massillon Tigers football.

Leo Strang grew up in Ashland, Ohio, where he was an All-Ohio halfback on that city's high school football team. He then played for three years at Ashland

▲ *Massillon's Jim Wood hauls in a pass from QB Joe Sparma against the Alliance Aviators in 1959. (Massillon Yearbook)*

College, where he majored in Art, before joining the U.S. Navy during World War II. After his wartime service in the Pacific Theatre, Strang finished his education at Western Reserve University and took his first coaching job at Caldwell High School, where his team went 4-5-1. After one year at Caldwell he took over as the head coach at Upper Sandusky High School, where Strang spent five years, and then on to East Cleveland Shaw for two seasons. In those latter two assignments, Strang had an overall record of 51-13-0 and his teams never finished lower than second in their respective leagues, winning four league championships. In 1955 Strang's Upper Sandusky team finished ninth in the AP Ohio poll, while his 1957 Shaw Cardinals finished eighth in the final poll.

From a football perspective, Strang was not afraid to make some changes and that is exactly what he would eventually do at Massillon. However, while the casual observer may not have noticed Strang's changes to Massillon's football technique, it was impossible to miss some of the other things that he did with the team. Using his art major background, Leo liked to dabble with how his team looked on the gridiron. Perhaps the most visible and certainly the longest-lasting idea he came up with was the leaping tiger logo design then used on the Massillon helmets, as well as the idea of using vinyl decals on football helmets. Strang gave away the rights to the vinyl decal idea to the company that designed the Massillon logo for him, a move that he was known to jokingly lament by saying, "I should be getting a nickel for every decal put on a helmet now, but I wasn't that smart."

Continuing along these sartorial lines, in 1959 Strang changed the Tigers' foot apparel to all-white spikes, the only school in the state so attired. He also came up with a uniform that consisted of three sets of pants in solid white, orange, or black, and three jerseys, also white, orange or black—the Tigers could go nine consecutive games without using the same uniform combination. Strang also introduced uniforms with multicolored stripes, v-neck jerseys with triple stripes, and outlined numbers.

Not only would the Tigers play excellent football under head coach Leo Strang, but they would look good doing it, too.

The results of Coach Leo Strang's first season in 1958 were quite similar to those of the preceding three seasons. After opening victories over Akron South and Canton Lincoln, the Tigers traveled to Alliance to face the Aviators. The Aviators had perhaps their best team ever in 1958. And when they marched 78-yards in 12 plays for a touchdown and an 8-0 lead on their first possession of the game, it looked like the Tigers were going to be in for a long day. After that initial march, however, defense ruled the day for both teams. The score remained 8-0 until the Tigers tied the score on the second play of the fourth quarter. There would be no more scoring over the balance of the game, which ended deadlocked at 8-8.

The Tigers would win their next three games, but the offense was not scoring like it had in the past. In fact, this would be the least-productive Massillon offense since 1947. In Week Seven against Warren Harding, the Tigers offense hit rock bottom by failing to score a single point for the first time in 101 games. Harding scored the only touchdown of the game in the second quarter and then made it hold up for a 6-0 victory. The Tigers actually out-gained Harding by about 100 yards for the game, but three Massillon turnovers proved to be fatal.

The Tigers closed out the season with three consecutive victories, including a 38-16 triumph over McKinley in the season finale, to finish 8-1-1. Despite the loss and the tie, the Tigers finished at #4 in the final AP Ohio poll, with the Alliance Aviators finishing at #1 and winning the school's only state championship.

Running back Bill Finney follows his blockers around the right side in this game action from the 1959 season. (Massillon Yearbook)

Wide receiver Bob Barkman makes a fantastic catch for a Massillon touchdown during the 1959 season. (Massillon Yearbook)

It was after the 1958 campaign that Leo Strang decided to make major changes to the Tigers' offense. He switched from the traditional T-formation and its balanced line to a winged-T and an unbalanced line (similar to the single wing), a formation that used the right halfback predominantly as a blocking back. His defenses varied, but his basic formation was a 5-4-2. Strang liked to refer to his somewhat unique system as "the goulash system." No matter what it was called, it worked. This totally revamped offense provided a completely new look for the Tigers opponents, one that they were not quite ready to handle. In 1958 the Tigers had scored just 220 points for the entire season. Using Strang's winged-T attack, they just about doubled that by scoring 431 points in 1959, including three games of 65 or more points.

The Massillon faithful got an inkling of what Strang's new offense could do in the team's first two games as the Tigers ran up 105 points in defeating both Akron South and Canton Lincoln. But, in the third game of the season, the Alliance Aviators again proved to be a tough nut to crack. The Tigers scored a touchdown in the second quarter and added a touchdown and two-point conversion in the final period as the Aviators held them to their lowest point output of the season. The Massillon defense, however, was just a tad better in shutting out the Aviators and the Tigers came away with a hard fought 14-0 win.

Coach Strang's new offense picked up some momentum the following week in handing Steubenville a 28-8 defeat, and then came back with a 30-6 lashing of Cleveland Benedictine on October 16.

All the Way to #1

The following Friday, October 23, Strang's offense showed what it was capable of when the conditions were right, if you can call a driving rain storm and a field of mud the right kind of conditions. The opponent that day was the Mansfield Tygers. Massillon and Mansfield had played many great games in the past, but this would not be one of them. Massillon gained 576 total yards, scored 10 touchdowns, and added five two-pointers as it completely manhandled the Tygers, 70-0. Mansfield never did get its offense going as it had one pass intercepted and lost four fumbles.

The game with Mansfield was supposed to be a preliminary to the "headliner" on October 30 against Warren Harding, but that game proved to be another one-sided affair. Before 21,092 fans, the game started off to be the battle everyone was expecting, with the Tigers leading by only 8-0 after one quarter of play. But Massillon broke the game open in the second quarter by scoring 22 points to take a 30-0 lead at the half. Out-gaining the Panthers by 422 yards to 149, the Tigers cruised to a 38-8 victory.

The following week, the combination of Massillon's powerhouse offense and its ball hawking defense led to a thorough thrashing of the Barberton Magics. The Tigers scored three touchdowns in every quarter and converted nine of 12 two-point conversion attempts as they totaled 90 points, the most points a Massillon team had scored since a 94-0 victory over Akron North in 1922. Despite using every player on the roster, most of them playing in all four quarters, Coach Strang's Tigers still ran up 608 yards of total offense to just 93 for Barberton. No doubt Barberton's eight turnovers adversely affected its chances of scoring.

▸ *Running back Bill Finney crashes across the goal line on a short touchdown run against Warren Harding during the 1959 season. (Massillon Yearbook)*

In their next-to-last game the following week, the Tigers doubled up on the Golden Rams of Akron Garfield in both points, 36-18, and yardage, 406-193, but it was not quite that easy. Garfield had lost just once in eight previous games—somewhat surprisingly to Barberton—and the Golden Rams did not back down from the Tigers, giving them a tough battle all the way to the final whistle.

The Canton McKinley Bulldogs entered the season's final game with a record of 6-3-0 and were a decided underdog, but it was a rivalry game so anything could happen. As it turned out, the Massillon defense kept the Bulldogs in check (67 total yards) until its own offense could get some points. After a scoreless first quarter Massillon scored late in the second to post an 8-0 lead at the break. Single touchdowns in both the third and fourth quarters added some insurance as the Tigers rolled to a 20-0 win.

Completing the season a perfect 10-0-0, the Tigers easily won the AP poll for Ohio champion. Leo Strang's Tigers were also named national champion that season by the National Sports News Service, the team's eighth national crown. Strang was named Ohio's high school football "Coach of the Year".

The 1960 campaign would bring new challenges for the Tigers in the form of four previously unplayed opponents and a schedule that had been expanded to 11 games.

Massillon opened the season with three comfortable victories to stretch its win streak to 16. The much-anticipated game with Alliance in Week Four proved to be all that it could be. After the Tigers had taken an 8-0 lead in the first quarter, the Aviators tied the game in the second and then used a safety to take a 10-8 lead in the third quarter. The Aviators were able to cling to that slim lead until there were

Massillon defenders Nick Daugenti (46), Lawson White (64), and Bob Oliver (80) try to catch up with future Pro Football Hall of Famer Paul Warfield during the Tigers game with Warren Harding in 1959. (Massillon Yearbook)

▲   *This great block springs*
Massillon running back Bob
Herring loose for a sizable
gain during the 1959 season.
(Massillon Yearbook)

just 57 seconds left on the game clock, at which point the Tigers' closed out a 65-yard drive by scoring a touchdown that gave Massillon a 14-10 advantage.

Despite the very limited time remaining, Massillon was far from locking up another "W". A great return of the ensuing kickoff, coupled with a 15-yard penalty against the Tigers, gave the Aviators excellent field position at the Massillon 45-yard line. The Aviators quickly moved the ball to the Tigers' 10-yard line, but time finally ran out before they could advance any further.

After something of a struggle in a 26-6 victory over Steubenville in their next game, the going got even tougher for the Tigers over the following three weeks. Cincinnati power Roger Bacon, one of the newcomers to the Tigers' schedule, held the Tigers to less than 150 yards of total offense and only one touchdown, but the Massillon "D" was equal to the challenge and shut out the Spartans in an 8-0 Tigers' triumph. Mansfield paid a visit to Tiger Stadium the following week; Massillon built up a 16-0 lead at the half, then held off the other Tygers for a 16-6 victory.

With their record now 7-0-0, the Tigers took to the road for a visit to Warren Harding. This would be a classic game of back and forth, with Massillon taking the early lead on Charlie Brown's 100-yard interception return for a touchdown in the first quarter. Harding tied the score at 6-6 in the second quarter, but the Tigers would regain the advantage, 12-6, just before the intermission. Harding again tied the game in the third quarter, but the Tigers went back on top 18-12 midway through the fourth period. Finally, with 1:34 left in the game, Harding scored a touchdown that again tied the score at 18-18, then won it 19-18 with the only extra point made during the contest. The loss stopped Massillon's win streak at 20 in a row.

Massillon running back Martin Gugov finds a big hole opened by the Tigers' offensive line in the Canton McKinley defense during the annual Massillon-McKinley game in 1959. (Massillon Yearbook)

After the Harding game, the Tigers breezed through the rest of their schedule, including a 42-0 victory over Canton McKinley—the biggest margin of victory in that series. The Tigers' final mark was 10-1-0 and, although they managed to retain their state championship, the loss to Harding cost them a second consecutive national title.

Leo Strang had another strong team of Massillon Tigers ready for the 1961 campaign, and they would need to be—the Tigers would again be playing one of the strongest schedules in the state.

Like the previous season, 1961 opened with three victories by comfortable margins, leading up to the Tigers' annual match with their old nemesis, the Aviators of Alliance High School. The Aviators would finish eighth in the final AP Ohio poll that season, but this week they were shot down by the Tigers, 26-0. After a relatively easy win over Steubenville, 38-14, the Tigers met another stubborn team from Cincinnati's Roger Bacon High School on Friday, October 13. Like the previous season's game, this one was also a tough defensive battle, but once again the Tigers held the Spartans, who would finish fourth in the final AP state poll, scoreless in a 12-0 Massillon victory.

Wins over Mansfield, 34-6, Warren Harding, 36-0, and Toledo Libbey, 56-0, followed in quick succession for the Tigers.

Massillon had now breezed through the first nine games of its 11-game schedule and ranked #1 in all nine AP Ohio weekly polls. With their final two games to be played against a couple of teams struggling to stay above .500, another state championship for the Tigers appeared to be an inevitability.

The first of those final two opponents were the Redmen of Parma High School, a suburb just south and west of Cleveland. The Redmen, the last of the four new teams on the Tigers' 1961 schedule, had been 18-1-0 the previous two seasons, but entered this game at 5-4-0. The previous year, the Parma junior varsity had defeated the Massillon jayvee team by 8 to 6; however, that fact did not seem to impress very many people and the Redmen entered this game as 40-point underdogs.

The game was played on Cleveland's lakefront at Municipal Stadium. When it was built in 1931, Municipal Stadium was the largest stadium of its kind anywhere in the world with a fixed individual seating capacity, as opposed to bleacher-style seats, of 78,819. Quite a venue for the Tigers to be playing in, and if their opponent had sported a better record there would not have been almost 70,000 empty seats for this game. However, those 10,219 who were present would see a game worthy of a full house.

All the Way to #1

The Massillon fans in attendance had to be just a little stunned when Parma took the opening kickoff and put together a methodical, 18-play, 79-yard march that ate up nine minutes and 15 seconds. The drive culminated with a touchdown on a one-yard pass, the two-point conversion giving Parma a surprising 8-0 lead. Massillon's only possession of the first quarter resulted in a three and out, Parma maintaining its 8-0 lead into the second quarter.

The Tigers finally got their offense going midway through the second period and were able to tie the score after a 53-yard drive that resulted in a touchdown and a two-point conversion at 6:28 of the second quarter. On their ensuing possession, the Redmen took 10 plays to march in for their second touchdown of the first

Massillon's Bill Finney is stopped by the McKinley defense after a short gain before a packed stadium in 1959. (Massillon Yearbook)

The very colorful Leo Strang was head coach of the Massillon Tigers from 1958-1963, winning three state and two national championships. (Massillon Yearbook)

Massillon QB Jim Alexander (23) completes a pass to his favorite target, Ron Schenkenberger, during the Tigers' game with the Alliance Aviators in 1961. (Massillon Yearbook)

half. This time the two-point conversion try failed, leaving Parma with a 14-8 lead with 3:26 left in the second quarter

Following the ensuing kickoff the Tigers attempted a pass on first down, but it was intercepted, giving Parma excellent field position at the Tigers' 45-yard line. The Redmen quickly added another six-pointer, taking only seven plays and a minute and a half to strike pay dirt. Again the Parma try for the two-pointer failed, but the Redmen had now increased their margin to 20-8 with 1:14 left in the second quarter, which is how the first half ended.

Midway through the third quarter the Tigers recovered a Parma fumble at the Redmen four-yard line. Fullback Ken Dean made Parma pay for the miscue when he crashed into the end zone on the very next play, the extra point cutting the Parma lead to 20-15.

Things continued to go the Tigers' way when, on the ensuing kickoff, Parma again fumbled the ball and it was recovered by the Tigers at the Redmen 30-yard line. It only took the Tigers six plays to again find the end zone. The two-point conversion try failed, but with 3:22 left in the third period, the Tigers had come storming back to take a 21-20 lead.

Neither team scored during the remainder of the game, the Tigers escaping with a one-point, 21-20, victory. Parma had only lost the ball twice, but the Tigers turned those miscues into a pair of touchdowns. Massillon had turned the ball over an incredible seven times, all on pass interceptions, making its come-from-behind victory even more remarkable.

Despite the somewhat less than impressive victory over Parma, the Tigers maintained a 29-point lead over second place Niles McKinley in the second-to-last AP poll tabulation.

Next up for the Tigers was their traditional season finale with Canton McKinley, this year played on Saturday, November 18, in Canton's Fawcett Stadium. McKinley entered the game with a record of 6-3-0 and, like Parma the week before, a considerable underdog by as many as 32 points. However, the Bulldogs had some extra incentive this time around as they were playing for more than just this one game, they would live with the results for all of 1962 as well. During the time between the 1960 and 1961 football seasons, a couple of McKinley boosters had enticed two players, brothers, away from Portsmouth High School to attend and play football for McKinley. When the superintendent of the Portsmouth schools complained to the Ohio High School Athletic Association, an investigation ensued. The OHSAA then determined that McKinley had violated the organization's bylaw against "undue influence". As a result, McKinley was barred from interscholastic football for the entire 1962 season, the so called "death penalty". McKinley tried to get the state's governor to intervene and even took the case all the way to the Ohio Supreme Court, but the Court ruled that the OHSAA was a private, independent organization and as a member McKinley must abide by its rules. The penalty remained and Canton McKinley did not play any varsity football during the 1962 season.

More than 20,000 fans showed up at Fawcett Stadium for the big game with Massillon in 1961. Massillon kicked off and then forced the Bulldogs to punt, going on offense for the first time from their own 47-yard line. The Tigers' 10-play drive resulted in a touchdown and an extra point to give them an early 7-0 lead. It would prove to be Massillon's only scoring threat of the game.

On the first play of the second quarter, Massillon misconnected on a pitchout and McKinley recovered the loose ball at the Massillon 49-yard line. Four plays later the Bulldogs were in the end zone as the result of a 36-yard TD strike. McKinley decided to go for the two-point conversion, but the run was stopped short of the end zone.

Leading by just a single point, 7-6, the Tigers never advanced beyond the McKinley 49-yard line for the balance of the game. The Bulldogs had four potential scoring threats over the final two-plus quarters, but they were never able to cash in. The 7-6 victory gave Coach Leo Strang's team its eleventh win of the season against no losses—a new record for victories for a Massillon football team.

The 1961 season had ended with two dramatic victories, but the drama was far from over.

Niles McKinley, which had been lodged in second place in the AP Ohio poll all season, finished with a perfect 10-0-0 record, extending its current winning streak to 28 in a row. When the final AP Ohio poll came out, Massillon had garnered 420 votes—but Niles McKinley had received 469. Apparently the voters in the AP poll had been negatively influenced by the Tigers' struggles in their final two games. This result made the Niles McKinley Red Dragons the 1961 AP Ohio poll champions, with Massillon finishing second.

Be that as it may, the final AP poll tally naturally did not sit well with the Massillon folks, especially since the Tigers had won one more game than the Red Dragons. When the final United Press International (UPI) poll came out, Massillon was ranked #1 and Niles McKinley #2. This only added more fuel to the Massillon fire. In an interview with the Cleveland *Plain Dealer* on November 25, 1961, Leo Strang claimed the "undisputed" state championship for his team. He noted that the Tigers were #1 in the UPI poll; they had been #1 for the first 10 weeks of the AP poll; and they had won more games, 11, than any other team in the state. Finally, he pointed out that his team had played perhaps the toughest schedule in Ohio that season, playing and defeating nine of the 90 teams that were ranked in the final AP poll, including two teams in the final Top 10, whereas Niles McKinley had only played two of those top 90 teams.

Coach Strang had one more salient point that he could have made in his team's defense, that being that the National Sports News Service had named the Tigers

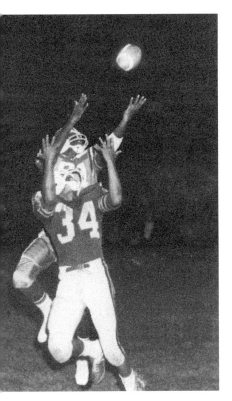

▼ *Massillon's Floyd "Duke" Pierce leaps high to intercept a pass during the Tigers' game against Alliance in 1961. (Massillon Yearbook)*

the 1961 national high school football champion—Massillon's record ninth such championship.

Massillon Washington High School may have had to share the Ohio championship, but it had sole possession of the national crown.

Over the next decade, the Tigers would have varied amounts of success. Leo Strang would remain at Massillon for two more seasons before moving on to the college ranks as the head coach at Kent State University. His 1962 Massillon team, hit with a ton of graduations the previous June, would win only six of its 11 games, the five losses being the most by a Massillon team in a single season since 1931, the year before Paul Brown took over the program. Strang's last team in 1963 would post a record of 9-1-0 and finish second in the AP Ohio poll—to #1 Niles McKinley.

Leo Strang would be followed at Massillon by Earl Bruce. In his two years at Massillon before taking over at Ohio State, Bruce would post a perfect record of 20-0-0, win a pair of AP state championships, and finish second in the country both seasons.

In 1967 the Tigers would finish second in the AP Ohio poll and in 1970, under head coach Bob Cummings, Massillon would win its 24th state title and again finish second in the country. In 1972 the Tigers finished first in the AP Ohio poll, but they would not be named state champion. 1972 was the first year of the new playoff format for determining Ohio football champions. Massillon played Cincinnati Princeton in one of two state semifinal games that season, with Princeton winning by a 17-14 score.

The 31 years of Massillon Washington Tigers football from 1935 to 1965 is one of the most incredible eras in the history of American high school football. Among the Tigers' accomplishments are the following:

- *A record of 274-27-11, a winning percentage of .896.*

- *13 undefeated and untied seasons.*

- *A 52-game winning streak, best in Ohio at that time.*

- *20 state championships, including twice winning seven in a row (part of a state record 24 titles).*

- *Nine national championships—more than any other high school in history.*

In almost 150 years of high school football in this country, no school has come close to this record, and possibly none will.

▲ *Massillon QB Jim Alexander picks up some much-needed yardage against Cleveland's Benedictine High in 1961. (Massillon Yearbook)*

▲   *Head Coach Leo Strang gets the traditional "ride" off the field after the Tigers defeated Canton McKinley, 7-6, in 1961. The victory clinched for the Tigers a third consecutive state title and their second national championship—a record ninth overall—in three years. (Massillon Yearbook)*

## CHAPTER 6

WRIGHT BAZEMORE'S VALDOSTA WILDCATS

Valdosta High School
Valdosta, Georgia

The Valdosta Wildcats were the winningest high school football team in the nation during the 20th century with 774 victories against just 156 defeats and 33 ties for a winning percentage of .821. The team suffered through only five losing seasons during that time (which does not include 1918 when the school did not field a football team due to both World War I and the worldwide Spanish flu epidemic).

Valdosta High School, located in the southernmost part of Georgia barely 10 miles from the Florida border, opened its doors in 1905. It was not until 1913, however, that the school fielded its first football team. In that first season Valdosta got off to a good start with three wins, a loss, and two ties. However, like every new venture, the team had its growing pains and during the next two seasons it was pretty much an average outfit with a record of 6-6-2. Although the Wildcats played under four different coaches from 1916 thru 1920 (with no football in 1918), it was during these years that they enjoyed their first real taste of gridiron success. The team compiled a record of 28-4-1 over those four seasons and posted its first undefeated campaign, 7-0-1, in 1919. In 1920, under Coach Arthur Cox, the Wildcats went 8-1-0 and are recognized in many circles as the state Class B champion for that season after defeating Athens High School, 20-13, in a "north-south" playoff.

After a decent 1921 season, 5-3-1, the team suffered through a 3-4-2 campaign the next year. However, the Wildcats rebounded nicely in 1923 to post their first undefeated, untied season at 9-0-0, but they were not considered good enough to gain any state championship recognition.

Over the next 17 years, the Wildcats played consistently good football and had two more undefeated, untied teams. In 1929 the Wildcats finished 11-0-0, but again without a state championship to go with it. In 1940 under head coach Bobby Hooks, the boys set a school record by winning 12 games while not losing or tying any and only allowing 20 points all season. This included a 21 to 0 victory over previously undefeated Cedartown in the annual North Georgia Football Assoc.-South Georgia Football Assoc. Class B state championship game.

Valdosta High School has been fortunate in having had two truly outstanding men as head coach of its football teams. The first of these took the reins in 1941.

▲ *Valdosta High School circa 1962.*
(Valdosta High School Yearbook)

The 1916 Valdosta Wildcats. (Valdosta High School Yearbook)

August Wright Bazemore, or simply Wright Bazemore as most knew him, was born on August 1, 1916, on a farm in Fitzgerald, Ga., about 60 miles from Valdosta. He attended Fitzgerald High School where he excelled in sports, playing on five school teams—football, basketball, track, tennis, baseball—earning a total of 16 letters. One of Bazemore's more unusual achievements while in high school was making it into "Ripley's Believe It or Not" when he scored 10 touchdowns in a single game his senior season at Fitzgerald High, not once but twice.

After graduating from Fitzgerald High in 1934, Bazemore moved on to Mercer University where he also played football and basketball. He graduated from Mercer in 1938 and immediately took a position as an assistant football coach at Waycross High School, remaining there for two years until he was hired as an assistant coach at Valdosta High School under Bobby Hooks.

Hooks had been the head coach at Valdosta since 1932. His overall record at Valdosta, 60-15-5, including the 1940 Class B state championship, got him into the college ranks when he was named the head coach at Mercer University beginning in 1941. It would be a short college career at Mercer for Hooks and it had little to do with the team's 3-6-0 record that first season. Less than two weeks after the team's final game in 1941, the Japanese attacked Pearl Harbor. One month later, on January 6, 1942, Mercer suspended football operations—and they were not resumed for more than 70 years, not until the 2013 season.

Named to replace Bobby Hooks at Valdosta was Wright Bazemore. Bazemore got off to a good start by leading the Wildcats to a 9-2-0 record his first season in '41 and then a 6-2-1 record in 1942. However, as it did in many lives, the war would intervene in Bazemore's coaching career. Being an educator who taught both math and science in addition to coaching several sports, Bazemore probably could have claimed an exemption from the military draft. However, that is not how things were done back then and Wright Bazemore, like many others in his situation, could not see sending young men off to war while he himself stayed behind. He enlisted in the U.S. Navy after the 1942 high school football season and served on a destroyer escort in the North Atlantic doing convoy duty.

Bazemore missed three seasons at Valdosta due to his military service, during which time the team was coached to a record of 18-11-1 by Buck Thomas. With his military commitment completed, Bazemore returned to Valdosta in 1946 to continue his pre-war teaching and coaching career. That first season back, the Wildcats won eight of 11 games. In 1947, Bazemore coached his first perfect campaign at Valdosta, leading the Wildcats to a 12-0-0 record and the Class B state championship—Bazemore's first state title, but certainly not to be his last. That '47 championship came in the last of the old "north-south" championship games when the Wildcats overcame a 12-12 tie in the third quarter to beat the previously undefeated team from Gainesville High School, 24-12

In 1948, the Georgia High School Association instituted a new playoff system for determining the state football champions. It would take the Wildcats three seasons to qualify for the playoffs. After the Wildcats finished with a record of 6-4-0

The 1940 State champion Wildcats accepting their trophy. #35 is team captain Glenn Ratliff; to his right is head coach Bobby Hooks; #47 is alternate captain Joe Davis. (Valdosta High School Yearbook)

in both 1948 and 1949, in 1950 (now playing in Class A) they ended the regular season at 9-1-0 and qualified for the state playoffs for the first time. In their first playoff game, the state semifinals, the Wildcats managed to just get by Tifton High School, 21-20. But in the finals it was a much different story. Playing undefeated Rockmart High School, the Wildcats fell behind 31-7 at the half and never recovered, losing their first trip to the state championship game by a score of 52-21.

Now that the Wildcats had gotten a taste of playoff football, they would become an almost yearly qualifier. Despite finishing the 1951 campaign with a record of 7-3-0, the Wildcats managed to again qualify for the postseason, then justified that selection by defeating Tifton in the Class A semifinal game, 20-7. The Wildcats went on to win their first playoff championship the next week with a 14-9 victory over previously undefeated Newman High School.

The Wildcats had finished the '51 season with four consecutive victories, which was just the start of the longest undefeated run in school history.

The 1952 Wildcats would be one of the most dominating teams in Valdosta history. They would outscore their opponents by 508-32, posting seven shutouts in a 13-0-0 season. And the Wildcats kept rolling along when they reached the playoffs, where they easily disposed of their three postseason opponents by a combined 115-7, including a 30-0 victory over LaGrange in the Class A title game.

With the team's win streak now at 17, there would be little let up for Valdosta in 1953 despite playing a schedule that would eventually include five opponents ranked in the Class A final top seven. Only a 0-0 mid-season tie with Moultrie High marred Valdosta's otherwise perfect regular season. The team then breezed through the playoffs, including another lopsided Class A championship game victory over LaGrange, this time by a 48-7 score. The team's final record of 12-0-1 pushed its undefeated streak to 30.

The 1954 season would again find Wright Bazemore's Wildcats playing some of the elite teams in Class A. The Wildcats would go through the first eight games of the season without a defeat, with just a 0-0 tie with Americus High School keeping them from being perfect. The team's undefeated string had hit a school record 38 in a row when Valdosta faced off against the top ranked team in Class A, Jesup High, in the next-to-last game of the regular season. It was a close defensive battle all the way, but Jesup would halt the Wildcats' win streak with a 13-7 win.

After the Wildcats closed out the regular season with a 33-0 victory over Waycross, they again faced Jesup in the Class A regional finals. Another tough defensive battle and another 13-7 Jesup victory ended Valdosta's championship hopes for 1954.

Playing seven teams ranked among the Class A top eight is an ambitious undertaking; the Valdosta Wildcats did that in 1955, but they paid the price. The Wildcats finished the regular season at 7-3-0, but still managed to qualify for the

Mercer University quarterback
Wright Bazemore in 1935.
(Valdosta High School Yearbook)

postseason. They avenged earlier losses to Jesup and Thomasville high schools in the first two rounds of the playoffs, but dropped the championship game to Athens High, 41-20.

Moving up to Class AA, both the 1956 and 1957 seasons would see the Wildcats continue their great success of the early 1950s while playing schedules sprinkled liberally with Top 10 opponents.

With the exception of a close call with Jesup, 12-6, during the second week of the 1956 season, the Wildcats had little trouble winning their first five games, which moved the team up to first place in the AA rankings. Then, a 6-0 victory over Moultrie High on October 23 notwithstanding, the team cruised through the rest of its regular season schedule to enter the playoffs at 10-0-0.

The playoffs in 1956, as they usually were, would be a real challenge for Valdosta since the Wildcats were now facing the top three teams in their class. In the regionals, a 13-0 win over third-ranked Jesup and an even closer 20-14 victory over fourth-ranked Thomasville in the semifinals sent the Wildcats into the Class AA championship game against #2 and undefeated (11-0-1) Druid Hills.

After a scoreless first quarter, the Wildcats took a 7-0 lead in the second and then pushed that margin to 27-0 with 3:36 left on the game clock. At this point, all of the electricity in the stadium went out. After an hour of futile effort failed to restore the power, the game was called, the Wildcats winning the Class AA title, 27-0. Coach Bazemore's Wildcats would again go 13-0-0 in 1957, extending their winning streak to 26. There would be no really close contests during the regular season as the Wildcats won their games by an average score of 32 to 6. (One game would be recorded as a 1-0 forfeit in Valdosta's favor when Berrien County had to cancel due to an outbreak of the flu at that school.)

The playoffs that season were not as easy for the Wildcats as the regular season had been. In the regional finals, Valdosta needed a 74-yard touchdown pass reception by Wildcats' halfback Johnny Welch and quarterback Dale Williams's 55-yard return of a punt for a touchdown to defeat Jesup High, 13-0. In a Class AA semifinal game, the Wildcats handed fourth-ranked Thomasville a 20-0 defeat to advance to the championship game for the fourth consecutive season. However, the Wildcats would have to play the AA championship game without All-State quarterback Dale Williams, who had suffered a kidney injury during the game with Thomasville and would be unable to play in the championship game against # 2 Rockmart.

After a scoreless first quarter, Rockmart took a 6-0 lead in the second period—it was only the second time all season that Valdosta had trailed in a game. Before the quarter was over, however, the Wildcats would go on top 7-6. In the third quarter Valdosta would add a second touchdown to increase its lead to 13-6, which

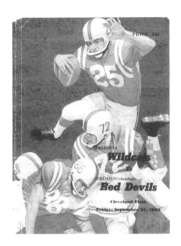

▲ *Game program from the Valdosta-Jordan game of Sept. 21, 1962. (Lowndes County Historical Society Archive)*

▾ *FB Walter Zant (arrow) finds a huge hole opened by his offensive line in the game against Jordan High on Sept. 21, 1962. (Lowndes County Historical Society Archive— Valdosta Daily Times)*

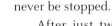

became the final score as the Wildcats came away with their second Georgia Class AA championship in as many seasons.

Valdosta closed out the decade of the 1950s without making the playoffs in either of the final two seasons, finishing 1958 with a record of 6-3-1 and 1959 at 5-5-0, but what a decade it had been for Wright Bazemore and his Valdosta Wildcats. Bazemore's record since taking over as the head coach at Valdosta in 1941 was 144-34-4, .802. For the years 1950-1959, Valdosta had won 98 games, lost just 19, and played three ties. The team had qualified for the playoffs eight times, made it to the state championship game seven times, and had won five titles (with a sixth, pre-playoff championship back in 1947). In the process, the Wildcats had set a still-standing team record of 38 consecutive games without a loss and had another streak of 30 consecutive victories.

That is quite a resume for any team or any coach. As the school's basketball coach, Bazemore had also posted a record of 176-26 thru 1959, with a Class B state championship in 1948. In recognition of his accomplishments at Valdosta High School, Wright Bazemore was inducted into the Georgia Sports Hall of Fame during the summer of 1960.

Getting selected to a Hall of Fame is an honor that one would normally associate with a coach who was retiring, or maybe even deceased, but Wright Bazemore was far from being either. Several factors combined to make this award, though well deserved, still somewhat unusual in its timing. For one, Bazemore was a relatively young man, not quite 44 years old. For another, he was still actively coaching—the only member of the Hall of Fame still "on the job". Finally, as incredible as it may sound, unbeknownst to anyone then, Wright Bazemore's best years as a football coach were yet to come.

While the decade of the '50s had ended on something of a sour note for Valdosta, the Wildcats came racing into the new decade of the '60s as if they would never be stopped.

After just two seasons in Class AA, in 1960 the Wildcats found themselves moved up to Class AAA. As that season rolled around, not too much was being expected of the Wildcats after a couple of mediocre campaigns. That the Wildcats would have a dozen sophomores and even a freshman among the 22 starters in 1960 certainly did not help perceptions. Many felt that the Wildcats were still "a year away" from having a truly good team.

Valdosta QB Rick Thomas eludes a Lanier High tackle and gains extra yardage against the Lanier Poets, on Sept. 27, 1962. (Lowndes County Historical Society Archive— Valdosta Daily Times)

The Wildcats fans were beginning to think that these youngsters were pretty quick learners when they opened the season with three victories, winning by an average margin of 28 points. Closer wins over Lanier, 19-7, and Athens, 7-0, followed as the Wildcats played their way into first place in the Class AAA state poll.

Over the following weeks the Wildcats added four more shutout victories to push their record to 9-0-0, the lone undefeated team in Region 1-AAA. On November 11, the last game of the regular season, they would face LaGrange, 8-1-0. A victory for the Wildcats would give them the Region 1-AAA championship, but a loss would force a playoff with LaGrange for the regional title and the Region 1 state semifinal playoff spot.

More than 6,000 fans were on hand in LaGrange for this one, a game that the newspapers would later call "the game of the year." The Grangers totally dominated the first half in taking a 13-0 lead; Valdosta had yet to cross the midfield stripe by halftime. The game was still 13-0 early in the fourth quarter when the Wildcats' Ken Ruffer finally got Valdosta on the scoreboard with a 65-yard punt return for a touchdown, the extra point cutting the Granger lead to 13-7. With about two minutes remaining in the game the Wildcats partially blocked a LaGrange punt, recovering the ball at the Granger 22-yard line. On the very next play the Wildcats tied the game on a 22-yard screen pass, then added the game-winning extra point with 1:16 left in the final quarter.

Having eliminated LaGrange, 14-13, Valdosta next faced undefeated Richmond Academy (10-0-0) on November 25 in a Class AAA semifinal game. The Musketeers, # 3 in the final AAA poll to the Wildcats' # 1, were nonetheless picked as a 1-2 touchdown favorite.

An overflow crowd estimated at 10,000 looked on as Richmond outplayed the Wildcats in the first two quarters; nonetheless the first half ended in a scoreless deadlock. In the second half, the tables were turned and the Wildcats dominated play. Early in the fourth quarter of a still scoreless contest, the Wildcats ground out a 14-play, 61-yard drive, picking up three first downs in the process. Although the Wildcats failed to get any points from this advance, it would still prove key to the outcome of the game.

When the final whistle was blown the score was still 0-0. There were no overtime periods at this time in the Georgia playoffs. The game would be decided on the basis of three statistical categories: total yards, total first downs, and the num-

▾ *Halfback Giles Smith leaps for
a few extra yards against Warner
Robins in this 1962 game action.
(Lowndes County Historical Society
Archive—Valdosta Daily Times)*

ber of penetrations inside the other team's 20-yard line. When everything was tabulated and totaled here is how it stood: total yards—Valdosta 187, Richmond 151; total first downs—Valdosta 7, Richmond 5; total penetrations inside the 20-yard line—Valdosta 2, Richmond 2. On the basis of winning two of the three tiebreaker categories the Wildcats were declared the winner and advanced.

The Class AAA state championship game, played at Valdosta's Cleveland Field, had the Wildcats taking on the second-ranked team in AAA, the Avondale Blue Devils (12-0-0). The Blue Devils were undefeated in 34 of their last 35 games.

Kickoff was at 8 P.M. on Friday night, December 2, in front of more than 9,000 high school football fans. Valdosta took a quick 14-0 lead by scoring on its first two possessions of the game, but Avondale came back to cut the lead to 14-7 at the half. In the third quarter, Avondale recovered a Valdosta fumble and then quickly went 80 yards in only five plays to tie the score at 14-14.

With about six minutes left to play and the score still deadlocked, Valdosta had the ball at its own 41-yard line following an Avondale punt. The Wildcats then ground out a time-consuming 17-play drive that culminated in a touchdown with just 29 seconds left on the game clock. The extra point try failed, but the Wildcats held on over those final 29 seconds to come away with a 20-14 championship game victory.

A couple of weeks later when the National Sports News Service (NSNS) issued its final national rankings for 1960, Valdosta came in at # 8 in the country.

Before the 1960 season had even begun, the word on the Valdosta Wildcats was that they were still "a year away" from doing anything substantial. Yet they went through that season undefeated, won the AAA state championship, and finished high in the final national rankings. The next year was supposed to be that "year away"; but 1961 and the following season as well would see all of those underclassmen from the 1960 team reach their full potential.

Unlike the previous year when they started out among the supposed also-rans, when the 1961 season opened the Valdosta Wildcats were the odds-on favorites to repeat as the Class AAA state champion. They were led by senior All-State quarterback Bruce Bennett, junior running back Ken Ruffer, and 32 other players who had either been starters or had seen substantial playing time the previous season.

Like a runaway locomotive, the Wildcats rolled over their first six opponents, totaling 206 points to just 27 allowed. In Week Seven they squared off against Moultrie, a team that had been known to give Valdosta fits in the past. The Packers were undefeated in six games thus far and entered the contest ranked # 6 in the latest AAA poll. More than 10,000 crammed into Valdosta's Cleveland Field, taking up every available viewing spot in anticipation of a great game—and a great game they got.

▲ *A typical observation pose for Wright Bazemore during a Wildcats game. (Valdosta High School Yearbook)*

▲   *Apparently surrounded*
by Richmond High defenders,
Valdosta HB Giles Smith
managed to break away for a
40-yard touchdown in this 1962
Class AAA semifinal game.
(Valdosta High School Yearbook)

The game was scoreless through the first quarter and into the second. Early in the second stanza, Valdosta took possession of the ball at its own 14-yard line and then marched 86 yards in 13 plays to take a 7-0 lead. Defense would rule the rest of the game as the Wildcats fought stubbornly to protect their slim lead. With the Valdosta defense holding Moultrie to just 52 yards rushing, the Packers offense only crossed the midfield stripe twice the entire game. When the final whistle sounded, Valdosta's 7-0 victory gave the Wildcats the best record in the region and broke the previous AAA record for consecutive wins, the Wildcats now at 19 and counting.

The Wildcats easily defeated their last three regular season opponents as they rolled into the playoffs having won six of their last seven games by shutout.

The Class AAA playoffs proved to be no more difficult for the Valdosta Wildcats than had the regular season. In a AAA semifinal game, they easily disposed of the fourth-ranked Musketeers of Richmond Academy, 26-0.

The 1961 Georgia Class AAA championship game would pit the top-ranked and undefeated Wildcats against # 2 and once-defeated Robert E. Lee, 10-1-1. Lee was a decided underdog; before the game Lee head coach Jim Cavan had told reporters that "our only chance is to play an outstanding game. Our first unit can stay close to their first unit, but where we play 13 or 14 boys, they play 30 or 40."

As Coach Cavan had predicted, the Rebels went toe-to-toe with the Wildcats and late in the third quarter Valdosta was clinging to a slim 14-13 lead. However, it was in the waning minutes of the third quarter that the Wildcats personnel advantage took its toll on the Rebels as the Wildcats scored 20 unanswered points over the balance of the game to come away with a 34-13 win. Valdosta's victory extended its winning streak to 24 and gave the team its second consecutive AAA state championship.

The 1961 Valdosta Wildcats were considered the best high school football team in the Peachtree State over the previous 20 years and by some perhaps the best team ever up to that time. The team's statistics were very convincing as they led the state in the following categories: rushing yardage, total offense, scoring, first downs, rushing defense, and fewest first downs allowed. When the National Sports News Service put out its final national rankings, Valdosta placed second; only Massillon Washington was considered a better team in the country than the Wildcats in 1961.

The always-packed Cleveland Field as it looked during the Wright Bazemore era at Valdosta High School. (Valdosta High School Yearbook)

Before the 1960 season, one in which the Wildcats were not expected to accomplish very much, Valdosta High School's veteran head coach Wright Bazemore had said, "Watch out for us in 1962." Bazemore not unexpectedly thought that his underclassman-laden 1960 squad would take some time to jell. What he and everyone else had not known was that the team would actually come together in 1960

and get even better over the next two seasons. Now 1962 was upon them and the team already had two consecutive state championships in its hip pocket and was looking for a third, not to mention that it was also ranked among the best teams in the country.

The 1962 Wildcats were loaded with talent, beginning with a large number of three-year lettermen, many with All-State and even All-America credentials. Players like ends Wally Colson and Billy Holtzclaw, tackle Bill Schroer, guards Bill Myddleton and Bill Holt, center Jimmy Robinson, former back-up quarterback and now starter Rick Thomas, halfback Red Reaves, and fullback Walter Zant. The Wildcats even had a few four-year players, most notably four-year starter at halfback/placekicker Giles Smith who was about to lead Class AAA in scoring for the second consecutive year. All in all the team had 15 veteran starters returning for the '62 campaign.

ONE LOCAL NEWSPAPER NOTED THE TEAM'S STRENGTHS WERE "EXPERIENCE, SIZE, DEPTH", WHICH DID NOT LEAVE TOO MUCH ON THE NEGATIVE SIDE.

One local newspaper noted the team's strengths were "experience, size, depth", which did not leave too much on the negative side. However, Coach Bazemore, in the best Knute Rockne tradition, always seemed to look on matters concerning his team with something of a jaundiced eye. His assessment of the team included a fear that, since many of his boys had never tasted defeat, what he called "senioritis" would set in; but, as he also noted, "It's my job to see that it doesn't."

Coach Bazemore would have to do "my job" in the Wildcats' very first game of the season against Baker High School. Baker had been playing football since 1948, but had yet to have a winning season and the Lions had never even come close to defeating the Wildcats. However, in the '62 season opener it appeared that the Wildcats may have been reading too many of their own press clippings. The first quarter ended scoreless. Late in the second quarter, the Wildcats finally got on the scoreboard to take a 7-0 lead at the halftime break. Apparently the Wildcats got "the message" from their coach at halftime because the second half was totally different. And all Valdosta. The Wildcats added three touchdowns in the second half to come away with a 28-0 victory.

With that first game safely tucked away, the Wildcats played up to expectations over the next five weeks as they rolled to five more victories, pushing their record to 6-0-0 and their win streak to 30.

On October 19 the Wildcats took on the always tough Moultrie Packers, 5-1-0, and a Class AAA Top 10 team at season's end. It was something of a sloppy game with penalties and turnovers hampering the effort of both teams, helping to keep the first half scoreless. Late in the third quarter Valdosta scored the first points of the game, but Moultrie managed to tie the score, 7-7, early in the final session after recovering a Valdosta fumble. Following the ensuing kickoff, the Wildcats had a second down at their own 26-yard line. Keeping the ball himself, quarterback Rick Thomas broke into the secondary, cut to his right and raced down the sideline 74 yards for another Wildcats touchdown. The extra point try failed, but the Wildcats had regained the lead, 13-7. The Valdosta defense dug in and stopped the Packers over the game's final minutes to give the Wildcats a hard fought 13 to 7 victory.

The following week Valdosta would confront another stiff challenge in a game that was billed as the feature game in Georgia that week. On October 26 at Cleveland Field, the Wildcats faced off against the Willingham Rams, who were undefeated at 5-0-2 and ranked sixth in Class AAA. In a game heavy on defense, the Wildcats scored single touchdowns in each of the first two quarters for the only points of the game. Their 12-0 victory pushed the Wildcats' win streak to 32.

Following the victory over Willingham, at least one national polling service elevated the Wildcats to the top spot in the country. Valdosta then closed out the regular season with victories over both Warner Robins, 47-7, and LaGrange, 20-0.

In a Class AAA semifinal the Wildcats took on Richmond Academy in a game to be played in Augusta. Like the previous 10 games, Valdosta's postseason games would prove to be of little difficulty. Against Richmond the Wildcats scored in every quarter and were only forced to punt on one occasion. The Valdosta defense completely stifled the Musketeers' running game, which netted minus-six yards; Richmond Academy had a net 28 yards of offense for the entire game.

Valdosta's 32-0 victory over Richmond Academy sent the Wildcats into the AAA state championship game against the second-ranked Murphy High Eagles, 11-1-0, of Atlanta. Despite this game featuring Georgia's two top ranked Class AAA teams, the rainy Friday night contest on November 30 was another one-sided affair as the guys up front in the Valdosta trenches dominated play. For the second straight playoff game the Wildcats completely stopped their opponent's ground game, limiting the Eagles to just one yard rushing and a paltry 64 yards of total offense. So dominant was the Valdosta defense that the Eagles never crossed the midfield stripe during the entire game.

On the other side of the ball, the Valdosta O-line opened the way for more than 300 yards of offense. The Wildcats had the ball eight times during the game and scored on six of those possessions, resulting in a resounding 39-0 victory for the Wildcats.

With that victory, Valdosta became the first team in Class AAA history to win three consecutive state championships, setting a team and AAA record with 36 consecutive victories.

▲ *The program from the 1962 Georgia Class AAA state championship game between Valdosta and Murphy high schools. (Lowndes County Historical Society Archive)*

'Cats Bury Eagles In Mud, 39-0, Win Third Straight State Title

▲ *The headline says it all in announcing another Valdosta Wildcats state championship, which in 1962 also included a national title. (Lowndes County Historical Society Archive—Valdosta Daily Times)*

After being ranked first in the country for the latter half of the season, it became official when the National Sports News Service named the Wildcats the 1962 national champion, the team's first such honor.

As so often happens when a great class graduates, the loss of so many Wildcats stars in June of 1963 gutted the football team. The Wildcats who took the field that fall won their first game to extend the team's win streak to 37, but that would prove to be one of only two victories for the entire season. The team's record of 2-7-1 would mark the only losing season in Wright Bazemore's long career at Valdosta.

The 1964 season would see a major improvement in Valdosta's gridiron fortunes. The team would sprint out of the gate by winning its first five games, but the Wildcats would miss the post-season after losing three of their last five games to finish with a record of 7-3-0.

A return to state and national prominence awaited the Wildcats in 1965. After opening with a 33-0 thrashing of Waycross, the Wildcats struggled a bit with Baker High, but emerged with a 13-0 victory. The next five weeks produced five more victories as the Wildcats improved to 7-0-0 and were ranked # 1 in Class AAA for the first time in three years.

On October 29 the Wildcats took on the Willingham Rams, also without a loss, 5-0-2. Playing on their home field, the Wildcats had most of the crowd behind them, but the offense could not get on track that night as the Rams shut out the Wildcats, 12-0. That loss cost the Wildcats their # 1 ranking in AAA, but they quickly regained that lofty perch with convincing victories over Northside (Warner Robins), 49-7, and LaGrange, 47-6, in the final two games of the regular season.

Finishing with a record of 9-1-0, the Wildcats were back in the Class AAA playoffs for the first time in three years. In a AAA semifinal game played on Thanksgiving Day at their own Cleveland Field, the Wildcats were pitted against the Savannah High School Blue Jackets, undefeated (10-0-0) and ranked seventh in the final AAA rankings. The Wildcats fell behind 3 to 0 early in the game. However, after that initial "shock" the Cats scored 32 unanswered points and routed the Blue Jackets by 32-3.

Valdosta's "reward" for defeating Savannah was a game on Saturday, December 4, against the second-ranked team in AAA, Athens. The Trojans were described in an article in the *Valdosta Daily Times*, "... [the] Trojans had been called by some

Georgia's greatest prep eleven. They had swept to the Region 5-AAA and North Georgia AAA titles without a close game. They had clicked off 13 straight wins this year ..."

The Trojans had the credentials to go along with those accolades, having won their 13 games by an average score of 42-6. Another win at the expense of the Wildcats seemed all but certain as the *Daily Times* noted, "They were supposed to waltz past the Wildcats." But, as the saying goes, that is why they play the games.

After a scoreless first quarter, the Wildcats drew first blood in the second. Capping off an 81-yard march that took 13 plays, quarterback Glenn Davis (not a bad name for a QB if you remember your West Point football) plunged the final yard for a Valdosta touchdown, the extra point giving the Wildcats a 7-0 lead. In the closing seconds of the first half Valdosta scored again on a screen pass, the extra point giving the Wildcats a somewhat surprising 14-0 lead at the intermission.

Early in the third quarter Glenn Davis had to leave the game with injured ribs, a situation that would greatly curtail the effectiveness of the Valdosta offense over the remainder of the game. Shortly after Davis's departure, Athens scored a touchdown to cut the Valdosta lead in half, 14-7. The game now became a defensive struggle. Late in the fourth quarter with the Wildcats still in front 14 to 7 and trying to run out the clock, they were forced to give up the ball on downs with 1:30 left in the game. Given one last chance, the Trojans quickly advanced to a first and goal at the Wildcats three-yard line. The Valdosta defense dug in and gave up ground grudgingly; but, on fourth and goal the Trojans finally cracked through for a touchdown, needing only the extra point to tie the game. This time the kick was no good as the Wildcats held on by a whisker to claim the 1965 Georgia AAA state championship, 14-13.

Not only were the Wildcats back atop the Georgia football world, but a short time later the National Sports News Service placed the Wildcats sixth in the country in its final national rankings.

The next season the Wildcats would allow more than one touchdown in only one game, the season opener, but that stat might be somewhat misleading because little in 1966 came easily for the Cats.

Valdosta opened its season on August 26 against Waycross. As so often happens, the first game was the usual feeling out process for both teams. The Wildcats scored all of their points in the first half, then held off Waycross's second half comeback effort to emerge with a 27-13 win. The following week, the Wildcats blitzed Baker High for 405 yards of offense and 49 points, while holding the Lions to just 56 yards in a 49-7 triumph.

The winning continued over the next several weeks, but the Wildcats had to work hard for every victory. They took the measure of Dougherty High, 19-6, bested Jordan, 27-7, and escaped with a 14-0 victory over Lanier.

The Albany Indians would pay a visit to Cleveland Field on the last day of September. The Indians were 4-1-0, having suffered their only defeat the previous week, and that by just a single point. After three quarters of scoreless football, Albany broke through to take a 6-0 lead late in the fourth period. Valdosta appeared to be marching for a possible tying touchdown when the game clock struck 00:00.

The loss to Albany cost the Valdosta its # 1 ranking in Class AAA, dropping them to fourth place. With a bye the following weekend, the Wildcats had an extra seven days in which to prepare for the second half of the season. The extra practice time paid off as the Wildcats ended the regular season on a four-victory roll and headed for the playoffs once again atop the Class AAA rankings.

On November 18, the Wildcats traveled to Savannah to take on the Warriors of Jenkins High School (9-1-0) in a Class AAA semifinal game. It would be a struggle, but the Wildcats took advantage of some poor play by the Jenkins punting unit to pull out a 16-7 victory.

In the AAA state championship game held on December 3, Valdosta faced off against the Marietta Blue Devils at Cleveland Field. The Blue Devils, ranked second in AAA, came into the game a perfect 12-0-0 and riding a 21-game winning streak. The Blue Devils were averaging 33 points per game and had not scored fewer than three touchdowns in any of their games. On the other side of the ball, Marietta's stingy defense already had five shutouts to its credit.

This game was a scoreless defensive duel until the final play of the first half when the Blue Devils' scored on a 30-yard field goal to give Marietta a 3-0 lead at the intermission. In the third quarter, Valdosta finally put up some points when John Copeland stunned the crowd by returning a punt 75 yards for a touchdown, the extra point giving Valdosta a 7-3 lead. The Wildcats added a second TD in the fourth quarter to come away with a tough 14-3 championship game victory.

Despite having one loss on its record, the National Sports News Service placed Valdosta second in its final national poll for 1966.

After two consecutive state championship seasons in 1965 and 1966, seasons in which the Valdosta Wildcats again placed high in the national rankings, 1967 saw the team fall back to earth. The Wildcats began that season with four consecutive victories, but did not win again until the final game of the season, finishing 5-4-1 and failing to make the Class AAA playoffs.

Wright Bazemore had been the head coach of the Valdosta High School football team since 1941, with three years out for military service during World War II. In 1968, he entered his 25th season at the helm of the Wildcats. Bazemore's teams had already won a dozen state championships and one national championship, he had been named the Georgia high school football "Coach of the Year" five times, and Wright Bazemore was the only member of the Georgia Sports Hall of Fame still actively coaching. Yet, incredibly, the next four seasons would prove to be not

▴ *Valdosta running back
Danny O'Neal runs over
and through Thomasville
defenders in the 1969 season
opener. (Lowndes County
Historical Society Archive—
Valdosta Daily Times)*

only the greatest in Wright Bazemore's long coaching career, but also the greatest in the history of Valdosta football.

Rebounding from their sub-par 1967 season, the Valdosta Wildcats in 1968 would begin a two season run in which they would totally dominate their opponents on both sides of the ball.

Valdosta's 1968 campaign opened on a humid 90-degree Friday, September 6, at Cleveland Field against the Thomasville Bulldogs, a team that Valdosta had been playing since 1914. This would be a good season-opening test for both teams. Thomasville was a Class AA team that would spend the season among the Top 10 of that class, most of the time ranked either first or second. Playing against a top notch opponent like the Bulldogs would give Wright Bazemore an indication of the progress his team had made since the previous season.

The Wildcats scored on their first offensive possession and maintained the lead till the final whistle. Holding Thomasville to a mere 41 yards of total offense, the Wildcats ground out a 19-0 victory in the stifling heat. While Coach Bazemore was no doubt pleased with the victory, the Wildcats' four turnovers and eight penalties totaling 80 yards still left room for improvement.

▲ *Valdosta guard Mike Dibois (66) helps clear the way for halfback Willie Jones against Thomasville on Sept. 5, 1969. (Lowndes County Historical Society Archive— Valdosta Daily Times)*

▸ *Valdosta quarterback Dan Golden scrambles for yardage during the 1969 season. (Lowndes County Historical Society Archive)*

That improvement came almost immediately as the Wildcats rolled over each new opponent in the weeks that followed. Dougherty High fell by a 40-0 count. Wayne County was kicked to the side, 35-0. Ware County was humbled by a score of 48-0. On October 4 against the Albany Indians the Wildcats had their best game of the season on defense, holding the Indians to minus-15 yards of total offense in a 28-0 victory.

The Wildcats had won their first five games and had yet to give up a point. It was more of the same in Game Six against Moultrie, always a tough opponent, which limited the Wildcats to 22 points, their lowest total of the season. However, like the five teams before it, the Packers failed to cross the Valdosta goal line as the Wildcats once again prevailed.

On October 25, the Tornadoes of Monroe High School (Albany) came calling at Cleveland Field. It was business as usual as the Wildcats took a 33-0 lead deep into the third quarter. It was at this juncture that the Tornadoes upset the apple-cart and did something no other Valdosta opponent had yet done—they scored a touchdown, the points coming on a 67-yard pass play. Other than that one play, the Tornadoes could muster only 55 yards of offense against the Wildcats as Valdosta saw its record go to 7-0-0 with its 47-6 victory.

The Wildcats, who had been ranked # 1 in Class AAA since the second week of the season, closed out the regular part of the campaign with three more one-sided victories, outscoring their opponents 130-6. Following their final regular season game, the Wildcats had a week off before starting postseason play.

The Wildcats' Class AAA quarterfinal game took place on Friday, November 29, against Lanier at Porter Stadium in Macon. Lanier was undefeated at 10-0-1 and ranked third in AAA. Valdosta scored a touchdown in the first quarter, but the extra point try failed. The score remained 6-0 until late in the second quarter when Lanier finally broke through to score a touchdown. The PAT gave Lanier a 7-6 advantage and put the Wildcats on the short side of the score for the first time all season.

As one newspaper later put it, "the Cats' reaction was swift and certain." Following the ensuing kickoff Valdosta promptly marched 61 yards in just eight plays to score its second touchdown; this time the extra point was good to give the Wildcats a 13-7 lead at the intermission. In the second half it was back to business as usual for Valdosta as the Wildcats added two more touchdowns while shutting out Lanier en route to a 27-7 victory.

Their AAA semifinal game would see the Wildcats playing another AAA Top 10 team, the Red Terrors of Glynn Academy, undefeated at 8-0-3 and ranked seventh in the state. This would be another road trip for the Wildcats, the game being played at Glynn Stadium in Brunswick.

▲   *Above: Valdosta defensive tackle Mike Everson leaps high to block this kick by the Wayne County High School punter on Sept. 19, 1969. (Lowndes County Historical Society Archive—Valdosta Daily Times)*

▸   *Following page, top: Running back Charles Daniels cuts behind a block by Mark Dibois to pick up substantial extra yards against Tift County on Nov. 7, 1969. (Lowndes County Historical Society Archive—Valdosta Daily Times)*

▸   *Following page, bottom: With blockers to his left and to his right, Valdosta end Tuffy Taylor (11) finds a big hole through which to run against the Savannah Blue Jackets in a Class AAA semifinal game on Dec.5, 1969. (Lowndes County Historical Society Archive—Valdosta Daily Times)*

Despite being a state semifinal game, this one was over almost before all of the spectators had found their seats. The Red Terrors won the pre-game coin toss and opted to kick off to open the contest. Valdosta's Larry Howell fielded the ball at his own 13-yard line and returned it the full 87 yards for a Valdosta touchdown. The PAT was good and the rout was on. The Wildcats held the Red Terrors to just 30 yards of total offense while managing almost 400 yards themselves in a 42-0 win.

The season's final game, the Class AAA state championship, was played on Saturday, December 12, in Atlanta at Georgia Tech's Grant Field. It was a bitterly cold day by most standards, but especially so for Georgia. The temperature barely hitting 20 degrees, a blustery wind of 15-25 mph brought the wind chill substantially lower and there were even snow flurries throughout the game for added "atmosphere." Despite the weather conditions, 12,476 hardy football fans showed up for the game.

Valdosta's opponent for the big game was the team from Forest Park High School. The Panthers were undefeated, 12-0-0, but had really only been tested in a couple of games. Valdosta, having outscored its opponents by 438-19, appeared to be the pregame favorite.

Call it luck or getting the breaks, but whatever it was it came Valdosta's way very early in the game. The Wildcats kicked off to open the contest and on the third play from scrimmage Forest Park fumbled the ball, the loose pigskin recovered by Valdosta at the Forest Park 37-yard line. It only took Valdosta one play to find the end zone via a 37-yard aerial, the extra point giving the Wildcats an early 7-0 lead.

As Yogi Berra might say, "it was déjà vu all over again." Following its touchdown Valdosta kicked off and again, on the third play from scrimmage, at the Forest Park 26-yard line the Panthers fumbled the ball. As the football skipped along the turf at the Panthers' 13-yard line, Valdosta's Jerry Neal grabbed it and raced into the end zone for another Wildcats' score that extended their lead to 14-0.

For the third time in the first quarter, the Wildcats kicked off. This time on the fateful third play, as the writer for the *Valdosta Daily Times* noted, "someone changed the script." On this third down, instead of giving the ball away, Forest Park completed a 67-yard pass that took the ball all the way to the Valdosta one-yard line. Forest Park scored on the next play, but the extra point try sailed wide left to leave the score 14-6.

That would end the scoring in a most entertaining and eventful first quarter. Turnovers would also play a big part in the second quarter, each team taking advantage of its opportunity to score a touchdown. At the half Valdosta still maintained the lead, 21-12. The second half was all Valdosta as the Wildcats added 13 points in the third quarter and a field goal in the final frame for a 37-12 victory.

The Wildcats had ended the season a perfect 13-0-0 (14 in a row including the previous season). The National Sports News Service named the Wildcats the # 2 team in the nation for 1968.

The 1968 Valdosta season had been one of the most dominating in the team's history; but with 18 seniors having graduated, 17 of them starters, the prospects for the '69 campaign were decidedly unknown. As head coach Wright Bazemore noted in one preseason interview, his team had potential, but it lacked experience.

There would be little time to tinker and experiment with players as the first game quickly arrived on September 5. The opponent was the Thomasville Bulldogs, who would again be a force to be reckoned with in Class AA, as the Wildcats were about to find out.

On another hot and humid September night in south Georgia, the game was played in Thomasville before a standing room only crowd of more than 8,000. All of the scoring in this one took place within a two minute span in the second quarter. The first points came when Valdosta's Curt Bazemore intercepted a pass at the Bulldogs 20-yard line. Bazemore returned the ball all the way for a Valdosta touchdown, the extra point giving the Wildcats a 7-0 lead. Following the ensuing kickoff, Thomasville went three and out and was forced to punt. Valdosta's Warrick Taylor caught the ball at his own 31-yard line and ran it back 69 yards for another Valdosta touchdown and a 14-0 lead.

And that was it for the game's scoring. Valdosta had emerged with a first-game victory, but despite 181 total yards the Wildcats' offense had not scored a single point.

If there was any concern about the offense's scoring ability after that first game it was soon dispelled over the following weeks:

Valdosta	42	Dougherty	0
Valdosta	34	Wayne County	0
Valdosta	63	Ware County	0
Valdosta	28	Albany	0
Valdosta	21	Moultrie	0
Valdosta	38	Monroe (Albany)	0
Valdosta	46	Coffee County	0

Eight games, eight shutouts, 34 consecutive shutout quarters going back to 1968. Averaging almost 36 points per game, the offense had obviously found its stride.

The Wildcats traveled to Tifton on Friday, November 7, to take on the team from Tift County High School. The Wildcats held a 14-0 lead as the game progressed into the third quarter. With the line of scrimmage at his own 11-yard line, Valdosta quarterback Danny O'Neal fumbled the ball, which was recovered by Tif-

ON THE VERY NEXT PLAY THE BLUE DEVILS SCORED "ON A PERFECTLY EXECUTED TRIPLE-OPTION" OVER THE RIGHT SIDE. THE HOME STANDS ERUPTED AS IF THE BLUE DEVILS HAD JUST WON THE STATE CHAMPIONSHIP—THE VALDOSTA GOAL LINE HAD FINALLY BEEN CROSSED FOR THE FIRST TIME IN 37 QUARTERS.

ton at the 11. On the very next play the Blue Devils scored "on a perfectly executed triple-option" over the right side. The home stands erupted as if the Blue Devils had just won the state championship—the Valdosta goal line had finally been crossed for the first time in 37 quarters.

Valdosta had given up seven points, but it was not the end of the world and the defense played its usual rock solid game over the remaining minutes of the game. The Wildcats' offense added single scores in both of the final two quarters and the team returned to Valdosta with a 28-7 victory and its record a perfect 9-0-0.

It was business as usual in the final game of the regular season on November 14 as the Wildcats defeated Lowndes County, 40-0.

The Wildcats now had an extra week to prepare for their Class AAA quarterfinal game on Friday, November 28. The game would be played at Valdosta's Cleveland Field against the Lanier Poets, the third-ranked team in AAA and undefeated at 11-0-0. As would be expected of an undefeated team, Lanier was solid in all facets of the game, winning by an average score of 31-5.

Playoffs or not, it was business as usual for the Wildcats. After a scoreless first quarter, Valdosta scored twice in the second to take a 14-0 lead. A field goal and a touchdown in the second half lifted the Wildcats to a 23-0 victory. Valdosta had held the Poets to minus yardage rushing until the last play of the game, and for the tenth time in 11 games the Wildcats had held an opponent scoreless.

On Friday night, December 5, Valdosta's AAA semifinal game would be played at Cleveland Field, the Wildcats hosting the Savannah Blue Jackets. Like Valdosta, Savannah entered the game a perfect 11-0-0, averaging 37 points per game and in fourth place in the final AAA rankings.

This game would come down to passing, and it would be the smothering Valdosta pass defense coupled with the Wildcats' passing duo of quarterback Don Golden and halfback Willie Jones that would carry the day. The Valdosta defense held the Blue Jackets to one completion in eight attempts for just seven yards. Meanwhile, the Golden-Jones tandem would provide the Wildcats with all of the

▲ *The Valdosta Wildcats even made headlines across the border in Florida. (Lowndes County Historical Society Archive)*

▼ *Valdosta fullback Danny O'Neal had to fight for every yard he gained against Athens in the 1969 Georgia Class AAA state championship game. (Lowndes County Historical Society Archive—Valdosta Daily Times)*

points that the team would need on touchdown aerials of 48, 36, and 74 yards, carrying the Wildcats to yet another shutout victory, 20-0.

The Wildcats' victory over Savannah sent them to the Class AAA championship game for the fourth time in the last five years. Their opponent would be the Trojans of Athens High School. Athens entered the game with a record of 11-1-0, on a 10-game winning streak, and ranked second in the state in the final poll before the playoffs.

The 11,000-plus who showed up at Cleveland Field on Saturday night, December 13, anticipated an exciting game. What these folks saw was one of the best state championship games in Georgia history, a game for the ages.

Valdosta opened the game by kicking off. Athens rushed down the field, 81 yards in just five plays; the touchdown came on a 43-yard run by fullback Benny Edmonds, but the Athens try for a two-point conversion failed. The Wildcats came right back with a lightning quick drive of their own, 74 yards in just four plays with the touchdown coming via a Don Golden to Willie Jones aerial that covered 63 yards. The extra point try was also no good, leaving the score tied 6-6 after one quarter.

In the second quarter, the Wildcats closed out an 84-yard drive with a touchdown and an extra point that gave the Wildcats a 13-6 lead. It looked as if that would be the halftime score, but on the final play of the half Athens quarterback Andy Johnson kept the ball himself and ran 68 yards for a Trojans touchdown. The Trojans extra point try was again no good, leaving Valdosta with a slim 13-12 lead at the half.

It had been an exciting first half, but these two teams were just getting started.

On the receiving end of the second half kickoff, Valdosta promptly marched 60 yards to pay dirt to increase its lead to 20-12. Athens immediately responded with a nine-play, 64-yard touchdown drive of its own, but a pass for the two-pointer that would have tied the game fell incomplete and left Athens trailing, 20-18.

As the game proceeded into the final quarter, erratic play and lost fumbles would hinder the efforts of both teams. Valdosta finally took advantage of an Athens fumble, recovering the loose

The final scoreboard tells the story of the 1969 Georgia Class AAA state championship game between Valdosta and Athens high schools. (Lowndes County Historical Society Archive)

ball at the Trojans' 11-yard line and needing only two plays to add to its total, but a missed extra point left Valdosta with a 26-18 advantage.

Late in the fourth quarter it was the Wildcats who again fumbled the ball, this time at their own 25-yard line, with Athens regaining possession of the ball with just one minute left to play. After making a few yards on the ground, Athens went to the air—completions on consecutive passes netted 72 yards and an Athens touchdown. Another pass for the two-point conversion was also successful and tied the game at 26-26.

Twenty-five seconds later the final whistle ended the game with the score still tied at 26-26. For the first time, Georgia's Class AAA had co-champions.

Despite being co-champion in Georgia, Valdosta's overwhelming dominance in 1969 was impressive enough to get the Wildcats named national champion. Head coach Wright Bazemore was named the national high school football "Coach of the Year"

Like the state championship, the national championship was an honor that Valdosta also had to share, but more on that later.

Coach Wright Bazemore described his 1970 Wildcats as the youngest team he had ever put on the field, with two freshmen among the 22 starters. With the Wildcats riding a string of 27 games without a defeat, it was hoped that these youngsters could keep the streak alive for many more weeks to come.

The season opened on September 4 against Thomasville, now playing in Class AAA. The former AA power Bulldogs had given the Wildcats some tough battles the last few seasons. It would be more of the same in this game, but this time the Wildcats only had themselves to blame as they struggled to defeat the Bulldogs, 35-21.

Valdosta then rolled through its next four games, allowing just seven points as the team raised its mark to 5-0-0 and ran its undefeated streak to 32. On October 16 the Wildcats traveled to Moultrie High for their annual game with the Packers. It was another tough game for Valdosta, but a pair of fourth quarter touchdowns produced a come from behind 19-12 victory.

The Wildcats cruised to victory in the final four games of the regular season to end with a perfect 10-0-0 record, extending the team's undefeated streak to 37 games. In the AAA quarterfinals, Valdosta defeated Kendrick High School, 28-12, tying the school record of 38 games without a loss and setting up a semifinal showdown with Richmond Academy in Augusta.

The Richmond Musketeers were 10-1-0 entering the game, but not ranked among the state's Top 10 Class AAA teams, while Valdosta was 11-0-0 and had been ranked # 1 all season. Although both teams were averaging 33 points per game, this game would be dominated by defense.

▲ *The 1969 Valdosta Wildcats—National Champions (Valdosta High School Yearbook)*

◂ Wildcats' quarterback Stan Bounds is about to pitch out against the Crisp County Cougars in this 1971 game action. (Lowndes County Historical Society Archive—Valdosta Daily Times)

▸ Valdosta tackle Paul Demersseman (84) throws a key block that springs fullback Pat O'Neal loose for a big gain against Moultrie High on Oct. 14, 1971. (Lowndes County Historical Society Archive— Valdosta Daily Times)

▴ The Valdosta Wildcats' defense (white jerseys) was a key element of the team's 1971 national championship season. (Lowndes County Historical Society Archive—Valdosta Daily Times)

▲ *In this 1971 game action, Valdosta defenseman Louie Goodin hit the Westover High quarterback in time to cause an errant throw, while teammates Randy Binford and Roger Roundtree rush to assist. (Lowndes County Historical Society Archive—Valdosta Daily Times)*

▸ *Valdosta quarterback Stan Bounds is just able to get off his pass as the Warner Robins defense closes in on him during a 1971 Georgia Class AAA quarterfinal playoff game. (Lowndes County Historical Society Archive—Valdosta Daily Times)*

The Wildcats had led throughout most of the game, but as the Valdosta High School yearbook would later note, the Wildcats were "sitting on a shaky 14-12 lead" as the game clock wound down to the final three minutes of the fourth quarter. At this point the Musketeers intercepted a Valdosta aerial and a little over a minute later turned it into a touchdown and an 18-14 Richmond lead. It was a lead that the Valdosta Wildcats were unable to overcome during the game's final minute and a half. The 18-14 defeat ended not only the Wildcats' season, but also their undefeated streak.

Wright Bazemore had been coaching at Valdosta High School since 1940, as the head coach since 1941. However, not even Coach Bazemore could have guessed the kind of success that his team would enjoy by the time the 1971 campaign was completed. In fact, if you listened to him before the season had begun, this was going to be another rebuilding year. Graduation the previous June had robbed the team of all but seven starters. Bazemore told reporters that, like the 1970 team, this was another "young team" that would have seven underclassmen starting on both offense and defense.

The season opened on September 3 with a game at Thomasville against the Bulldogs. Led by quarterback Stan Bounds, who would be an All-America selection

▲ *The program for the 1971 Georgia Class AAA semifinal game between two teams of Wildcats, those from Valdosta High and from Laney High. (Lowndes County Historical Society Archive)*

▼ *Valdosta's Scott Griffin (80) saved the moment when he recovered teammate George Roundtree's fumble in the Class AAA state championship game against Avondale High on Dec. 11, 1971. (Valdosta High School Yearbook)*

at season's end, the Wildcats romped to a 49-0 victory. As the season unfolded, results like that would become common place.

In the preseason polls Valdosta had been picked either first or second in Class AAA, but that opening victory left the team firmly in control of first place.

The next four weeks produced similar results for the Wildcats as they averaged 41 points per game while allowing a total of just 22. Next, the Wildcats prepared for a home game against the Moultrie Packers, who were also 5-0-0. It would be a close game through three quarters as Moultrie nearly equaled the total number of points that Valdosta had allowed thus far in the season, but this was the Wildcats year. Final score: Valdosta 42, Moultrie 21.

The following week Valdosta traveled to Albany to take on the Monroe Tornadoes. Monroe actually took a 6-0 lead early in the game, but Valdosta had yet to go on offense. Even though he cleared the bench of all 81 players, Wright Bazemore's team went on to a 75-22 triumph, the most points that one of his teams had ever scored. In quick succession, Valdosta then took the measure of Westover, 47-6, Tift County, 60-28, and cross-town rival Lowndes County, 40-0, to close out the regular season 10-0-0.

The Wildcats would have the home field advantage throughout the playoffs, but this is one season when they did not need any kind of advantage. On November 26 they played Warner Robins in a Class AAA quarterfinal game. Warner Rob-

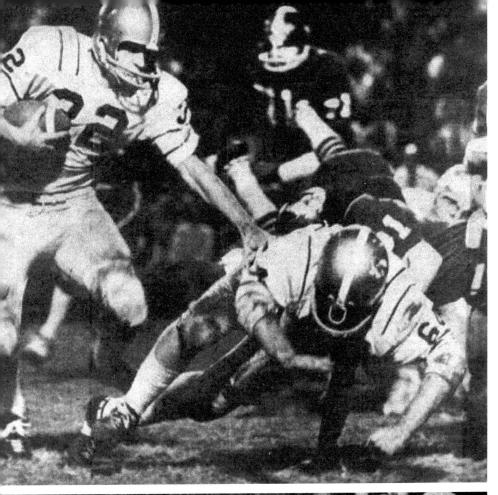

‹ Valdosta guard David Register's great block opened up a lot of running room for fullback Pat O'Neal during the 1971 state championship game against Avondale. (Lowndes County Historical Society Archive—Valdosta Daily Times)

‹ It seems like the entire Valdosta defense is in on this sack of Avondale quarterback Doug Elstad during the 1971 Georgia Class AAA championship game. (Lowndes County Historical Society Archive— Valdosta Daily Times)

▲ *The 1971 national champion Valdosta Wildcats are always part of the conversation when it turns to the greatest high school football teams of all-time. (Valdosta High School Yearbook)*

▲ *Valdosta wide receiver George Roundtree (88) leaps high to battle for the ball against this Avondale defender in the 1971 Class AAA championship game. (Valdosta High School Yearbook)*

ins was ranked second in Class AAA, but that did not impress Valdosta as the team rolled to a 35-6 victory.

The following week, Valdosta faced Class AAA's third-ranked team, Laney High School, which entered the game with a record of 10-1-0. Once again Valdosta dominated as the Wildcats smashed their way into the Class AAA championship game with a 54-20 triumph.

In the 1971 Georgia Class AAA state championship game, the Wildcats played Avondale, now the second-ranked team in AAA and sporting a record of 11-1-1. However, Avondale was undefeated in Georgia, its lone defeat coming in the first game of the season to Butler (Ala.) High School, a team that would play in Alabama's 4-A state championship game later in the season.

Before more than 11,000 fans at Cleveland Field, the Wildcats would put an exclamation point on their already incredible season. Valdosta scored early and often and led 21-0 just over seven minutes into the game. By halftime that lead had grown to 35-6 and Coach Bazemore had already used 55 different players. Finishing with 637 yards of total offense (349 yds. rushing, 288 yds. passing), 29 first downs, nine touchdowns, and not a single punt, the Wildcats came away with a stunning 62-12 victory. It was the 15th state championship of Wright Bazemore's career at Valdosta and the eighth in the last 12 seasons.

It had been an incredible season filled with superlatives and gaudy numbers. Accomplishing something few teams anywhere have ever done, the Valdosta Wildcats in 1971 were a point-a-minute team, averaging 48.4 points per game while setting a then-state-record by scoring 629 points for the season. In the playoffs against the best teams in Class AAA, the Wildcats were even better, averaging an unbelievable 51.3 points per game.

Whether it was on the ground or in the air, it was almost impossible to stop the Valdosta offense that incredibly averaged 200 yards rushing and 231 yards passing over the entire season. Leading the charge was All-America quarterback Stan Bounds who passed for 2,758 yards (a record that stood for 18 years) and 30

▸ *Valdosta senior quarterback Stan Bounds in front of the final scoreboard for the 1971 Georgia Class AAA state championship game. Valdosta was the Home team. (Lowndes County Historical Society Archive)*

The Dosta Outlook

BAND WINS
MARDI GRAS

GO CATS
WIN REGION

Vol. XXXVIII, No. 6

VALDOSTA HIGH SCHOOL, VALDOSTA, GEORGIA

February 15, 1972

WILDCATS NO. 1 IN NATION

▲ *The Dosta Outlook, the Valdosta High School newspaper, proudly proclaims the football team's elevated status. (Lowndes County Historical Society Archive)*

touchdowns and ran for 485 yards and 23 touchdowns. On the receiving end of 72 of those passes was sophomore wide receiver Stan Rome, whose catches totaled 1,573 yards (a record that stood for 29 years) and 21 touchdowns.

On the defensive side of the ball, Valdosta was not as smothering as some teams in its past, but they more than got the job done as the opposition was limited to just 10.5 points per game. The opportunistic Wildcats defense averaged more than four takeaways per game, twice coming up with seven turnovers in a single game.

This time, unlike 1969, there would be no sharing of the national championship. In 1971 the National Sports News Service named the Valdosta Wildcats as their unanimous choice for national champion—Valdosta's third such honor in the last 10 seasons.

The 1971 Valdosta Wildcats are considered by many to be the greatest team in Georgia high school football history. And when the conversation turns to the country's all-time greatest teams, the '71 Wildcats are usually in the mix.

The last four seasons were a great run for the Wildcats as they posted a record of 49-1-1, 38 consecutive games without a loss, three state championships, twice named national champion, and one second place finish.

The 1971 season was the crowning glory. It was almost as if Wright Bazemore's whole career had been pointing to this one incredible season, as if he had been saving the best for last. For about the last year, there had been rumors floating around town that Wright Bazemore was going to hang up his cleats, retire from coaching. That rumor became a reality less than a week after the Class AAA championship game. Coach Bazemore was retiring from coaching after 33 years, all but two of them spent at Valdosta, 28 as the Wildcats' head coach. When interviewed, Bazemore often cited the intense pressure that he felt while coaching and that no doubt played a part in his decision. But the greater part, and one he tended to down play, was most likely the advice from his doctor.

▲   *The back cover of the program from the retirement banquet honoring Valdosta head coach Wright Bazemore. Pictured are Bazemore and his wife Betty, as well as the coach's outstanding record. (Lowndes County Historical Society Archive)*

In his 28 seasons as the head coach at Valdosta High School, Wright Bazemore compiled a record almost unmatched in Georgia, or anywhere else for that matter. His final mark included 265 victories against 51 defeats and seven ties, a winning percentage of .831—only four coaches in Georgia high school football history have posted a better mark. His teams won 15 state championships and three national crowns and were ranked among the nation's top eight teams seven times—a combination unsurpassed by any other coach in the country. Over the course of his career, Wright Bazemore also coached the basketball team to at least one state championship and the tennis team to several state titles. And he even spent one season as the baseball coach.

Wright Bazemore has been described as being "outwardly quiet and calm, (but with a) competitive spirit, a demand for perfection and a seemingly boundless knowledge of football..." That intense pressure he felt was most likely self

COACH WRIGHT BAZEMORE
Valdosta High School
1940-1971
Won 290—Lost 43—Tied 6
15 State Championships
3 National Titles

"IT HAS TO BE A TEAM EFFORT; YOU CAN'T GET THIS JOB DONE ANY OTHER WAY."

imposed in his striving to succeed. When asked the secret to his success, Bazemore's usual reply was something like this, "It has to be a team effort; you can't get this job done any other way." He also credited his success to "good working conditions, good luck, and the good Lord."

Wright Bazemore remained as a teacher and Athletic Director at Valdosta High School for seven more years before taking his full retirement. In 1988 he was inducted into the National High School Sports Hall of Fame. Wright Bazemore passed away in 1999 at the age of 82.

## CHAPTER 7

THE STINGAREES

Miami High School
Miami, Florida

(Miami High School Yearbook)

Miami High School was that city's first, opening in 1903 with just 15 students. As the city's population grew, more high schools were added, until in 1931 the school's name was officially changed to Miami Senior High School. However, despite the "official" name change the school and its teams have always been referred to in the local newspapers, and virtually everywhere else, as "Miami High School" or "MHS".

In fact, if you were to try finding the school on the MaxPreps website by using the name "Miami Senior High" you will get the response "no schools match your search criteria." Therefore, in keeping with this long-standing tradition, in this book the school will also be referred to as Miami High School, along with the team's most-unique nickname, the "Stingarees".

While Miami High opened in 1903 it did not field its first football team until 1911. That somewhat informal aggregation played one game that year and again in 1912. Both games were played on Thanksgiving Day on the grounds of the Royal Palm Hotel against a team of militiamen known as the Miami Military Athletic Association. Not too surprisingly, the high school boys lost both games, the first 10-3 and the second 12-0.

The school did not field another team for almost the next decade, but on December 3, 1921, the boys from Miami High met and defeated a team representing the local American Legion Post by a score of 12-6. In a rematch on January 2, 1922, the high schoolers again got the better of the legionnaires, 6 to 0. In the fall of 1922, Miami High played what can be considered its first regular schedule of games, against mostly local high schools and one church team. The boys won their first six games handily, five by shutout. They closed out the season playing the team from Gainesville High School in a game designated as having been for the state championship. Apparently the Miami team was playing well out of its league in this one as Gainesville, described by the Miami yearbook as "a veteran team long on experience," handed Miami High a 58-0 thumping.

Over the balance of that decade the Stingarees played winning football, but not championship football, until 1929. That season, against a schedule of exclusively Florida teams, MHS went 8-0-1 in its first nine games. The Stingarees then defeated both Charlotte (N.C.) High School, 12-7, and Salem (Mass.) High School,

7-6, to earn the title of Eastern United States Champion, but somehow the designation of Florida state champion eluded them.

During the decade of the 1930s, the Great Depression forced virtually every school in the country to make cutbacks. However, this was apparently not the case at Miami High for the Stingarees football team, especially in regard to its travel budget. And the Depression definitely did not adversely affect the team's on-field performance.

In 1930 the Stingarees played a schedule entirely composed of Florida teams, defeating all 10 of the high school teams, but dropping a 12-0 decision to the University of Miami freshman squad. Although the Stingarees won the Big 12 Conference championship, there is no mention of them being named state champion. Again in 1931, the Stingarees went undefeated against Florida high school opponents, posting a record of 8-0-2 and this time being named Florida's state champion—a title they would pretty much own throughout the balance of the decade and well beyond. At the end of the season the team accepted the challenge of Chicago's Harrison Tech for a postseason game, which Tech won by an 18-7 count. It was Miami High's first loss in 32 games against high school opponents. (In some circles it is believed that this game was played for the national championship; but, because Ashland (Ky.) High School is the recognized title holder for 1931 that was apparently not the case.)

That game with Harrison Tech appears to have set in motion at Miami High a desire to play interstate and intersectional games. In fact, for the balance of the decade, 1932-1939, under the direction of head coach Jesse "Mule" Yarborough, fully 65% of the Stingarees' games would be against opponents from outside of Florida. For most of that period the team played seven to nine out of state opponents each season, which made for an interesting situation when it came to deciding the Florida state champion.

Taking on a large slate of out of state opponents was at first not a successful venture for the Stingarees. In 1932 the team finished with a record of 8-3-0 and defeated Palmetto High, 13-0, for the Florida championship. However, in four games against non-Florida teams, Miami lost three times, including a 13-7 defeat at the hands of Toledo Waite in that year's national championship game.

Miami High had indeed picked a tough row to hoe by venturing outside of Florida, but in the long run it served to enhance the team's reputation, not only in its home state, but throughout the country. Playing teams from all over the eastern half of the nation, and even venturing west of the Mississippi River on a couple of occasions, the Stingarees won 67% of their interstate contests from 1933-1939. In addition they were named Florida state champion in six of those seven years and the Southern champion in 1939. In fact, so great had the team's reputation become in Florida that in 1936, with a record of only 5-5, the Stingarees were named state champion after having gone undefeated against the only two Florida teams on their schedule.

As good as the Stingarees had become, however, the first half of the 1940s would prove to be something of a "golden era" for Miami High football.

Coach Yarborough's defending state and Southern champions opened the 1940 season with victories over a pair of Florida opponents before knocking off the team from Savannah (Ga.) High School, 13-0. After rolling over Andrew Jackson High of Jacksonville, Fla., 26-6, the Stingarees cruised past a trio of teams from Alabama, Georgia and South Carolina. Thanksgiving Day produced a 28-7 victory over Edison High School of Miami, raising the Stingarees' record to 8-0-0.

Miami High finished the campaign with games against a couple of out of state teams. The always formidable Boys High of Atlanta put a halt to Miami's winning ways when it handed the Stingarees a 13-0 thumping. Miami High then closed out the season with a game against Fenger High School of Chicago, the Stingarees ending the season on an up note with a 19-0 win. With a final record of 9-1-0 and undefeated against Florida foes, the Stingarees were named Florida's state champion for 1940.

That last game victory over Fenger High would be just the first in what would become the longest undefeated streak in Miami High School football history.

Jesse Yarborough's Miami Stingarees rolled through the first eight games of the 1941 season like few Miami High teams had ever done before. Defeating teams from Florida, Georgia, North Carolina, and Virginia, the Stings averaged just under 38 points per game while allowing a total of just 13, posting six shutouts. On Thanksgiving Day, the Stingarees played their traditional game with Edison High. Although the Stingarees had won every game in the series that had started in 1925, it was never an easy go for them and this edition of the rivalry was no different. Edison scored 13 points to equal what Miami had allowed all season, and held the Stingarees to their lowest point total of the year. However, it was not enough to upset Miami's applecart as the Stingarees came from behind and scored 14 points in the game's final two minutes to come away with a 26-13 victory.

For the third straight season the week after Thanksgiving found the Stingarees playing Boys High of Atlanta. Like many championship caliber teams, Miami High was not averse to playing good opponents and Boys High was a perfect example. Like the Stingarees, Boys High had been enjoying great success throughout the decade of the 1930s. Under head coach R. L. "Shorty" Doyal, the Purple Hurricanes had won five Georgia state championships since 1932. Since the beginning of the 1939 season Boys High had won 31 games, lost just once, and played three ties—and that one loss had been to Miami High.

To nobody's surprise it was a great game as the Stingarees and the Purple Hurricanes battled up and down the field. Both teams managed to score a single

touchdown and both teams converted the extra point—final score, 7-7. Boys High, its season now over, finished with a record of 11-0-2 and its third consecutive Georgia state title, sixth overall.

Miami High still had one more game to play and it was against another powerful opponent. Baltimore City College High School of Maryland was on a streak like few schools have ever even approached. Since 1934 the Knights had gone 54 consecutive games without a loss under head coach Harry Lawrence, winning four Maryland state championships in the process.

This game was played in mid-December in Miami's Orange Bowl. (Miami High had been playing on the site of the Orange Bowl since around 1936, first under the stadium's original name of Roddy Burdine Stadium and then, after the stadium was expanded, as the Orange Bowl when it was renamed shortly after World War II.) It is said that the temperature that day hit 90 degrees, which may have been a little too warm for the boys from up north. Be that as it may, the Stingarees defeated the Knights 26 to 0, finishing the season at 10-0-1 and winning another Florida state championship.

▴ *Miami High's great running back Arnold Tucker flies through an opening made by his offensive line during the 1942 season. (Miami High School Yearbook)*

As we have seen with men like Paul Brown of Massillon and Wright Bazemore of Valdosta, Miami's Jesse Yarborough left the team after the '41 season to do his bit for the war effort, eventually rising to the rank of major in the U.S. Army Air Corps. Taking over direction of the Stingarees for the 1942 season would be J. Lyles Alley, who had been the head basketball coach and an assistant football coach at the school since September of 1940. Coach Alley had a senior-laden team led by quarterback Arnold Tucker and All-Southern halfback Bruce Smith, who played behind a veteran, all-senior line.

Despite wartime restrictions on travel and the rationing of items such as gasoline and rubber tires, there would be little change in the make up of the Stingarees football schedule during the war. During the seasons of 1942 thru 1944, Miami High played 14 of its 27 games against teams from outside of Florida.

The Stingarees' 1942 campaign opened on Saturday, September 26, with a game in the Orange Bowl against Miami's Andrew Jackson High. It was the first game in 10 years in which Jesse Yarborough was not pacing the sidelines for Miami. Not to worry as Lyles Alley's Stingarees began the season by scoring in every quarter en route to a 25-6 victory. The only downer may have been the job done by the Miami pass defense, which allowed eight receptions for 124 yards and all eight Jackson first downs—definitely something to work on at practice.

On Saturday, October 3, the Stingarees took on the Generals of Robert E. Lee High School from Jacksonville. As they had done the previous week, Miami's tandem of quarterback Arnold Tucker (two touchdowns) and halfback Bruce Smith (155 yards passing, one touchdown scored) led the assault as the Stingarees came away with a 19-7 victory.

The following Saturday, October 10, found the Stingarees traveling to Petersburg, Virginia, to play that city's high school. The previous season Miami had taken the measure of Petersburg, 40-0, in the Orange Bowl, but this was a different Golden Wave team that was now playing in front of 6,000 hometown fans. The Petersburg team made a game of it and hung with the Stingarees throughout the contest; but, despite losing the battle of the statistics, the Stingarees returned to Florida on the long end of a 13-7 score.

With their record now 3-0-0, the Stingarees played the balance of their schedule in the friendly confines of the Orange Bowl. However, due to an open week and a pair of cancellations, it would take six weeks for MHS to get in its next three games.

On Saturday, October 17, the Stingarees squared off against the Blue Jackets of Savannah (Ga.) High School. Coach Alley cleared his bench and the defense came up with five pass interceptions to help keep the Blue Jackets off the scoreboard as MHS came away with a 58-0 win.

After an open week, the Stings played the Knoxville (Tenn.) Trojans on Friday, October 30. The Trojans were one of the best teams in Tennessee that season,

▲ The "Sophomore Flash" as he was known around Miami High, halfback Pete Williams, was a major factor in the Stingarees' gridiron success not only in 1942, but the following two seasons as well. (Miami High School Yearbook)

▸ Next page: Arnold Tucker was perhaps the greatest football player to ever play for the Stingarees. A triple-threat man and a member of the College Football Hall of Fame, Tucker played on the national champion 1942 Miami High team, then topped that by starring on three national championship teams—1944-45-46—at West Point. (Miami High School Yearbook)

coming to Miami boasting a perfect 8-0-0 record and having outscored the opposition 246-33. Despite falling behind 7-0 very early in the first quarter as a result of its own fumble, Miami literally ran all over the Trojans to the tune of 326 yards rushing. Arnold Tucker led the Miami assault with four touchdowns, including one on an 89-yard run, as the Stingarees delighted their home town fans with a 43-19 victory over the Knoxville team that would be declared the 1942 Tennessee state champion.

The Stingarees would have to wait another three weeks to play their next contest as games scheduled with Lanier High of Macon, Ga., and with Memphis (Tenn.) Tech were cancelled. Finally, on Thursday, November 18, the Stingarees once again took to the gridiron, this time against Ensley High School of Birmingham, Ala.

The *Miami Herald's* report that "Ensley High of Birmingham ... put on the best aerial show of the season at the Orange Bowl Thursday afternoon" might lead one to believe that the Stingarees had been in for a long night, but such was not the case. Despite an aerial attack that completed 18 of 35 passes for 153 yards, all of that passing failed to generate a single point for the Yellow Jackets. The Miami defense intercepted four of those aerials, and recovered a pair of fumbles, to more than keep the Ensley offense in check. Led by Arnold Tucker's three touchdowns, including an 88-yard return of the second half kickoff, the Stings cruised to a 57-7 victory.

On Wednesday, November 25, a crowd numbered at 13,119 was on hand at the Orange Bowl for the annual Miami High-Edison High Turkey Day battle. With 420 total yards of offense, the Stingarees easily maintained their dominance over the Red Raiders with a 40-6 triumph.

Saturday, December 5, had the Stingarees lined up opposite Atlanta's Boys High (8-2-0) in the Orange Bowl before another large crowd—more than 10,000 fans. This was currently one of the hottest interstate rivalries in the country, with Miami winning four of the previous nine games, the Boys High Purple Hurricanes winning three and two contests ending in ties.

Pacing the sidelines for the Stingarees would be a different, but most familiar, face. Taking over the coaching duties at Miami High for the last two games of the 1942 season would be Lt. Jesse Yarborough, USAAC. Yarborough had been granted a special leave from his Air Corps duties to coach the Stingarees since Lyles Alley had gone on active duty with the U.S. Navy with the rank of lieutenant (j.g.).

It was a typical Miami High-Boys High game, one of the more exciting games of the season, hard fought and close until the end. However, led by the tandem of Arnold Tucker and Bruce Smith, who scored two touchdowns apiece, the Stingarees recorded their 20th consecutive victory by a score of 31 to 20.

The season came to an end for Miami High on Saturday, December 12, with a game against Lee H. Edwards High School of Asheville, N.C. At the time the Maroons of head coach Ralph James were recognized as perhaps the best team in the South. In 1941 they had finished the season with a record of 11-1-0, losing only to Boys High; the Maroons were ranked as the second-best team in the nation that year, second only to Chicago's Leo High School, the first parochial team to ever be named as national champion.

The Edwards High Maroons were right back at it in 1942, entering their game against Miami with a record of 9-0-0 and having outscored their opponents 441-6. The Maroons were led by one of the greatest high school and college football players of all-time, Charlie "Choo Choo" Justice, a future college football Hall of Famer. Justice was a true triple-threat man who was averaging an incredible 18.63 yards every time he carried the ball that season. Justice ran behind a line that averaged 191 lbs. per man, giving them an average 21 lbs. per man advantage over the Stingarees.

While this game is not recognized as having been played for the national championship, for all practical purposes that is exactly what it was. Unfortunately, the field conditions were not what one would like for such an important game, rain having turned the Orange Bowl surface into muddy turf. The inclement weather no doubt also kept the crowd down to a somewhat meager 5,401 spectators (and limited the teams to a total of just six forward passes).

For the last time in his high school career, it would fall to Miami's Arnold Tucker to be the hero of the game. Late in the first quarter and again with just five minutes left to play, after finding his receivers covered, Tucker scrambled into the end zone for the touchdowns that gave Miami a 13-7 win.

▲ *The 1942 Miami High*
Stingarees—National Champions.
(Miami High School Yearbook)

That win over Edwards High gave the Stingarees victories over teams from six different states. Already the Florida champion, Miami High was also named the Southern champion and, for the first time in its history, the national champion for 1942.

Arnold Tucker, who led the 1942 Stingarees with 20 touchdowns and 122 points, was perhaps the best athlete to ever attend Miami High. He played all four years on the football team, as well as playing basketball and running track. After graduation he went on to West Point, where in 1946 he not only earned All-America recognition playing in the same backfield with the legendary Doc Blanchard and Glenn Davis, but he also won the Sullivan Award as the country's top amateur athlete.

Because of the war there were many changes to American life, like the previously mentioned rationing. Some changes were not quite that dramatic, but nonetheless affected certain groups of people. One example of these less dramatic changes is that there would be no designated high school football national champion for the years 1944 and 1945; not the greatest sacrifice in the world for sure, but definitely a change from the norm. There could be any one of several reasons for this. For example, as we have seen numerous coaches, among them many of the country's best, had joined the military; and many players, even at the high school level, had also enlisted in the armed forces; and some schools had simply stopped playing the sport until after the war.

But 1944 and 1945 were still a little ways down the road. The Stingarees had been named the national champion for 1942; now the question was "Could they defend that title?" during the '43 season. Defending any championship is never easy under the best of circumstances, but the Stingarees would have to do it without many of their best players from the '42 team. Both Arnold

DEFENDING ANY CHAMPIONSHIP IS NEVER EASY UNDER THE BEST OF CIRCUMSTANCES, BUT THE STINGAREES WOULD HAVE TO DO IT WITHOUT MANY OF THEIR BEST PLAYERS FROM THE '42 TEAM.

Tucker and Bruce Smith and all but one starting lineman were members of the Class of 1943 and had graduated that June.

Also, for the third year in a row the Stingarees would be playing for a new head coach. Lyles Alley was, as mentioned, in the Navy and Jesse Yarborough was back with the Army Air Corps. Taking over as head coach at Miami High School would be Tom Moorer, a former Clemson star who had coached the last two seasons at Griffin High School in Georgia. In those two seasons Griffin had achieved a record of 15-4-1, with a splendid 10-1-0 in 1942, the team's best mark in 44 years of interscholastic football. Moorer's offense at Miami would employ the single wing, a major change from the short punt formation offense of his two predecessors.

Miami High's '43 season opened on Friday, September 24, in the Orange Bowl against Miami's Andrew Jackson High. The Stingarees took a 6-0 lead less than four minutes into the game and it looked as if the team might not be as green as first thought. However, those would be the only points of the game until the Stingarees scored another touchdown early in the fourth quarter to give Miami High a 13-0 opening day victory.

With no games scheduled for the intervening two weeks, the Stingarees next took to the gridiron on Friday, October 15, traveling north to Tallahassee to play the undefeated Lions of Leon High School. After Miami had fallen behind 7-6 in the first quarter, a 95-yard punt return by halfback Pete Williams on the first play of the second period put the Stingarees ahead to stay. Miami added a second quarter safety and an insurance touchdown in the fourth quarter to go back to Miami with a 20-7 victory.

On Thursday, October 21, the Stingarees were in West Palm Beach to play the West Palm Wildcats. Miami led 7-0 at the half before turning it into a romp with five touchdowns in the fourth quarter as the Stingarees came away with a 46-0 victory.

Returning to the Orange Bowl for the first time since their opening game, the Stingarees were scheduled to play what the *Miami Herald* called "the No. 1 prep football game of the state with the Florida championship hanging on the outcome ...." The Stingarees opponent that Thursday, October 28, would be the undefeated Generals from Robert E. Lee High School of Jacksonville. Lee High was the last Florida team to defeat the Stings back in 1938, and the Generals were now favored to defeat the defending state and national champion.

The starting offense for the 1943 Miami High Stingarees. (Miami High School Yearbook)

Before more than 12,000 fans, Miami took advantage of a poor Lee High punt and the interception of a Lee aerial to take a 12-0 lead at the halftime break. A Miami fumble midway through the third quarter allowed the Lions to make it a 12-7 game. It would take a successful goal line stand by Miami on the game's final play to preserve the 12-7 victory for the Stingarees.

The first Saturday of November presented MHS with something of a breather as they defeated Miami's Andrew Jackson High, 39-6, but that relatively easy game would prove to be the exception rather than the norm over the balance of the season.

On Friday, November 12, the Stingarees played host to the team from Columbus (Ga.) High School at the Orange Bowl. Fumbles by the Stingarees on their first two possessions put them into a quick 6-0 hole, but after that shaky start things began to settle down for Miami and by the intermission MHS had taken a 12-6 lead. The two teams traded second half scores as the Stingarees held on for an 18-12 victory.

November 25—the day after Thanksgiving—another game with the Edison Red Raiders—another big crowd, 21,067—another Miami victory, this year by a 25-12 score.

On Friday night, December 3, the Stingarees played Boys High of Atlanta in the Orange Bowl, a game that was billed as being for the Southern prep championship. Boys High was almost unbeatable from 1939-1945, posting a record of 70-6-4. Thus far during the season the Purple Hurricanes were undefeated in 10 games, outscoring the opposition 289-6. They had already been declared the Georgia Interscholastic Athletic Association champion for 1943, the team's seventh title in the last 11 years. According to the *Miami Herald*, Boys High had "an acknowledged

▼ *The 1943 Miami High National Champion team. (Miami High School Yearbook)*

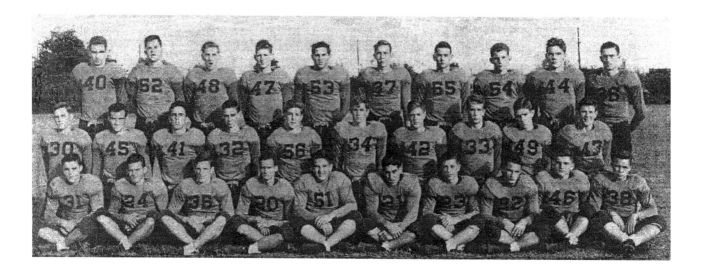

All the Way to #1

Stingarees halfback Jerry Newcomer comes up with a big gain and a first down against Coral Gables during the 1960 season. (Miami High School Yearbook)

edge in speed and experience, and have been made a slight pre-game favorite" over the Stingarees.

With the top teams in Georgia and Florida facing off against each other, game tickets were in high demand as an overflow crowd of just over 24,000 jammed the Orange Bowl to witness the action. Miami scored twice in the first quarter and once in the second to settle the issue early. The Stingarees' 27-7 victory gave them the Southern prep title, but the Stingarees still had one game to play.

On December 10, Miami High lined up for the second week in a row against the champion of a neighboring statve. Charlotte Central High was the North Carolina State Class AA (big school) champion, but that mattered little to the Stingarees. An Orange Bowl crowd of 14,283 looked on as the Stingarees totally dominated the champions of the Tar Heel state, 45-0.

The victory over Charlotte Central was the 30th consecutive game without a loss for Miami High, and the 41st victory in its last 42 games. The team had now won eight consecutive Florida state championships and, more importantly, had successfully defended its national title.

In 1944 Miami High slipped to 7-2-0, losing the third game of the season to Atlanta's Boys High, 20-0, a defeat that halted the Stingarees win streak at 32 in a row. Ironically, the Purple Hurricanes had also been the last team to defeat the Stingarees before they went on their long winning streak. Despite those two defeats Miami High was again named the Florida champion for a ninth consecutive season. In 1945 Miami High finished 7-1-1, but saw its run of state championships come to an end.

In the decade and a half following World War II, 1946-1959, Miami High continued to field very good football teams. The Stingarees averaged just over seven wins and fewer than two defeats per season, with an outstanding winning percentage of .784. In those 14 seasons they were also named state champion seven more times. However, if the early part of the 1940s is considered the first "golden era" of Stingarees football, then the early 1960s was the team's second "golden era".

The Stingarees of head coach Ottis Mooney, who had been guiding the Miami High football fortunes since 1956, opened the 1960 season with a trio of lopsided victories, games in which Miami averaged 36 points per game while yielding a total of just seven. The Stingarees' fourth game, played on Thursday, October 6, was against Jacksonville's Robert E. Lee High School. The Generals were then ranked second in the state, but proved to be of little difficulty to the top ranked Stingarees who again came away with a big victory, 28-6.

On Saturday, October 15, Miami High played the Benedictine Military School of Savannah, Ga., the Stings' first game against a non-Florida team in four years. It proved to be the Stingarees' toughest game of the season thus far, at least as far as

▲ *Miami quarterback Jim Angel gets the pass off...*

scoring points was concerned. However, with the Miami defense pitching its third shutout of the season (and holding Benedictine to minus-three yards rushing), 14 points from the Miami offense was more than enough to ensure another MHS win.

The following Thursday the Stingarees faced off against North Miami High in the Orange Bowl before more than 6,500 fans. Three North Miami fumbles led to a pair of Stingarees' first half touchdowns and a 13-0 lead at the intermission. Miami High opened the second half with two more touchdowns within the first two and a half minutes of the third quarter to put the game away. The Stingarees' 26-7 victory solidified their hold on the top spot in state, a position they had held since the first week of the season.

It was not supposed to be a difficult game for Miami High when the undefeated Stingarees met the Lakeland Dreadnaughts (3-2-0) on Friday, October 28, but each time the Stingarees scored, the Dreadnaughts came right back with a touchdown of their own. Both teams punched across four touchdowns and both missed a crucial extra point. The *Miami Herald* called it the "season's prep shocker" when the game ended in a 27-27 tie.

The Stingarees had two weeks to get over the let down of the tie with Lakeland and to get ready for an even more formidable foe. Also located in Miami, and less than five miles away, was Coral Gables High School. After a sub par 3-4-1 1959 season, one in which they had been beaten by Miami 40-7, the Cavaliers (6-1-0) were

... and end Dick Emerson makes the catch for a Miami High touchdown during the 1960 season. (Miami High School Yearbook)

on the rebound in 1960 and were now the # 2 ranked team in Florida—behind # 1 Miami High. In one of the most exciting games of the season, witnessed by 15,589 at the Orange Bowl, the Stingarees and the Cavaliers played a well-executed game that saw only one turnover and just 15 yards in penalties by each team. Reminiscent of the Lakeland game two weeks before, both teams scored a pair of touchdowns and both missed an extra point kick, the game ending in a 13-13 tie.

Because of all of the work and effort that their respective teams had put into the preparation for and the actual playing of this game, both coaches were upset with the result. Miami's Ottis Mooney probably spoke for both coaches when he told the *Miami Herald*, "We played our hearts out. You can't ask for more. Except maybe a game that doesn't end in a tie."

After two grueling games, the Stingarees now had two weeks off to prepare for their annual Thanksgiving Day game with Edison High, in which Miami High was as much as a 21-point favorite. However, Edison had won its last four games after dropping three of its first four; and this was a rivalry game, so anything could happen. And anything did when the Red Raiders jumped to an early 7-0 lead. Late in the second quarter, the Stingarees bounced back to tie the game at 7-7. In a game that was dominated by defense, Miami finally broke the deadlock with a touchdown late in the fourth quarter to come away with a 14-7 victory.

▲ *Stingarees halfback*
Butch Poe battles a couple of
Brockton (Mass.) defenders
and makes the catch for a
touchdown in the annual
Miami FOP Charity Classic
on Dec. 9, 1960. (Miami
High School Yearbook)

With their record now at 7-0-2, the Stingarees played their final game of the season on Friday, December 9, against Brockton (Mass.) High School in the annual Fraternal Order of Police Charity Classic postseason game in the Orange Bowl. Brockton came to Miami with a perfect 9-0-0 record and undefeated in its last three seasons, 23 contests in all. The Shoemakers were a powerhouse team that featured seven All-State selections in their line-up and outweighed the Stingarees by an average of 20 lbs. per man. Unlike Miami, which was strictly a two-platoon team, all but three of head coach Chester Millett's Brockton starters played both offense and defense.

Just under 8,900 fans were on hand for the 8:15 P.M. kickoff. After a scoreless first quarter, Brockton was first to get on the scoreboard with a touchdown in the second period that gave the Shoemakers a 7-0 lead at the intermission. Brockton added another touchdown in the third quarter and as the game entered the final 12 minutes the Stingarees had yet to score, trailing 13 to 0.

The Stingarees had been hurting themselves the whole game, having suffered three interceptions and a pair of lost fumbles, but the Miami offense finally started to click early in the final frame. After successfully converting a fourth and 10 from the Brockton 16-yard line, the hometown team got its first points to cut the Brockton lead to 13-7 with 8:54 left on the game clock.

Following the ensuing kickoff, Miami held Brockton to a three and out, going back on offense at its own 39-yard line following the Brockton punt. Using a 15-play drive, the Stingarees marched right down the field for the game tying touchdown. The Stingarees were then forced to try for the extra point without their placekicker, who had suffered a back injury early in the game. The Stingarees run for the extra point was successful to give them a 14-13 lead with 2:01 left on the game clock. The Stingarees defense did the rest to enable Miami High to come away with an exciting come from behind 14-13 victory.

▲ *Ottis Mooney was the head coach at Miami High School from 1957-1962, leading the team to national championships in both 1960 and 1962. (Miami High School Yearbook)*

▲ *1962 Miami High quarterback Tom Tarbert shows here that he could pick up yardage on the ground when necessary. (Miami High School Yearbook)*

The Stingarees finished the 1960 season with a record of 8-0-2, were again named state champion and, despite the two ties, the National Sports News Service (NSNS) picked Miami High as the best team in the nation.

Miami High had another good season in 1961, finishing with a record of 8-1-1 and being named the Florida state champion for the second consecutive time.

Head coach Ottis Mooney's Miami High Stingarees opened the 1962 campaign in fine style on Friday night, September 14, by downing the Eagles of Southwest High by 34-7. The Stingarees' offense appeared to be in mid-season form as Miami gained 336 yards on the ground. The defense was also humming along, limiting the Eagles to just 75 yards of total offense and coming up with four turnovers.

Miami High, already Florida's top ranked team this early in the season, was a 26-point favorite over Miami Jackson the following week; but, as Miami head coach Ottis Mooney would say after the game, "Things get equal real fast when you play in a sea of mud and rain." Torrential rain before, after and especially during the game turned the Orange Bowl into a quagmire that hampered the play of both teams. After slogging through the muck and mud for four quarters, each team had managed to score just six points, the game ending in a surprising 6-6 deadlock.

With no game scheduled the following week, the Stingarees next took the field at the Orange Bowl on Saturday night, October 6, against Lee High School of Jacksonville. The Miami defense played another fine game in limiting the Generals to 101 total yards and only three first downs, but the Miami offense was still not clicking like it should. With just eight seconds left in the second quarter, the Stingarees broke open a scoreless game by finally hitting pay dirt to take a 6-0 lead at the half. Miami added an insurance score late in the fourth quarter for a 12-0 victory. The loss was Lee High's first of the season and marked the sixth consecutive season in which the Generals had suffered their first loss at the hands of the Stingarees.

The Stingarees traveled to Tallahassee the following week to take on Leon High. Three Leon fumbles were turned into early Miami touchdowns and catapulted the Stings to a 26-0 halftime advantage, en route to a 32-7 victory.

Returning home to the Orange Bowl on Friday night, October 18, Miami High had its hands full against the North Miami Pioneers. After a scoreless first quarter, North Miami shocked the Stingarees in the second period by marching 92 yards to take a 7-0 lead. Miami High took the ensuing kickoff and promptly marched 65 yards to answer the Pioneers' score with one of its own; however, the extra point

▲ Stingarees running back Jim Finnell leaves defenders floundering in his wake as he races into the end zone during the 1962 season. (Miami High School Yearbook)

▲ Stingarees defensive back Pat Kelly goes airborne to break up this pass against Leon High of Tallahassee during the 1962 campaign. (Miami High School Yearbook)

try failed, leaving the Stingarees down by a point, 7-6, at the intermission. After a scoreless third quarter the Stingarees took the lead in the fourth, Miami High holding on for a 13-7 victory.

A 21-point first quarter outburst by Miami the following week against Jacksonville's Andrew Jackson High propelled the Stingarees to a 34-7 win and prepped the Stingarees for their final three contests of the season.

Miami High squared off against the Cavaliers of Coral Gables High, one of the best football teams in Florida at this time, on Saturday, November 1. The *Miami Herald* described the weather as "crisp wintry air"—but how crisp could the wintry air have been in Miami?

After a scoreless opening session, the Stingarees used a pair of second quarter pass interceptions to not only stymie the Cavaliers, but to also get on the scoreboard with the only points of the first half. Miami added single scores in both the third and fourth quarters to offset a late touchdown by the Cavaliers as the Stingarees came away with a 19-7 victory.

With their record a now very fine 6-0-1, the Stingarees were ready for their annual Thanksgiving game with the Red Raiders of Edison High. One of the oldest rivalries in Florida, this was the 41st meeting in a series that had been continuous since 1925 (in 1925, 1928, and 1938 the teams had met twice). In 1962 the two teams were about as statistically even as they could be. Miami High was ranked # 1 in Florida and Edison (7-1-0) was ranked # 2; the two teams were only 98 yards apart in total offense, while on defense they had limited their respective opponents to about 150 yards of offense per game. Scoring totals both for and against each team were virtually identical.

Although it was one of the most lopsided of rivalries as far as total wins and losses go, Miami High holding a 35-3 "edge" with two games ending in ties, it was still considered one of the premier games every season. This season in particular there was a lot riding on this one game for the winner: the city and state championships were both up for grabs, as well as an invitation to play in the FOP postseason Charity Classic in the Orange Bowl. Put it all together and it is not surprising that more than 31,000 Miami area high school football fans showed up at the Orange Bowl for the 8:15 P.M. kickoff that Thanksgiving night.

Just three minutes into the game, the Stingarees turned an interception into a touchdown and a 7-0 lead. After fumbling away a couple of potential scoring opportunities the Stingarees put it all together again late in the second quarter, quickly going 74 yards in just six plays for a touchdown that increased their lead to 14-0. With its defense continuing to shut out the Edison Red Raiders, the Stingarees added a final TD in the fourth quarter. Miami High's 21-0 victory ensured the Stingarees of the city title and yet another Florida state championship.

All that remained now for the Stingarees was to play in the postseason FOP Charity Classic on Friday night, December 7. From a field of 15 possible opponents emerged four finalists: undefeated Boston English, the oldest public high school in the country; undefeated, but once tied, Everett (Mass.) High School; Gulfport (Miss.) High School, 8-1-1; and Baltimore Polytechnic Institute, 9-0-0, Maryland's 1962 state champion.

On Saturday morning, November 24, the announcement was made that Baltimore Poly would be facing Miami High in the Charity Classic. This was a game that would also have an effect on the national championship because both teams were highly placed by the pollsters that rated the high school elevens—Miami ranked as high as sixth in the country and Baltimore Poly topping out at seventh. Both the National Sports News Service and the Imperial Sports Syndicate would be watching this game closely as they made their final decisions as to which team would emerge as their respective choice for the nation's top high school gridiron eleven.

Unfortunately for the Stingarees, they would have to play the Polytechnic Engineers without the services of one of their best players. Quarterback Tom Tarbert injured his knee during prac-

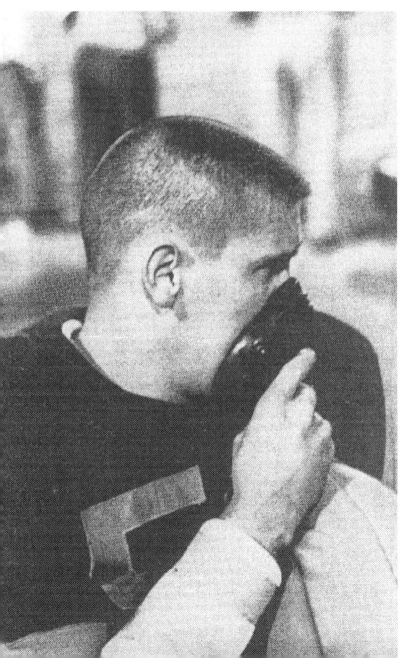

▼ *Even in the fall it can get hot and humid in Miami, so the Stingarees' Ed Bell is getting some extra aid with a dose of oxygen. (Miami High School Yearbook)*

▲ *Bob Carlton took the Miami High Stingarees to the 1965 national championship in his first year as head coach. (Miami High School Yearbook)*

tice the week before the game and would be unable to take the field. Taking over for Tarbert as the Miami signal caller was back-up Dave Thomas, who had played exactly one quarter at that position the entire season. Thomas had only three days in which to prepare for the biggest game of his high school career.

Before an Orange Bowl crowd of 9,617 and a Baltimore regional television audience of about a half-million, the Poly Engineers struck swiftly. On the game's second play from scrimmage, Baltimore halfback Ernie Torain raced around his right end 78 yards for a Baltimore Poly touchdown. The extra point gave the visitors a shockingly quick 7-0 lead. Just before the intermission Miami was able to finally score a touchdown of its own, but the extra point try failed, leaving the Stingarees down by a point, 7-6, at the intermission.

At 9:26 of the third quarter the Stingarees gained possession of the ball at their 23-yard line. In a drive that was the definition of ball control, Miami marched 77 yards in 20 plays, using up nine minutes and two seconds of the clock before scoring the go-ahead touchdown. The successful extra point try put the Stingarees out in front, 13-7, with just 24 seconds left in the third quarter.

Following the ensuing kickoff Baltimore Poly moved the ball out to its 35-yard line, but there they were forced to punt. The snap from center went sailing over the punter's head and was recovered by the Stingarees all the way back at the Baltimore 16-yard line. On their first two plays the Stings were tossed back a total of 10 yards to the Baltimore 26-yard line, but on third down a 26-yard touchdown pass gave Miami another six points. The Miami defense did the rest in keeping Baltimore Poly at bay and Miami went on to win the game, 19-7.

After the game Baltimore Poly head coach Bob Lumsden told reporters, "... Miami High (has) the best football machine we have played in five years. They specialize in the fundamentals of winning football ... running, tackling and blocking with great skill. Then they throw their superb speed at you—and dare you to beat them."

Meanwhile, as the *Miami Herald* reported, "on the other side of the field proud Miami High students were chanting: 'We beat Poly...we're national champions.'" And they were. In a double split decision, the National Sports News Service named the Wildcats of Georgia's Valdosta High as its top team. Meanwhile, the Imperial Sports Syndicate named co-champions for 1962, the Stingarees of Miami High and the Wildcats of San Francisco's St. Ignatius High School.

Following the '62 season, head coach Ottis Mooney left Miami High School to accept a coaching position on the staff of the University of Florida. In his seven seasons at Miami High, Mooney had compiled a record of 54-6-8, .853, while leading the Stingarees to five Florida championships and two national titles.

Taking over as the new Miami High head football coach was Harold Sawyers, who had been an assistant coach there for the past eight years. The competition in the Miami area was heating up, as Sawyers found out in his two seasons as the Stingarees mentor. In that time Sawyers's teams went 5-3-0 and 8-3-0, losing twice to new area powerhouse Coral Gables and once to Edison.

After the 1964 season, Sawyers, like Ottis Mooney before him, moved on to the college ranks, becoming an assistant coach at the University of Miami. Taking Sawyers's place as the new Miami High head coach was Bobby Carlton, who had been a star lineman for the Stingarees during the early 1950s. In something of a departure from the past, where the Stingarees tended to favor power football between the tackles, Coach Carlton used a lot of ball movement in his offensive scheme. Now the Stingarees would be throwing the ball much more often than past teams, even on first down, and running outside via the pitchout. On defense the Stingarees added a blitz package to their attack.

The Stingarees' first game of the '65 season was played in the Orange Bowl on Wednesday, September 15, against the Eagles of Southwest High School. Coach Carlton's new look offense and defense resulted in a 20-0 opening day victory for Miami; the new offensive schemes generated 135 yards through the air, the most passing yardage in a game by a Miami High team in the last three seasons. But the team's new offense was not without a few early problems. All of Miami's points were scored in the first half, the team's second half performance marred by numerous turnovers, totaling five for the game. It would take a few weeks for the Stingarees to work out the kinks.

No doubt to Coach Carlton's great dismay, it seemed to be taking a little longer than he had planned for the Miami High team to settle into his new systems, and it almost proved costly in the Stingarees' very next game against Miami Jackson on September 23. As the *Miami Herald* reported, "As late as 15 minutes into the first half Thursday night, Miami High was so confused it lined up on the wrong side of the Orange Bowl for a Jackson kickoff."

At this point of the game, less than three minutes into the second quarter, the state's second-ranked Stingarees already trailed 13-0 and were not looking good at all. Both Jackson touchdowns had come as the result of Miami fumbles, the second coming off of an errant pitchout that Jackson returned 78 yards for a touchdown. But as the *Miami Herald* also noted, "When officials waved MHS to the other

▾ *Miami's All-City cornerback Carlos Arocha stops this Southeast Eagle running back dead in his tracks during this 1965 game. (Miami High School Yearbook)*

▸ *This bone jarring tackle by Miami's George Mekras prevented this Jackson High receiver from making the catch during the 1965 Miami-Jackson game. (Miami High School Yearbook)*

▾ *Miami's Al Consuegra batters the North Miami defense for some tough yards during the Stingarees 21-0 win in 1965. (Miami High School Yearbook)*

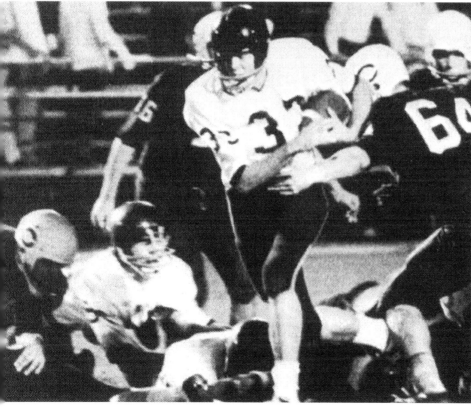

◄ *Miami High running back Gabe Michelena leaves a trail of Fort Lauderdale defenders in his wake during the Stingarees' 35-0 victory in*

▼ *Miami fullback Dave Hardy breaks through the Columbus High defense for good yardage during the Stingarees' 44-0 win in 1965. (Miami High School Yearbook)*

side of the field (for the ensuing kickoff), they also may have awakened the state's No. 2 team."

Once that kickoff was made, the Miami offense proceeded to score a pair of touchdowns in just under three minutes, going into their locker room at the half with some new-found momentum and the game now tied at 13-13. That momentum continued into the second half, which belonged to Miami. After turning the ball over five times in the first two quarters, the Stingarees only coughed it up once in the second half while adding 13 more points. The defense held Jackson to 77 total yards for the game and completely slammed the door on the Generals over the game's final two quarters as the Stingarees came away with a 26-13 victory.

On Friday, October 1, the Stingarees traveled to Fort Lauderdale to play the Flying Ls of Fort Lauderdale High School before more than 6,000 fans. This time it was the Stingarees who were able to take advantage of turnovers as they recovered three Flying L fumbles, intercepted a pair of passes, and blocked one punt—resulting in four Miami High touchdowns. The Miami offense added a fifth score on its own as the Stings came away with a 35-0 victory.

After a week off the Stingarees were on the road again for a game on Friday, October 15, traveling to West Palm Beach to play the Falcons of Forest Hill High School. A 20-point second quarter highlighted an explosive first half by the Stingarees as they scored all of their points and gained 198 yards against the Falcons in just the first two quarters. Miami's first team offense sat out the second half and the defense had four takeaways while limiting the Forest Hill offense to just 77 total yards as Miami High raised its record to 4-0-0 with a 27-0 win.

It was more of the same over the next three weeks as the Stingarees pushed their record to 7-0-0 with three more convincing victories. North Miami played MHS tough, limiting the Stingarees to just a 7-0 advantage at the half, but the third quarter was all Miami High—literally. Taking the second half kickoff Miami methodically marched 70 yards to a touchdown. Following the kickoff, the Stingarees intercepted an aerial on North's first play, Miami High using the rest of the quarter and part of the fourth to march 51 yards to the game's final touchdown in Miami's 21-0 victory.

The following week the Columbus High Explorers were completely out manned by Miami—Columbus had only 34 boys on the squad—as the Stingarees rolled to their most one-sided win of the season, 44-0. Coach Bobby Carlton cleared his bench for the second half, but the onslaught continued nonetheless. The Explorers netted just 18 yards of total offense against the Stingarees. It would have been a lot worse for Columbus had the Explorers not intercepted four Miami aerials and recovered one Stingarees' fumble.

On November 4, Palmetto High gave the Stingarees a brief scare when they pulled to within a point, 7-6, early in the second quarter; it was only the second

▲ *Leading an all-out Miami rush, defensive back George Mekras (52) and middle guard Skip Thomas smother this Palmetto High ball carrier for a big loss during the Stingarees' 27-6 victory in 1965. (Miami High School Yearbook)*

game all season in which the Stingarees had been scored upon, and just the first successful scoring drive against the Miami defense. However, the Stingarees immediately responded with another touchdown drive, increasing their lead to 14-6 at the half. Palmetto never threatened thereafter, Miami adding a pair of scores in the third quarter to come away with a 27-6 victory.

After seven games the Stingarees were not only undefeated, they were virtually untouchable. Miami High was averaging 28.5 points per game, a decent amount, but certainly not overwhelming. Where the team really impressed was on defense. Of the 28 quarters played thus far, the Miami High defense had been scored upon in only two, and one of those was a short field affair set up by a Miami fumble. Not only were teams not scoring on Miami, they were not even moving the ball. In the seven games played thus far, opposing offenses had gained a total of just 486 yards, a mere 69.4 yards per game in total offense. The Stingarees would need that rock solid defense, and much more, in their eighth game.

The biggest high school football game in the Miami area in almost two decades took place on Thursday, November 11, 1965, when the Stingarees lined up opposite the Cavaliers of Coral Gables High School. Both teams came in undefeated and untied with seven victories apiece. Miami High was the state's # 2 ranked team. Coral Gables, in the midst of the greatest success its football team would ever enjoy, was ranked # 1 in Florida and was the two-time defending state champion, as well as being the current national champion and on a 28-game win streak.

As stated above, Miami had a great defense, but Coral Gables took a back seat to no one in that phase of the game. As the *Miami Herald* noted, the Cavaliers had "given up two harmless fourth quarter scores" in winning their seven games. Coral Gables came into the game with Miami High having shut out their last four opponents, giving the Cavaliers five whitewashes on the season. The Coral Gables

▲ *Miami's Ray Smith springs Carlos Arocha free with a key block that allowed Arocha to return this punt 99 yards for a touchdown against Miami Edison in 1965. (Miami High School Yearbook)*

▲ *Seemingly kicking under the spotlight, Don Ricigliano's PAT in a 1965 state semifinal playoff game provided the margin of victory in the Stingarees' 7-6 win over Tampa's Plant High School. (Miami High School Yearbook)*

offense was slightly more potent than that of Miami, but not by much, scoring just under 34 points per game.

As rivalries go, this one had been as close as any of late. Over the previous 12 seasons each team had won four times and four games had ended in ties.

The largest crowd that had ever seen a high school football game in Florida, 44,571 filled the Orange Bowl that Thursday night. Miami struck first in the opening quarter, scoring on a 55-yard aerial from quarterback Richard Hormel to wide receiver Jack Lauramore. It was the first touchdown given up all season by the Coral Gables starting defense.

Late in the second quarter the Stingarees recovered a Cavalier fumble at the Coral Gables 40-yard line. Miami went for it all on first down and the Richard Hormel to Joey Fernandez aerial was good for 40 yards and another Miami touchdown.

Now trailing 14-0, a big return of the ensuing kickoff started the Cavaliers on a drive that took the ball to the Miami one-yard line. It took Coral Gables two plays to get the six-pointer, scoring only after center John Haviland fell on a fumble in the end zone for the touchdown. The extra point made it a 14-7 game at the half.

Neither team was able to score during the second half. Twice Coral Gables recovered Miami fumbles deep in the Stingarees' end of the field, but both times the Miami High defense rose to the occasion and stopped the Cavaliers cold. When time finally expired, the Stingarees had held on for a 14-7 victory over the nation's # 1 team, claiming Florida's top spot in the process.

The Florida high school football playoffs had begun in 1963, but the Stingarees had yet to play in them. With its victory over Coral Gables, Miami High was now primed to make the postseason for the very first time. The Stingarees had two games yet to play, but their remaining opponents, Hialeah and Edison high schools, had but four victories between them. Neither proved to be much of a problem. Against once-victorious Hialeah High School the Miami defense and special teams each scored a touchdown in the second quarter, spurring the Stings on to a 33-7 victory. On Thanksgiving night the Stingarees used their stonewall defense to roll to a 17-0 victory over Edison's Red Raiders.

Having finally qualified for the postseason, Miami High's first Class AA playoff opponent would be the Panthers of Tampa's Plant High School (8-1-1) in a semifinal game to be played at Phillip's Field in Tampa on Friday night, December 3. This would be a game that featured exceptional defense by both teams, beginning with the game's very first offensive series.

The Panthers were on offense first and had advanced the ball out to their 32-yard line, but at that point the Stingarees forced a fumble that they recovered. Five plays later Miami High closed out the short drive to take a 7-0 lead. The balance of the first half was scoreless, the Panthers never able to advance beyond their own 44-yard line during the game's first two quarters. In the third quarter,

▸ Quarterback Richard Hormel pitches out to halfback Mike Goldfarb and Goldfarb races 30 yards around the right side for a touchdown in Miami's 44-12 victory over Melbourne High in the 1965 state championship game. (Miami High School Yearbook)

the Panthers had their best field position of the game thus far when they gained possession of the ball at their own 49-yard line. Grinding out a 12-play, 51-yard drive, the Panthers finally found the end zone, but a missed extra point left them trailing Miami, 7-6.

Plant had a huge scoring opportunity later in the third quarter when the Panthers recovered a Stingarees fumble at the Miami 23-yard line. The Panthers drove to the Miami five-yard line, where on the second play of the fourth quarter they were facing fourth and three. The Panthers gambled on a field goal try, but as the *Herald* reported, "Alfieri's 22-yard attempt—from an angle and against the wind—was wide."

The balance of the fourth quarter was scoreless, the Stingarees hanging on to preserve a razor thin 7-6 victory.

Moving on to the Class AA championship game, the Stingarees faced the Bulldogs of Melbourne High School, the surprise playoff entry from Class AA's Region 3 and an even more surprising 7-0 upset victor over Region 2's Jacksonville Wolfson in the other AA semifinal contest. Miami High (representing Region 4) was a big favorite to win its first playoff championship.

After watching a couple of the Miami games in person, as well as films of the Stingarees, Melbourne head coach Byrd Whigham

THE STINGAREES' GREAT SUCCESS HAD FIRMLY ENTRENCHED FLORIDA HIGH SCHOOL FOOTBALL ON THE NATIONAL SCENE.

thought that he had detected a flaw in the Miami defense that he hoped his team would be able to exploit. Whigham's game plan was to utilize his quick pitch offense and run outside of the Miami defensive ends, which he felt were susceptible to such a maneuver.

Having seen the Stingarees offense held pretty much in check in three of its last four games, the Miami High fans among the 8,438 in the Orange Bowl on Friday night, December 10, had to be more than a little pleased as to how the championship game started for their team. The Miami offense was hitting on all cylinders as it scored touchdowns on each of the Stingarees' first three possessions to give Miami a 21-0 lead early in the second quarter. The Stingarees later tacked on another touchdown and a 33-yard field goal to take a commanding 30-6 lead at the intermission.

Miami scored a touchdown in each of the last two quarters to come away with a very convincing 44-12 victory in its first playoff championship game. The Stingarees' aerial attack had accounted for 296 yards of offense and four touchdowns, with no interceptions.

As for Melbourne head coach Byrd Whigham's plans to run outside on the Miami defense, while his team had the best game of the year against the Stingarees with 234 yards passing, the Bulldogs netted just one yard on the ground against a Miami defense that refused to let the Panthers' runners get outside.

Not too many coaches have a first season like Miami High's Bobby Carlton had in 1965. His team went undefeated, qualified for the postseason playoffs for the first time, and then won both of its playoff games to capture the state championship. Miami High's 12-0-0 record was the team's first perfect season since 1943, and the most wins ever for a Miami High football team.

When the final tally was made by the National Sports News Service the Stingarees were also named the country's # 1 team for 1965.

From 1931 thru 1965, the Miami High School Stingarees football team had a record of success like few other teams have ever had; not one losing season as they totaled 270 victories against only 57 losses and 22 ties for an .805 winning percentage. In those 35 seasons, the Stingarees captured an incredible 24 Florida state championships and five national titles.

Playing against teams from throughout the eastern half of the country and a few west of the Mississippi, the Stingarees' great success had firmly entrenched Florida high school football on the national scene.

TWO GREAT TEAMS, FIVE CHAMPIONSHIP SEASONS

Coral Gables Senior High School
Coral Gables, Florida

John H. Reagan Early College High School
Austin, Texas

Of the 17 national championships awarded from 1960-1971, four different teams, all from the southern part of the country, took home no fewer than 13 of those titles. We have already told the story of two of those teams, the Stingarees of Miami Senior High School and the Wildcats of Valdosta High School. We will now look at the other two teams.

Coral Gables Senior High School opened on the southern fringe of Miami in 1950 when the former Ponce de Leon High School was converted into a middle school. The school's first football team took the field in 1951 as the Cavaliers wearing crimson and gray and posting a record of 3-5-1. After that first season, Nick Kotys was hired as the head coach and the Cavaliers' fortunes took a decided up swing for the next two decades.

Nick Kotys was born in Monessen, Pa., on April 3, 1913, the oldest of six children of Ukrainian immigrants. He starred in football at Monessen High School and earned a scholarship to Villanova University where his coach was Harry Stuhldreher, one of Knute Rockne's famed Four Horsemen. At Villanova, Kotys played football well enough to earn All-East and All-America Honorable Mention recognition in 1935.

Kotys graduated from Villanova University in 1936 and with the help of Harry Stuhldreher got his first coaching job at Schickshinny High School in Pennsylvania. For the next 13 years he coached football at three different high schools in Pennsylvania, compiling an outstanding record of 98-24-7, .787.

In 1949 Kotys joined the football staff at Yale University as the offensive coordinator and backfield coach. However, it did not take long for Nick to realize that he missed the high school game, both the teaching aspect and the opportunity to positively influence young men. As Kotys told the *Miami Herald* in 1969, "Like any young coach, I had college aspirations, but frankly I wasn't happy at Yale. I found out in one month that there's no molding the player like in high school. It's almost entirely a matter of recruiting."

Kotys was in Miami in December, 1951, to help coach the North All-Stars in the annual North-South Shrine game. During his stay there he ran into Jim Norton, a former adversary on the basketball court back in Monessen. During one of their conversations, Kotys inquired as to the availability of any coaching openings in the area and was told by Norton that Coral Gables High School was looking for a football coach. As an article in the *Miami Herald* in September of 1969 later noted, when Kotys showed some interest in the opening, "Norton tried to discourage Nick at first, pointing out that the Gables job was far from the plum of the area."

Norton also told Kotys how Miami High had dominated the local football scene for the past 40 years, not having lost to a local Dade County team in more than 20 years. Kotys's response to Norton was, "If I get this job I'll catch up with this team in three years."

Kotys arranged several meetings with Coral Gables' principal Harry Rath, who especially liked Kotys's ideas about the school in general. Rath's main problem in hiring Kotys, however, was with the County School Board trustees, who had to approve all coaching hires and who did not like the idea of hiring an outsider, especially one who was a "damn Yankee." But Rath persisted and Nick Kotys was hired as Coral Gables' head football coach and Athletic Director.

▼ *Coral Gables' John Norris (34) often led the interference for halfback Alan Scott (7) during the Cavaliers' 1964 season. (Coral Gables High School Yearbook)*

As the folks in Miami, Dade County, and eventually the rest of Florida and the country as a whole would eventually learn, Nick Kotys's teams would soon become a reflection of their coach. First and foremost was Nick's quest for perfection, which he accomplished by keeping his teams in top physical shape and insisting that everyone hustle. As former University of Miami head coach Andy Gustafson once said of Kotys, "He quick-steps. Everything he does is quick. He's high-strung, gung-ho. His teams are that way, too... You can always tell Nick's team by conditioning and hustle."

Nick was a disciplinarian at Coral Gables both on the gridiron and in the hallways. He had a genuine feeling for the individual, something that would allow him to scold and inspire at the same time. As the *Miami Herald* once noted, Nick Kotys cut a player from his team for only three reasons, and none of them had anything to do with that player's overall

▲   *The Coral Gables coaching staff during the Cavaliers' 1964 national championship season. Head coach Nick Kotys on the extreme left. (Coral Gables High School Yearbook)*

athletic ability: 1) poor grades, 2) breaking training rules, 3) failure to show up for practice.

When Nick Kotys took over the Cavaliers, he wanted to install the still popular Notre Dame box formation offense, but since his players did not have the physical size that the formation required, he kept the T-formation that the team had been using. After the Cavaliers' 3-5-1 record in 1951, Nick's first team in 1952 finished 6-3-0, the school's first winning season in seven years going back to the Ponce de Leon High School days. In 1953 the Cavaliers slipped ever so slightly to finish at 6-4-0.

The Cavaliers' first really big year came in 1954. That season the team won eight times while losing just once, with one tie. However, the tie was a truly significant event for the Cavaliers' program. In that game the Cavaliers played the Stingarees of Miami High to a 14-14 deadlock. It was not a victory, but true to his word, Kotys's team had caught up with the Stingarees in just three seasons.

In 1955 the Cavaliers finished with a very good 8-2-0 record, but again lost to Miami High, this time by a 12-0 count. However, the Cavaliers were on the brink of the greatest era in their history. And the team's rivalry with Miami High over the next 17 seasons would be one of the most intense anywhere in the country.

The Cavaliers opened the 1956 campaign with victories over North Miami, 21-6, and Miami Edison, 34-7. In its third game, Coral Gables went to 3-0-0 with a 33-6

…CORAL GABLES HEAD COACH NICK KOTYS CUT A PLAYER FROM HIS TEAM FOR ONLY THREE REASONS, AND NONE OF THEM HAD ANYTHING TO DO WITH THAT PLAYER'S OVERALL ATHLETIC ABILITY: 1) POOR GRADES, 2) BREAKING TRAINING RULES, 3) FAILURE TO SHOW UP FOR PRACTICE.

victory over the Lakeland Dreadnaughts. Coach Kotys no doubt liked the fact that his defense had another good game in holding Lakeland to just 73 yards of total offense, but he could not have been too pleased with the 110 yards in penalties assessed against the Cavaliers.

On October 5, the Cavaliers traveled to Jacksonville to play that city's Jackson High (3-0-0) in the Gator Bowl. This was the first time that these two teams had ever played each other. At the time, Coral Gables was ranked # 1 in the state polls and Jackson # 2; the *Miami News* wrote that this very well could be "the high school game of the year."

While the numbers after the game indicated a pretty even contest, the final total on the scoreboard told another story: Coral Gables 20, Jackson 0. Miami High School head coach Ottis Mooney, whose Stingarees would be playing Coral Gables the following week, was on hand to scout the Cavaliers (his team had already been upset by Jackson). After the game he told reporters, "The scoreboard doesn't indicate how bad Coral Gables beat them. It was worse."

The October 20 game between Coral Gables and Miami High in the Orange Bowl was much anticipated. Miami (2-1-0) was the defending state champion and Coral Gables was off to one of the best starts thus far in school history. Coral Gables fell behind after the first two quarters, but a big second half comeback that was sparked by a blocked punt in the third quarter carried the Cavaliers to a huge 20-13 victory. It was the first victory over Miami High for a Nick Kotys team in six tries—the first ever by a team representing Coral Gables High School.

By the time October 26 and the Cavaliers sixth game of the season rolled around, the Cavaliers' faithful were beginning to wonder if perhaps they had offended the schedule maker in some way. First they had played Jacksonville Jackson, then Miami High, and now they had to face off against Lee High School of Jacksonville—games with three of the toughest teams in the state back to back to back.

All of the scoring in this one took place in the first half. The Cavaliers notched single touchdowns in each of the first two quarters, closing out long drives to gain each score. The Generals' Doug Davis returned the kickoff after the Cavaliers' second touchdown 79 yards for his team's only points of the game. Coral Gables' 14-6 victory gave the Cavaliers a perfect 3-for-3 against some of the state's toughest teams and raised their record to 6-0-0.

The Cavaliers cruised to the finish line, winning their last three games by a combined 114-12.

With a final record of 9-0-0, Coral Gables became the first major team in the Greater Miami area to finish the season undefeated and untied since 1943. That accomplishment garnered for the Cavaliers their first state championship as they finished first in all of the state polls. Nick Kotys was named the Greater Miami "Coach of the Year" while halfback Mike Harrison was named a high school All-American.

The Cavaliers entered the 1957 season riding the crest of a 15-game winning streak. They opened against the Palm Beach Wildcats. Five turnovers by the Cavaliers was not the way to preserve a win streak, and the Wildcats took advantage of the Coral Gables miscues to come away with a surprising 14-7 victory. Coral Gables would go on to have a good season, but not a great one, finishing 7-2-1.

In their 1958 opener, the Cavaliers avenged their defeat of the previous season at the hands of the Palm Beach Wildcats. The Cavaliers next faced Miami Edison, the other team that had defeated Coral Gables in 1957. This was a big early season match-up because Edison was the defending state champion while Coral Gables was ranked # 1 in the first statewide poll of 1958. With the Red Raiders having lost 42 players to graduation, as well as losing their head coach and three of his assistants, things were looking good for a Cavaliers victory. A "W" looked to be even more secure when Coral Gables took a 7-0 lead after the first two quarters, but a second half surge by the Red Raiders carried Edison to a 14-10 triumph.

After that somewhat stunning defeat, Coach Kotys's crew rolled to victory in its next five games. With their record now at 6-1-0, but still ranked # 1 in Florida, the Cavaliers next game took place on Thursday, November 13, against the 6-0-1 Stingarees of Miami High. Miami High was still the big kid on the block as far as Florida high school football was concerned, but the Cavaliers had not lost to them since 1955 and were hoping to continue that trend.

A large and boisterous crowd of just under 16,000 fans was on hand at the Orange Bowl for this always big game. The action started right from Miami's opening kickoff, which Coral Gables fullback Ted Saussele returned 90 yards for a Cavaliers touchdown and a quick 6-0 lead. However, Miami would dominate play over the balance of the first quarter and into the second to take a 12-6 lead. Late in the second quarter, Coral Gables would take advantage of a recovered Miami fumble to regain the lead, 13-12, at the intermission.

There would be no more scoring in the game as the Cavaliers held on for a 13-12 victory.

In their final game of the regular season, behind Ted Saussele's 172 yards rushing and three touchdowns and a defense that held the Southwest Eagles to just two yards rushing, the Cavaliers rolled to a 19-7 victory.

However, this season Coral Gables still had one more game to play, a newly established postseason contest. In 1958 the Miami chapter of the Fraternal Order of Police (FOP) decided to hold a charity high school football game, pitting the two best teams from the Miami area against each other in a game to be held on Friday, December 12. Those two teams in 1958 were the Cavaliers of Coral Gables (8-1-0) and the Miami High Stingarees (8-1-1), who had played each other just one month before.

The 18,000-plus who showed up at the Orange Bowl that day were no doubt expecting to see another hotly contested game. The Cavaliers would have liked that as well, but the game did not go that way. After a scoreless first quarter, the Stingarees scored single touchdowns in each of the remaining three quarters. Meanwhile the Miami defense completely bottled up the Coral Gables offense, allowing it to cross the midfield stripe only once during the entire game. When the final whistle sounded, the Cavaliers found themselves on the short end of a 20-0 score. The final poll results had come out before this game was played—naming Coral Gables as the 1958 state champions. With the results of this game, both teams are recognized as the 1958 Florida state champion.

The next four seasons would be the least productive for Coral Gables under head coach Nick Kotys. Player losses due to graduation cut deep into the veteran ranks of the Cavaliers football team in 1959, resulting in a disappointing 3-4-1 record, the only losing season during Nick Kotys's tenure as the Cavaliers' head coach. The team's fortunes improved a bit in 1960 (7-1-1), but declined in 1961 (5-1-3), and again in 1962 (5-4-1). While it may have looked as if the team was gradually slipping back into the pre-Kotys mediocrity, this was not to be the case. In fact, over the balance of the 1960s, the Cavaliers would enjoy the greatest era, not only in their history, but of any team in the history of Florida high school football.

Something new was added for the 1963 Florida high school football season. After having discussed the idea for years, the Florida High School Activities Association finally decided on a playoff system for football to determine the state champion, beginning with the 1963-64 school year. While the state's high schools were divided into three classes—AA, A, B—only the schools in AA would participate in the playoffs the first year so that any problems that cropped up could be dealt with before the rest of the schools joined in. A system of points was set up, different points awarded to a team for defeating an opponent in its class, in a higher category, or in a lower category. The state was divided into four regions, which were expanded to eight regions in 1967, and the leading point getter in each region would qualify for the playoffs at the end of the season.

The Coral Gables Cavaliers were looking forward to better times with the coming of the 1963 season and like every other school in Class AA, they had their sights set on a spot in the playoffs at season's end. The season opened with a pair of encouraging victories over Palmetto, 27-6, and Miami Edison, 23-0,—games that told a lot about what the Cavaliers would be like for the entire season. On offense the Cavaliers were steady without running up a big score; in those first two games they scored in seven of the eight quarters. The team's forte, however, would be defense, and especially run defense. Both opening opponents had been held to less than 50 yards rushing and less than 75 yards of total offense.

On October 3, the Cavaliers took on the team from Key West High School (1-1-0) at home in Central Stadium. As four-touchdown underdogs, nobody including the Conches' head coach gave Key West much of a chance. But this game did not go according to the "script" and at the half it was still a scoreless tie. Finally, in the third quarter, Coral Gables junior quarterback Larry Rentz broke the scoreless deadlock when he went 76 yards down the east sideline for the first touchdown of the game. A botched snap on the extra point try prevented the Cavaliers from making the PAT for one of the few times all season. Early in the fourth quarter, Key West got on the scoreboard via a 37-yard touchdown pass, the extra point giving the Conches a 7-6 lead with 11:05 left in the game. There would be no more scoring in the game as Key West came away with a huge upset victory.

The *Miami News* called it "the end of a dream" for Coral Gables and team head coach Nick Kotys, who for years had been a prime backer of a playoff system. Now, with a loss, Kotys felt that his team's chances of reaching the playoffs in the very competitive Region 4 were all but gone. As Kotys told the *News*, "We're out of it now." But with 70% of the season yet to be played, it was probably a bit too early to be throwing in the towel.

The following week against Hialeah High, the Cavaliers' defense, especially cornerback Vince Romano, proved just how valuable they were to the team's success. Romano blocked a first quarter Hialeah field goal attempt, which minutes later became a 28-yard field goal by the Cavaliers' Larry Davidson. In the third quarter, Romano blocked a Hialeah punt attempt, the ball being grabbed out of the air by defensive tackle Art Lloyd and returned for a 35-yard touchdown to secure Gables' 10-0 victory.

The Cavaliers next three games were not quite as dramatic as they rolled to wins over South Broward, 35-7, Miami Beach, 42-0, and Christopher Columbus, 28-7. With their record now 6-1-0, the Cavaliers next had their annual showdown with Miami High. The Stingarees entered the game with a record of 4-2-0 and were picked as two-touchdown underdogs.

As the Cavaliers should have learned from their game with Key West, don't read the newspaper clippings. This game was scoreless until the final play of the first half when Miami scored a touchdown, but a failed extra point try left the Stingarees with only a 6-0 lead. Miami High added a second touchdown, and the extra point, in the third quarter to enter the final 12 minutes with a 13-0 advantage. Early in the final frame, the Cavaliers finally got on the scoreboard as Larry Rentz went around the right side for a 13-yard touchdown, the extra point making it a 13-7 game. Later in the quarter, after

As the yearbook caption says, "Larry Rentz (1) rolls to his left, cuts back sharply, and leaves (Jacksonville) Lee defenders flatfooted" during the 1964 state championship game. (Coral Gables High School Yearbook)

converting a fourth and 12 from the Miami 40-yard line, the Cavaliers advanced to the three-yard line. With just 13 seconds left on the game clock, Larry Rentz scored the tying touchdown and placekicker Larry Davidson calmly booted the game-winning point.

Having overcome that last big hurdle, the Cavaliers cruised by Miami Jackson, 33-0, and outlasted Southwest High, 24-14, to end the season with a record of 9-1-0. In doing so, they edged out North Miami for the Class AA Region 4 championship and the right to play Region 3 champion Gainesville in a Class AA semifinal game on Friday, December 6, at Gainesville.

The semifinal game got off to a fast start for the Cavaliers as they took the opening kickoff and marched 72 yards to take an early 7-0 lead. On the ensuing Gainesville possession, the Cavaliers forced a fumble; the ball was picked up by Vince Romano for Coral Gables and returned 45 yards for another early Cavaliers touchdown. Coral Gables added 14 more points in the third quarter to come away with a comfortable 28-6 victory.

The Cavaliers' victory set up a state championship game with Robinson High School of Tampa, at 11-0-0 the last undefeated team in Class AA. The Robinson Knights had allowed only 20 points all season, just seven in their last eight games, while putting up eight shutouts. The game was played in perfect weather at Tampa's Phillips Field before more than 15,000, along with a television audience of about half a million.

Not too unexpectedly in a game between two defensive powers, the first half ended scoreless. Robinson broke the deadlock early in the third quarter on an 11-yard pass for a 7-0 lead. On the final play of that quarter, the Cavaliers' Larry Rentz raced 43 yards for a touchdown, Larry Davidson's PAT tying the score at 7-7.

Early in the final quarter, following a Coral Gables pass interception Larry Rentz went 13 yards for the go-ahead touchdown, but the PAT was missed, leaving the Cavaliers with a 13-7 lead.

Robinson High came roaring back on the strength of its passing game and took a 14-13 lead with just 4:05 left in the game. Taking the ensuing kickoff, the Cavaliers marched from their own 40-yard line to the Robinson 24, overcoming a fumble along the way. With just 15 seconds left on the game clock, Larry Davidson's field goal attempt split the uprights from 35 yards away to give Coral Gables a 16-14 championship game victory.

When the final National Sports News Service nationwide listing came out the Cavaliers were ranked sixth in the country.

As the 1964 season rolled around, three teams were considered to be the cream of Florida's Class AA crop: Miami High, Hialeah High, and the defending state champions from Coral Gables. Because the other two teams were on the Cavaliers' schedule, the Region 4 entry for the postseason playoffs would most definitely be decided on the gridiron.

Like the 1963 edition of Nick Kotys's Cavaliers, the '64 team, with 11 returning starters, would feature another outstanding defensive unit and an offense that, in a word, got the job done. And then there was senior quarterback/halfback Larry Rentz; by season's end Rentz would attain All-America status, more than living up to the phrase coined by a local Miami newspaper sportswriter that "there's no defense for Larry Rentz."

Coral Gables opened the season on Thursday, September 17, against the Explorers of Christopher Columbus High School. The previous season, this small, all-boys Catholic school had hung with the mighty Cavaliers thru the first three quarters of the game, and it would be more of the same this time around. Played before a crowd of 9,000 at Central Stadium, the game was scoreless until the Cavaliers tallied twice in the game's final nine minutes to come away with a 13-0 victory.

It was another nail-biter for the Cavaliers the following week against Miami Edison. The first half appeared to be ending without a point having been scored when the Cavaliers' intercepted an Edison aerial at the Red Raiders' 48-yard line with just 18 seconds left. On the final play of the second quarter, a 37-yard Larry Rentz touchdown pass gave the Cavaliers a 7-0 lead. The final two quarters were dominated by Edison, but the Red Raiders were unable to score until just 1:20 was left in the game. Amazingly, the Red Raiders' kicker missed the PAT wide left, leaving Coral Gables with a 7-6 lead—which was good enough for the win.

The following week Larry Rentz threw for two touchdowns and ran for a third as the Cavaliers defeated Key West, 21-6, and thus avenged their lone loss of the previous season.

Before 11,000 fans on Thursday, October 8, the Cavaliers met the first of the two teams that were believed to have the best chance of derailing their playoff hopes, the undefeated Thoroughbreds of Hialeah High School. With the Hialeah defense keying on Larry Rentz, the Coral Gables signal caller countered by continually handing the ball off to his backfield tandem of halfbacks Phil Tracy and Pat Phelan. The two responded by rushing for a combined 191 yards and a pair of

▲ *Coach Nick Kotys poses with the seven Cavaliers named to the 1964 All-City team. The following four were also All-State: quarterback Larry Rentz (1), guard Rick Bishop (55), linebacker Carlos Luis (59), and halfback Phil Tracy (16). (Coral Gables High School Yearbook)*

▲ *Defensive back Ed Merlano (8) makes an interception against Southwest during the Cavaliers Homecoming Game on Nov. 23, 1967. (Coral Gables High School Yearbook)*

touchdowns. Rentz added a touchdown on a 56-yard punt return as Coral Gables came away with a key 21-13 victory.

Coral Gables won its next four games, three by shutout, as the Cavaliers raced through their opponents' defenses for an average of 283 yards rushing. With their record now 8-0-0, Coral Gables had moved into first place in the state poll and, more importantly, in the race for the regional playoff spot.

Friday, November 13, brought the game that many in the Miami area had been awaiting all season, the showdown between Coral Gables and Miami High. The Stingarees had just suffered their first loss in seven games the previous week, so they would like nothing better than to upset the Cavaliers' playoff chances. A huge crowd of 28,360 filled the Orange Bowl that night and saw a game that was more than worth the price of admission.

After a scoreless first quarter, Miami High took a 6-0 lead early in the second. Larry Rentz returned the ensuing kickoff 77 yards to put the Cavaliers right in the shadow of the Miami goal posts. Four plays later, the Cavaliers found the end zone to tie the score at 6-6, but the missed PAT prevented them from taking the lead and the game remained tied at the intermission.

A third quarter touchdown by Larry Rentz proved to be the only scoring of the second half as Coral Gables came away with a big 13-6 win. A Miami comeback was short-circuited by five turnovers.

The Cavaliers now had a two week break until their next game against the Eagles of Southwest High on Thanksgiving morning. With that game still scoreless late in the third quarter, Larry Rentz intercepted a deflected Southwest pass near midfield and returned it all the way to the Eagles 18-yard line. Three plays later, Rentz was on the receiving end of a halfback pass, which he took all the way for a touchdown and a 7-0 Cavaliers lead. The Cavaliers added a field goal in the fourth quarter and, despite only 79 yards of total offense, it was enough to give them a 10-0 victory.

Having finished the regular season a perfect 10-0-0 and run their win streak to 19 in a row, the Cavaliers' next stop was the Class AA semifinals and a game against Orlando's Colonial High School. After having been held in check for the most part by Southwest, this game was a breath of fresh air for Cavaliers fans. Taking a 7-0 lead in the first quarter, Coral Gables blew the game open with a 20-point second quarter. Six Colonial turnovers (five interceptions and one fumble) definitely hurt the Grenadiers' cause, as the Cavaliers took advantage of the extra possessions to run up almost 400 yards of total offense.

When the final whistle blew, the Cavaliers had whitewashed the Grenadiers, 39-0, to again move on to the Class AA state championship. This time their opponent in the Orange Bowl would be the once-defeated Generals, 9-1-0, of Jacksonville's Lee High School.

A Larry Rentz touchdown pass gave the Cavaliers a 7-0 lead midway through the first quarter. In a defense-oriented game, neither team would score again until the fourth quarter when another Coral Gables touchdown pushed the lead to 14-0. The Lee Generals avoided a shutout by scoring a touchdown with a little less than three minutes to play, but their attempt at an onside kick was recovered by Coral Gables, which then ran out the game's final 2:37.

The 14-7 victory gave Coral Gables a 12-0-0 record for the season; the win was the team's 21st consecutive victory, tying them with Miami High (1941-1944) for the longest win streak in state history. Not only did the Cavaliers win the state championship, but when the final rankings were announced by the National Sports News Service, Coral Gables was also named the national champion, the third time that a Miami area team had taken home the top prize since 1960.

Although All-American Larry Rentz had now graduated, Nick Kotys appeared to have another solid team in 1965. After seven games the Cavaliers were undefeated, having run their win streak to 28, and the first team defense had yet to yield a point.

All of that was put on the line on Thursday, November 11, in what had now become Florida's biggest annual encounter, Coral Gables vs. Miami High. Coral Gables and Miami High were both 7-0-0 and Miami's defense had five shutouts to its credit, yielding but 19 points all season. Both teams were about as even as two teams could be, making the prospects for a great game in the Orange Bowl something that 44,571 fans, the largest crowd in Florida high school football history, could not afford to pass up.

As was to be expected, defense dominated the game. After Miami scored on a 55-yard pass play in the first quarter, the Stingarees turned a Coral Gables fumble into a second touchdown in the second period. The Coral Gables defense also got into the scoring in the second quarter by recovering a Miami fumble in the end zone for a touchdown, cutting the Miami lead to 14-7 at the halftime break. That is how the score remained until the final whistle and Coral Gables' 28-game win streak had come to an end.

The Cavaliers split their remaining two games to finish the '65 season at 8-2-0, while Miami High went on to win both the state and national championships. By Nick Kotys's standards, 1966 would be another off year, the Cavaliers slipping to 7-3-0. The Cavaliers failed to make the playoffs both seasons.

In large part because of what was taking place off the gridiron, the 1967 high school football season in Florida would be one of the most remarkable ever, definitely one of some change. This was a time of desegregation in the south. In 1966, Carver High School in Coconut Grove, a previously all-black school, was converted into a middle school and its students integrated into Coral Gables High School. In an effort to ease that transition, Nick Kotys at one point set up a table outside

The Coral Gables defense, led by George Jahn (81), stopped the Southwest Eagles quarterback before he could get his pass away during the Cavaliers' homecoming game Nov. 23, 1967. Coral Gables won the game, 40-0. (Coral Gables High School Yearbook)

Carver High School and used a microphone to welcome the Carver kids to their new school at Coral Gables.

While the transition was not always as smooth as one would hope off the field, things went much better on the gridiron. For one thing, the former Carver players now on the Coral Gables squad soon realized that football is football and that Coach Kotys and his methods were not much different than the coach they had played for at Carver. Even more important, Nick Kotys never played favorites with the kids on his teams; like Paul Brown 30 years earlier, the best players would start and the color of their skin was irrelevant. Even so, putting that maxim into practice at this time in Florida had to take more than a little "intestinal fortitude", especially when Kotys named former Carver player Craig Curry as the starting quarterback for Coral Gables in 1967 (he had also seen some action as the signal caller the previous season).

What opponents could expect to see from the Cavaliers in 1967 was evident from the very first kickoff. As it had for the last several seasons, Coral Gables opened against the Explorers of Christopher Columbus High. Unlike the last couple of times these two teams had met, there would be no waiting until the final quarter to determine the game's outcome, the Cavaliers jumping out to an early 14-0 advantage on the way to a 39-0 victory.

As that score might indicate, this had not been a game dominated solely by the Cavaliers' offense. Eight returning starters on the defensive side of the ball had more than their fair share of an impact on the outcome. The defense held the Explorers to minus-20 yards rushing, in part by sacking a pair of Columbus quarterbacks for a total of 36 yards in losses. The Explorers did not cross the midfield stripe until the fourth quarter and then only once.

After a couple off seasons, Coral Gables was again primed and ready to go.

Against Miami Edison the following week, the Coral Gables offense scored in each of the last three quarters, but it was the defense that had the big day. The Cavaliers' "D" held Edison to just 46 total yards and two first downs, allowing only one pass completion out of 16 attempts while making three interceptions. In their 23-0 victory Coral Gables never allowed the Red Raiders to advance beyond their own 39-yard line.

It was more of the same when Key West came to town, the Conches managing just a single late score against the Coral Gables reserves in an otherwise dominating performance by the Cavaliers in a 26-6 victory. The state's top-ranked Cavaliers made it four in a row with a 13-6 victory over the first-year team from Killian High School, but it was not as dominating a performance as the team's three previous victories, marking the first time during the season that the Coral Gables starting defense had been scored upon.

The close game with Killian cost Coral Gables its top ranking in Florida as the team slipped to # 2 in the state poll. Whatever Coach Kotys said to his team during practice the following week had the desired effect. Playing the Coral Park Rams on October 12, the Cavaliers scored five of the first six times they had the ball en route to a 36-0 halftime lead. So dominant was Coral Gables in this game that Coach Kotys was already taking out his starters in the first quarter. The Rams managed to avoid a shutout with a touchdown against the Gables reserves as the Cavaliers' record climbed to 5-0-0 with their 39-7 win. The victory moved Coral Gables back into the state's top spot after a short one week absence.

Coral Gables then breezed past Palmetto, 34-0, Miami Springs, 27-0, and Pompano, 40-0, raising the team's record to 8-0-0 just in time for the annual showdown with Miami High.

Another huge crowd of just over 39,000 was on hand at the Orange Bowl on Thursday, November 9, for the highly anticipated battle between the state's top-ranked Coral Gables Cavaliers and the second-ranked and also undefeated, 7-0-0, Miami High Stingarees. The game developed into a defensive battle worthy of two top teams.

After a scoreless first quarter, Coral Gables took a 7-0 lead with a little more than a minute remaining in the half. After the intermission Coral Gables promptly marched 70 yards on the opening possession of the third quarter, quarterback Craig Curry closing out the drive with an 11-yard touchdown run. A fourth quarter Cavaliers field goal closed out the game's scoring and the Coral Gables defense continued to show why it was the best in the state as it kept the Stingarees on the Miami side of the field for all but one possession in the Cavaliers' 16-0 victory.

A 40-0 thumping of the Southwest Eagles on Thanksgiving Day closed out the Coral Gables season at a perfect 10-0-0 and qualified the Cavaliers for the Class AA playoffs for the first time since 1964. Class AA had expanded to eight regions in 1967, resulting in four district playoff games, followed by the two semifinal games and then the state championship contest.

Coral Gables' district playoff opponent on December 2 would be the team from McArthur High School (7-3-0) of Hollywood, Florida. Due to several turnovers, the Cavaliers got off to a slow start, but still managed to hold a 13-0 lead at the intermission. Putting it all together in the second half, Coral Gables cruised to

◄ Fullback Roberto Alvarez (5) leads the blocking for halfback Dick Whittington (27) around the right side against Southwest High on Nov. 23, 1967. (Coral Gables High School Yearbook)

a 36-0 victory. The defense did its usual fine job, limiting McArthur to just 93 yards of total offense while intercepting four passes.

On Friday night, December 8, the Cavaliers lined up opposite Robinson High (10-1-0) of Tampa in one of the Class AA semifinal games. Back in the first state championship game in 1963, the Cavaliers and the Knights had played one of the all-time great Florida championship games; unfortunately for the Knights, this would not be another. The tone of this game was set early when Coral Gables halfback Richard Whittington ran 41 yards for a touchdown on the second play from scrimmage. "Long distance" would be the order of the day for Coral Gables as the Cavaliers scored six touchdowns from an average of 49.5 yards away. Toss in two short touchdown bursts and seven PATs and Coral Gables had itself a play-off-record 55-0 victory. Not to be outdone, the Cavaliers' defense came up with five interceptions, including Ed Merlano's team-leading eighth, which he returned 35 yards for a touchdown.

Winning the semifinal game sent Coral Gables to the Class AA state championship game for the third time in five years. The team's opponent would be the state's fourth-ranked Wolfson High (11-0-1) of Jacksonville, in a game played before 16, 652 in Jacksonville's Gator Bowl on Friday, December 15.

Wolfson held Coral Gables to just 46 yards of offense during the first two quarters and, although the Wolfpack dominated the action by running 33 plays to just 13 for Coral Gables, the Cavaliers' defense would bend but not break and the half ended with the game still scoreless.

As he had done all season however, quarterback Craig Curry stepped up for Coral Gables during the second half. An interception and 47-yard return by John Clifford (one of two he had in the game) gave the Coral Gables offense excellent field position at the Wolfson 17-yard line. Three plays later, Curry ran the ball into the end zone from five yards away; Bill Emmons added the point for a 7-0 lead. Wolfson came right back to tie the game, marching 60 yards in 12 plays. That touchdown and extra point were the first points allowed by the Coral Gables first team defense in 32 quarters.

Curry continued his fine play late in the game by putting the Cavaliers back into the lead with a nifty 43-yard touchdown run just one minute into the fourth quarter. Curry then put an exclamation point on the game and the season with a four-yard touchdown scramble with just two seconds remaining on the game clock. Bill Emmons added both placements to make the final score 21-7.

The victory gave Coral Gables its third state championship in the last five seasons; the Cavaliers had yet to lose a playoff game.

Coral Gables ended the season a perfect 13-0-0, the best record the team would ever have. Immediately after the game Nick Kotys told reporters that this was the best team he had ever coached, the complete package of offense, defense, and special teams. The Cavaliers had outscored the opposition 410-26, including nine shutouts, and the defense had a team-record 33 interceptions. Apparently a lot of people shared Coach Kotys's opinion of his team for in 2007 the FHSAA named the 1967 Coral Gables Cavaliers as the state's "Team of the Century."

Adding a little icing to Coral Gables' championship cake, the National Sports News Service named the Cavaliers as the # 1 team in the country for 1967, the team's second such honor in four years. However, this time around, Coral Gables was not the only team that NSNS thought was good enough to be ranked #1 in the country.

———————

While all of this championship football was transpiring in Florida there was an event taking place far to the west that at the time gained little, if any, notice outside of its immediate vicinity. Located about 1,400 miles west and just a bit north of Coral Gables High School, John H. Reagan Early College High School of Austin, Texas, first opened its doors in the fall of 1965. Although there were no seniors that year, a football team was formed even though the Raiders, as they were known,

▼ *Coral Gables head coach Nick Kotys is carried off the field by his players after the team's 21-7 victory over Jacksonville Wolfson in the 1967 Florida Class AA state championship game. (Coral Gables High School Yearbook)*

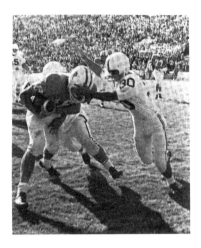

▲　*Above: Reagan High School quarterback Dale Rebold picks up crucial yardage against Bellaire High in a state semifinal game on Dec. 9, 1967. (Reagan High School Yearbook)*

▸　*Following page, top: Finding himself bottled up, halfback Don Ealey pitches the ball back to quarterback Dale Rebold in a 1967 state semifinal game against Bellaire. (Reagan High School Yearbook)*

▸　*Following page, bottom: Reagan halfback Don Ealey scampers into the end zone against Abilene Cooper in the Texas Class 4A state championship game on Dec. 16, 1967. (Reagan High School Yearbook)*

were not eligible for the state playoffs that first season. The varsity was composed of ninth, tenth, and eleventh graders.

During their first half-dozen seasons, the Raiders were under the direction of head coach Travis Raven. Raven was born in Austin on August 31, 1923, and remained an Austin resident most of his life. He attended Austin High School, where he was an All-State fullback for the Maroons in 1939 and 1940. After graduation, he enrolled at Schreiner Institute in the fall of 1940; at the time Schreiner was a junior college located about 100 miles west of Austin. Raven played football that season, helping the Schreiner team win the state junior college championship. In 1941 Raven enrolled at the University of Texas at Austin, but with the coming of World War II he joined the Army Air Corps, in which he served for the duration of the war. After mustering out of the Air Corps (now known as the U.S. Air Force), Raven went back to school at UT Austin where he again played football and graduated in 1948.

Upon graduation from college, Travis Raven began his high school coaching career as the head football coach at Yoakum and then Lockhart high schools, before moving on to Austin High School in 1953 where he coached several sports. The highlight of these years occurred when Raven coached the Austin High baseball team to the 1958 state championship.

When Reagan High School opened in 1965, teachers from various Austin schools were selected for the new school and Travis Raven was named the school's first head football coach. Raven soon earned a reputation as a defensive specialist. He always maintained a positive attitude while coaching and, unlike many coaches who think louder is better, his former players will tell you that screaming and hollering was not Raven's way.

Considering the situation, the Reagan Raiders did well to finish with a respectable 5-4-0 record in 1965, and improved to an even better 6-3-1 the following season.

It is not surprising that there were no lofty expectations for the still fledgling Raiders of Austin's John T. Reagan High School with the coming of the 1967 campaign. After all, this was only the team's third season, just the second with a true varsity squad. And despite some mild success during those first couple of years, the team had yet to even qualify for the state playoffs. Also, a coach does not build a team or a program overnight and Travis Raven was still in the process of installing his offensive and defensive schemes and imparting his philosophies—with only a couple of assistant coaches to help him.

The Raiders had closed 1966 on a positive note by defeating Killeen High School, 13-6. This gave the team a little momentum on which to build for the '67 campaign, but no one could have predicted what was about to happen.

Reagan opened 1967 with a very impressive 42-6 thrashing of San Antonio's Churchill High, followed the next week by an even more impressive 53-0 rain-soaked rout of the team from Lockhart High. After its next game with King High School of Corpus Christi was washed out, literally, due to road flooding in Corpus Christi in the wake of Hurricane Beulah, Reagan continued its winning ways by rolling through its next four games by a combined 149-29.

With its record now 6-0-0, Reagan's next opponent would be the Maroons of Austin High School, this game with the team from across town quickly taking on the status of a rivalry game. This 1967 contest with the Austin Maroons was the first truly big game in Reagan's short history, a major stepping stone to a possible first playoff appearance if the Raiders could pull out a victory. Both teams featured high scoring offenses coupled with defenses that yielded little, the Reagan defense having allowed only five touchdowns (and none on the ground) to just six for the Austin defense.

Early in the first quarter, Reagan grabbed the advantage by recovering a fumble at the Austin 30-yard line, which a short time later turned into a touchdown and a 6-0 lead. There would be no more scoring until just 19 seconds remained in the first half, when Reagan quarterback Dale Rebold hooked up with halfback Don Ealey on a 36-yard touchdown strike to give the Raiders a 12-0 lead at the half.

The Austin Maroons cut the lead to 12-7 in the third quarter, but later in the period Reagan scored again to push its advantage out to a more comfortable 18-7. Austin came back again with 1:47 left in the fourth quarter to cut the margin to 18-14. The Maroons quickly regained possession of the ball for one last chance to move ahead, but on the final play of the game Reagan's Randy Humphrey intercepted an Austin aerial to kill the threat and preserve an 18-14 victory for the Raiders.

Reagan then closed out the regular season with shutout victories over Lanier, 21-0, and McCallum, 35-0, a game in which the Raiders totaled 496 yards of offense.

Having qualified for the postseason for the first time in school history, the Raiders opened the playoffs against Temple High in the District 13 championship game. Behind four touchdown passes by quarterback Dale Rebold, three of which wound up in the hands of end Mike Bayer, Reagan came away with a convincing 27-7 win.

Jesse Thompson (44) kicks an extra point for the Reagan Raiders in the 1967 Texas 4A state championship game against Abilene Cooper. (Reagan High School Yearbook)

The Coyotes of Alice High School, ranked # 4 in Class 4A, were the heavy favorites to end the fifth-ranked Raiders' playoff run in the Bi-District championship game on Friday, November 24. Although both teams entered the game with perfect 10-0-0, records the Coyotes were the playoff-tested team, having reached the Bi-District championship game for the third consecutive season. The game was played at the Alice High School field where the Coyotes owned a 36-game unbeaten streak.

As befits a game between a pair of strong defensive teams, this one was scoreless after the first half and remained so deep into the third quarter. At that point Reagan had the ball at its own 25-yard line when halfback Don Ealey took a pitchout and raced 75 yards for the game's first touchdown and a 7-0 Raiders lead at 2:10 of the third quarter.

Those would prove to be the game's only points as the Raiders shocked the Coyotes and moved on to the Class 4A quarterfinals with their 7-0 victory.

In that quarterfinal game played on December 2, the Reagan Raiders were again on the road, traveling just over an hour south to San Antonio to play that city's Brackenridge High School Eagles (11-0-0). The Raiders' defense was again in top form and so was halfback Don Ealey. The Raider "D" held the Brackenridge ground game to just 57 yards and 145 yards of total offense. When the Raiders had the ball, Don Ealey tore through the Brackenridge defenders for 167 yards and a pair of touchdowns, leading the Raiders to a 20-0 win.

In its first-ever Class 4A state semifinal game, Reagan hosted the sixth-ranked Cardinals of Houston's Bellaire High School (12-1-0) before 22,800 fans in Austin's Memorial Stadium on Friday afternoon, December 9. Both teams possessed stingy defenses, while the Reagan offense held a slight statistical edge on the Cardinals.

Halfback Johnny Kleinert outruns the Cooper defense to score what would prove to be the winning touchdown in Reagan High's 20-19 victory in the Texas 4A state championship game on Dec. 16, 1967.(Reagan High School Yearbook)

The two teams had one common foe, the Austin High Maroons, Reagan having defeated the Maroons, 18-14, and the Cardinals winning by 21-15.

A state semifinal game is supposed to have been closer than this one was, but Reagan provided the hometown crowd with a great performance and showed just how good it had become in a very short time by flying past highly regarded Bellaire by a lopsided score of 40-7. In doing so, the Reagan defense held the potent Bellaire running attack to a net of just two yards.

Unbelievably to many, the Reagan Raiders in only their second year of playoff eligibility had defied the odds and were now playing for the Texas Class 4A

state championship. Once again taking to the road, the Raiders traveled just under 200 miles to the north to play the championship game in Fort Worth at Texas Christian University's Amon Carter Field. Their opponent on Friday, December 16, would be the Cougars of Abilene's Cooper High School. Like Reagan, Cooper was undefeated at 13-0-0, but unlike the surprising Raiders, Cooper had been the preseason pick by many to win the 4A championship.

As the *Austin American-Statesman* noted in a pregame article, the 1967 Abilene Cooper football team was regarded by many "as the finest high school football team to come out of Texas."

▲ *This is the goal line stand that preserved Reagan's one-point victory as the Raiders stopped Abilene Cooper at the one-yard line on the last play of the 1967 Texas 4A state championship game.(Reagan High School Yearbook)*

Favored by three touchdowns and despite the preseason predictions, the Cougars were something of a surprise themselves. The school, like Reagan, was not yet 10 years old, having opened in 1960. Not including the current season of 1967, Cooper had posted a less than impressive record of 17-37-7 in its previous six seasons of varsity football; this was only Cooper's second season with a winning record. Like Reagan, this was also the first season that Cooper had ever qualified for the playoffs. Having finished 1966 with a record of 9-1-0, the Cougars had now won 15 in a row and 22 of their last 23 games. For the '67 campaign, they were averaging 38 points per game, but allowing only six.

The state championship game was played in less than pristine conditions. Drizzle throughout the game, coupled with near freezing temperatures, made the grassy gridiron slick at best.

The Cougars and all of their supporters who had come east from Abilene had to be just a bit stunned when Reagan's Johnny Kleinert fielded the opening kickoff at his own three-yard line and returned it all the way, 97 yards, for a touchdown. Jesse Thompson's PAT gave the Raiders a 7-0 lead before many in the crowd had even found their seats.

After that initial shock, the Cougars settled down to play their game over the balance of the first half. They shut out the Reagan offense while mounting a comeback that resulted in a 19-7 Cooper lead at the intermission, leaving the Reagan yearbook to later remark, "It looked as if all the predictions were going to come true."

▲ *The scoreboard makes the result official in the 1967 Texas 4A state championship game. (Reagan High School Yearbook)*

After the halftime break, however, with their defense holding Cooper at bay and out of the end zone, what one reporter called the "opportunistic Raiders" came charging back. Late in the third quarter, Reagan took advantage of an errant Cooper punt and a short 31-yard field to score a touchdown and cut the Cooper lead

IF EVER THERE WAS A CINDERELLA FOOTBALL TEAM IT WAS THE 1967 REAGAN HIGH SCHOOL RAIDERS. IN ONLY ITS SECOND SEASON REAGAN HAD PLAYED SIX TEAMS RANKED AMONGST THE CLASS 4A TOP NINE AND DEFEATED EVERY ONE OF THEM, WINNING THE STATE AND NATIONAL CHAMPIONSHIP IN THE PROCESS.

▲   *The 1967 National Champion Reagan Raiders. (Reagan High School Yearbook)*

to 19-14. With time running out in the fourth quarter, a spectacular 41-yard pass reception by Don Ealey led to another Reagan touchdown and a 20-19 Raiders lead.

In the game's final minutes the Cougars would get one more scoring opportunity. They advanced the ball down the field and were at the Reagan one-yard line with no timeouts left and just seconds to play. With time for just one more play, the Cougars had no choice but to try for a touchdown. Leaving the ball in the hands of their all-everything quarterback Jack Mildren, the Cougars tried a quarterback sneak into the middle of the line. When the officials unpiled the players the ball was still short of the goal line. With time having expired, the referee is reported to have turned to Reagan defensive back Johnny Kleinert and said, "Boy, you're State Champs."

In July of 1984, *Texas Football* magazine called this game the greatest high school football upset in Texas of the previous 25 years.

If ever there was a Cinderella football team, it was the 1967 Reagan High School Raiders. Three years previously, the school did not exist. In 1965 Reagan fielded its first team, in essence a glorified junior varsity squad composed of sophomores and juniors. In 1966 the Raiders' first true varsity team finished with a respectable 6-3-1 record. Now in only its second season of playoff eligibility, Reagan had survived a grueling regular season and playoff schedule. In their last eight games the Reagan Raiders had played six teams ranked among the Class 4A top nine and defeated every one of them, winning the state championship in the process. The team's success earned for head coach Travis Raven 1967 Texas "Coach of the Year" honors.

Even more amazing, the same National Sports News Service poll that had ranked Coral Gables as # 1 placed the Reagan Raiders right there beside them— naming the Raiders as 1967 national co-champion. Incredibly, the Raiders had done something no other team has ever done before or since by rising to the top spot in the country in only its second true season of varsity football.

▼ *Coral Gables halfback Bertie Taylor returns the opening kickoff for a touchdown against Key West in 1968. (Coral Gables High School Yearbook)*

By the late 1960s Miami, Fla., had suddenly become the center of the country's high school football universe. Not only were teams from that area dominating Florida high school football, but five times between 1960 and 1967 teams from that city had either won outright or shared the national championship. Little would change in that regard over the balance of the decade, but the Raiders from Reagan High School in Austin would also remain in the thick of it.

Having swept the field for a perfect season and both the 1967 Florida championship and a national co-championship, Nick Kotys and his Coral Gables Cavaliers were primed and ready for the 1968 campaign. But, as usually happens in high school athletics, graduation takes a toll on the returning team. The Coral Gables offense was in pretty decent shape for the new campaign with running backs Bertram Taylor, Gerald Tinker (the defending state 220m dash champion), Richard Whittington, and future (1969) high school All-America selection Jack Brasington back for another season. Offensive tackle Mitchell Berger, another future high school All-American, was also returning. However, on the other side of the ball there were only two returning

▲ *Above: In this game
action from the 1968 season,
Dick Whittington of Coral
Gables breaks thru for a 19-
yard touchdown run against
Killian High. (Coral Gables
High School Yearbook)*

▸ *Following page, top:
Coral Gables' Jack Brasington
blasts through a huge hole
made by his offensive line
on this play against North
Miami in 1968. (Coral Gables
High School Yearbook)*

▸ *Following page, bottom:
Quarterback John Benitez (11)
and halfback Bertie Taylor (20)
made a great combination for
the Coral Gables Cavaliers
during the 1968 season. (Coral
Gables High School Yearbook)*

starters in defensive end Roger Peaco and safety John Clifford.

Coral Gables opened its '68 schedule by
blasting Christopher Columbus, 44-0. The Cavaliers held the Explorers to a total of 62 yards
of offense, so the new guys on defense seemed
to be working out right from the start. In their
next game the Cavaliers rushed for 295 yards,
but it almost was not enough against the Edison Red Raiders; a 14-point second quarter
provided the bulk of the Coral Gables scoring in the team's 21-6 win. Key West
also played the Cavaliers tough, but the Conches could only muster a fourth quarter touchdown on their home field as Gables raised its record to 3-0-0 with a 27-7
triumph.

Coral Gables next took on the Cougars of Killian High School before more
than 13,000 fans in the Orange Bowl on Thursday, October 10. Coral Gables scored
the only points of the first half to take a 6-0 lead at the intermission. In the second
half the lead see-sawed back and forth, with Killian taking a 7-6 lead and then
Coral Gables going back on top 13-7. Finally, with a pair of fourth quarter tallies,
the clincher coming with just 50 seconds remaining, Killian took a 19-13 lead and
held it till the end. In this game, Coral Gables was hurt by the lack of a passing
game (only two attempts with no completions) and too many penalties (totaling
117 yards).

The defeat halted the Cavaliers' win streak at 19 and dropped them from first
place all the way down to sixth in the next state poll.

Before more than 8,000 at Central Stadium, Coral Gables started another winning streak on Monday, October 21 (Columbus Day), against Coral Park. After a
tight first two quarters that found Coral Gables leading by only 7-6 at the intermission, the Cavaliers' defense kept Coral Park on its own side of the 50-yard line the entire second half and the Gables offense added two more touchdowns for a 21-6 win.

With its record now at 4-1-0, Coral Gables found itself in a three-way race with
Killian and Jackson high schools for the District 8, Class AA playoff spot. With every game a must win, the Cavaliers proceeded to take care of business.

Coral Gables took the field against Palmetto High on Saturday, October 26,
the team's second game of the week. Racing to a 21-0 lead after one quarter, the
Cavaliers tallied in every period as they humbled Palmetto, 44-19. Against Miami
Springs on Halloween night, Coral Gables amassed 433 yards of offense and again
scored in every quarter to post a 28-13 victory.

On Friday, November 8, the Cavaliers came up with a pair of crucial fumble
recoveries, then held off a late rally by North Miami to down the Pioneers, 21-14.

▸ *Coral Gables' Jack Brasington follows the blocking of Dick Whittington in the Cavaliers' 1968 game against Edison High. (Coral Gables High School Yearbook)*

A week later, Coral Gables lined up opposite the Stingarees of Miami High. Miami was experiencing its first losing season in 48 years and had only a single win and a tie in seven previous outings. The Cavaliers made it tough on themselves by turning the ball over five times, but a 14-point fourth quarter finally salted away a 24-0 Coral Gables victory.

On Thanksgiving morning against Southwest High, head coach Nick Kotys cleared his bench, using all 100 members of the varsity, plus a few junior varsity players, as Coral Gables roared to a 49-7 victory before more than 10,000 Turkey Day fans at Central Stadium. But those Cavaliers loyalists had much more than the team's ninth victory to be thankful for that morning. The Coral Gables victory had insured that the Cavaliers would emerge as the top team in Class AA, Region 8 and thus qualify for the state playoffs.

Coral Gables started its playoff run on Friday, December 6, against the Thoroughbreds of Hialeah High School in the Orange Bowl before 14, 915. On the game's first play from scrimmage, Coral Gables quarterback John Benitez fumbled the ball away, Hialeah eventually turning it into a touchdown and a 6-0 lead at the end of one quarter of play. If the Cavaliers faithful were worried, they need not have been. Coral Gables came roaring back, rolling up just under 600 yards of total offense, including an incredible 490 yards on the ground, as they steamrolled to a 49-18 playoff victory.

The following week on Friday the 13th, Coral Gables met Sarasota High School in a Class AA semifinal game in the Orange Bowl. The Cavaliers appeared to be a bit sluggish after their huge victory the week before and were fortunate to hold a 13-6 lead over the Sailors at the halftime break. Although Coral Gables would score in every quarter, it was not until the team had added a pair of touchdowns in the game's final 1:47 that they could relax a bit.

The Cavaliers' 32-6 victory over Sarasota sent them to the Class AA state championship game for the second consecutive year and, like the previous season, they would again be facing Jacksonville's Wolfson High for the state title.

If you were a fan of old school football, then this game was just your cup of tea. Wolfson's hard hitting defense caused Coral Gables all kinds of problems throughout the game, resulting in seven fumbles by the Cavaliers, three of which they lost. The first of those fumbles proved to be the most costly as Wolfson took a 6-0 first quarter lead with a 28-yard touchdown run on the very next play.

Still trailing 6-0 as the second half got under way, Coral Gables held the Wolfpack to a three and out to open the third quarter and then marched 69 yards down the field for its first touchdown of the game, the extra point giving Coral Gables a 7-6 lead. Coral Gables still led by that single point with just five seconds remaining when Wolfson completed a pass to the Coral Gables 48-yard line. It was the only pass completion by either team during the entire game and the first time that the Wolfpack had crossed midfield during the second half—but time expired before the Wolfpack could run another play.

Coral Gables' 7-6 victory gave the Cavaliers their second consecutive Class AA Florida state championship; Nick Kotys's team was now undefeated in 10 straight playoff games.

Despite finishing the season with a loss, 12-1-0, Coral Gables was still in the running for the 1968 national championship. To see how that situation would play out we have to return to Austin, Texas, and the Raiders of Reagan High School.

Like Coral Gables, Coach Travis Raven's Reagan High team had some major holes to fill in its 1968 roster after the graduation of 27 seniors the previous June. Most notably, Raven would have to find replacements for a couple of outstanding backfield men in quarterback Dale Rebold and halfback Johnny Kleinert. The whole offensive line in '68 would be manned by new faces and injuries would keep the O-line from becoming a truly cohesive unit until halfway through the regular season. The Reagan defense also suffered

▾   *Reagan High's All-State defender Howard Shaw brings down a Wheatley High ball carrier during the Raiders' 1968 Class 4A semifinal game. (Reagan High School Yearbook)*

Reagan's Gene Sanders leaves his blockers and Wheatley defenders in his wake during the 4A semifinal game on Dec. 7, 1968. (Reagan High School Yearbook)

heavy losses, but veteran two-way players would again be the core: future high school All-America selections Don Ealey and Mike Bayer, as well as Howard Shaw who alone averaged 16 tackles per game in 24 previous varsity contests. Another plus for the Reagan Raiders was a large number of experienced juniors now turned seniors who would move into starting roles; in fact, seniors would again make up the bulk of the team, 23 out of a total roster of only 44. Also on hand to back up the starters was a fine corps of experienced receivers who had seen a lot of playing time the year before.

Reagan opened its season on Friday, September 13, on a wet and muddy grid-iron against San Antonio's Churchill High. It looked as if Friday the 13th would be a jinx for the Raiders when the Churchill Chargers took a 7-0 lead just three minutes into the game. However, after tossing off some first game jitters, Reagan came roaring back. The defense shut out the Chargers over the balance of the game, holding Churchill to minus-10 yards rushing. Meanwhile, Reagan halfback Don Ealey's first touchdown of the season would tie the game, halfback Gene Sanders would add a pair of TDs, and wide receiver Mike Bayer scored another on a 42-yard pass from quarterback Emory Bellard, Jr., as Reagan opened its season with a 28-7 victory.

Reagan went methodically through the rest of its regular season schedule. The Raiders never really blew anyone away as they averaged a relatively modest 24.4 points per game, but they did not have to score a lot as the defense posted six shut-outs and allowed a total of just 27 points.

Only the Austin High Maroons gave Reagan a real battle, but even that game was one-sided despite the low score. Played in the mud of Austin's Nelson Field, the Raiders out-gained the Maroons 314-45, with all of that yardage coming on the ground. Despite this overwhelming offensive superiority, the Raiders did not get on the scoreboard until Don Ealey found the end zone from 10 yards away with 9:37 left in the game. Sophomore Billy Schott added the PAT and later a 24-yard field goal to close out the scoring in Reagan's 10-0 win.

Finishing the regular season a perfect 10-0-0, the Reagan Raiders had again qualified for the Class 4A playoffs. For the most part, the playoffs would prove to be no more difficult for Reagan than the regular season had been. In the District 27 championship game, Reagan took advantage of six turnovers and a short 19-yard punt by the Seguin High Matadors to score five touchdowns and a pair of field goals as they posted a season-high point total in humbling Seguin, 40-0. Miller High School of Corpus Christi was the next to fall before the Raiders as Reagan captured the Bi-District crown with another shutout victory, its eighth of the season, 25-0.

Having advanced to the Class 4A quarterfinals, Reagan faced Wheatley High of San Antonio in a classic top offense vs. top defense clash. With 409 points, the Wheatley Lions were the second highest scoring 4A team in the state, while Reagan had the best defense, having allowed just 27 points in 12 games. In this instance it would be the defensive team that came out ahead. While the Reagan first team defense was on the field the Lions could only manage 27 yards of total offense. Meanwhile, the Raiders took a 10-0 lead at the half and then exploded for 20 points in the third quarter en route to a very convincing 37-6 victory.

In the 4A semifinals on Saturday, December 14, Reagan traveled to Houston for a 2 P.M. game with that city's Washington High School in Rice University Stadium. Like the game with Wheatley High, this would be another match-up between an outstanding offense and an equally outstanding defense. The Eagles of Washington High (13-0-0) had been lighting up the scoreboard all season with a state-high 429 points, while the Reagan defense, as we have seen, had been more than stingy. If Reagan was to win this game it would have to stop the passing attack of the Eagles quarterback Larry Foster, who had drilled opponents for 2,527 yards and 30 touchdowns.

After a scoreless first quarter, Reagan took a 7-0 lead on an Emory Bellard, Jr., to Gary Morrison 30-yard touchdown pass, but the Washington Eagles came right back to tie the score on Larry Foster's 20-yard pass to end James Cain. Don Ealey then gave Reagan a 14-7 halftime advantage with a 13-yard TD scamper just before the intermission. The only scoring of the third quarter was by Washington on another Foster to Cain connection, this time covering 15 yards. However, Reagan retained a razor thin lead, 14-13, when the Raiders' Jackie Linam broke through and blocked the PAT try after the Eagles' second score.

The Reagan Raiders would put the game on ice by exploding for 17 points in the final frame. And they would turn Washington High's main weapon against the Eagles in doing so. A pair of interceptions by the Raiders midway through the final frame would result in 10 Reagan points, while a third Washington turnover, a fumble, would result in a Don Ealey touchdown with less than two minutes to play.

▸ *Reagan High's All-State end Mike Bayer makes a catch for big yardage against Odessa Permian in the 1968 Texas 4A state championship game. (Reagan High School Yearbook)*

Reagan's 31-13 victory extended the team's win streak to 29 games, but more importantly it sent the Raiders to the Class 4A championship game for the second straight season.

The 1968 Class 4A title game would be played on Saturday afternoon, December 21, in San Angelo's Bobcat Stadium. More than 14,000 turned out to see the Reagan Raiders do battle with the Black Panthers of Odessa's Permian High School for big school state supremacy. Permian had won the Class 4A championship in 1965 and came into this game with a record of 11-3-0. Reagan entered the game as a slight favorite based primarily on a solid statistical advantage over the Panthers.

Turnovers would play a major part in the scoring of this defense-oriented game. Late in the first quarter, Permian broke on top 3 to 0 on a 32-yard field goal by Kent Husley; Permian had recovered a fumble by Reagan fullback Howard Shaw to set up the scoring play. With 2:51 left in the first half Reagan tied the score on a 23-yard field goal by Billy Schott, his 11th three-pointer of the season. The Raiders' field goal climaxed a 10-play drive that began when linebacker Hap Feuerbacher recovered a Permian fumble.

After the ensuing kickoff, Reagan held the Panthers to a three and out, a short Permian punt giving Reagan excellent field position at the Permian 39-yard line. It only took the Raiders two plays to cash in, the touchdown coming on a 27-yard pass from quarterback Emory Bellard, Jr., to wide receiver Mike Bayer. Billy Schott's PAT gave the Raiders a 10-3 lead at the half.

The first time it had the ball in the third quarter Reagan marched 56 yards in 11 plays, all on the ground, with Don Ealey going the final 13 to push the Reagan lead to 17-3. Permian came right back with a 76-yard drive that culminated in a 10-yard Steve Cox to Dennis Duckworth touchdown pass. Cox then connected with his halfback Stewart on a pass for the two-point conversion, and with 1:41 left in the third quarter the Reagan lead was down to just six points, 17-11.

The teams would battle ferociously over the game's final 13-plus minutes, but neither would add to its point total.

By a final tally of 17-11, the Raiders of Reagan High School had won their second consecutive Texas 4A state championship. The Raiders had also gone undefeated for a second straight season, this time finishing with a perfect 15-0-0 record—the first high school team in Texas history to win 15 games in a single season. In doing so, Reagan had pushed its winning streak to 30 (since the final game of 1966).

A huge part of Reagan's success had been the play of its defense, which finished the season as the best in Texas. The Raiders' "D" had allowed only 57 points all season, giving up less than 65 yards per game rushing and an even more paltry 62.8 yards passing.

With the close of the 1968 high school football season, it was again time to determine a national champion. In 1967, we recall that honor was shared by the undefeated teams from Coral Gables and Reagan high schools. While Reagan was again undefeated in 1968, Coral Gables had lost once. However, according to Art Johlfs of the National Sports News Service, that Coral Gables had lost a game did not necessarily knock the Cavaliers out of contention for the national championship. In an interview with Johlfs printed in the December 28, 1968, edition of the

▾ *1968 4A State Champs*
and National Co-Champs.
(Reagan High School Yearbook)

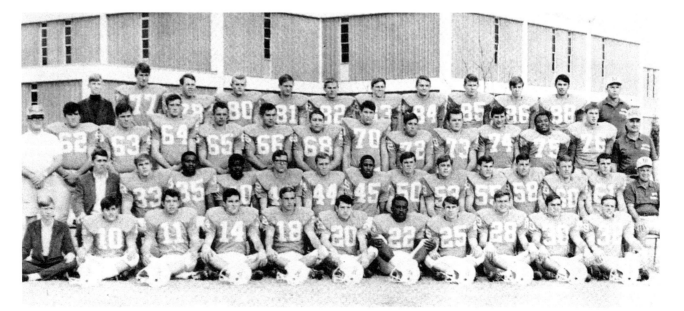

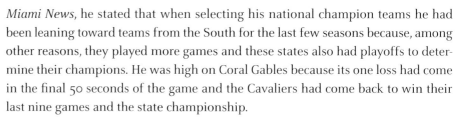

▾ *Coral Gables' Glenn
Cameron battles for some
tough yardage against the
Miami High Stingarees on
Nov. 13, 1969. (Coral Gables
High School Yearbook)*

Miami News, he stated that when selecting his national champion teams he had been leaning toward teams from the South for the last few seasons because, among other reasons, they played more games and these states also had playoffs to determine their champions. He was high on Coral Gables because its one loss had come in the final 50 seconds of the game and the Cavaliers had come back to win their last nine games and the state championship.

Johlfs was considering a few teams for national champion honors in 1968, among them Valdosta (Ga.), Upper Arlington (Oh.), and Rockville (Md.). While Reagan appears to have been an easy choice for him, Johlfs could not leave Coral Gables out. He cited the team's record of 63-7-0, four state championships, and two national titles—all within the last six seasons. When all was said and done, for the second consecutive season the National Sports News Service named the Reagan Raiders (15-0-0) and the Coral Gables Cavaliers (12-1-0) as co-national champions for 1968.

The Reagan Raiders were looking for a three-peat as both state and national champions in 1969. The Raiders opened the season as if that would indeed be the case, extending their winning streak to 36 by posting five shutouts while winning their first six games, outscoring the opposition 176-14. In Week Seven, however, the Raiders hit a huge snag in McCallum High School and dropped an intense defensive battle by a 10-7 count. The Raiders rebounded the next week to hand Lanier High School a 47-0 thrashing. But against the Maroons of Austin High, they were held to just seven points for the second time in three weeks, losing to their cross town rival, 27-7.

Reagan closed out the season with a 51-0 win over Anderson High, ending the campaign with a record of 8-2-0. However, their two losses in district play kept the Reagan Raiders out of the state playoffs and the national championship picture for 1969.

In Florida, the Coral Gables Cavaliers were also trying for a three-peat at both the state and national level.

Coral Gables, ranked # 1 in the preseason Florida polls, opened the defense of its back-to-back state (and national) championships with a pair of shutout victories over Northwestern, 21-0, and the Edison Red Raiders, 27-0. The team's rock solid defense had allowed a combined 126 yards in total offense in the two victories.

On October 4, the Cavaliers traveled to Gainesville to take on the Gainesville High Purple Hurricanes. In a game heavy on defense by both teams, the Cavaliers

▲ *Coral Gables halfback Bernie Kitteriell eludes several Southwest High defenders in this game on Nov. 27, 1969.*

▲ *The Miami High defense finally catches up with Cavaliers halfback Bernie Kitteriell in this 1969 game action. (Coral Gables High School Yearbook)*

▸ *Leaving players in his wake, Coral Gables' Glenn Cameron runs away from pursuing Miami High tacklers on Nov. 13, 1969. (Coral Gables High School Yearbook)*

managed to scratch out a 13-0 lead as the contest proceeded into the fourth quarter. The Purple Hurricanes finally broke through to cut that lead to 13-7 with 9:26 left to play, but the Cavaliers were able to hold on to make that the final score.

In its next game on October 9, Coral Gables faced the Killian High Cougars, the only team to defeat the Cavaliers in their last 33 games, before more than 10,000 fans at Central Stadium. Despite holding Killian to just 100 yards of total offense, Coral Gables had to stage a second half rally to keep its record clean. The Cavaliers' four turnovers probably had something to do with keeping the game close.

After a scoreless first quarter, Killian took advantage of an interception midway through the second period, turning it into a touchdown and a 6-0 lead—the extra point try blocked by the Cavaliers' Ralph Ortega. Coral Gables came right back to score a touchdown of its own to take a 7-6 lead at the half. Early in the third quarter, Killian regained the lead, 12-7, again thanks to the largesse of the Coral Gables offense that fumbled the ball away at its own 13-yard line. Coral Gables immediately responded by marching 57 yards in 12 plays to regain the lead, 14-12. The Cavaliers' defense held Killian to just five yards of total offense over the game's last 19 minutes, while the Coral Gables offense added an insurance tally with a touchdown in the game's final 34 seconds for a harder-than-it-should-have-been 21-12 victory.

In a total mismatch, Coral Gables next shut out the winless, and still scoreless, Rams of Coral Park High School by a score of 35-0. The Cavaliers had averaged just 20.5 points per game in winning their first four outings, but the 35-point outburst against Coral Park must have set the Coral Gables offense in motion as they would go on to average 38 points per game over the balance of the season.

▲ *Coral Gables placekicker Rick McCord was a busy man during the Cavaliers' 1969 campaign. (Coral Gables High School Yearbook)*

▸ *The Coral Gables defense stopped this Miami High ball carrier dead in his tracks during their 1969 game. (Coral Gables High School Yearbook)*

On October 23, Coral Gables blitzed Palmetto by a 47-14 score. The following week, Gables actually trailed Key West at the end of the first quarter, 7-3, but then exploded for 28 points in the second quarter as they sloshed across a sea of mud at Central Stadium to a 45-7 victory.

The Cavaliers next faced the Pioneers of North Miami High on Thursday, November 6. North Miami riddled the Coral Gables defense for 247 yards through the air, but on the ground the Pioneers were held to minus-seven. The game was still close after the first quarter, Coral Gables leading by just a point at 7-6. But then North Miami would fall victim to its own turnovers and Coral Gables middle guard Ellis Statom. All of those passing yards by North Miami were pretty much canceled out by its six turnovers, and Statom was in the middle of most of them as he recovered a pair of fumbles and intercepted a pass, as well as blocking the extra point try after the Pioneers' lone touchdown. An 18-point second quarter gave Coral Gables a commanding halftime lead as the Cavaliers rolled to a 32-6 victory.

With its record now 8-0-0 and its win streak at 17, Coral Gables next played Miami High on November 13. Coral Gables had little trouble with the still slumping Stingarees, who were held to only 68 yards of offense in dropping their seventh game in eight outings, 35-7.

In its final regular season game, Coral Gables rolled to a 34-14 victory against Southwest High. Coral Gables quarterback Ed McDougal threw for four touchdowns and halfback Jack Brasington (a 1969 high school All-American) scored a pair on an 85-yard run and a 59-yard pass reception.

With its record now a perfect 10-0-0 and having extended its winning streak to 19 in a row, one would think that the next stop for Coral Gables would be the Class AA playoffs. Unfortunately for the team and their supporters, this was not to be the case. For Coral Gables to make the playoffs, the team had to win the Class AA District 8 championship. The two best teams in the district, Coral Gables and

Just one of the many great catches made by Jack Brasington for Coral Gables during the 1969 season. (Coral Gables High School Yearbook)

Miami Jackson, finished the season with identical 10-0-0 records. The tie breaker in this case was the total victories by each team's opponents. Coral Gables opponents had won a total of 34 games, but Jackson's had been victorious 40 times—therefore Jackson got the playoff spot and the two-time defending state and national champion, despite an undefeated season, went home with nothing.

Well, almost nothing. Adding even more irony to the situation, in the final Florida Class AA state poll Coral Gables (291 points, 16 first place votes) finished first by a healthy margin over second-place Jackson (234 points, 5 first place votes).

Coral Gables did, however, have one postseason game to play, against Hialeah High School for, of all things, the Greater Miami Athletic Conference runner-up spot. Coach Nick Kotys did not really want to play in this basically meaningless game, which would prove disastrous to his team should they lose. However, as Kotys told the local newspapers, they had a commitment to the conference and would keep it.

Coral Gables scored single touchdowns in the first, second, and fourth quarters, taking a 19-0 lead to the final play of the game, when Hialeah returned a fumble 66 yards for a touchdown and then added a two-point conversion for a 19-8 final. The Coral Gables effort was aided by Hialeah's six turnovers, including four interceptions by Cavaliers' safety Cornelius Colzie.

The victory left Coral Gables with a 1969 final record of 11-0-0, a 20-game win streak, and the top spot in the Class AA state poll. Adding to their laurels, a national computer ranking system called the Junior Super Bowl ranked the Cavaliers as the nation's top team. The National Sports News Service also named Coral Gables its national champion, but this time they had to share top billing with Georgia's Valdosta Wildcats. Not bad for a team that had not won its conference championship.

Coral Gables High School had now been named national champion for three consecutive seasons: 1967, 1968, and 1969. Only one other team during the entire 20th century had gained top national honors three consecutive times and that was Oak Park, which held the top spot for four consecutive seasons from 1910 to 1913.

The Cavaliers' offensive line gave placekicker Rick McCord plenty of protection on every PAT and field goal try during the 1969 season. (Coral Gables High School Yearbook)

▲ *The Coral Gables 1969*
football banquet program.

With the close of the 1969 season, the curtain came down on Coral Gables' supremacy over Florida and national high school football. In Nick Kotys's final two years at the helm, 1970 and 1971, the Cavaliers finished a combined 16-4-1. Over the balance of the 20th century the team would play decent, though not spectacular, football. Coral Gables never again won a state or national championship, seldom even qualifying for the state playoffs.

Nick Kotys retired from coaching after the '71 season at the relatively young age of 58. From 1952 through 1971, Kotys's Coral Gables Cavaliers had posted the best record in the state of Florida, 162-35-9, .786. From 1963 through 1969, his team was one of the most dominant in the country with a mark of 74 wins, seven defeats, and no ties, a winning percentage of .914; four playoff state championships, and four national championships (his teams also captured two non-playoff state championships in 1956 and 1958). In 1984 Nick Kotys was inducted into the Florida Sports Hall of Fame and in 2007 Kotys was named one of the greatest coaches in state history. Nick Kotys died in 2005 at the age of 92.

————————

After back-to-back state and national championships in 1967 and 1968, the Raiders of Reagan High School dipped to 8-2-0 in 1969 and failed to make the Texas Class 4A playoffs. Full of enthusiasm and hope for the 1970 campaign, the team's spirits were somewhat dampened during its first two games—the Raiders had seemingly forgotten how to score.

The season opener pitted the Reagan Raiders, second-ranked in Class 4A, against Houston's Springwoods Tigers, also ranked among the top five. The Raiders' defense proved to be as solid as ever as it held the Tigers to just 66 yards of offense (minus-three yards passing), but that was almost not enough as Springwoods showed up with a pretty good defense of its own. In the first quarter, Springwoods took advantage of a botched Reagan snap on a punt attempt, turning the ensuing field position into a 25-yard field goal and an early 3-0 lead. Reagan countered with a pair of Billy Schott three-pointers in the second frame to lead 6-3 at the half. And that was it, no scoring by either team in the second half of this defense-dominated game as Reagan opened the season with a 6-3 victory.

The Raiders traveled to Houston the following week to take on the Bears of Spring Branch High School. The only scoring in the first half was another Billy Schott field goal that gave the Raiders a 3-0 lead at the intermission. The rest of the game's scoring came in the fourth quarter. Early in that quarter the Bears moved ahead 7-3, but Reagan came back to regain the lead, 10-7, on a 10-yard pass from quarterback Larry Miller to Mike Epperson. With 4:10 left in the game, Spring Branch added a second touchdown, but missed the extra point to take a 13-10 advantage. This time Reagan was unable to answer and the team's record fell to 1-1-0 with the 13-10 defeat.

In the first two games of the season the Reagan offense appeared to be lost, still trying to find itself. Following the loss to Spring Branch, the whole team went through a strong week of practice in preparation for its next game with Churchill High, a week that no doubt included a bit of soul searching as well. That week of intense practice quickly bore fruit, because before the game with Churchill High was even half over it was clearly evident that the entire Reagan team was back on track.

Churchill High was mowed down by a 53-7 score and Reagan went on to win the following five games by a combined 216-19. Week Nine brought cross town rival Austin High, which had defeated the Raiders the previous season. This time around it was a much different story as Reagan jumped to a 35-7 halftime lead and coasted to a 52-25 victory. Reagan completed the regular season with a 24-6 win over Anderson High.

With a record of 9-1-0, Reagan had once again qualified for the Class 4A playoffs. Reagan's postseason run began on Saturday, November 21, against the Buccaneers of Brazoswood High School. Like Reagan had been just a few short years previously, Brazoswood was in its first year of varsity competition, but had come on strong with a perfect 10-0-0 record.

With a strong wind at their backs to open the game, the Reagan Raiders took a 13-0 lead after the first quarter on a pair of Billy Schott field goals and short touchdown run by halfback Waymon Clark. Brazoswood scored a second quarter safety to make it 13-2 at the half, and then added a touchdown early in the third quarter to close the gap to 13-9 as the Reagan faithful began to get a little nervous. With the game still in the third period, the Buccaneers were driving for the go-ahead score when the Reagan defense rose up and stopped them cold at the Reagan three-yard line. The Raiders then came right back and marched 97 yards for the clinching touchdown, adding a late insurance tally to make the final score 27-9. Before some 15,000 fans, the Buccaneers had given Reagan a real battle, but in the end experience won out.

Immediately after the game there was a coin flip to determine the site of the next playoff game. Reagan lost the flip and had to travel to Corpus Christi the following Saturday afternoon to play that city's Ray High School Texans in a regional final. Ray High had won the 1959 state championship and like Reagan entered the regional final with a record of 10-1-0.

The tone of this game was set on the opening kickoff. Ray High was on the receiving end, but fumbled the ball which was recovered by Reagan's Cary Hill at the Ray three-yard line. Two plays later, quarterback Larry Miller scored from the one and Reagan had jumped to a quick 7-0 lead, pushing it to 17-0 by halftime. Reagan, which dominated the game on both sides of the ball, added a pair of touchdowns in the final quarter to come away with a convincing 31-0 victory.

On Friday night, December 4, Reagan was again on the road, this time traveling to San Antonio for a 4A quarterfinal match-up with that city's Roosevelt High. The Roosevelt Rough Riders had opened the season by losing their first four games, but since then had come charging back by winning eight in a row. Unfortunately for the Rough Riders, for this game they would be without the heart and soul of their offense, quarterback Richard Salley, due to a back injury suffered the previous week.

While the Reagan defense played a great game throughout, the Raiders led only 7-0 at the half due to some sloppy play and several turnovers by its offense. Adjustments made at halftime did the trick and, behind three touchdowns by quarterback Larry Miller, the Reagan Raiders rolled to a 28-0 victory and advanced to the state semifinals.

In that semifinal game, Reagan would be taking on the undefeated (13-0-0) Yellow Jackets of Port Arthur's Jefferson High School; like Reagan the Yellow Jackets were a two-time state champion. Both teams had powerful offenses and brick wall defenses; it looked to be a pretty even contest.

On a cold but clear Saturday afternoon, December 12, more than 30,000 hardy fans showed up at Houston's Rice Stadium for this game. Whatever these fans were expecting, it probably was not the scoring blitz with which Reagan opened the action.

On the third play of the game, Reagan halfback Waymon Clark burst through the line and into the Jefferson secondary, racing 64 yards for the first touchdown of the contest just 1:16 after the opening kickoff; a run for the two-pointer failed. Jefferson's Yellow Jackets came right back and marched to a first and goal at the Reagan three-yard line. Four plays later, they gave up the ball on downs at the two after a great goal line stand by the Raiders' defense.

Going back on offense, Reagan ran four plays, all on the ground, moving the ball out to the 17-yard line, but an offside penalty pushed the Raiders back to their 12. On the next play halfback, Ed Attra took the handoff and went wide around the right side, picked up a couple of blocks, and was gone—88 yards for another electrifying Reagan touchdown. This time the two-pointer was successful and Reagan had grabbed a 14-0 lead at 2:09 of the first quarter.

The Reagan defense would stage another goal line stand in the second quarter that stopped Jefferson at the four-yard line, but the Yellow Jackets finally broke through to score later in the quarter to cut the Reagan lead to 14-6. Just before the intermission, a five-yard pass from Larry Miller to wide receiver Mike Foster closed out a 75-yard drive to give Reagan a 21-6 lead at the half.

▾ *Reagan running back Robert Easley powers through the Churchill High defense during the 1970 season. (Reagan High School Yearbook)*

The Raiders pushed their lead to 28-6 in the third quarter. The Jefferson Yellow Jackets added a touchdown in the fourth quarter, but that only served to lower the final deficit from 22 to 16 points. Reagan's 28-12 victory allowed them to move on to the Texas Class 4A state championship game for the third time in four years.

As they had in their last trip to the Class 4A state title game in 1968, in 1970 the Reagan Raiders would again be facing the Black Panthers of Permian High School at San Angelo Stadium. Permian entered the game with a perfect 14-0-0 record and in the midst of a 17-game win streak. Statistically both teams were almost even, neither showing much of an advantage in any one category of offense or defense, with the possible exception of the placekicking game. That category definitely belonged to Reagan's Billy "Sure" Schott, who had missed on only four of 64 PATs during the season and had converted 10 field goal tries to give him 90 points scored.

With the temperature a brisk 47 degrees, the weather was near perfect for football as almost 18,000 filed into the stadium in San Angelo on Saturday afternoon, December 19, for the 2 P.M. start. Reagan kicked off to get the game underway and, after forcing Permian to punt, took over the ball at its own 36-yard line. Reagan's opening drive was a beauty as the Raiders marched right down the field, 64 yards in 13 plays. Fullback Doug Mitchell closed out the drive with a three-yard

touchdown run, Billy Schott's extra point kick giving Reagan a 7-0 lead at 5:16 of the first quarter.

It did not take long for the Raiders to double their advantage. Following the ensuing kickoff, Permian put the ball into play at its 34-yard line. On first down, Panther's quarterback Ben Montgomery faked the handoff up the middle and pitched back to running back Collins Rice. Instead of Rice catching the lateral, however, there to take the pitchout was Reagan's Scottie Senter, who grabbed the ball out of the air and sped 34 yards into the end zone for another Reagan touchdown almost before the Panthers knew what had happened.

▲ This Reagan High ball carrier is just yards away from the end zone in the Raiders' 1970 Texas 4A state championship game against Odessa Permian. (Reagan High School Yearbook)

Billy Schott's PAT made it a 14-0 game—only 13 seconds had elapsed between the two Reagan touchdowns.

In the second quarter, Permian cut the Reagan lead in half with a 78-yard, five-play drive that made the score 14-7 with 8:33 left in the first half. The Reagan Raiders came right back to answer that touchdown with an 81-yard drive of their own, a drive that ate up almost six minutes of the clock. Doug Mitchell closed out the 13-play march with an 18-yard burst up the middle for his second touchdown of the game. Billy Schott's PAT gave the Raiders a 21-7 lead at the half.

Reagan had dominated play in the first half, running 38 offensive plays to only 12 for Permian. Several Permian turnovers had already squelched possible scoring opportunities, while the Raiders would not have a single turnover the entire game. Permian made something of a comeback in the third quarter, holding the Raiders without a first down while adding a touchdown of its own to close the gap to 21-14. However, the Reagan defense held the line in the fourth quarter and did not allow Permian to add to its total.

When the final whistle sounded, the Reagan Raiders had a 21-14 victory and their third state championship of the last four seasons. And, despite the one defeat on its record, Reagan was chosen as the national champion by the National Sports News Service—and this time they did not have to share the honor with anyone.

Following the 1970 season, Reagan head coach Travis Raven decided to forgo coaching and took the position as Athletic Director for the Austin Independent School District. While Raven had been at the helm of the Reagan Raiders, he had led the team on a path of remarkable and almost unprecedented growth and accomplishment. Under his direction, the Raiders had grown from a first-year, basically junior varsity aggregation to a team that was recognized as being among the

▾   *This Permian ball carrier is lifted high off the ground and held for no gain by the Reagan Raiders' defense during the 1970 Texas 4A state championship game. (Reagan High School Yearbook)*

top three or four all-time in Texas high school football history. Over his last five seasons, Travis Raven had coached Reagan High to a record of 57-6-1, .898, a mark that at one point included a string of 36 consecutive victories. The Raiders played in 14 Class 4A playoff games and had won every one of them, earning for Reagan High School three Texas 4A state championships. In those three state championship seasons, the Raiders were also named national champion. It was an incredible record of achievement, made all the more so considering that 1) it was done at a brand new school and 2) like Coral Gables High School with the retirement of Nick Kotys, since Travis Raven stopped coaching at Reagan High School the team has had decent success, but never since has it won a state or national championship.

## CHAPTER 9

THE MOELLER MYSTIQUE

Archbishop Moeller High School
Cincinnati, Ohio

As has just been seen, the battle for the national championship was dominated by schools from the southern part of the country during the 1960s and into the '70s. It was during this same time that another school was just getting started, one that would soon bring the focus of the high school football championship back to the Midwestern part of the country.

▾ Moeller quarterback Tim Koegel (14) led the Moeller offense from 1974-76, compiling a record of 34-1 while winning two Ohio Division I and one national championship. (All photos in this chapter are from the Moeller High School yearbook.)

In September of 1960, a new Catholic high school first opened its doors in Cincinnati, Ohio. Run by the priests and brothers of the Society of Mary, the Marianists, the school was named in honor of the fourth Roman Catholic bishop of that city, Archbishop Henry K. Moeller. Archbishop Moeller High School would take as its nickname the Crusaders, with blue and gold as its colors.

In those earliest days, the school had a faculty that included six members of the Marianist order and two lay men, led by the school's principal, Brother Lawrence Eveslage, S.M. Bro. Larry, as he was more popularly known, made a selection in one of his first hiring decisions that would affect the history of Moeller High School to this day. To better understand that decision we need to take a step back and look at some of the history of Marianist high schools in Ohio and how that history affected Bro. Larry's hiring decision.

Bro. Larry had been involved in teaching and administration at several Marianist schools around Ohio for more than 30 years before taking his assignment at Moeller. From his experience at these schools, one of Bro. Larry's beliefs was that a successful beginning of the school year by a school's football team definitely contributed to creating both a positive atmosphere and positive results in every phase of school life over the balance of the year. He could cite three prime examples from his own experience. At Dayton's Chaminade

Moeller placekicker Ken
Naber seldom missed on
PAT or field goal attempts.

Wide receiver Bob Massong
leaps to make another catch
during the Crusaders first state
championship season in 1975.

High School, head coach Gerard "Fuzzy" Faust had led the football team from 1933-1953, compiling a record of 123-49-10 and winning 13 City League championships. Even more impressive was the record of head coach Herb Eisele at Cleveland's Cathedral Latin School, where Eisele's Latin Lions had won nine city championships from 1927 to 1946, as well as three consecutive state titles in 1944, 1945 and 1946. At another Cleveland area school, St. Joseph High School, Bill Gutbrod was doing great things with the football team, including compiling the third-best record in the entire state from 1957-1969.

All of these schools were also rated at the top in academics and other areas of high school life. The connection for Bro. Larry was no accident; by working at these schools he had seen first hand how this success on the gridiron early in a school year had engendered pride in a school and enhanced all of its activities. As Dick Beerman notes in his book about Moeller athletics, *We Are the "Big Moe"*, Bro. Larry "was determined that the school years at Archbishop Moeller High School would enjoy that advantage as well."

Bro. Larry had also noticed one other thing: all three of these head coaches had played football at, and were graduates of, the University of Dayton. Over the years the Dayton Flyers had enjoyed a fine reputation for gridiron success and had produced many of Ohio's finest high school coaches. That the University of Dayton was also a Marianist school was not lost on Bro. Larry.

For all of the above stated reasons, when Bro. Larry went looking for a football coach for the new Moeller High School, one man soon stood out, Gerry Faust, the son of his long time friend "Fuzzy" Faust. Born on May 21, 1935, Gerry Faust was the product of a Marianist education. He graduated from Chaminade High School where he was a two-time starting quarterback for his father and named All-Ohio his senior year in 1953. Gerry then moved on to the collegiate ranks at the University of Dayton where he became a three-time letterman at quarterback, graduating in 1958.

After graduating from Dayton, Faust returned to his high school alma mater, Chaminade, where he taught English and history and joined the football coaching staff as a backfield coach for both the offense and defense. After the 1959 football season, Bro. Larry called Faust and offered him the head coaching job at Moeller. As Gerry Faust would later recall, "I didn't even know the school existed. On the phone, I told him I wasn't interested. Then he asked me to come to the school and talk with him. I saw the school and found out where the kids would be coming from. I took the job even though I had no previous intentions of doing so."

▾ *Top: The Moeller defense did an excellent job during the '75 season in chasing down opposing ball carriers before they could advance very far.*

▾ *Bottom: The Moeller defense smothers a St. Edward ball carrier during the 1975 Ohio Division I championship game.*

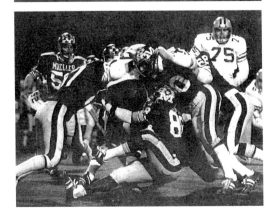

When that first school year at Moeller started in September of 1960, so did the school's first football team. Of necessity it was composed of all freshmen and coached by Faust and one assistant, then Athletic Director Bill Daily, and one volunteer, Bill Clark, who had an expertise in weight training.

That freshman team finished with a modest 4-4-0 record, but the team progressed to 8-2-1 as jayvees the next season. The 1962 squad, which now included juniors in its line-up, finished 4-6-0. The 1963 Moeller Crusaders are considered the school's first true varsity team, the first team that had both seniors and a schedule composed of all varsity level opponents. Giving an indication of what might be expected in the future, that season Gerry Faust's team finished with a record of 9-1-0. After dipping to 8-2-0 the following year, the Crusaders put it all together in 1965 with a perfect 10-0-0 season—the first of seven perfect campaigns under Gerry Faust. The Crusaders also finished third in the AP state poll that season, their first state ranking.

In a state with as rich and competitive a football tradition as is found in Ohio, the new kid on the block still had to pay his dues. Over the next half-dozen or so years, Moeller continued to play good football and posted a record of 57-11-2 from 1966 thru 1972; however, the Crusaders only finished the season state ranked in 1969 (10-0-0) at # 3 and 1971 (9-1-0), when they placed fifth. Moeller's major stumbling blocks during those years were the other members of Cincinnati's Greater Catholic League (GCL), primarily Roger Bacon, Elder, and St. Xavier high schools, which handed the Crusaders eight of their 11 defeats. Adding even more significance to Moeller's soon to be success, the GCL (and later the GCL South) would become known as one of the nation's toughest high school football leagues, annually being ranked among the top five leagues in the country. Moeller's strength of schedule would be undeniable and go a long way in legitimizing the team's success.

▲ Moeller defender Jim Gross (53) is about to lower the boom on St. Edward quarterback Dan McHugh during the 1975 Ohio Division I championship game.

Moeller's gridiron reputation was also enhanced during this period as no less than seven Crusaders had earned high school All-America recognition.

In 1972 the Ohio High School Athletic Association instituted its football play-off system. That first playoff season, Moeller finished with a record of 8-2 and failed to make the playoffs. However, the 1973 season would mark the beginning of an era in which the Moeller Crusaders would be recognized as one of the truly legendary high school football aggregations of the 20th century, and for that matter in the entire history of the high school sport.

After squeaking by Cincinnati Princeton, 13-12, in their 1973 season opener, the Crusaders rolled over Walnut Hills 61-0. In Week Three it was a close call, but Moeller escaped with an 8-7 victory over St. Xavier. After that it was smooth sailing as the Crusaders won their last eight games by a combined 261-14, with five shut-outs, to finish the regular season a perfect 10-0 and ranked # 2 in the final Class AAA state poll. It also marked the beginning of an unprecedented run in which Moeller would finish either first or second in the final AP Ohio poll.

With its perfect record, Moeller had also qualified for the state playoffs for the first time. It was, however, a much different story when the Crusaders took the field for their first-ever Class AAA playoff game. Going up against Youngstown's Cardinal Mooney High School, the Crusaders suffered a 34-7 thumping at the hands of the eventual state champions.

The 1974 campaign was almost a carbon copy of the previous season. While Moeller was not quite as dominant as in 1973, the Crusaders

▸ Head Coach Gerry Faust celebrates with his team after the Crusaders won their first state championship in 1975.

▲ The 1975 Moeller Crusaders—the school's first championship team.

held off Findlay High, 21-20, in the second game of the season and GCL foe Elder, 24-20, in the regular season finale to again finish 10-0. This time, in qualifying for the Class AAA playoffs, the Crusaders were ranked # 1 in the final Class AAA AP state poll. Although Moeller did a little better this time in the AAA semifinals, the result was the same as they dropped a 20-10 decision to the eventual state champions from Warren's Harding High School.

After having completed two of the most successful, but also heartbreaking, football seasons in school history, Gerry Faust's Moeller Crusaders approached 1975 with a renewed "can do" mind set. In the opener against Clayton Northmont, Moeller rolled to a 42-0 victory. While many may have thought that the Crusaders would now roll through the season, Cincinnati power Princeton brought the team back to earth. Moeller did win the game, but they had to fight all the way for the 12-10 victory.

Three more victories quickly followed, but a trip to Cleveland for a game on Friday night, October 10, against St. Joseph High School almost proved to be Moeller's undoing. The Crusaders fell behind 7-0 in the first quarter and still trailed 7-6 at the half, having missed the extra point try after a second quarter touchdown. The score remained at 7-6 until the 1:16 point of the fourth quarter when the Crusaders pulled the game out with a touchdown for a 13-7 win.

Moeller took no prisoners over the final four weeks of the season as it posted shutouts in three of the four games and outscored the opposition 156-8. For the third consecutive season, Moeller had finished a perfect 10-0 and qualified for the state playoffs ranked # 2 in the final Class AAA state poll. The Crusaders fought off a valiant effort by Findlay High School and posted its first playoff victory, 28-16, in a Class AAA semifinal game.

On Friday night, November 21, the second-ranked Crusaders played Class AAA's # 1 team, 11-0, Cleveland-area power St. Edward Eagles for the state championship in the Akron Rubber Bowl. After a scoreless first quarter, Moeller took

It is "student body left" as QB Tim Koegel pitches back to one of his backfield mates during the Crusaders' 1976 season.

Another point, or three, is on its way off the foot of Moeller placekicker Ken Naber in 1976.

a 7-0 lead in the second, but St. Edward came right back with a touchdown of its own. The Eagles then tried for a two-point conversion, but the pass attempt failed and Moeller held a 7-6 advantage at the half.

In the fourth quarter the Crusaders pushed their lead to 14-6, but again St. Edward came back and answered with a touchdown with 5:44 left on the game clock. This time the Eagles were forced to go for the two-pointer to tie the game, but the pass attempt was overthrown in the end zone. St. Edward later got the ball for one last attempt to pull out the win and had marched to the Moeller 16-yard line, but there they fumbled the ball and Moeller's future All-American Bob Crable recovered the loose pigskin at his own 18-yard line with 1:21 left to play. The Crusaders then ran out the clock.

Moeller's 14-12 victory gave the Crusaders a perfect 12-0 season and the team's first Ohio Class AAA state championship. The team would also finish the season as the country's fourth-ranked team. But they were just getting started.

The last three seasons had been quite a ride for Gerry Faust's Moeller football team. Three perfect regular seasons, three playoff appearances, and finally that elusive first state championship. The still relatively new Crusaders may have been a surprise to many after that first playoff season in 1973, but by 1976 they were quickly becoming the big kid on the block that everyone was gunning for. And that block had just expanded a bit. A new national sports magazine, "Joe Namath's National Prep Sports", had named the Moeller Crusaders as its 1976 preseason # 1 team in the country.

There were the usual losses to graduation that every high school team has to deal with, but the '76 Crusaders seemed to be in pretty good shape. The entire starting backfield of three-year quarterback and All-American Tim Koegel and running backs Bob Massong (All-Ohio) and Steve Givens would again be lining up behind the offensive line. That O-line would be the big question mark with only one returning starter, but what a starter he was in 6'5", 270 lbs. soon-to-be All-American Jim Brown, who also started on defense. The defense had a few holes to fill, but five veteran returnees led by Brown and All-American Bob Crable would give the "D" the leadership that it needed.

Once the season had gotten underway, it did not take long before everyone had come to the same conclusion, Gerry Faust was not in a rebuilding mode for

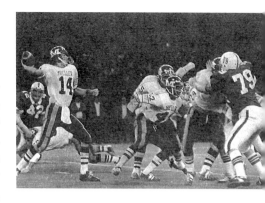

A familiar sight to Moeller fans in 1976, QB Tim Koegel gunning the ball downfield behind a wall of blockers.

1976, he had simply reloaded. In the season lid lifter against Clayton Northmont on Friday, September 10, the Crusaders jumped to a 35-0 halftime lead and scored in every quarter en route to a 49-0 triumph. Princeton High was always a tough game for Moeller and this year would be no exception. The Crusaders trailed 9-7 as the game made its way into the final 12 minutes, but Moeller rallied for a pair of late touchdowns that carried the team to a 21-9 victory.

Moeller's September 24 game at undefeated Middletown was billed in some circles as an early-season showdown for the region's Class AAA playoff spot. Moeller jumped out to an early 7-0 lead, but the Middies came right back, returning the ensuing kickoff 55 yards to the Moeller 35 and then scoring on the very next play to tie the game at 7-7. As it turns out, that was the end of the showdown. Moeller scored the game's next 23 points while Middletown added a late touchdown to make it a 30-13 final. The Middies could take some solace in that they would be the only team all season to score in double digits against the Crusaders.

After just three weeks of the season, Moeller was now 3-0 and had outscored the opposition 100-22 in what would prove to be the toughest part of the Crusaders schedule. They would go on to close out the regular season schedule with five shutouts in seven games, outscoring the opposition 299-13.

The 1976 Ohio Class AAA playoffs would begin for Moeller with a semifinal game against Youngstown's Cardinal Mooney (10-0) at Dayton's Welcome Stadium on Friday, November 19. In Moeller's first playoff appearance back in 1973. this same Cardinal Mooney had humbled Moeller by 34-7 and the Crusaders were out to even the ledger. This game would not be nearly that close. The *Cincinnati Enquirer* headlined its game story as a "Semifinal Mismatch" totally dominated by the "Moeller Avalanche". The Crusaders jumped to a 14-0 lead after one quarter and never looked back. Scoring in every quarter, the Crusaders rolled to a playoff-record 48 points in shutting out Mooney, 48-0.

In the Class AAA state championship game, Moeller would be playing the Gahanna Lincoln Lions (10-0), a strong defensive team that had allowed only four touchdowns and a field goal during the regular season. The Lions had continued with their strong defensive play the previous week by shutting out St. Edward, 28-0, in the other Class AAA semifinal game.

Strong defense or not, Gahanna Lincoln was no match for the steamroller known as the Moeller Crusaders. Led by quarterback Tim Koegel's three touchdown passes and

The 1976 Moeller defense, aka the "Crunch Bunch", showing how they earned that name.

▲ *The official signals
"Moeller's ball!" as the Crusaders
come up with a fumble
recovery against Youngstown
Cardinal Mooney in a 1976
Division I semifinal game.*

▼ *The official signals
"Touchdown!" as the Crusaders
score six of their 48 points
against Cardinal Mooney in their
1976 Division I semifinal game.*

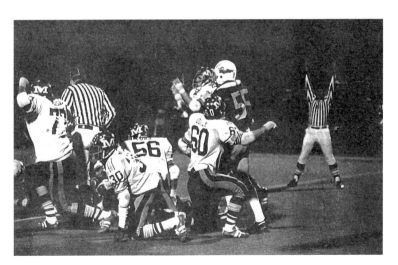

tailback Steve Given's two running touchdowns, the Crusaders scored in every quarter as they crushed Gahanna Lincoln by 43-5. During the first half when the game was still undecided, the Moeller defense held Gahanna to just five yards of total offense.

The victory gave Moeller its second consecutive Ohio Class AAA state championship, the first team in any class during the short history of the Ohio playoffs to win back-to-back titles. The Crusaders were also named the nation's top team in the final National Sports News Service rankings, an honor they shared that season with Warner Robins High School of Georgia.

Moeller, with its win streak now at 24 consecutive games, had gone through the 1976 season with an unbeatable combination of great offense and outstanding defense. While the Moeller defense was limiting opponents to a total of just 40 points for the entire season, the Crusaders had scored 490 points, averaging 40.8 points per game.

The 1977 campaign would bring its own set of challenges for the Crusaders to overcome. Lost to graduation was three-year starting quarterback Tim Koegel, along with running backs Bob Massong and Jack Givens, two-way all-everything lineman Jim Brown, and many more first line seniors. In addition to a three-way scramble to replace Koegel at quarterback, Gerry Faust had many fine players coming back, both '76 starters and those stepping up to first team roles, led by All-American Bob Crable.

Gerry Faust's team, playing what the *Cincinnati Post* dubbed "the toughest schedule in the nation", would have to be ready from the very first kickoff to meet this extraordinary challenge. In their first game, the Crusaders would be having their annual battle with the Princeton Vikings, now Moeller's primary rival, who were ranked # 12 in the country in the preseason polls. Next Moeller would take on Findlay and Middletown high schools, both ranked in Ohio's top 15. On September 30, Moeller would be stepping out of the relative security of Ohio high school teams to take on Monsignor Farrell High School of New York City, the country's 18th ranked team. And those were just the first four games of the season, with the brutal GCL schedule to follow.

Moeller and Princeton had been enjoying one of Cincinnati's best rivalries for the past dozen years, and that Moeller was the preseason pick as the # 1 team in the nation and Princeton was # 12 only enhanced that. In fact, there were those who thought that this season-opening game might actually decide the state championship, still 11 weeks away.

Be that as it may, the game got off to a wild start. Princeton got its crowd going when it returned the opening kickoff all the way inside the Moeller 15-yard line. On the first play from scrimmage, it was the Moeller crowd's turn to cheer as linebacker Bob Crable picked up a Princeton fumble and took it 85 yards in the other direction for a touchdown and a quick 7-0 Moeller lead. Princeton came back to

▼ *Moeller defensive back Russ Huesman (44) picks off an opponent's aerial during the 1977 season and starts back up field with defensive back Bill Long (13) providing some interference.*

tie the score later in the period, but after that it was all Moeller as the Crusaders scored 28 unanswered points to open their season with a 35-7 thumping of the Vikings.

It would be more of the same when Moeller traveled to Findlay and played the Trojans before more than 12,000 fans. Findlay had been undefeated in 1976 and opened the season in Ohio's top 10, but that meant little to Moeller. The Crusaders amassed 406 yards of offense as they rolled to a 51-7 victory. On September 23, Moeller posted its first shutout of the season as it limited Middletown to 83 yards of total offense in a 42-0 victory.

In what was billed as a key intersectional match-up, Moeller took on New York's Monsignor Farrell High School on September 30 in the University of Cincinnati's Nippert Stadium before a huge crowd of more than 22,000. Moeller showed just how good it would be this season by scoring in every quarter en route to a 30-0 victory. For the second time in four weeks the Crusaders had easily disposed of a nationally ranked opponent, tightening its hold on the nation's top spot.

▲ *Quarterback Mark Schweitzer gets ready to fire a pass downfield for Moeller during the Crusaders' 1977 season.*

On October 7 the Crusaders would venture cross town to one of the most iconic football stadiums in the country, "The Pit" at Elder High School. If ever a stadium provided a team with a home field advantage, it was Elder's "Pit", rated by "Sports Illustrated" as one of the 10 best high school football venues in the country. Elder had only defeated Moeller once in the past eight years, but this was the season that many felt the Panthers just might do it again.

Elder would actually out-gain Moeller in this one, 361-240, but games are won by the points on the scoreboard and not yards gained. Moeller took a 7-0 lead late in the first quarter, then doubled that advantage with a touchdown on its first drive right after halftime. Elder finally got on the scoreboard with a touchdown and two-point conversion with just under two minutes to play, but Moeller's Bill

▲ *Moeller quarterback Mark Schweitzer hands the ball off to tailback Tom Schroeder during this 1977 game.*

Long (a 1977 All-America selection) recovered the Panthers' onside kick and the Crusaders ran out the clock to preserve the close 14-8 victory.

Elder's eight points would prove to be the only points that Moeller would give up over its last eight games. The Crusaders closed out the last five games of their regular season schedule with shutouts, winning by a combined 180-0.

For the fifth consecutive year Moeller had finished the regular season a perfect 10-0, running its regular season win streak to 52 games. The undefeated season also earned for the Crusaders a second-straight Ohio Class AAA AP poll championship, but to take home the true championship hardware they would now have to win it all in the playoffs.

Facing Moeller in one of the two 1977 AAA semifinal games were the Fighting Irish of Toledo Central Catholic (9-1), in a game played at Dayton's Welcome Stadium on Friday night, November 18. Moeller took it right to Central Catholic very early in the game as the Crusaders raced out to a 21-0 lead after just seven and a half minutes of the opening quarter. The game then settled down a bit, and the Fighting Irish were even able to make the game look respectable thanks to Moeller errors; Central Catholic turned a Moeller fumble into one touchdown and then added a second score via a pass interception to pull to within 21-14 at the half. But Moeller would make no more errors over the game's final two quarters. The Moeller offense added three more touchdowns in the second half while its defense shut down and shut out the Fighting Irish.

Moeller's 42-14 victory sent it into the Class AAA state championship game against Canton McKinley (10-1), on Friday night, November 25, in Akron's Rubber Bowl. McKinley had one of the most storied football programs in the state, while the Crusaders were still building their history.

More than 11,000 chilled fans sat through a first half snow storm as they took in the action on the gridiron below them, with the wind not only swirling the snow but dropping the wind chill to a less-than-seasonal 16 degrees. The snow, wind, and cold affected the play of both teams. Moeller quarterback Mark Schweitzer, like most of the ball carriers, had a difficult time gripping the ball and completed only two passes during the entire game and none until the fourth quarter. The wintry conditions adversely affected McKinley long snapper Mike Randazzo in the second quarter when he sent the ball high over his punter's head, the Crusaders recovering the errant pigskin at the McKinley 13-yard line. A few plays, later Moeller's Tom Schroeder scored from the one-yard line to give the Crusaders a 7-0 lead. McKinley was able to put up a couple of points before the half on a safety

▲ *The Archbishop Moeller Crusaders have a joyful celebration after winning the 1977 Ohio Division I state championship game.*

when Moeller's Mark Schweitzer was called for intentional grounding while in the end zone.

With the score still 7-2, Moeller added a late fourth quarter touchdown. The Moeller defense did not let the Bulldogs do much with the 106 yards of offense that they generated during the game and the Crusaders' goal line was seldom threatened.

By a score of 14-2, Moeller added its third consecutive Ohio Class AAA state championship. And with it a second straight national title—and this time the national championship was all theirs.

The 1977 Cincinnati Moeller football team truly owes its success to its phenomenal defensive play. Not to slight an offense that generated 34 points per game, but the defense was the best in the school's history. During the 10-game regular season, the Crusaders "D" allowed only 22 points, the best ever by any Moeller team. They did allow 14 points in the playoffs (two more points were scored on a

The 1977 national champion team from Archbishop Moeller High School.

safety) for a season total of 36 points in 12 games; the school season record is 33 points (1965), but that was set in only 10 games.

The 1978 football season got off to a good start for the Crusaders when they came from behind twice to down a game Findlay team, 28-16. The next week Moeller had its annual showdown with Princeton. The Vikings led 10-0 at the half, but Moeller came back with a pair of third quarter touchdowns to take a 12-10 lead as the game headed into the final stanza. Late in the fourth quarter, Moeller had the ball and was trying to run out the clock, but a failed third down conversion forced them to punt on fourth and two with less than a minute left on the game clock. The kick went only about 25 yards, leaving Princeton with a relatively short field to work with. After two plays, the Vikings called their last timeout with the ball just inside the Moeller 30-yard line. When play resumed, the Vikings nailed a 38-yard field goal on the game's last play for a thrilling 13-12 victory.

The loss snapped Moeller's overall win streak at 36 and its regular season string at 53. The Crusaders went on to win their next eight games, including a 37-7 victory over Jesuit High School of Dallas, Texas, in an intersectional game, but the damage had been done. Despite finishing second in the Class AAA state poll—and 20th in the nation—Moeller was unable to garner its region's playoff spot. (When the Ohio High School Athletic Association instituted its football playoffs in 1972, only the top team from each region qualified for the postseason. In 1980 the playoffs were expanded to include the top two teams, in 1985 the top four, and finally in 1999 the top eight.)

Like 1977 when many thought that the state championship had been decided with the Moeller-Princeton game, the same might have been said about 1978. Princeton went on to finish the season a perfect 12-0 and capture the Ohio Class AAA state championship. The Vikings also finished ninth in the NSNS final national rankings. With two teams in the final national Top 20, Cincinnati's and Ohio's reputation for outstanding high school football soared.

Once again in 1979, the Moeller Crusaders of head coach Gerry Faust would be playing a monster schedule, one that included cross-border games with a couple of powerhouses in Pittsburgh's Penn Hills and Detroit's Brother Rice high schools. And the Crusaders also had their Ohio opponents to contend with, which included St. Edward from the Cleveland area and Moeller's GCL foes. After three preseason scrimmages in which Moeller had out scored its opponents 131-7, including a 42-0 thrashing of Louisville powerhouse and defending Kentucky champion St. Xavier, the Crusaders were feeling very confident, but now the games were for real.

Unlike a lot of teams that open the season with a powder puff opponent, Moeller started right at the top with the nationally ranked Penn Hills Indians. Moeller was the preseason pick for number one in the country, but three-time defending Pennsylvania champion Penn Hills was ranked 12th.

Moeller and Penn Hills squared off before a huge crowd at Nippert Stadium on Friday night, September 1. Late in the first quarter, Moeller's Mark Edmondson recovered a fumbled punt by Penn Hills at the Indians' 49-yard line. Three plays later the Crusaders deposited the ball in the end zone for a 7-0 lead at 1:30 of the first period. The Indians fumbled the ensuing kickoff and the loose ball was again recovered by Moeller, this time by Mike Larkin, at the Penn Hills' 15-yard line. Five plays later, Moeller was again in the Penn Hills' end zone and its lead was 14-0.

▸ Running back Mark Brooks takes a pitchout from quarterback Tom Lockwood during the Crusaders' 1979 campaign.

Penn Hills would never recover from those early miscues. Moeller went on to a 21-7 lead at the half and a 30-13 final. The Moeller defense, about to have another great season, shut out the Penn Hills' offense, the Indians touchdowns coming off an interception and a fumble return.

The following week the Crusaders were on the road at Findlay High School, but the travel did not seem to hurt their performance. Moeller amassed 472 yards of offense and 25 first downs while holding Findlay to just 15 yards and no first downs in a 48-0 victory.

Unbeknownst to those in attendance, the 1979 Moeller-Princeton game would once again go a long way toward determining the state's Class AAA champion. Before the game, Princeton head coach Pat Mancuso told reporters that this was the best Moeller team to date, and he knows because his team had played against most of them. The more than 24,000 high school football fans who packed Nippert

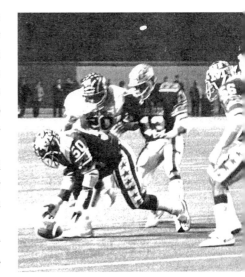

Stadium that day soon found out that Coach Mancuso was not exaggerating. As Randy Holtz of the *Cincinnati Enquirer* noted, "From the game's outset it was obvious. Moeller was too big. Moeller was too quick. Moeller was too many." And in the end, Moeller had too many points. Final score: Moeller 34, Princeton 7.

Three games into the season and the word was already starting to spread: this Moeller team is the best high school football team in the country.

Moeller's next big challenge was Michigan power Brother Rice High of Birmingham, just west of Detroit. Brother Rice started playing football in 1961 and the Warriors did not win a game until the last week of their third season in 1963, but now they seldom lost and had won two state titles in the last five seasons. (Head Coach Al Fracassa would finally retire after the 2013 season and his tenth state championship.)

But Moeller was on a roll in 1979 and the guys from "that state up north" were not going to slow them down. In a dominant first half in which they out-gained the Warriors 282-64, Moeller built a 19-7 lead and finished with a 33-14 victory.

On September 29, the Crusaders again took to the road, traveling north to Finney Stadium on the campus of Baldwin-Wallace College (now Baldwin-Wallace University) to take on the state's fifth-ranked Eagles from St. Edward High School.

Moeller tight end Phil Roach comes up with another great catch during the 1979 season.

The game got off to a good start for St. Edward as the Eagles marched right down the field the first time they had the ball. The drive stalled deep in Moeller territory, but St. Edward managed to grab an early 3-0 lead on a 22-yard field goal. Moeller came right back on its first possession to take a 6-3 lead on a four-yard touchdown run by Eric Ellington. After that quick start by both teams, there would be no more scoring during the first half.

It was a much different story in the second half. After Moeller added a touchdown in the third quarter, the Crusaders blew the game open in the fourth on a 53-yard touchdown run by Eric Ellington, followed by another score that was set up by a Moeller pass interception. St. Edward added a late touchdown to make the final score a little more respectable at 27-9. Holding the Eagles to just 39 yards rushing and intercepting four passes certainly helped the Moeller effort.

Moeller's next four games were against its GCL opponents. First up was La-Salle, which fell by a 31-0 score. Next came St. Xavier, going down by a similar count, 34-0. Facing Elder in "The Pit" is always a tough assignment as Moeller's 7-0 halftime lead would indicate; but halftime adjustments by the Crusaders led to 20 unanswered second half points and a 27-0 victory. Eric Ellington's two touchdowns and 127 yards rushing propelled Moeller to a 33-0 victory over Roger Bacon High and a clean sweep of GCL opponents. As good as Moeller had been over the last 10 seasons, this was the first time that the Crusaders had shut out all of their GCL opponents in the same season.

Tailback Joe Lima takes the handoff from QB Tom Lockwood as the Moeller offensive line surges forward during Moeller's 34-7 Homecoming Game victory over Cincinnati Princeton in 1979.

In the regular season finale against Mount Healthy High School, played in the mud and muck of a rain-soaked Sycamore High School Field, the Crusaders exploded for 23 first quarter points to salt this one away early. Moeller's 37-6 victory over Mount Healthy gave it a 10-0 record for the regular season, the team's sixth perfect regular season mark in the last seven years. The victory earned for the Crusaders the # 1 ranking in the final AP Ohio Class AAA poll and also clinched a postseason berth for the Crusaders, beating out Princeton for the regional playoff spot—once again the Moeller-Princeton game had been key to the postseason.

On Saturday, November 17, Moeller opened its quest for its fourth state championship against the Panthers of Toledo's Whitmer High School, ranked 10th in the final AP Ohio poll, in a Class AAA semifinal game played at Dayton's Welcome Stadium. Whitmer had just signed a four-year home-and-home deal with the Crusaders that would begin the next season, so this was something of a preview of how that series might go.

Before more than 13,000 at Welcome Stadium, Moeller showed Whitmer why it was ranked as the top team in both the state and the country. On its first three possessions Whitmer ran a total of nine plays, which included two punts and a lost fumble. By the time the Panthers got the ball for the fourth time Moeller had already built up a 19-0 advantage, on the way to a 25-0 lead at the half. After Whitmer scored a touchdown in the third quarter, the Crusaders turned another recovered Whitmer fumble into a three-play, 27-yard touchdown drive in the fourth quarter that closed out the scoring in Moeller's 31-7 victory. Playing its usual brand of superb defense, the Crusaders had limited Whitmer to just 43 yards of offense.

In the Ohio Class AAA state championship game, Moeller went up against Padua Franciscan High School of Parma in the Akron Rubber Bowl on Saturday, November 24. The Bruins, 10-1, had been something of a surprise 12-0 winner over Massillon Washington in the other AAA semifinal game.

▲ *Running back Eric Ellington cuts to his left en route to another great run during the Crusaders' 1979 season.*

All the Way to #1

▾ *Moeller's Matt Uecker
gets away another successful
extra point try during the
'79 campaign as a couple of
opposition defenders make
a valiant effort to block it.*

To most, this was the 1979 Class AAA state championship game, but to the Moeller Crusaders it was just another game, business as usual. On the first offensive possession of the game, Moeller marched 70 yards to take an early 7-0 lead. That long drive would set the tone for Moeller's offensive strategy for the game, but not before the Padua Bruins made the game at least a little bit interesting. On its ensuing possession, Padua went 62 yards in just two plays to tie the score at 7-7 with 2:57 left in the opening quarter. The Bruins made it look too easy, but looks can be deceiving—Padua would not score again.

Moeller responded to that Padua touchdown with a 20-point second quarter outburst on three lengthy drives. Leading by 27-7 at the half, Moeller then scored single touchdowns in each of the final two quarters to bring home its fourth state championship by a score of 41-7.

The game had been as lopsided as the score indicated, with Moeller setting an Ohio Class AAA/Division I state championship game record with 536 yards of total offense, a record that still stands. The Crusaders' defense held Padua to just 97 total yards, another championship game record that still stands.

After the game, Padua head coach Tom Kohuth told reporters, "If there is a better high school team in the country, I'd like to see it. But I'd like to see it from the stands." When asked if he thought anyone could defeat the Crusaders, Kohuth replied, "That would depend on which college you're talking about."

Now that the Ohio state championship had been decided, the only thing remaining was the naming of a national champion for 1979. The National Sports News Service had been ranking Moeller # 1 ever since its preseason list had come out. Immediately after the state championship game, Barry Sollenberger, who ran the NSNS out of Phoenix, Ariz., was asked if this clinched the national title for the Crusaders. Because the NSNS was not going to make its official announcement until the week after Christmas, Sollenberger was unwilling to let the cat out of the

WHEN ASKED IF HE THOUGHT ANYONE COULD DEFEAT THE CRUSADERS, KOHUTH REPLIED, "THAT WOULD DEPEND ON WHICH COLLEGE YOU'RE TALKING ABOUT."

▸ *The Moeller defense gets through to Padua quarterback Dan Schodowski during the Crusaders' 41-7 victory in the 1979 Ohio Division I state championship game.*

bag just yet. He told the *Cincinnati Enquirer*, "I'd rather not say, but I don't know who in the world we could rate over them."

When the final NSNS rankings came out, the answer to Sollenberger's question was "Nobody." The Crusaders were officially named the national champion for 1979—the team's third such honor in the last four seasons.

Since Moeller's championship run began in 1975, the team's record was an impeccable 57-1. The Crusaders had been so dominant over that span that you could count on one hand the number of times they were truly threatened in a game. During the 1980 campaign, Moeller would be in more tight games than it was used to dealing with during a single season, and it began with the very first game.

Moeller's 1980 season opened on Friday night, August 29, in Nippert Stadium against the Elks of Centerville High School. After neither team could move the ball on its first possession, Centerville closed out a short 40-yard drive to take a 7-0 lead with just five seconds remaining in the opening quarter. The Crusaders came right back on their ensuing possession and marched 87 yards to a touchdown, then added a second touchdown just before the intermission to take a 14-7 lead into the locker room.

Defensive back John Rains returns an interception for Moeller during the 1980 season.

On the receiving end of the second half kickoff, Moeller raced 83 yards in just seven plays to push its lead to 20-7 and it looked as if this game might be close to being over. However, the Elks were not going away and a touchdown later in the third quarter pulled Centerville to within six points, 20-14. Centerville came close to scoring several times over the last quarter-plus of the game, but the Crusaders held on for a 20-14 opening night victory.

The following Saturday, Moeller traveled north to Canton for a game with the Bulldogs of McKinley High School. For the second consecutive week Moeller would allow the opposition to twice cross its goal line, but a series of miscues by McKinley during the middle part of the first half would prove to be fatal for the Bulldogs. A fumble, a pass interception, and a shanked punt by the Bulldogs on consecutive possessions led to three Moeller touchdowns and a 21-7 Crusader lead at the intermission. Each team scored a touchdown in the second half as the Crusaders kept their slate clean with a 27-14 victory.

Running back Mark Brooks (35) sweeps wide around the right side for Moeller during this 1980 game.

The next three games would be more of what Moeller fans had come to expect from their Crusaders. On Saturday, September 13, the Crusaders played an intersectional contest against Maryland power Dematha Catholic before 12,000 fans at Nippert Stadium. Holding the Stags to minus-11 yards of total offense in the first half, Moeller jumped out to a 21-0 lead and cruised to a 34-0 victory. It was more of the same the following week against Toledo Whitmer in the first of their four game regular season series. Rolling up 381 yards of offense while holding Whitmer to just 90, Moeller again had an easy time of it in posting a 32-0 win.

The LaSalle Lancers had never defeated Moeller in 16 previous meetings, but when the two teams met on Friday, September 26, in the first GCL game of the season the Lancers appeared ready to do just that. The first half ended in a scoreless deadlock and some in the crowd were wondering aloud if this might actually be LaSalle's year. Early in the third quarter, however, the Moeller defense dropped LaSalle quarterback Marty Rueve in the end zone for a safety and a 2-0 lead. Fol-

Moeller's Hiawatha Francisco flies through a big hole left by his offensive line against Cincinnati Princeton during the 1980 season.

lowing the Lancers free kick Moeller marched 47 yards to a touchdown, the two-point conversion giving the Crusaders a 10-0 lead. The Crusaders added a fourth quarter field goal to close out the 13-0 victory—and LaSalle would have to wait another nine seasons to finally get that first win over Moeller.

On Friday, October 3, the Crusaders squared off with Elder in another GCL game. The game was not played in "The Pit", but it might as well have been. As Gerry Faust would later say, "That was one great high school football game", and few in the crowd of better than 14,000 at Nippert Stadium would have disagreed with him.

Elder was first to score, taking a 7-0 lead late in the opening quarter. Undeterred, Moeller came charging back to score 21 points in the second quarter to take what appeared to be a comfortable 21-7 lead at the intermission.

Unfazed, Elder came out of the halftime break and scored a touchdown on its second possession of the third quarter. The Panthers missed the extra point try, leaving Moeller with a 21-13 lead. Moeller later went on a drive that carried to the Elder one-yard line, but running back Mark Brooks fumbled the ball (even All-Americans can make a mistake) and it was recovered in the end zone by the Panthers for a touchback.

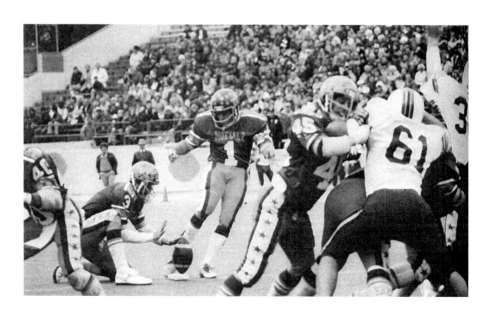

Placekicker Tony Melink gets plenty of protection as he puts his foot into another field goal attempt during the 1980 season.

▲ *Moeller's Mike Lane (32) does not appear to need any assistance as he brings down this opposition ball carrier during the Crusaders' 1980 season.*

Late in the fourth quarter, Elder added its third touchdown to cut the Moeller lead to 21-19 with 2:23 remaining. Because of a penalty on Moeller, Elder actually had two tries at making the game-tying two-point conversion, but failed both times.

Moeller ran out the last 143 seconds of the game and was happy to escape with a 21-19 victory.

On Friday, October 10, St. Xavier led Moeller 7-0 early in the first quarter, but that may have been the most deceiving statistic to ever appear in a Moeller game, certainly in 1980. Behind a record-breaking performance by All-America running back Mark Brooks and a defense that held St. Xavier to just 34 yards of total offense, Moeller coasted to a 35-7 victory. In this game, Brooks set a team single game rushing record of 254 yards, became Moeller's all-time rushing leader with three regular season games and possibly the playoffs still to go, and scored three touchdowns on runs of 80, 74, and 3 yards.

The following week Roger Bacon High played the Crusaders tough. As the game headed into the final frame, Moeller was clinging to the same 3-0 lead it had taken way back in the opening quarter. However, a pair of fourth quarter touchdowns gave Moeller a 17-0 victory and made the game look a little easier than it had been. The next-to-last game of the regular season, against Walsh Jesuit of Stow, Ohio, was more to the Crusaders' liking as the 42-0 score would indicate.

In the 1980 season finale on Friday, October 31, Moeller would have its annual showdown with the Princeton Vikings at Princeton Stadium. After a scoreless first quarter, Moeller made the scoreboard early in the second quarter on a short touchdown pass to take a 7-0 lead. The Crusaders had other opportunities in the first two quarters, but Halloween "tricks" in the form of four turnovers killed those efforts. Moeller was fortunate that Princeton was only able to capitalize on one of those turnovers, leaving the score tied 7-7 at the half.

Late in the third quarter, Princeton scored another touchdown to take the lead, but a bad snap from center prevented the Vikings from adding the extra point. Now trailing 13-7, Moeller then went on a 17-play drive, all on the ground, resulting in a touchdown and PAT that gave Moeller a 14-13 lead with 8:55 to play. Princeton came right back and drove to the Moeller 23-yard line, but at that point an errant Vikings pitchout turned the ball over to the Crusaders. The game clock read 3:55 and Princeton never had the ball again as Moeller hung on for a 14-13 victory.

▲ *Moeller running back Mark Brooks (35) follows offensive lineman Jeff Cooper (60) as he works his way downfield during the 1980 season.*

Another thriller in the Moeller-Princeton series, but they were not finished with each other quite yet.

The Ohio High School Athletic Association expanded the playoffs in two ways for 1980. The OHSAA had dropped the previous three classifications of Class AAA, AA, A and replaced them with five Divisions: I, II, III, IV, V. Also, instead of just the top team in each Division qualifying for the postseason, now the top two teams were in. (In a somewhat strange occurrence that would remain until the 1987 season, the AP weekly polls still ranked the teams by the old AAA, AA, A classifications.)

As fate and the football gods would have it, not only did Moeller and Princeton finish 1-2 in the final AP poll, but they also finished 1-2 in Region 4 and thus would face each other in the postseason in a state quarterfinal game to be played on Friday night, November 7, the Friday after their first meeting.

In the week between the two games with Princeton, the Moeller staff had been watching the films of the first game and had spotted a few things that they were confident they would be able to take advantage of in the playoff game.

A near-capacity crowd of almost 27,000 Cincinnati high school football fans packed Nippert Stadium to see what was being called "THE GAME". Instead of "THE GAME", however, what they saw was just "another game" by the Moeller Crusaders. A touchdown in the first quarter followed by two more in the second period carried Moeller to a 21-3 halftime lead, en route to a 28-3 final.

Moeller defensive back Rob Brown (21) intercepts a pass against Massillon Washington in the 1980 Ohio Division I state championship game.

Moeller's Hiawatha Francisco (43) looks for an opening as he heads up field against Upper Arlington in a 1980 Ohio Division I semifinal game.

That victory sent Moeller into a Division I semifinal game against Upper Arlington High School out of the Columbus area. Upper Arlington had been one of the best teams in the country in the late 1960s and early 1970s (ranked as high as #4 nationally) and had lost in the Class AAA state championship game in 1974. The Golden Bears had qualified for the 1980 semifinals by defeating Sandusky High School, 42-6. However, this week at Dayton's Welcome Stadium the shoe would be on the other foot for Upper Arlington. Right from the start, Moeller was in control and never let up as the Crusaders out-gained the Golden Bears 399-82 and finished with a decisive 36-0 win.

In the 1980 Division I state championship game Moeller played Massillon Washington, a team that already owned two dozen Ohio championships. At the last minute the game had been moved from Dayton's Welcome Stadium to Cincinnati's Nippert Stadium. The reason: Welcome Stadium only held 11,500 people and Moeller and Massillon had each been allocated 8,000 tickets to sell. As it turned out, this was a fortuitous move, even though it gave Moeller something of a home field advantage, because on game day, Sunday, November 23, more than 25,000 fans filled Nippert Stadium to watch the game.

The previous season, Massillon had lost in the semifinals to Padua, 12-0, and then watched as Padua got clobbered 41-7 by Moeller in the title game. After that game, several Massillon players were quoted as saying that they were better than Padua and would not have lost by such a huge score. Now, a year later, they would have a chance to prove it. It took the Massillon Tigers a very short time, less than a quarter, to realize that they may have misspoken the previous year. Moeller took the opening kickoff and quickly went down the field 62 yards for a touchdown and a 7-0 lead. A pass on Massillon's first play from scrimmage was intercepted and two plays later the Moeller lead had jumped to 14-0. After holding the Tigers on their next possession, Moeller again marched 62 yards to a third touchdown and a quick 21-0 lead. A championship game record 49-yard field goal by Moeller placekicker Tony Melink gave the Crusaders a 24-0 advantage at the half and the Massillon Tigers were trying to figure out what had hit them.

The second half still needed to be played, but this game was pretty much over. When the final whistle sounded, Moeller's victory had been complete. In their 30-7 victory the Crusaders defense had limited Massillon to minus-5 yards rushing and 98 total yards for the game, just one yard short of the record the Crusaders had posted in the previous year's title game.

With a team-record 13 victories, Moeller had won its fifth state championship in the last six seasons. When the final NSNS 1980 national rankings came out at the end of December, Moeller was the national champion for the fourth time in the last five seasons. Mark Brooks, Mike Larkin, and Doug Williams had earned All-America honors.

All the Way to #1

Winning the state championship and even the national championship were becoming somewhat old hat at Moeller, but after the 1980 season there was some real news to digest. For a few months the rumors had been flying, but on Monday afternoon, November 23, the day after the Crusaders' state championship victory over Massillon the word was out—Gerry Faust, the only football coach that Moeller had ever known, was leaving. Moving on to the job he said he had always wanted, Faust had been named to succeed Dan Devine as the head coach at the University of Notre Dame.

In 18 years as the Crusaders' head coach, Gerry Faust had taken a brand new and unknown team of all freshmen and turned it into a true high school football dynasty, creating what had become known around the country as the "Moeller Mystique." His teams had posted a record of 174-17-2, .907—one of the very few coaches in the country for his length of service to have lost fewer games (17) than

IN 18 YEARS AS THE CRUSADERS' HEAD COACH, GERRY FAUST HAD TAKEN A BRAND NEW AND UNKNOWN TEAM OF ALL FRESHMEN AND TURNED IT INTO A TRUE HIGH SCHOOL FOOTBALL DYNASTY, CREATING WHAT HAD BECOME KNOWN AROUND THE COUNTRY AS THE "MOELLER MYSTIQUE."

years coaching (18). Over his last five seasons at the school, 1976-1980, Gerry Faust had led Moeller to 70 victories in 71 games, five big school state titles, and four national championships.

Upon learning that Faust would be moving on to the college ranks, the superlatives flowed like the waters over Niagara from friends and on-the-field foes alike, many of whom were both. Long time Princeton head coach Pat Mancuso told the *Cincinnati Enquirer*, "... one trademark of Moeller is its enthusiasm, its rah-rah attitude. And that's the trademark of Gerry... When you think of the legend of Moeller, he is the legend. When that man leaves, the personality leaves. It's like Knute Rockne or Woody Hayes."

The search for the Crusaders' new head coach did not take long, nor did it stray from the Moeller campus. Being named as the Crusaders' new mentor was long time assistant coach Ted Bacigalupo. While Ted brought his own style to the job, he inherited virtually Gerry Faust's entire coaching staff and a team still laden with talented players—and Bacigalupo would need them all because the Moeller schedule was not getting any easier.

◄ *Moeller's Mark Brooks (35) takes the handoff before powering his way into the end zone for the Crusaders' second touchdown against Massillon in the 1980 Ohio Division I state championship game.*

▲   *Defensive back Ben Thamann goes high to break up this pass against Cincinnati's Roger Bacon High School during the 1982 season.*

As so many teams had learned before them, after many years of outstanding success the Crusaders were having a problem filling their schedule outside of the games with the GCL and the Princeton Vikings. None of the more local teams that would normally be expected to be on the schedule were willing to play Moeller. Only state powers and similar teams from outside of Ohio, teams that thought they had a legitimate shot at defeating Moeller, were willing to put the Crusaders on their schedule.

In 1981, Moeller would open its season with four of those top notch teams, but like the old saying, the beat goes on. Centerville 21-7, Bethel High (Hampton, Va.) 17-0, Massillon Washington 24-6, and Toledo Whitmer 37-0—all fell before the Crusaders. Next came the four teams of the GCL; except for a 15-7 squeaker over the Elder Panthers in the infamous Pit, Moeller swept aside the other three teams by an average of 30 points per game. With their record now 8-0, the Crusaders then took on perennial state power Lakewood St. Edward—and put up a season-high 42 points against just eight for the Eagles.

In the regular season finale, Moeller took the field against Princeton in the biggest game of the season. A standing room only crowd of better than 10,000 was on hand at Galbreath Field to witness the annual showdown, with a trip to the postseason hanging in the balance.

With less than nine minutes remaining in the game, Moeller was trailing by 10 points, 17-7, and was forced to punt. Kicking with a strong wind, the Crusaders punt sailed deep into the Princeton end of the field. The Crusaders defense stepped up and stopped the Vikings cold, forcing them to punt into that strong wind from deep in the Princeton end of the field. The relatively short kick resulted in excellent field position for Moeller at the Princeton 36. Moeller quickly worked the ball over those 36 yards and into the end zone for a touchdown, but a failed two-point conversion left the team's deficit at four points, 17-13.

Following the ensuing kickoff, Princeton tried to run out the clock, but the Moeller defense again stopped the Vikings and the Crusaders regained the ball at the Princeton 37-yard line with 1:07 left on the game clock. With the clock down to just 16 seconds, Moeller tight end Bobby Hill in the left corner of the end zone made a spectacular one-handed catch of a ball that appeared to be over his head. The PAT gave Moeller one of the most dramatic wins in school history, 21-17.

That victory qualified Moeller for the Division I playoffs with a 10-0 record. In the 1981 Division I quarterfinals Moeller would be seeing GCL rival St. Xavier for the second time in five weeks. Moeller had won their first meeting by 37-3. This game would not be as easy, but the Crusaders advanced with an 18-7 triumph.

For the second consecutive year, Moeller played Upper Arlington in a Division I semifinal contest. This would be another tough playoff game, but as they had done in the previous season's semifinal game, the Moeller defense held the Golden

Bears without a point. The Crusaders advanced to the Division I championship game with a hard-fought 14-0 victory.

In that championship game, Moeller faced the 12-0 Canton McKinley Bulldogs, the same team that Moeller had defeated in the 1977 state title game. Not only would this game decide the Ohio Division I title, but it would go a long way toward deciding the national championship because both teams were placed high in the national rankings.

McKinley entered the game with one of the best defenses in the state, having already shut out eight of 12 opponents, and that defense would prove to be the difference in the game. The Bulldogs took a 7-0 lead midway through the first quarter, then added another touchdown in the second period to lead 13-0 at the intermission. Those would prove to be the only points of the game as McKinley avenged its 1977 title game loss to the Crusaders with a 13-0 victory.

The McKinley victory was considered to be a huge upset at the time, but in retrospect perhaps not. Held to just 99 yards of total offense, Moeller saw its win streak halted at 45. It was also the first time that the Crusaders had been shut out in 107 games going all the way back to the eighth game of the 1972 season. In a well played game by both teams, the win by the McKinley Bulldogs was no fluke.

A strong case could be made that the winner of this game, no matter which team it was, should have also been named the national champion. McKinley had come through a very tough schedule unscathed, having allowed only 32 points in a 13-game schedule while shutting out nine. In the Ohio Division I playoffs, recognized as perhaps the toughest playoffs in the country, the Bulldogs had allowed only six points and had shut out the two-time defending Ohio and national champions. However, Barry Sollenberger and the National Sports News Service settled on Warner Robins of Georgia as the nation's top team in 1981, with McKinley ranked second and Moeller still in the mix at # 5.

▲ *Moeller All-American Hiawatha Francisco (43) tries to elude the tackle of a defender from California's Servite High School during the 1982 season.*

After having had the same head coach for its first 18 seasons, Moeller was about to get its third coach in the last three. A private business venture that Ted Bacigalupo had been working on for several years was finally starting to take off and he had to choose between coaching and that business. He decided that the best thing for his family was to pursue the business venture, so he resigned as the Crusaders' head coach. As it did when Gerry Faust left, the Moeller administration was able to find its new football coach "in house". Steve Klonne, who had been an assistant at Moeller since 1979, was selected to take over the reins of Moeller football. Klonne would eventually hold the job for a year longer, 19 years, than Gerry Faust had.

If anyone thought that because Moeller was on its third coach in as many years that the quality of play would drop off, they were in for a rude awakening. The Crusaders had advanced to the state championship game in six of the previous seven seasons and that kind of success was not about to change. As Ted Bacigalupo had done the year before, Steve Klonne took over a team with a first class, experienced coaching staff and still loaded with talent that included 46 seniors and players like All-America

▲ *Moeller defender Don Duckworth nails the Elder quarterback just as he releases the ball during Moeller's 31-7 victory in 1982.*

linebacker Shane Bullough and the outstanding running back tandem of the Francisco brothers, senior All-American Hiawatha and sophomore D'Juan. While the Moeller-Princeton match-up in the last game of the regular season was still the big game on the schedule, in a phrase it was back to "business as usual" for the Crusaders during the 1982 campaign.

If there was any doubt as to the quality of this Crusaders team, the first two games put those doubts to rest. For their opener on Friday night, August 27, the Crusaders traveled to Toledo for their game with Whitmer High School. Led by the Francisco brothers and their four touchdowns, and a solid defense that had three interceptions, Moeller rolled to a very convincing 42-0 victory.

The following week the Crusaders were even more impressive. In a game billed as a rematch of the previous year's Division I championship game, the contest proved to be more "mismatch" than "rematch". Playing Canton McKinley in Cincinnati, Moeller actually trailed by a score of 3-2 after the first quarter, but then the Crusaders offense really took off. Moeller exploded for 21 points in the second quarter and added 21 more after the intermission to come away with a very convincing 43-10 victory.

▸ *The Moeller defense (white jerseys) is ready for action against Gahanna Lincoln in this 1982 Ohio Division I semifinal playoff game.*

In one of the most anticipated games in school history, on September 18 the Crusaders played host to the Servite High School Friars from Anaheim, Calif. One of that state's powers and soon to be 1982 California champion, Servite like Moeller was also a nationally ranked team. The Friars were led by senior quarterback Steve Beuerlein, who would go on to have a successful college career at Notre Dame and then play 17 seasons in the pro ranks.

Behind the passing of Beuerlein, Servite led 6-0 after the first quarter, but a Moeller touchdown aerial in the second quarter gave the home team a 7-6 lead at the half.

In the third quarter, the lead seesawed back and forth. Servite regained the lead on a 30-yard field goal, but on its next possession Moeller went back on top, 14-9. Still in the third quarter, Beuerlein led Servite back to the lead, but a missed PAT left that lead at just a single point, 15-14.

The Crusaders finally put some distance between themselves and Servite with a pair of touchdowns within the first two minutes of the fourth quarter to take a 29-15 lead. With the Moeller defense digging in and intercepting a pair of Beuer-

▸ *Dave Springmeier races into the end zone with Moeller's second touchdown against Massillon Washington in the 1982 Ohio Division I state championship game.*

lein aerials, the Crusaders held off a possible Servite comeback to preserve the 29-15 victory.

On Friday, September 24, the Crusaders were again on the road and headed north to take on the Magics of Barberton High School in the first meeting between the two schools. Moeller raced to a 35-0 halftime lead, cleared the bench during the last two quarters, and coasted to a 35-8 final. Moeller's next four games were against its GCL opponents, the Crusaders winning all four—by an average score of 33-7—with only LaSalle giving them any real trouble. In that game, Moeller led 13-0 at the half and 19-0 early in the third quarter. LaSalle then scored two quick touchdowns to make it a five-point game at 19-14. A touchdown in the fourth quarter insured that Moeller would keep its record clean against La-Salle with a 26-14 final.

A 38-14 victory over the St. Edward Eagles the following week set the stage for the Crusaders' annual showdown with Princeton. Like Moeller (9-0), Princeton was also undefeated (8-0).

Despite the fact that Princeton's backfield was manned by a pair of 1,000-yard rushers, the much anticipated showdown never materialized. With the Crusaders scoring by land and air and running up 419 total yards to just 19 for Princeton, Moeller took a 42-0 lead—and those were just the halftime stats. In those first two quarters, Moeller had scored more points against Princeton than any team had scored against the Vikings in a whole game in more that 25 years of football.

With Moeller clearing its bench in the second half the Crusaders went on to a 56-7 victory.

Almost before the Vikings could lick their wounds from that horrendous loss, they would have to take the field the following Saturday and again face Moeller in a Division I quarterfinal game. This time the score would be a bit more respectable, but the outcome remained the same. The Crusaders jumped to a 20-7 halftime lead en route to a 33-20 victory; the Francisco brothers scored all four of the Moeller touchdowns.

Advancing to the Division I semifinal round, Moeller would be taking on Gahanna Lincoln, 10-1, at Dayton's Welcome Stadium on Saturday, November 20. Like

▸ *The younger of the Francisco brothers, D'Juan (44), rushes for some of the 123 yards that he gained against Massillon in the 1982 Ohio Division I state championship game.*

the two games against Princeton, Moeller simply overpowered and out manned Lincoln, scoring in every quarter of a 38-0 victory.

With that victory, the Crusaders advanced to the Division I state championship game for the seventh time in the last eight seasons. Playing Moeller for the second time in three years in the Division I finals would be the Tigers of Massillon Washington High School. Like Moeller, Massillon was also 12-0 and ranked high in the national polls by both the National Sports News Service and the newly established *USA Today* Super 25. Moeller and Massillon had played two common opponents. Moeller defeated Canton McKinley, 43-10, while Massillon just got by the Bulldogs, 7-0, in their annual rivalry game. Both teams also played Barberton, with Moeller coming away with a 35-8 win and Massillon defeating the Magics, 43-0.

This was one of the biggest Ohio state championship games yet to be played, with both the Division I title and the national championship riding on the outcome.

In 1982, getting a ticket to the big game would not be a problem since it was being played in the Horseshoe at Ohio State University, the third largest college football stadium in the country. When the game kicked off at 2:30 P.M. on Saturday, November 26, an all-time state championship game crowd of 31,412 was on hand.

Following a Massillon fumble Moeller took a 7-0 lead at 7:26 of the first quarter, but the Tigers came right back to tie the score about three minutes later. A pair of second quarter touchdowns by the Crusaders seemed to insure a 21-7 lead heading into the halftime break, but a Massillon touchdown just before the intermission cut the lead to 21-14 and appeared to give the Tigers some momentum.

Unfortunately for the Massillon Tigers, their new-found momentum did not carry over into the third quarter. The second half belonged entirely to Moeller, which scored a touchdown in each of the last two quarters while the Crusaders' defense kept the Tigers in check.

The major difference in this championship game was to be found in the respective running games. Moeller very nearly had three 100-yard rushers as it rolled up 337 yards on the ground. On the other hand, Massillon did not have one runner rush for more than 30 yards and totaled only 77 yards on the ground.

With their 35-14 victory, the Crusaders had claimed their sixth state championship in the last eight seasons.

When the final accounting was made for the national rankings, both Moeller and Massillon were high among the country's best teams. Moeller finished first in both the NSNS rankings and the *USA Today* Super 25 poll while Massillon finished sixth and seventh, respectively, in the two polls.

Moeller's exceptional run of success would last for three more seasons. In 1983 the Crusaders would again go 10-0 in the regular season, defeating Princeton in the final game, 28-21. The next week in the Division I quarterfinals, Princeton would return the favor by defeating Moeller by the exact same score. In 1984 Moeller would again finish 10-1, dropping a 10-7 game to Centerville in the state quarter-finals. The 1985 Crusaders finished the season 13-1 and won their last Division I state championship of the 20th century. The Crusaders lone loss that season came in their fourth game and halted at 71 the team's regular season winning streak.

The "Moeller Mystique" was no fluke and the numbers prove it. In 38 years of football during the 20th century, the Moeller Crusaders never had a losing season and only finished 5-5 once. For the 13 years from 1973 to 1985 the Crusaders finished first or second in the final AP Ohio Class AAA poll every season. Similarly, for the 11-year period from 1975 thru 1985, the Moeller Crusaders finished in the national Top 20 each season. No other team during the entire century in either Ohio or across the nation comes close to matching those streaks.

Finally, no team has ever won more national championships in a shorter period of time than the Crusaders of Cincinnati's Archbishop Moeller High School—five national championships in just seven seasons, 1976 thru 1982.

▾   *The 1982 Moeller Crusaders, the school's fifth national championship team in the previous seven seasons.*

## CHAPTER 10

VALDOSTA
THE NICK HYDER YEARS

Valdosta High School
Valdosta, Georgia

When Wright Bazemore retired from coaching at Valdosta High School after the 1971 season and took over as the Athletic Director, he left behind a legacy unlike any before him. Looking back more than a half century later, Bazemore's years with the Wildcats can now be called the "first golden era" of Valdosta High School football.

However, back in 1971 the folks in Valdosta did not have a crystal ball to tell them what the future would bring. As far as they knew, this was it, the end of the line. Bazemore had set the bar so high that another "golden era" seemed remote at best, as did possible silver or even bronze eras. The idea that someone could have even better success with the Wildcats was pure fantasy.

Like the fans of other teams that have enjoyed extraordinary success, the people of Valdosta had been spoiled by their team's exceptional accomplishments under Coach Bazemore. When Bazemore retired from coaching, the next man to take the job was one of his long-time assistants, Charlie Greene. Greene was a good coach and his teams won 85% of their games, finishing 17-3 under Greene in 1972-1973; but the Wildcats failed to make Georgia's playoffs either year. Good-bye, Mr. Greene.

Charlie Greene resigned as the Valdosta head coach following the '73 season. With Wright Bazemore leading the way, the search for the next Wildcats' head coach immediately got under way. The man that Bazemore selected already had something of a reputation in Georgia as a top-notch high school coach. However, nobody could have known that one Georgia high school coaching legend was about to hire another.

Nick Hyder was born on March 17, 1935, in Elizabethton, Tenn. At Elizabethton High School he played both fullback and linebacker on the school's football team, leading the team in both rushing and scoring his senior year. However, Hyder was not simply a football player but graduated sixth in his class academically.

Following high school, Hyder went to Tennessee's Carson-Newman College on a football scholarship, playing all four years in both the offensive and defensive backfields. As he had done in high school, Hyder led Carson-Newman in scoring

his senior year. After graduation Nick went to the University of Tennessee where he earned a Master's Degree.

Nick Hyder began his teaching and coaching career in Georgia at the newly opened West Rome High School in 1958. While teaching six classes daily (math, algebra, geometry), he started his coaching duties with both the jayvee football and jayvee girl's basketball teams, as well as being the school's head baseball coach. His baseball teams did extremely well with an overall record of 124-67 and state championships in both 1960 and 1962; Hyder was named the Georgia baseball "Coach of the Year" in 1962. His varsity football coaching career began in 1960 when he became an assistant coach at West Rome, remaining in that position until 1968, at which time he was named both the school's Athletic Director and head football coach.

The West Rome Chieftains football team got off to a quick start under Hyder, winning their first six games in 1968; a three-game losing streak followed, and then the Chieftains closed out the season with a 14-6 victory over cross-town rival East Rome. The team slipped to 5-4-1 the following season, but then hit real success over the next four years. From 1970 to 1973, Hyder's West Rome team posted a combined 41-5-2 record, advancing to the Class AA quarterfinal game in 1970 and the AA semifinal game in both 1971 and 1972. For his efforts, Nick Hyder was named the Northwest Georgia "Coach of the Year" four consecutive times, 1970 thru 1973. His overall record with the Chieftains was an excellent 53-12-3, .801.

Wright Bazemore and Nick Hyder were not total strangers to each other by 1974, having first met in 1962 at a Georgia coaches association banquet where each was being honored, Bazemore as the football "Coach of the Year" and Hyder receiving the same award for baseball. Nick Hyder was high on the list of possible candidates to replace Charlie Greene. He had been offered the head coaching job at several other schools, but when Valdosta came calling he accepted, officially becoming the Wildcats head coach on February 9, 1974.

Each new coach has to install his own system and run the program as he feels is best. In doing so, not everything goes as smoothly as one would hope. Being the new guy, Hyder had to establish his system of play even while he was establishing who the boss was, and if that meant stepping on a few toes—or more than a few— that was OK with him if it got the point across. Before the Wildcats' first game in 1974, therefore, a showdown of sorts took place and Nick Hyder bounced a dozen senior lettermen from the team for disciplinary reasons.

To no one's surprise, the loss of so much talent adversely affected the team's results on the gridiron. Hyder did start out his Valdosta career with a 3-0 victory over Crisp County the first weekend, but the team would win only two more games that first year and finished with a 3-7-0 record. Even the revered Wright Bazemore had a losing season, but that came after three consecutive perfect-season state championships and a national title. This was Hyder's first year and, knowing what the Wildcats fans expected of their football team, it was not all that surprising that Nick Hyder may have been looking over his shoulder every weekend. Despite the unimpressive start, Hyder still felt that the Wildcats would "be the best football team playing in the best football town in America." Before he was finished he would deliver on that promise.

With that first season mercifully out of the way, Valdosta's football fortunes picked up immediately. In 1975 the Wildcats won their first five games before dropping a 28-20 decision to traditional rival Moultrie High. They then closed out the regular season with four consecutive victories and made it five in a row with a 3-0 win over Thomasville in the regional finals. The season came to an end with a heartbreaking 15-14 defeat at the hands of Wayne County High in a Class AAA quarterfinal game.

It was more of the same in 1976, another 9-1-0 regular season and on to the playoffs; but this time the Valdosta postseason run ended in the first playoff game.

The winning continued in 1977 and only a 7-2 upset defeat at the hands of cross-town rival Lowndes High School prevented Valdosta from having a perfect regular season. That year, however, the Wildcats played deep into the postseason. They defeated Thomasville, 39-20, in the regional final, and then shut out Benedictine, 13-0, in a Class AAA quarterfinal match up. A 27-8 victory over Warner Robins in a semifinal game sent Valdosta to the Class AAA state championship game for the first time since 1971.

▲ *Wildcats quarterback Berke Holtzclaw (15) scrambles for positive yardage against Dougherty High on Oct. 26, 1984. (Valdosta High School Yearbook)*

▲ *Valdosta Wildcats Darrell Leonard (89) and Jimmy Lewis (92) literally jump for joy after Derrick Folsom (5) had returned a pass interception for a touchdown against Lowndes County in the 1984 edition of Valdosta's annual "Winnersville Classic". (Lowndes County Historical Society Archive-Valdosta Daily Times)*

The Wildcats' opponent in the 1977 championship game was the undefeated Gladiators, 13-0, from Clarke Central High School of Athens. The game, played on a very cold night in Athens, was very even throughout, but with the game clock winding down in the fourth quarter, Valdosta found itself on the short end of a 16-14 score. With 1:23 remaining, Valdosta tried to take the lead with a field goal, but the try missed wide left, leaving the Wildcats on the short end of a 16-14 final.

For the 1978 season, there was a slight realignment of schools and Valdosta found itself in the newly formed big school category of Class 4A. Following its fine season of the previous year, Valdosta was ranked # 1 in the state in the preseason 4A polls. Living up to that lofty ranking, Valdosta went through the regular season virtually unscathed, outscoring the opposition 362-28 while posting six shutouts. A 21-7 regional semifinal victory over Lowndes and a 12-7 win over Thomasville in the regional championship game proved to be more difficult than most of the previous 10 games, but this was the playoffs.

Playoffs or not, once they were out of their region the Wildcats found the going a bit less difficult. From 1960 through at least the end of the Hyder era at Valdosta, the majority of the Class 3A and Class 4A state champions came from the region in which Valdosta played, so winning the region during the playoffs was a key to winning state. In a 4A quarterfinal game on Friday, November 24, the Wildcats crushed Westside High of Augusta, 52-0. It was not as lopsided against Benedictine in a 4A semifinal game the following Friday, but Hyder's Wildcats again kept the opposition scoreless in a 23-0 victory.

The 1978 Class 4A state championship game had Valdosta playing the Griffin High School Bears, who came into the game unranked with a record of 12-2-0. The state's top-ranked Wildcats took a 7-0 lead midway thru the first quarter and it looked as if Valdosta might be on its way. After that, however, the defenses of both teams took over and dominated play. Griffin finally broke through to tie the game, but not until 11:19 of the fourth quarter after a lengthy drive that had started in the third period. Griffin had one last chance to win the game with 10 seconds remaining, but the Bears' 50-yard field goal try fell short.

The game ended in a 7-7 tie with both teams being declared Class 4A state co-champions. After the game Nick Hyder told reporters, "I'd like to play it off; there are no ties in life. You either win or lose."

The 1978 season was the first truly big year for the Valdosta Wildcats under Nick Hyder. In addition to the state co-championship, the 14 victories was a new single season team record and the Wildcats had also placed in the final national rankings for the first time since their national championship season of 1971, finishing 17th in '78. On a personal note, Nick Hyder was named Georgia "Coach of the Year" for 1978.

The following season was a tough one for Valdosta. After winning its first two games of 1979, the team dropped a 9-0 decision to Thomasville High. It was the Wildcats' first shutout in five seasons; ironically enough, the last one had also come at the hands of Thomasville. After winning its next two games, Valdosta dropped back-to-back one-point decisions, losing 13-12 to Tift County and then 15-14 to cross-town rival Lowndes.

Finishing the regular season with a 7-3-0 mark, the Wildcats still managed to make the postseason. In the regional semifinal game they avenged their loss to Lowndes by downing the Vikings 24-21. But the next week they were unable to duplicate that effort against Tift County, losing again to the Blue Devils, this time by a 24-6 score.

The 1980 edition of the Valdosta Wildcats started off the season ranked #10 in Class 4A, but steadily worked their way up toward the top. While the team had its moments on offense, defense was the key this season as the Valdosta defenders only allowed three of 10 regular season foes to score. The big showdown came in Week Eight when Valdosta squared off with cross-town rival and Class 4A's # 1 team, the Vikings of Lowndes High. In posting their 6-0-0 record, the Vikings had outscored their rivals by an average of 42-10, but this night defense would rule— the Valdosta defense. Holding the Vikings to a single touchdown, Valdosta pulled off the upset with a 17-8 victory.

Valdosta would run its winning streak to 11 when, on Friday night, November 21, they would again meet Lowndes, this time for the regional championship. The game would be another defensive battle and the Wildcats' defense would hold Lowndes to just six points. However, the Lowndes Vikings were just a tad better this time around and did not allow Valdosta to score any points as the eventual 1980 4A state champion Vikings came away with a 6-0 victory.

After that less-than-impressive start in 1974, Nick Hyder's Valdosta Wildcats had averaged almost 11 victories per season in the six years since, and that success would continue in 1981. A steady but not spectacular team that season, Valdosta averaged a little more than 27 points per game in winning nine of ten regular season contests. The team's lone defeat came in the fourth game, a 14-3 loss at the hands of always tough Thomasville. Qualifying for the playoffs for the seventh consecutive time, Valdosta defeated Westover High, 21-7, in a regional semifinal game before extracting a bit of retribution from Thomasville by handing the Bulldogs a 24-6 defeat in the regional finals.

That victory sent the Wildcats to the state quarterfinals where they would face the undefeated Demons of Warner Robins High School. Valdosta had won all six of its previous meetings with Warner Robins, but this Demons team was unlike any that had preceded it. It was a great game and one of the toughest that the Robins team would play that year, but in the end the Demons prevailed, 17-14. Warner

▲ *Valdosta tackle Johnny Crook's great block takes out a pair of Thomasville Central defenders and springs loose running back Willie "Loopy" Lewis during this encounter on Oct. 12, 1984. (Valdosta High School Yearbook, Photo by Mike Dowse)*

Robins would go on to win the state Class 4A championship and be named the 1981 national champion as well.

Since Wright Bazemore's retirement from coaching after the 1971 season, the Valdosta Wildcats' football fans had been patiently waiting for the "magic" to strike again. From 1972 to 1981 the team had played some very noteworthy football, but had only two trips to the state finals, and one co-championship, to show for it. All of that would change with the coming of the 1982 campaign.

Nick Hyder's Wildcats opened 1982 as the # 2 ranked team in the state. On August 27, the Wildcats defeated Waycross, 42-14, in the season opener and promptly moved up to first place in the polls. Except for a tight 17-14 victory over Dougherty High on October 8, Valdosta cruised through its regular season schedule averaging almost 33 points per game while allowing just six in posting a perfect 10-0-0 record.

Valdosta opened its 1982 playoff run with a regional semifinal contest against Thomasville, 7-3-0, playing the Bulldogs for the second time. In the first meeting between the two teams, Valdosta had come away with a well-earned 19-10 victory.

This game would be even tougher, but with the Wildcats' defense playing its usual top notch game, Valdosta moved on to the regional championship by the margin of a field goal, 10-7.

The regional championship on Friday, November 19, would be another rematch. Just two weeks previously, Valdosta had defeated Tift County, 8-3-0, by a 21-7 margin. Now playing the Blue Devils at Cleveland Field, Valdosta duplicated that first game with another 21-7 victory to win the regional championship.

In the Class 4A quarterfinals Valdosta traveled to Douglas, Ga., to take on the undefeated, 12-0-0, Trojans of Coffee High School. The Trojans had an explosive offense that was averaging more than 38 points per game and a defense that had already shut out four opponents. Playing a team like this on the road was a tall order, but one the Valdosta Wildcats were up for. Coffee's season came to an end before its hometown fans by a final score of 29-18.

Having now advanced to the Class 4A semifinals, Valdosta would have to face the defending state and national champion from Warner Robins. The Demons had lost two of their first three games in 1982, but got back on track and were still a dangerous team as their current 10-game winning streak would attest. However, there would be no repeat for Warner Robins as Valdosta moved on to the 4A state championship game with a well-earned 14-7 victory.

That championship game would be played at Valdosta's Cleveland Field against the third-ranked team in 4A, the 14-0-0 Patriots of Peachtree High School from Dunwoody. The Patriots were a solid though not spectacular team that relied heavily on its defense; Peachtree opponents had been shut out six times and held to just a single field goal on two other occasions.

Saturday night, December 11, was a rainy night in Valdosta, which no doubt contributed to keeping the score down. Each team had put across a touchdown and the extra point, but no more, and as the final minutes were ticking off the game clock it appeared that Valdosta was heading for its second tied championship game in five years. However, those who thought that had failed to take into account the right foot of placekicker Herbert Lowe. With just 33 seconds left in the game, Lowe booted home a 24-yard field goal that gave the Wildcats a 10-7 victory.

The dramatic win gave Valdosta its first 15-victory season and the team's first unshared state championship since 1971. As Nick Hyder remarked after the game, "Valdosta is Valdosta again".

When the final national rankings for 1982 were announced, the Valdosta Wildcats were listed as the nation's second best team, right behind Moeller.

With the coming of the 1983 season, the Wildcats took up right where they had left off the previous year. In running through the regular season and stretching their win streak to 25 the Wildcats averaged almost 40 points per game. Only in the regular season finale with Tift County did Valdosta have a real fight on its

▲ *Putting the "gang" into "gang tackling" are Valdosta defenders Dwayne "Moon" Hart (32), Derrick "Cool" Folsom (on the ground), and Kelvin Miller (94) as they team up to bring down this Tift County ball carrier during a regional semifinal game in 1984. (Valdosta High School Yearbook, Photo by Laura Harris)*

◄ *Valdosta tight end Darrell Leonard makes a nice catch during the Wildcats' 45-0 victory over Statesboro in a Class 4A semifinal game in 1984. (Valdosta High School Yearbook)*

▲ *Valdosta reserve quarterback Greg Talley hands off to Scott Braswell (35) during the 1984 Class 4A semifinal game against Statesboro. (Valdosta High School Yearbook)*

hands, but they managed to pull that one out by a 14 to 10 score.

When the playoffs started, the Wildcats were matched in the regional semifinals with Thomasville, a team they had previously defeated by 28-0. As the saying goes, the playoffs are a whole new season and teams step it up a notch. That was the case in this game; Thomasville played tough, but Valdosta managed to hold off the Bulldogs and emerge with a 16-6 victory.

The regional final game was another rematch, this one with Tift County, which the Wildcats had defeated only two weeks prior at Cleveland Field. Tift County had apparently learned something in that first encounter as the Blue Devils turned the tables on the Wildcats in their own stadium to come away with a 17-13 victory. Three weeks later Tift County would emerge as the Class 4A state champion.

Despite the heartbreaking defeat that ended the dreams of the '83 campaign, the Valdosta Wildcats' hopes for a championship season were again high at the start of the 1984 campaign. The team was ranked # 1 in the preseason Georgia Class 4A polls and they intended to make that ranking hold up for the entire season.

Valdosta's opening game was played on August 31 at Cleveland Field against the Thomasville Bulldogs. The Bulldogs had been the last team to hand Valdosta a regular season defeat on their home field three years previously, and when Valdosta lost a pair of fumbles inside its 25-yard line early in the first quarter it was not looking good for the Wildcats. However, Thomasville managed only a 34-yard field goal from those "gifts" as the Valdosta defense stepped up to stop the Bulldogs' offense. With the Valdosta "D" holding Thomasville to just 92 yards of total offense, the Wildcats' offense came back to take a 7-3 lead later in the opening session, made it 14-3 at the half, and finished on the long end of a 21-3 score.

Turnovers plagued Valdosta early in the season as the team coughed up the ball an average of four times per game in its first four games. However, with the defense playing faultlessly and the Valdosta offense unstoppable when it managed to hang on to the ball, the turnovers became nothing more than irritating distractions in the overall scheme of things. The Wildcats' record raced to 5-0-0 as they won their next four games by an average score of 46-7.

On Friday night, October 5, Valdosta met Tift County on the Blue Devils' home field. Tift had been the only team to defeat Valdosta the previous year, but the defending state champions were having a rough time of it one year later and had already dropped two of their first five games. Make that three losses in their first six games as Valdosta jumped to a 21-0 lead at the half on the way to a 28-0 final.

Valdosta easily put away its next three opponents by a combined 143-14, including a 68-0 trouncing of Dougherty High. In that game, Valdosta led by only 7-0 after the first quarter, but that was only the calm before the storm, or perhaps the thunderstorm, as the Wildcats exploded for a team-record 40 points in the second quarter.

With their record now 9-0-0, the Wildcats closed out the regular season at Cleveland Field against cross-town rival Lowndes in a game that was now known as the Winnersville Classic. As the Valdosta newspaper would later report, the Lowndes High Vikings "put up a gamely battle," but this season that would not be nearly good enough. Final score: Valdosta 28, Lowndes 6.

On Friday, November 16, Valdosta opened its postseason play in a regional semifinal game at Cleveland Field. The Wildcats would be hosting the Tift County Blue Devils; this game marked the third consecutive season in which these two teams had met during both the regular season and the playoffs. Since losing to Valdosta, 28-0, back on October 5, Tift had played like a renewed team in finishing the season with four consecutive victories, raising its record to 7-3-0.

The Cleveland Field crowd had to be just a bit stunned when the whistle blew to usher in the halftime break and Valdosta found itself on the short end of a 7-0 score. However, with the Valdosta defense playing another strong game (allowing Tift only 17 yards rushing), the Blue Devils were shut out during the second half while the Valdosta offense was able to mount a comeback to pull out a 16-7 victory.

In the regional finals, Valdosta had another rematch from the regular season, this one with the Colquitt County (formerly Moultrie High) Packers. The Packers entered the game with a very good 9-1-1 record, that lone loss a 40-7 drubbing at the hands of Valdosta. Colquitt County did not fair much better in the regional finals, losing to the Wildcats 35-7.

Advancing to the Georgia 4A quarterfinals, the state's top-ranked Wildcats found themselves on the road as they traveled to Warner Robins to take on the fifth-ranked Demons of Warner Robins High School, 10-1-1. The game was an 8 P.M. kickoff on Friday night, November 30, at the home team's

Valdosta safeties David Thomas (12) and Derrick "Kool" Folsom combine for a touchdown-saving tackle in the 1984 Class 4A state championship game against Clarke Central. (Valdosta High School Yearbook)

International City Stadium before more than 11,000 fans. The Valdosta defense would bend but not break during the first half and, despite allowing the Demons 154 yards of offense, Warner Robins was unable to score. Meanwhile, Valdosta had managed to cross the Demons' goal line once to lead 7-0 at the intermission.

After making some adjustments during the halftime break, the Valdosta defense was almost impenetrable in the second half. Warner Robins made only 36 yards on the ground over the final two quarters and never advanced beyond its own 48-yard line. Despite playing in a heavy downpour, the Valdosta offense came alive to score 21 unanswered points in the second half as the Wildcats advanced to the semifinal round with a 28-0 victory.

Valdosta was back in the friendly confines of Cleveland Field for its Class 4A semifinal game. How friendly you might ask? Over the past 10 seasons the Wildcats played a total of 68 games at Cleveland Field and had lost only six times. Not too surprisingly, therefore, Cleveland Field had been named "Death Valley" by opposing teams.

Playing Valdosta in that semifinal game was the team from Statesboro High School, meeting Valdosta for the very first time. The Blue Devils had opened the season by losing two of their first three games, but were now on a 10-game winning streak. Over its last four games the Statesboro defense had allowed only three points.

Played on Friday night, December 7, the game got off to a poor start for Statesboro when Valdosta All-American linebacker John Porter intercepted the Blue Devils' first pass and returned it 35 yards for a touchdown and an early 7-0 Valdosta lead. Statesboro never recovered from this early reversal as the Wildcats went on to a 45-0 victory.

The Georgia 4A state championship game was played at Cleveland Field on Saturday, December 15. Valdosta's opponent was the Gladiators of Clarke Central High School. This was the first meeting between these two teams since Clarke Central had defeated Valdosta, 16-14, in the 1977 state championship game. The Gladiators entered this game with a record of 13-1-0; ironically, that one loss had come at the hands of the other team that called Valdosta home, Lowndes High School.

This was one of the most important games that the Valdosta Wildcats had ever played because the Georgia championship was not the only title riding on the game's outcome. The Wildcats were currently

It seems like every member of the Valdosta defense is in on this tackle of a Clarke Central ball carrier during the 1984 Georgia Class 4A state championship game. (Valdosta High School Yearbook, Photo Mike Dowse)

▲ *Valdosta quarterback Berke Holtzclaw (15) goes around the right side during the Wildcats' 21-14 victory over Clarke Central in the 1984 Class 4A state championship game. (Valdosta High School Yearbook, Photo by Garner Walker)*

the top-ranked team in the country and a victory over Clarke Central would also clinch the national championship for Valdosta.

Before a crowd of more than 12,500 fans, Valdosta kicked off to open the game. Forcing the Gladiators to punt on their first possession, the Wildcats then marched 44 yards in just five plays, tailback Tony Anderson scoring the game's first touchdown as Valdosta took an early 7-0 lead.

Having moved the ball smartly down the field on its first possession, it looked like Valdosta was set to put Clarke Central away early, but such was not to be the case. Over much of the next three quarters, the Clarke Central defense kept the Wildcats in check. Meanwhile, Clarke Central tied the score with a touchdown midway through the second quarter and added a second TD late in the third to take a 14-7 lead.

Following that second Clarke Central score, the Valdosta offense finally started to move the ball. Taking the ensuing kickoff and putting the ball into play from their own 20-yard line, the Wildcats marched 80 yards in 18 plays, a drive that took almost eight full minutes off the game clock. The drive, which started in the third quarter and finished in the fourth, ended with Tony Anderson scoring on a two-yard run, John Porter adding the PAT that tied the game.

After the ensuing kickoff, Clarke Central went on offense at its own 20-yard line. After moving out to the 30 on first down the Gladiators then went backwards; a holding penalty followed by an intentional grounding call put the Gladiators back at their own three-yard line. Two plays later, Clarke Central was forced to punt from its own four-yard line; Tony Anderson fielded the ball at the Clarke Central 40-yard line and returned it 37 yards to the Gladiators' three. It took three

▲   *This cartoon commemorating head coach Nick Hyder and Valdosta's 1984 national championship season was drawn by Valdosta alumnus Bill Malone, Class of 1969, and appeared in the 1985 Valdosta High School yearbook, Sandspur.*

VALDOSTA HEAD COACH
NICK HYDER

▲ *Head coach Nick Hyder led the Valdosta Wildcats to seven state championships and three national titles. (Valdosta High School Yearbook)*

plays, but with 6:22 left in the game, Anderson finally pushed the ball over from the one-yard line. John Porter again added the PAT to give Valdosta a 21-14 lead.

Clarke Central was forced to punt on its next possession and Valdosta then ran out the last few minutes of the clock.

Valdosta's 21-14 come-from-behind victory gave the Wildcats the 1984 Georgia Class 4A state championship. When the final national rankings were announced a few days later it became official—the Valdosta Wildcats were the national champion for the first time during Nick Hyder's tenure as head coach, and the fourth time in school history.

Repeating as a champion in consecutive seasons is always tough, especially at the high school level, as Valdosta found out in 1985. The Wildcats won their first six games that year, but it was primarily on the play of a defense that recorded four shutouts and allowed only 13 points. The Cats also won in Week Seven, but it had been a struggle to pull out a 7-3 victory over Thomas County Central. Valdosta then lost two of its next three games, suffering a rare shutout, 10-0, in the last game of the regular season against cross-town rival Lowndes High. Despite the two defeats, the Wildcats qualified for the Class 4A playoffs for the 11th consecutive year. In the regional semifinals they avenged an earlier loss to Colquitt County with a 14-13 victory, but lost for the second time to Lowndes, this time 14-7, in the regional finals to finish the season with a 9-3-0 record.

As had been the case at Valdosta every season, the arrival of the new 1986 football season was greeted with great optimism and high hopes. The Wildcats were primarily a running team on offense. However, should second year quarterback Greg Talley decide to drop back to pass, he would have plenty of protection behind an offensive line that averaged about 250 lbs., led by 310 lb. tackle John Wheeless. The ground game would be in the very capable hands, and legs, of senior running back Jerome Calloway, while four-year starter at defensive end Seaborn Williams and three-year starter at linebacker Bill Kirby anchored the always formidable Valdosta defense.

Nick Hyder's Wildcats opened the '86 campaign at Cleveland Field at 8:30 P.M. on Friday night, September 5. Ranked # 2 in the preseason Class 4A poll and # 14 in the preseason national polls, one would normally expect that Valdosta would be a heavy favorite to win. Not so this year. Valdosta's opening game opponent was the LaGrange Grangers, the first meeting between these two teams in 19 years. LaGrange was coming off a 12-2-0 season and had 14 returning starters. They were also the top-ranked team in Class 4A and were # 4 nationally. Somewhat unusual for the Wildcats, Valdosta found itself the underdog in the season opener.

After an exchange of possessions to open the game, LaGrange jumped out to a 6-0 lead midway through the first quarter. Valdosta came right back with a nine-play, 71-yard touchdown drive that resulted in a touchdown with 1:42 left

▲ *The Valdosta defense was all over the Tift County running backs during the Wildcats 35-14 victory on Oct. 3, 1986. (Lowndes County Historical Society Archive-Valdosta Daily Times)*

▲ *The Wildcats battered down the goal posts against all comers during the 1986 season, as this Bill Malone drawing from Valdosta's 1987 yearbook shows.*

in the period. Like the Grangers, the Wildcats missed on their PAT try, leaving the score tied at 6-6 after the first quarter. With quarterback Greg Talley picking up sizable yardage through the air Valdosta took a 13-6 lead at 8:05 in the second quarter. The Wildcats added a field goal at 4:06 of the third quarter to close out the game's scoring. Valdosta's 16-6 upset victory was greatly aided by its opportunistic defense that forced five LaGrange turnovers.

The victory moved Valdosta up to # 1 in Class 4A and enhanced its national ranking as well.

Over the next couple weeks, Valdosta followed up that huge win with victories over Fulton High, 30-6, and Waycross, 31-0, raising the Wildcats' record to 3-0-0 as they prepared to travel to Florida to take on Leon High School of Tallahassee. According to the *Valdosta Daily Times*, this game would match the winningest teams of Florida and Georgia. Valdosta and the Leon Lions were not total strangers to each other. They had played before, but that first meeting was 60 years ago when Valdosta traveled to Tallahassee in 1926 and handed Leon High a 10-0 defeat.

More than 20,000 people were on hand at Florida State University's Doak Campbell Stadium on Friday night, September 26, for the big interstate game. With the Lions' defense playing tough against the run, Valdosta responded with an aerial attack by Greg Talley that opened things up. Talley's aerials hit their mark for 211 yards and two touchdowns as the Wildcats scored single touchdowns in each quarter. The Valdosta defense, which limited Leon to just 36 yards rushing, had a shutout all wrapped up until the Lions kicked a field goal with just six seconds left in the game to make the final score 28-3.

Returning to Georgia, Valdosta ran through its next five opponents by an average score of 39-7. With its record now 9-0-0, Valdosta's next game would be the now traditional season finale with Lowndes. The Vikings had suffered three defeats in their previous nine games, but local pride was at stake in this rivalry game and despite the fact that they were a heavy underdog in this one the Vikings had no intention of simply rolling over.

Defense ruled the day as play in the first half showed. Valdosta jumped out to a quick 7-0 lead just four minutes into the game, but those would prove to be the only points of the first half. After Valdosta pushed its lead to 14-0 in the third quarter, Lowndes immediately responded with a 72-yard touchdown pass on its first play from scrimmage following the Wildcats' ensuing kickoff. That one play was

▲   Top: Valdosta tailback Jerome Calloway
runs through a big hole in the Waycross defense
during the 1986 season. (Lowndes County
Historical Society Archive-Valdosta Daily Times)

▲   Bottom: Tailback Jerome Calloway (11)
on his way to a few of the 102 yards that he
gained against Leon High (Tallahassee, Fla.)
on Sept. 27, 1986.(Lowndes County Historical
Society Archive-Valdosta Daily Times)

▲   Valdosta fullback James Roberts follows offensive lineman
John Wheeless (75) during the 1986 season. (Lowndes County
Historical Society Archive-Valdosta Daily Times)

▲ *Jodie Sprenkle (79) and Troy Wells (77) anchored Valdosta's offensive line during the Wildcats' 1986 championship season. (Lowndes County Historical Society Archive-Valdosta Daily Times)*

the only mistake that the Valdosta defense made as the Lowndes offense would net only nine more yards the entire game.

Still in the third quarter, the Wildcats added a field goal to close out the game's scoring, Valdosta emerging with a hard-earned 17-6 victory.

Valdosta began its playoff run at Cleveland Field with a regional semifinal game and "28" would seem to be the team's "magic number" during the postseason. The Blue Devils of Tift County came ready to play and gave Valdosta a much better battle than during their first meeting about two months earlier. However, the Wildcats had just too much talent and emerged with a 28-16 victory.

The regional championship game brought the Vikings of Lowndes High back to Cleveland Field for the second time in 14 days. Lowndes continued its fine play of the first meeting through the first half, which ended in a scoreless deadlock, but the Vikings could not hold Valdosta down forever. The Wildcats exploded for 21 points in the third quarter as they rolled to a 28-0 regional championship game victory.

Valdosta took to the highway for its Class 4A quarterfinal game, traveling to Columbus, Ga., to take on the Tigers of Carver High School. Despite Carver's less-than-impressive 6-4-0 record, the game was still scoreless at the half; turnovers and penalties by both teams short-circuiting their offenses. In a game that was a carbon copy of the previous week's game as far as the box score was concerned, Valdosta blitzed Carver for 21 points in the third quarter en route to a 28-0 victory. The Valdosta defense had now strung together nine consecutive shutout quarters in the playoffs, this time by making 14 tackles for loss and holding Carver to minus-seven yards rushing.

On Friday night, December 12, the Wildcats returned to the friendly confines of Cleveland Field for a Class 4A semifinal game, also referred to as the South Georgia Championship. Lining up opposite the Wildcats would be the Tigers of Bradwell Institute in the first-ever meeting between these two teams. Bradwell entered the game with a prefect 13-0-0 record. Like Valdosta, Bradwell was playing excellent defense with seven shutouts to its credit and having allowed only 50 points all season.

The story of this game would be the Valdosta defense and tailback Jerome Calloway—and the outcome would be all but decided with the first offensive series of both teams.

Valdosta kicked off to open the game, held Bradwell to four yards and went on offense at its own 20-yard line following a Bradwell punt. On first down, quarterback Greg Talley handed the ball off to tailback Jerome Calloway. Calloway went

Valdosta safety Derek Shaw (8) brings down a Carver High running back during the Wildcats' 28-0 Class 4A victory in 1986. (Lowndes County Historical Society Archive-Valdosta Daily Times)

up the middle and, by the time he crossed the 30-yard line, he was in the clear and seconds later he had completed his 80 yard touchdown run.

What had all of the makings of a great game between a pair of undefeated teams, as the *Valdosta Daily Times* noted, "turned out to be a rout." Bradwell managed to score a touchdown in the second quarter, but it was not nearly enough. Led by Jerome Calloway's 280 yards rushing and two touchdowns (the other covering 90 yards), Valdosta piled up 450 yards on the ground as it crushed Bradwell by a 49-7 score.

It is often said when two teams meet that they have "identical records"—but in the case of the 1986 Georgia Class 4A state championship game it was truer than most might have thought. Meeting for the state championship for the third time in the past 10 seasons, and second time in the last three, Valdosta would be playing defending Class 4A champion Clarke Central on Saturday, December 20, at Cleveland Field. Both teams entered the game with identical 14-0-0 records and solid defenses, but the similarities did not end there. Over the past 11 seasons, from 1976 thru their 1986 semifinal games, each team had won 129 games, lost 15 (Valdosta also owned a tie game) and won three Georgia 4A championships. In addition to this, Clarke Central entered the game with a 29-game winning streak, its last loss coming in the 1984 Class 4A championship game—at the hands of Valdosta.

Valdosta won the pregame coin toss and opted to kick off to open the game before more than 13,000 fans. After forcing a Clarke Central punt, the Wildcats marched 60 yards with their first possession of the game to take a 7-0 lead at 6:34 of the first quarter. The score would remain that way until the last five minutes of the half when Valdosta scored two quick touchdowns to take a commanding 21-0 lead into the locker room at the break.

Valdosta scored the only touchdown of the second half as the team won its fourth state championship in the last nine seasons, 28-0. Defense had truly been a huge factor in Valdosta winning this title, as the Wildcats "D" allowed only seven points over the last 17 quarters of the playoffs.

HIGH SCHOOL FOOTBALL FINAL SUPER 25 WHERE THE TEAMS ARE

1 Valdosta, Ga. (15-0)

Last week: 1. USA TODAY's top-ranked team for the second time in three years. Won 19th state championship with a 28-0 victory, ending Athens Clarke Central's 29-game winning streak before 13,000. Greg Talley passed 40 yards to Charles Steward for a touchdown and ran for two 1-yard TDs. Bill Kirby had 10 first hits.

The Valdosta Wildcats finished atop the final USA Today Super 25 rankings as the undisputed # 1 high school team in the country for 1986.

When the final national polls were issued the following week, Valdosta was ranked # 1 by both the National Sports News Service and the *USA Today* Super 25, the Wildcats' second national title in the last three seasons. Valdosta was also the first repeat champion in the five years of the still young *USA Today* Super 25.

From 1982 thru 1986, the Valdosta Wildcats had been one of the best, if not the best, teams in the country. Three perfect 15-0-0 seasons, three Georgia big school titles, two national championships, and a second place finish—it does not get much better than that. The next couple of seasons would also be good, but they would soon have the Valdosta faithful wondering if there really was a 13th game jinx.

The Wildcats were ranked # 1 in Georgia's Class 4A to open both the 1987 and 1988 campaigns and held on to that ranking throughout the regular season with perfect 10-0-0 records. Each season they had also won the regional semifinal and final games, but then lost in the Class 4A quarterfinal game—the season's 13th game.

The 1989 campaign started off with some adversity and then hit a few bumps along the way, but nothing comes easy in high school football.

On the first day of practice in August, projected starting quarterback senior Jason Nichols suffered a broken leg. Back-up signal caller Deric Cotton was still recovering from a knee injury suffered in the spring. Head coach Nick Hyder's unlikely choice as the team's quarterback was junior wide receiver Alton Hitson, described as "a good student and athlete with a good attitude ...(who had) played some quarterback on his junior high and 9th grade teams."

Perhaps not the greatest pedigree for a Valdosta quarterback, but Valdosta fans were not all that worried about the Wildcats' offense because they had "THAT DEFENSE".

The season got underway on Friday night, September 1, at Cleveland Field with a game against Camden County High. Not too surprisingly, the Valdosta offense was slow to start, but a 20-point fourth quarter put an exclamation point on the team's 34-0 opening night victory. However, the real buzz that night was for the Wildcats' defense, which held Camden County to no first downs and minus-25 yards of total offense. That was a huge start for the Wildcats' defense and it would be next to impossible for them to repeat that level of performance each week during the season—but they came darn close.

Over the next five weeks, the steadily improving Valdosta offense averaged 32 points per game as the team improved to 6-0-0. The defense was rock solid, adding three more shutouts and holding Game Six opponent Bainbridge to minus-11 yards of total offense.

On Friday, October 20, the Colquitt County Packers came to Cleveland Field with a record of 3-3-0 to take on the state's second-ranked Wildcats. Who knows what happened? Many blamed the bright lights of ABC-TV's "20-20" television show, which was in Valdosta to do a feature story on the Wildcats. Whatever the cause, Valdosta came out on the short end of a 7-0 score, the team's first regular season home shutout in 15 years.

Over the next three weeks, the Valdosta offense seemed to lose some of its zip, averaging slightly fewer than 14 points per game. However, thanks to their outstanding defense, which never missed a beat, the Wildcats won those three games and headed into the playoffs with a record of 9-1-0.

It has often been said that the playoffs are a second season and this second season came none too soon for the Valdosta Wildcats. Despite some erratic play, they defeated Shaw High, 21-12, in the regional semifinal and avenged the loss to Colquitt County, 20-7, in the regional championship game—ironically enough, the game was played on the very day that "20-20" aired its previously recorded Valdosta segment.

On December 1, Valdosta faced Brunswick High in a Class 4A semifinal game, the only playoff game that the Wildcats would play at their home stadium, Cleveland Field. This was also the season's 13th game, but the Wildcats blew that "jinx" out of the water with a 42-0 victory.

The 4A semifinal game would not be nearly that easy. First there was the four-hour bus drive to LaGrange to play the LaGrange Grangers. Then the game, played in wind, rain, and sleet with the temperature in the 30s and the gridiron a field of mud. The 13-12 halftime deficit was also something that Valdosta had to overcome. Despite all of that, the Wildcats' defense shut down the Grangers in the second half while the Valdosta offense rallied for a pair of touchdowns to pull out the game by a 24-13 count.

Advancing to the 1989 Class 4A state championship game, Valdosta would be facing Clarke Central, 12-2-0, for the state title for the third time in the last six seasons. The Gladiators had advanced to the finals despite losing their first three games of the season (one later returned on a forfeit) and then overcoming top-rated Southwest DeKalb in the semifinals, 21-20.

More than 4,000 Valdosta faithful made the trip to Athens to take in the game on a night when the mercury dipped to a cold 22 degrees. Valdosta immediately took advantage of a huge break when Clarke Central fumbled the opening kickoff, the Wildcats recovering the loose pigskin and then taking it in for an early 7-0 lead. With Valdosta playing perhaps its best game of the season, the Wildcats built up a commanding 33-7 lead, only to have the Gladiators make it seem a bit closer by scoring a touchdown on the game's final play.

Valdosta's 33-14 championship game victory, the team's 20th state title since 1940, allowed the Wildcats to close out the 1980s with a state-record 125 victories against only 10 defeats. That outstanding Wildcats defense set what was believed to be a state record by holding its opponents to an average of only 34 yards rushing per game.

▲ *This Bill Malone drawing commemorates the Valdosta Wildcats' twin championships for 1986. (Valdosta High School Yearbook)*

Despite the one loss, Valdosta also finished 1989 high in the national rankings, placing seventh with the National Sports News Service and 11th in *USA Today*.

The Valdosta Wildcats opened the decade of the 90s with a season unlike most that they had enjoyed over the past several decades. The Valdosta faithful were used to seeing their team win big in a majority of the games played, but during the 1990 season virtually every game would be close enough to have gone either way. Having most of the previous year's record-setting defense graduate no doubt contributed to the closeness of these games. A schedule loaded with quality opponents, from both Georgia and beyond its borders, also helped to make the season interesting.

The season got off to a relatively normal Valdosta beginning when the Wildcats defeated McEachern High School, visiting from the Atlanta area, by 28-6. The next week Camden County High played at Cleveland Field and things went much differently. Valdosta found itself trailing 14-0 at the half, but rallied in the second stanza to score a pair of touchdowns. A victory eluded the Wildcats, however, when the game ended in a 14-14 deadlock.

On September 14, the Wildcats traveled to Jesup to take on the Wayne County Yellow Jackets, a game that Valdosta easily won, 38-6, but that big win would prove to be the exception this season.

Valdosta's game on Friday night, September 21, would introduce something new to the Wildcats' schedule. Beginning in 1990 and continuing at least through the balance of the decade, Valdosta added two strong out of state teams to its schedule. This night the first of two opponents from Alabama stopped by Cleveland Field, the Tigers of Jess Lanier High School from Bessemer. Providing some added excitement, this interstate contest was broadcast live on Sports Channel America.

As the Valdosta Media Guide related, "Lanier shocked Valdosta with two quick scores before most fans were in their chairs." Overcoming that two touchdown blitz, the Valdosta team soon settled in and pulled to within 16-7 at the half, Lanier having added a safety. The Valdosta defense continued to dominate the visitors throughout the second half, while the Valdosta offense scored just enough to pull the game out, 17-16.

▲ *Valdosta's Tommy Speed (21) dives for a first down during the Wildcats' 1992 season. (Valdosta High School Yearbook)*

The following week, Robert E. Lee High School, also from Alabama, paid a visit to Cleveland Field. Another defensive struggle, the Wildcats led 7-0 at the intermission and then added a late field goal for a 10-0 final.

The balance of the Valdosta schedule involved Georgia teams, and the close games continued. A second quarter field goal by Valdosta's Dow Drury provided the game's only points as the Wildcats defeated Bainbridge, 3-0. On October 19, against one of its oldest rivals, Colquitt County, Valdosta played one of its most exciting games of the season. After a 3-3 first quarter, Valdosta never trailed, but the Packers were never far behind. A late touchdown by Valdosta made the final 28-18 and made the game appear to be more of a big win than it actually was.

The following week, five Valdosta interceptions spelled doom for Tift County in a 23-7 Wildcats victory. Against Coffee County in their next encounter, the Wildcats saw an 11-point halftime lead slip away, but held on for a 30-29 victory. In the regular season finale, cross-town rival Lowndes needed a win to land a playoff spot and fought the Wildcats tooth and nail, but Valdosta managed to pull out a come-from-behind 16-7 win.

The 1990 season saw a revamping of the Georgia playoff format, skipping the former regional semifinal and final games and going directly to a new four-game state playoff format. Opening the playoffs on November 23 at Cleveland Field, Valdosta shut out Northside High of Warner Robins by a 21-0 score.

The Class 4A quarterfinal game at Cleveland Field was not as easy for the state's top-ranked Wildcats when they played Statesboro High. The game was tied at 10-10 with less than two minutes to play and it looked like one of the newly instituted overtime contests was in the offing. But Valdosta managed to pull the game out with a last minute touchdown and advanced to the semifinals with a 17-10 victory.

Clarke Central and Valdosta had been "regulars" in the Class 4A title game over the last few years, but the new playoff system had the two teams meeting this season in a semifinal contest. Not too surprisingly, it was a game heavy on defense. With the game still scoreless, the Wildcats scored a third quarter touchdown to take a 6-0 lead and later made it 8-0 with a safety. With the Valdosta defense holding Clarke County to only 56 yards of total offense, those eight points proved sufficient to send Valdosta to another state championship game, 8-0.

On Saturday, December 15, Valdosta took the field against Southwest DeKalb in the Class 4A state championship game. With the Wildcats jumping out to a 17-0 lead midway through the second quarter, this game proved to be the least difficult of the Wildcats' four playoff contests as Valdosta played on to a 31-0 victory and the team's 21st state championship.

With its victory over DeKalb, Valdosta became the first Class 4A team to win back-to-back state championships since Class 4A was established in 1978. It was also the first time since 1968-1969 that the Wildcats had won consecutive state titles. Valdosta again finished high in the national polls, coming in at # 11 in the National Sports News Service rankings and # 8 in the *USA Today* Super 25.

Valdosta had lost only one regular season game in the previous five years, so it should not have been a surprise that the Wildcats were once again the preseason Georgia Class 4A top pick for 1991. Living up to that ranking, Nick Hyder's team rolled through its 10-game schedule by an average score of 29-7. The only opponent that really threatened Valdosta was its old adversary, Tift County, which held Valdosta to a season low of 10 points, but could muster only six of its own. Even the rematches with the two teams from Alabama proved to be less of a challenge than their first meetings, with Valdosta taking the measure of Jess Lanier High, 35-0, and downing Robert E. Lee, 17-3.

In the first round of the playoffs, Valdosta crushed Northeast High of Macon, 49-19. It would be a much different story when the undefeated Wildcats took on undefeated LaGrange, 11-0-0, in the 4A quarterfinal round. After a scoreless first half, LaGrange broke on top in the third quarter by way of a 39-yard touchdown pass. Those six points were the only points scored that night, Valdosta seeing its undefeated string halted at 33. LaGrange went on to win the Georgia Class 4A championship and was also named the national champion by *USA Today.*

As had almost become the norm for both Valdosta and Georgia's Class 4A, the Valdosta Wildcats were again named the state's top team in the 1992 preseason rankings. Having lost only eight games over the past 10 seasons, there was no reason to think that the '92 campaign would be any different. The Valdosta offense, which would average 27 points per game, was not as potent as some in the recent past; but, as in previous years, the defense that Valdosta was able to put on the field meant the Wildcats' offense would not need to score many points.

The season got off to a great start for Valdosta on September 4 when the Wildcats defeated Augusta's Richmond Academy, 39-7. The game was a season highlight in that this proved to be the most points Valdosta scored in any game during the '92 season. The Wildcats saw their record climb to 3-0-0 with shutout victories

**Valdosta Wildcats
Milestone Wins**

1st win - 1913
14-0 over Sparks Institute

50th win - 1923
14-8 over Bainbridge

100th win - 1930
41-0 over Cordele

150th win - 1937
61-0 over Perry, Fla.

200th win - 1944
18-13 over Cairo

250th win - 1950
14-7 over Moultrie

300th win - 1955
27-12 over Baxley

350th win - 1960
7-0 over Albany

400th win - 1965
32-3 over Savannah

450th win - 1970
47-0 over Westover

500th win - 1976
30-0 over Monroe

550th win - 1980
27-14 over T'ville-Central

600th win - 1984
28-0 over Warner Robins

650th win - 1988
35-14 over Kendrick

700th win - 1992
17-7 over Northside-WR

▲ *The Valdosta Wildcats were the first high school football team in the country to reach 700 victories, achieving that feat on Dec. 4, 1992. (Lowndes County Historical Society Archive*—Valdosta Daily Times*)*

over Camden County, 21-0, and Cedar Shoals, 35-0, before facing a couple of out of state powers.

For that first cross-border game, Valdosta traveled to Lake City, Florida, to play Columbia High. Scoring in every quarter and holding Columbia to just 10 yards rushing and 39 total yards for the game, the Wildcats returned to Georgia with a 31-7 victory.

On Friday, October 2, Valdosta hosted the Bulls from Pennsylvania's Glen Mills High School. In Glen Mills, the Wildcats would be taking on one of the best teams in the Keystone State. This game, being an intersectional battle, was huge for the Wildcats as far as the national championship picture. Valdosta was currently the # 2 team in the nation according to *USA Today*, right behind # 1 Berwick High, also a Pennsylvania team. Earlier in the season, Berwick had handed Glen Mills it's only defeat, 33-7, so comparisons between Valdosta and Berwick as a result of this game were only natural; Valdosta needed to do at least as well against Glen Mills to maintain or improve its current national standing.

Giving Glen Mills a taste of the Valdosta style of "Southern hospitality", the Wildcats came up with seven turnovers and scored in every quarter in soundly defeating the Bulls, 35-0.

Since Glen Mills was the only team that would be playing both Valdosta and Berwick during the '92 season, it was quite natural for Bulls' head coach Joe Ferrainola to be asked to compare the nation's two top-ranked teams. His reply, "Eleven for eleven, Valdosta probably has the edge. The passing game I have to give to Berwick. Running game and total offense and defense I give to Valdosta."

Following the Glen Mills game, Valdosta had a two week layoff before its next scheduled game, an October 16 meeting with Bainbridge High. While a break like this in the middle of the season is often welcomed to help injured players get back on their feet, this layoff almost cost Valdosta its season. While the Valdosta defense never missed a beat in holding the Bearcats to 64 total yards, the Wildcats' offense had a hard time hanging onto the ball as it coughed it up seven times. Valdosta was fortunate that only three of the fumbles were lost, but one of those was returned for a Bainbridge touchdown that put the Wildcats on the short end of a 7-0 score early in the first quarter. In spite of itself, the Wildcats offense rallied for a pair of first half touchdowns to take a 13-7 lead at the intermission. That would end the scoring for the day as the Valdosta defense did its usual fine job in preserving the 13-7 victory.

On Friday, October 23, a 17-point second quarter outburst carried Valdosta to a 24-0 victory in Moultrie over the stubborn Packers of Colquitt County. The game had been scoreless until 11:20 of the second quarter when Valdosta closed out a drive and went up 7-0. Just 55 seconds later the Wildcats capitalized on a Packers turnover to add a second touchdown and a couple of minutes after that tacked on a field goal—17 points in three and a half minutes. The defense did another splen-did job in limiting Colquitt County to just 51 yards of total offense.

As had become the norm this season, Valdosta's next game, against Tift Coun-ty, was also close—for a while. The Wildcats led by only 10-3 at the half; but, three interceptions by the Valdosta defense and 410 yards of total offense propelled the Wildcats to a big second half and a 31-3 victory.

On a cold Friday, November 6, Valdosta was finally back at the friendly con-fines of Cleveland Field for the first time in three weeks. The opponent was the Coffee High Trojans and it was homecoming for the 11,000 in attendance. After fumbling the ball away on its first play from scrimmage, Coffee came back to take a 10-0 lead in the first quarter and held that margin at the half.

Coffee High was seemingly having its way with the Valdosta defense, which would yield an uncharacteristic 353 yards of offense in the game. The Trojans' first quarter touchdown was the first yielded by the Valdosta defense in 30 quarters, not since the first week of the season. However, at other times the Trojans were their own worst enemy as they lost four of five fumbles during the game.

After the intermission, Valdosta scored on its first two possessions of the third quarter, getting a field goal to cut the lead to 10-3, then recovering a Trojans fumble and turning it into the touchdown that tied the game at 10-10. The two teams than battled back and forth until Valdosta's Ryan Sanderson nailed a 33-yard field goal at 6:49 of the fourth quarter. Over the final six and a half minutes of the game, the Valdosta defense got back to playing its brand of football, shutting down the Tro-jans and preserving the Wildcats' heart stopping 13-10 victory.

In the regular season finale against Lowndes, it was business as usual when Valdosta completed its schedule with a journeyman-like 31-0 victory.

Over the last several seasons, Nick Hyder and his Valdosta Wildcats, despite their continued outstanding success, had come to learn that the games were get-ting harder and harder to win. The other teams were getting better, the Wildcats were playing a schedule that on average contained stronger opponents, and being the best team around they were marked men—everyone wanted to be the team that knocked off Valdosta. As the Wildcats were about to find out, this was even more true in the playoffs.

The first round of the 1992 Georgia Class 4A playoffs began for Valdosta on Friday, November 27, against the Bears of Griffin High School. The game was played at Valdosta's Cleveland Field, where the Wildcats would enjoy the home field advantage for as long as they were in the playoffs.

After a scoreless first quarter of an evenly played game, Valdosta scored twice in a span of about three minutes to take a 10-0 lead into the halftime break. Neither team scored in the third quarter, but Griffin closed the gap to 10-6 with a touch-down early in the final frame. Five minutes later, Valdosta's Steve Emerson scored

▲ *Valdosta quarterback*
Steven Emerson connects with
John Bell (8) on a flanker screen
pass during the Wildcats' 31-0
victory over Lowndes County
on Nov. 13, 1992. (Lowndes
County Historical Society
Archive-Valdosta Daily Times)

from seven yards out, then added the two-point conversion to give the Wildcats the 18-6 advantage that they would hold until the final whistle.

This victory held more significance for Valdosta than simply allowing the team to advance to the Class 4A quarterfinals. The victory was the 269th in Nick Hyder's 25 years of coaching in Georgia, 19 of those with the Wildcats. It moved him into fifth place on the all-time Georgia victory list, passing the man who had hired him at Valdosta, the legendary Wright Bazemore.

Advancing to the Class 4A quarterfinals, the Wildcats hosted the Eagles of Northside High from Warner Robins on Friday, December 4. Like Griffin the week before, Northside entered the game with a record of 9-3-0, but they had lost those three games by a total of only eight points.

After a scoreless first quarter, Valdosta erupted for 17 points in the second. Those would prove to be the Wildcats' only points of the game. However, with the Valdosta defense playing its usual bang-up game, 17 points was more than enough. Northside pushed across a touchdown with less than a minute remaining in the game to make the final a bit more respectable at 17-7.

Like the previous week, this victory was also a significant milestone in not only the history of Valdosta football, but also high school football nationwide. By defeating Northside High, Valdosta had reached a plateau that no other high school football team in the country had ever achieved—700 victories.

In the 4A semifinals scheduled for Saturday, December 12, Valdosta's Wildcats would be taking on another team of Wildcats, those representing Dunwoody High School, which entered the game with a record of 10-2-0.

The deeper one goes into the playoffs, the tougher the games become. Offense is hard to come by and defense tends to be king. Both teams would find that to be true this day.

A Ryan Sanderson 25-yard field goal gave Valdosta a 3-0 lead with 45 seconds left in the first quarter. The score remained at 3-0 thru the second quarter and the third as the Wildcats' defense took over the game. Finally in the fourth quarter the Valdosta Wildcats put the game out of reach with a 45-yard touchdown strike from quarterback Steve Everson to tight end Shadrick Green. The PAT gave Valdosta a 10-0 lead, which remained the score until the final whistle.

In the Class 4A state championship on Saturday, December 19, Valdosta would be hosting the Gladiators of Clarke Central. This would mark the fourth time in the last nine seasons that these two teams had met for the 4A championship, with another meeting during that time in the semifinals. Clarke Central entered the game at Cleveland Field with a record of 12-2-0, just barely advancing to the finals with a 22-21 overtime victory over Warner Robins in the semifinals. This would also be the first state championship game to be televised live across Georgia.

Before a sellout crowd at Cleveland Field, Clarke Central took an early 7-0 lead at 6:12 of the first quarter. Less than four minutes later the Gladiators were in the end zone again, having recovered a Valdosta fumble near midfield and turning it into a touchdown just three plays later to take a 14-0 lead.

The Valdosta Wildcats may have been down, but with more that three quarters of the game yet to be played they were hardly out. Sparked by a fumble recovery early in the second quarter, the Wildcats took less than a minute to get back into the game with a touchdown and extra point, adding a Ryan Sanderson field goal just before halftime to make the deficit a more manageable 14-10 at the intermission.

After that first quarter outburst by Clarke Central, the Valdosta defense put the clamps on the Gladiators' offense, just waiting for its own offense to catch up. The third quarter was scoreless, but 49 seconds into the fourth period Valdosta got the points it was looking for since early in the game on a 13-yard touchdown run by Nakia McMullen, Sanderson's PAT giving Valdosta a 17-14 lead.

With more than 11 minutes left in the game, three points was hardly a secure lead, but the play of the Valdosta defense made it secure—and a missed 28-yard field goal try by Clarke County in the closing minutes of the game certainly helped. When the final whistle sounded, Valdosta still had that 17-14 advantage, and its 22nd state championship trophy.

Before the year was out, the Valdosta Wildcats would pick up more championship hardware when both the National Sports News Service and the National Prep Poll both named Valdosta as their national champion for 1992, with *USA Today* ranking the Wildcats second behind Pennsylvania's Berwick High School. With this national title, Valdosta now had six to its credit, more than any other school except Massillon's Washington High School, which had been named national champion nine times.

As so often happens after a run of success, especially at the high school level, comes the inevitable down turn. After 12 seasons in which Valdosta had won 141 games while losing just eight with one tie, that down turn came in 1993. Although Valdosta started the season with three consecutive victories, the Wildcats lost four

▲ *Valdosta quarterback Steven Emerson (1) rolls out behind the blocking of Jamie Griffin (54) and Brad Grant (55) during the Wildcats' 1992 state and national championship season. (Valdosta High School Yearbook)*

of their next five games and finished the season with a 6-4-0 record, missing the playoffs for the first time since 1974.

However, it is tough to keep the country's winningest football team down for long, and Valdosta rebounded dramatically in 1994. Finishing the regular season with a more Valdosta-like 9-1-0 record, the Wildcats again found themselves in the postseason. They defeated Bainbridge, 33-6, and Brunswick, 28-8, to advance to the Class 4A quarterfinals. In that game, a high scoring shootout, Valdosta held off Northside High, 42-32. In the 4A semifinals played at the Georgia Dome in Atlanta, Valdosta found itself in another high scoring game, this time with 13-0-0 Southwest DeKalb. This game was much closer, but Valdosta managed to hang on for a 40-37 win.

Advancing to the Georgia 4A state championship game for the fourth time in the last six seasons, the Wildcats saw their season end with a 23-10 defeat at the hands of the new 4A champion, Colquitt County.

The 1995 season was another good one for Valdosta with the team again winning nine of ten regular season games, only a 21-10 loss at the hands of defending state champion Colquitt County marring the Wildcats' record. Valdosta made its way thru the first two rounds of the 4A playoffs with victories over Lowndes, 10-3, and Effingham County, 28-14. However, against Forest Park High School in the quarterfinals, Valdosta saw its season come to an end with a heart breaking 22-21 defeat, the Wildcats final record slipping to 11-2-0.

That quarterfinal playoff game would prove to be Nick Hyder's last time roaming the sidelines for Valdosta High School. On May 16, 1996, while having lunch in the Valdosta High School cafeteria, Nick Hyder suffered a heart attack and died within a few hours.

FROM 1982 TO 1992, THE VALDOSTA WILDCATS WERE THE BEST TEAM IN THE COUNTRY—A RECORD OF 141-8-1, .943; THREE NATIONAL TITLES; AND SEVEN NATIONAL TOP 20 FINISHES.

Nick Hyder is considered by many to be the greatest high school football coach in Georgia history and his accomplishments speak for themselves. His overall record was an exceptional 302-48-5, .858. In 22 seasons as the Valdosta head coach, Hyder compiled a record of 247 wins, 36 defeats, and two ties, .870., won seven Georgia Class 4A state championships, and saw his team named national champion three times. Hyder was the first Georgia coach to win 200 games in 20 seasons and 300 games in 30 seasons—reaching that second milestone in just 28 years as a head coach.

From 1982 to 1992, the Valdosta Wildcats were the best team in the country—a record of 141-8-1, .943; three national titles; and seven national Top 20 finishes.

While many considered Hyder to be a tough coach, and he probably was, what he was most of all was consistent in his beliefs and not afraid to put his job on the line for those beliefs. In fact, Nick Hyder did that his very first year at Valdosta, before the team had even played its first game under his direction, when he cut 12 seniors for failing to follow his practice schedule. Despite seeing the team finish 3-7-0 that year, the only losing season any of his teams would ever have, one person noted after his death that Hyder "wasn't happy about losing (that first year), but he was thinking about more than that one season; he was building a program."

Nick Hyder was not just another "football guy." He was active in many areas of school life, always willing to help any student. He was a deacon in his church, taught Sunday School, and was involved with the Fellowship of Christian Athletes. Hyder had his priorities, lived by them and was not afraid to let people know what they were. As Nick Hyder often told people, "A lot of people have rules and a playbook. We have a priority system. Number one is our Creator; Number two is family; Number three is academics; Number four is friends; and Number five is the Wildcats."

In 1996, Valdosta High School's Cleveland Field was renamed "Cleveland Field at Bazemore-Hyder Stadium" in honor of the school's, and Georgia's, two greatest coaches.

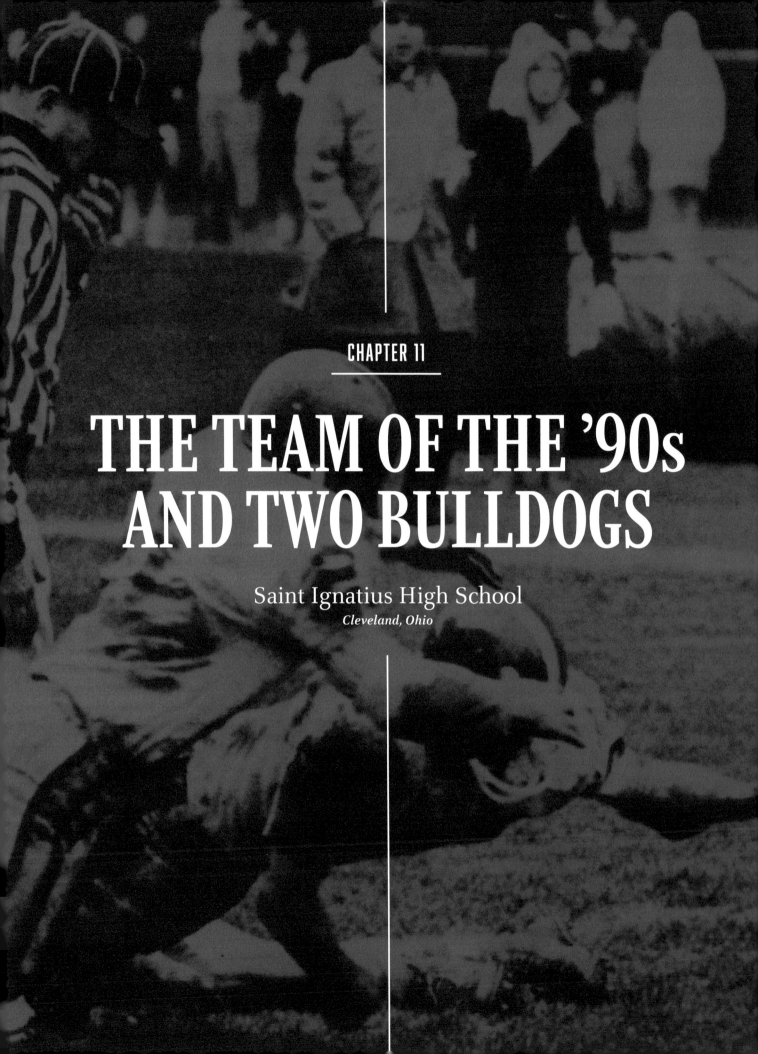

CHAPTER 11

THE TEAM OF THE '90s AND TWO BULLDOGS

Saint Ignatius High School
Cleveland, Ohio

One of the oldest schools represented here, Saint Ignatius High School of Cleveland, Ohio, was founded by German priests and brothers of the Society of Jesus, better known as the Jesuits. They came to Cleveland from Buffalo, N.Y., at the request of Cleveland's Catholic bishop and opened the school's doors to 40 students on the city's near west side on September 6, 1886. Known at the time as Saint Ignatius College, the school was a combination high school and college established to educate Catholic boys of the city.

While the school was known for its strong academic standards and spiritual base, the Jesuits knew that a well rounded student had to grow in both mind and body. Physical activities and limited sports were part of the curriculum; soccer was one of the early team sports enjoyed at the school. As the game of football began moving across the country from its origins in New England, it was inevitable that the sport would eventually reach Cleveland, where the first high school football game was played in 1890. It would not be for another 21 years, however, that the game was played by the boys of Saint Ignatius High School. A loosely formed team representing the high school lads first took to the gridiron on November 8, 1911, defeating a team from Cleveland's West Commerce High School, 18-0. Saint Ignatius High School has fielded a team every year since with the lone exception of 1913.

The progress of the team at this small all-boys high school at first was haphazard and slow, but it received a big boost in 1917 when Saint Ignatius High School formally established the football team as something of a "feeder" system for the "varsity", i.e., the Saint Ignatius College team. A short time later, the high school team adopted its first nickname. Like virtually every Catholic school in the country in those early days, the team was usually known as the "Saints". However, based on the success of Cleveland native John Heisman and his 1917 national championship team from Georgia Tech, the Saint Ignatius teams became known as the Golden Tornadoes and held that name for about the next 20 years.

The Golden Tornadoes enjoyed their first real success from 1923-26 under the direction of head coach Ralph Vince. Posting a record of 29-6-0 in those seasons, Saint Ignatius claimed its first Cleveland city championship in 1925. That 1925

The 1925 Cleveland city champion Golden Tornadoes of Saint Ignatius High School, the school's first championship football team. (Saint Ignatius High School Yearbook)

team was one of the school's all-time best and still holds the record for points allowed per game with 2.8.

The college and high school divisions at Saint Ignatius became wholly separate entities in the early 1920s and by the early 1930s the college, renamed John Carroll University, had relocated to University Heights on Cleveland's east side.

After Ralph Vince left Saint Ignatius High School, the football team fell on hard times and enjoyed only five winning seasons during the next 21 years. Finally, in 1949 the team's fortunes started to pick up under the direction of second-year head coach Fred George and his assistant, John Wirtz. Saint Ignatius, now known as the Wildcats, won its second Cleveland city championship that season. In 1950 the Wildcats again claimed a share of the Cleveland championship and earned the school's first state ranking, finishing eighth in that year's International News Service (INS) Ohio poll.

When Fred George left Saint Ignatius after the 1950 season, John Wirtz moved up to become the head coach, a position he retained for the next 20 years. Those seasons produced a level of success previously unknown by the Wildcats. While most of that success was on the local level, the Wildcats also began to make a name for themselves statewide. From 1952 to 1970, the team was ranked in the final state polls ten times, finishing in the Top 10 six times.

The high point of the Wildcats' success during those two decades came from 1962-1964 when the team posted a record of 29-1-0, 27-0-0 during the weeks when the various statewide polls were taken. That was the best won-lost record of any team in Ohio during those three seasons, but the best poll ranking that the Wildcats could muster was a fifth in 1963.

There were many across the state who for years had felt that the wire service polls, unscientifically based on the opinions of coaches and sportswriters, were not the most accurate or unbiased in their results. The 1963 poll results only added more fuel to that fire. The Saint Ignatius Wildcats were 9-0-0 and on a then school record (and state best) 19-game winning streak when the final 1963 poll results were issued, but the Wildcats finished a relatively low 7th (UPI) and 5th (AP) in the polls. However, a new scientific computerized poll known as the Conley System made its debut that season. Posted in the November 1963 issue of "Hi-School Sports" magazine, the results of this unbiased computerized poll ranked the Saint Ignatius Wildcats as the state's best team, while the poll champion team from McKinley High School in Niles came in third.

Polling discrepancies like this would lead to the Ohio High School Athletic Association adopting a playoff system for football less than ten years later.

John Wirtz retired from coaching after the 1970 football season, but the Wildcats would continue to enjoy success over the next eight years, gaining Top 20 ranking in the state polls three more times. However, in 1978 a change took place that has altered the fortunes of Saint Ignatius High School football ever since; initially not so well, but eventually taking the team to heights never before dreamed of.

In 1937 Saint Ignatius High School had joined Cleveland's Senate League, for most of the first half of the 20th century one of the best, if not the best, interscholastic football leagues in the country. However, by the 1950s the level of competition in the Senate had fallen off, not only as regards the private versus public school members of the league (where the private schools dominated), but also between many of the league schools and teams from other area conferences (with the Senate League schools becoming increasingly less competitive). The situation was deemed to be unbeneficial to both the public and private schools in the league, and the private schools slowly withdrew. Saint Ignatius was the last of the private schools to move on, which it did beginning with the 1979 season.

With the Senate League teams no longer a major part of the Saint Ignatius schedule, the level of the Wildcats' competition dramatically increased, virtually over night. Where once Saint Ignatius was playing set ups like former Senate League foes Cleveland West and Cleveland South high schools, now their opponents included regional and state powers like St. Edward, Youngstown Cardinal Mooney, Canton McKinley, and Pittsburgh's Penn Hills High School. Not too surprisingly, the team's won-lost record suffered accordingly, with the Wildcats barely staying above the break-even point.

When the 1982 team finished with a record of 4-6-0, the Wildcats' first losing season in 36 years, a change at the top was made. The search was long, taking four months, and thorough. Selected to be the new head coach for the Saint Ignatius Wildcats beginning with the 1983 season was Saint Ignatius alum Charles Kyle, Class of 1969.

More commonly known as Chuck, Kyle was born in Munster, Ind., in 1951, the youngest of four boys. His father, Fred, was a superintendent for Republic Steel and his mother, Dorothy, a kindergarten teacher. Being educated people themselves, Kyle's parents insisted that their sons also get a good education. Chuck credits his father with teaching him how to win and that success comes through hard work and doing a job right.

In 1955 a job transfer sent the Kyle family to Cleveland. When they reached high school age, all four Kyle boys went to Saint Ignatius High School and all participated to various degrees in sports. Chuck and his brother Fred had the most athletic success; Fred's coming as a starting lineman on the football team and as a member of the school's 1962 city championship squad, the first Saint Ignatius football team to enjoy a perfect season, 10-0-0.

▲ *Saint Ignatius Wildcats halfback Chuck Kyle diving on his own fumble to score a touchdown in the Cleveland city championship Charity Game, Nov. 28, 1968. (Saint Ignatius High School Yearbook)*

Chuck Kyle entered Saint Ignatius High School in the fall of 1965 and played football all four years at halfback. As a junior in 1967, he had hoped to be a starter, but a change in the offensive scheme that year relegated him to a backup role. The next year as a senior, Kyle finally was the starter. In helping to lead the Wildcats to a city co-championship with a record of 9-0-1 he rushed for just over 1,000 yards, led the team in scoring with 15 touchdowns and 90 points, and was named to Cleveland's All-Scholastic team.

Upon graduation, Chuck Kyle began his college career at Xavier University in Cincinnati, but when that school dropped football after his freshman year, Kyle transferred to Cleveland's John Carroll University. Chuck was on the Carroll varsity for three seasons, but an injury during his senior year ended his playing days—and started his coaching career when he volunteered with the coaching staff at Saint Ignatius.

In the spring of 1973, Chuck Kyle was offered a job at his alma mater as an English teacher and an assistant football coach for defense. On the day he went to the school to sign his contract, Athletic Director John Wirtz, Kyle's old football coach, saw Chuck in the hallway and asked him if he would like to be the new track coach. That was the entire "interview"; Kyle accepted right then and there ("You didn't say 'No' to Coach Wirtz.") and he has been the head track coach at Saint Ignatius ever since.

In his last four seasons as an assistant football coach, Chuck Kyle had moved up to defensive coordinator. His defenses were among the stingiest in school history, allowing an average of just 8.4 points per game. However, upon becoming the head coach in 1983, Kyle would now be responsible for the entire program. It was a dream come true for Chuck Kyle; but, as many were about to tell him, be careful what you wish for.

Like any new head coach, Chuck Kyle had high aspirations for his team, but he also knew that there were those who doubted that the Saint Ignatius football team would or could be a success. Some came right out and told him that he should not take the job because he could not win at a school like Saint Ignatius. Those naysayers compared Wildcats football to that of another team of Wildcats, the North-

CHUCK KYLE'S CHALLENGE WAS THAT OF TAKING ACADEMICALLY GIFTED KIDS, WHO ALSO HAD A STRONG MORAL AND SPIRITUAL CONVICTION, AND PROVING THAT THEY COULD ALSO BE PHYSICALLY TALENTED.

western University teams of the 1980s, a team of brainy kids that could not beat the Michigans and Ohio States of the world. Instead of discouraging Kyle, this became his motivation and driving force. His challenge was that of taking academically gifted kids, who also had strong moral and spiritual convictions, and proving that they could also be physically talented. Chuck Kyle felt that it was an insult to the human spirit to think that you could not do all three, so it was his goal to prove that it could be done.

To help his team meet these challenges against the toughest batch of opponents that a Saint Ignatius football team had ever had to face, Chuck Kyle took several key steps. For one, he continued the weight training program that his predecessor had started to help build his team physically. He then combined the varsity and junior varsity teams into one, insuring that the players and their coaches were all on the same page and eliminating the need to "retrain" jayvee players when they advanced to the varsity squad.

Another change involved the offense. Kyle's team was not yet ready, i.e., big enough, to battle it out for four quarters with many of the physically bigger teams that were now populating the Wildcats' schedule. Traditionally, Ohio high school football favored a run-based offense and, since most defenses were designed primarily to stop a ground attack, Kyle switched the Wildcats offense to one that was pass oriented. This may have been his biggest gamble, since a passing attack requires much more coordination and split second timing. However, Kyle was confident that his players could overcome this challenge with their God-given intelligence. After reviewing the best collegiate passing programs in the country, Chuck Kyle and his staff, especially offensive coordinator Nick Restifo, came up with an attack that initially featured just 10 basic patterns and a three-step drop by the quarterback. Eventually the Wildcats' passing attack would evolve into more than 90 pages of the team's 130-page offensive playbook. (Ironically, the birthplace of John Heisman, one of the earliest proponents of the forward pass, is a mere 600 feet from Chuck Kyle's school office.)

A further aid to the new Wildcats passing attack came five years after Kyle took over as the head coach in the form of a new rule that liberalized pass blocking, further enhancing the ability of the Wildcats to attack through the air.

All of these changes, and more, would take time to implement; in the meanwhile there were football games to be played.

The Wildcats' Barry Alvis tackles Cincinnati Princeton quarterback Johnny Mattress on the last play of the 1988 Ohio Division I state championship game to insure the first state championship for Saint Ignatius. (Saint Ignatius High School Yearbook)

Chuck Kyle's first season at the helm of the Wildcats, 1983, proved to be successful as his team reversed the results of the previous season by finishing 6-3-1. Of even more significance to the Saint Ignatius faithful was that for only the second time since 1957, the Wildcats had not lost to their arch rival St. Edward High School. Granted, the game did end in a 14-14 tie, but it was not a loss—a step in the right direction.

The next season, the Wildcats improved to 8-2-0, followed by seasons of 7-3-0, 6-4-0, and 6-4-0; winning seasons that had produced an overall record of 33-16-1 in Kyle's first five years.

After the 1987 season, in which the Wildcats had finished 6-4-0 for the second consecutive time, Chuck Kyle, as he had done every year since becoming head coach, sat down with each player for a 10-minute postseason interview. During these brief sessions Kyle would get the player's thoughts on that player's performance during the just completed season, tell the player where he needed to improve, and get the player's goals for the coming campaign. At the post-1987 meetings, Chuck Kyle started to hear one thing repeated over and over: that the Wildcats could be state champions. Not that they wanted to be, or hoped to be, but that they *could* be state champions in 1988.

The Ohio high school football playoffs had just completed their 16th year and the Saint Ignatius Wildcats had never qualified for the postseason, had yet to play in their first playoff game. This declaration by his players struck Chuck Kyle as pretty heady stuff, though he could not complain about his players' confidence. Therefore, he tossed the challenge right back at them: Talk is cheap, go out and do it.

But the Wildcats were not the only ones who felt that the 1988 season might be something special for Saint Ignatius High School football. The local newspapers in their preseason forecasts noted that the Wildcats had 26 returning lettermen, which gave the team a great deal of experience and incredible depth to overcome any injuries that might strike the team during the season.

Saint Ignatius would need all of that depth and experience if they hoped to survive a regular season schedule that included six of the area's Top 20 rated teams. After defeating Lake Catholic, 24-7, in the season opener, the Wildcats faced their first truly big challenge in their second game. The opponent was the Panthers of Euclid High School, who would end the season as the state's fifth-ranked Division I team and were led by future collegiate and pro star tailback Robert Smith. Smith, who would be named Northeastern Ohio's top player of the past 50 years in 2013, ran all over the Wildcats the previous season as Euclid posted a 30-7 victory. In 1988 the Wildcats defense keyed on Smith and, although he gained 102 yards, he did not score a single point from scrimmage as Saint Ignatius cleared its first big hurdle with an impressive 21-12 win.

Three consecutive shutouts followed, in which Saint Ignatius outscored the opposition 123-0. On Saturday, October 8, the Wildcats took on the Patriots of Valley Forge High School. Valley Forge entered the game with a less-than-distinguished record of 2-3 (with overtime periods now being played in Ohio, no more need to leave a space for ties), while the Wildcats were coming off a 75-0 victory, the most lopsided win in school history. Perhaps a bit over confident, the Wildcats found themselves on the short end of a 13-7 score with just 7:44 left in the game before rallying to pull out a 14-13 victory.

Saint Ignatius cruised through its next four games, including a 14-7 victory over the St. Edward Eagles, to finish the regular season a perfect 10-0—the team's first perfect campaign since 1964. To make things even sweeter, in the closest AP Ohio poll vote ever, Saint Ignatius was ranked # 1 in Ohio Division I, edging out Sandusky High School by a single point. Cincinnati Princeton, the defending Division I champion, had been # 1 all season until losing its final game and dropping to third place in the poll.

Having come through its tough Northeastern Ohio schedule unscathed, Saint Ignatius now had to venture into the unknown—Ohio Division I playoff football. The Wildcats' first playoff game took place on Saturday, November 12, a rematch with Robert Smith and the Euclid Panthers. Holding Smith to his lowest rushing total in two seasons, a mere 22 yards, the Wildcats notched their sixth shutout of the season, 17-0, and advanced to the Division I quarterfinals. The victory over Euclid also sent the Wildcats somewhere they had never been before—into the national rankings, coming in at # 18 that week.

Saint Ignatius's quarterfinal game took place on Saturday, November 19, against Stow High School, 10-1, at Finnie Stadium on the campus of Baldwin-Wallace College in Berea, Ohio. Stow had played a relatively weak schedule and it showed when the Wildcats handed them a 35-8 thrashing.

With its record now 12-0, Saint Ignatius had now advanced to the Division I semifinals. The Wildcats' opponent was the Panthers of Toledo's Whitmer High School, the game set for a 1 P.M. kickoff at the Toledo Glass Bowl. However, in one of the more unusual decisions ever made by the Ohio High School Athletic Association, Saint Ignatius was designated as the home team. As Chuck Kyle noted, "To be honest, I do not understand it. To say that we're the home team and then schedule us at 1 P.M. (more than 100 miles away) in Toledo is a little puzzling."

Bottom line, you play the hand you are dealt. The Wildcats simply played their game, putting up 28 points by halftime en route to a 31-8 victory.

Saint Ignatius defensive back Kareem Ingram (44) stops Euclid's Robert Smith in the backfield in this nationally televised game on Sept. 2, 1989. (Saint Ignatius High School Yearbook)

At the end of the 1987 season, Chuck Kyle's players had told him that they were going to win the 1988 Division I state championship, and now that championship game had arrived. It was played on Saturday, December 4 at 1 P.M. in the stadium at Ohio State University. Befitting a game for the Ohio Division I state title, it featured two of the best teams, not just in Ohio, but in the country. The Wildcats' opponent that day was the Vikings of Cincinnati Princeton High School. Princeton, the defending Division I champion, was one of Ohio's premier high school football teams at this time. The Vikings were veterans of not only the playoffs, their seventh time, but also the championship game—five title game appearances and three Division I state championships in the last 11 seasons. In the national rankings, Saint Ignatius had now entered the Top 10 while Princeton was ranked as high as 13.

In a game that featured a pair of high powered offenses and brick wall defenses, it would be defense that ruled this day. After a scoreless first quarter, the Wildcats took a 3-0 lead on a 24-yard field goal at 11:44 of the second period. About five minutes later Princeton finally got on the scoreboard, taking a 7-3 lead that they carried into the halftime break.

The third quarter was also scoreless, but on the second play of the final period Wildcats quarterback Joe Pickens called an audible and hit wide receiver Mike Buddie with a pass down the middle for a 42-yard touchdown, the PAT giving the lead back to Saint Ignatius, 10-7, with a little more than 11 minutes to play. The

Wildcats held onto their lead, but it would take an incredible goal line stand over the game's final 80 seconds to preserve the first Division I state championship for Saint Ignatius.

When the final national polls came out about 10 days later, Saint Ignatius had moved up to # 5.

Having accomplished something no other Saint Ignatius High School football team had ever done in winning both a state football championship and being ranked in the national top five, it remained to be seen if the Wildcats would be "one and done" or if they could sustain their excellent play for another season. The 1989 squad lost 31 seniors to graduation, including 13 starters, but the depth that was highlighted on the previous year's team would again be there for the '89 Wildcats. Leading the returning players was senior quarterback Joe Pickens, who would be joined by a number of veteran seniors and juniors, as well as a few top notch sophomores who would fill out the varsity line-up.

Having won the last two games of the 1987 campaign and gone undefeated in 1988, the Wildcats opened 1989 with their win streak at 16. It quickly went to 17 when the Wildcats opened the new season with a 43-2 victory over Mentor High School's Cardinals.

One of the most anticipated and highly publicized high school football games in Northeastern Ohio history was played the next week on Saturday, September 2, at Lakewood Stadium. Again bringing together the Wildcats with the Panthers of Euclid High School and their star Robert Smith, this game had the makings of an instant classic as it matched a pair of regional and state powers. If all of that were not enough, the game's audience jumped to the millions, literally, when it was announced that Sports Channel America would broadcast the game live, making it the first ever nationally televised regular season high school football game.

Euclid struck first, turning a Wildcats fumble into a touchdown and an early 7-0 lead. The Cats came back to score a touchdown of their own, but the missed extra point try left Saint Ignatius down by a point, 7-6, at the end of the first quarter. After that shaky early start, the middle two quarters belonged entirely to the Wildcats as they outscored Euclid 35-6 to take a commanding 41-13 lead into the fourth quarter.

Both teams added a pair of touchdowns during the final 12 minutes as the Wildcats showed the national television audience with a 55-26 victory why they had started the season ranked # 3 in the country. After the game, Euclid head coach Tom Banc told reporters, "I'd like to see the team that can stop those guys."

The Wildcats easily won their next three games, pushing their win streak to a school-record 21 and counting. On October 7, the Wildcats faced off against Cleveland's St. Joseph Vikings, the # 1 ranked team in Ohio's Division II. It was a tough game, but Chuck Kyle's Wildcats came away with an historic 23-6 victory. Not only

▲ *Saint Ignatius wide receiver Mark Ruddy leaps high to go over a Euclid defender to make this spectacular catch on Sept. 2, 1989. (Saint Ignatius High School Yearbook)*

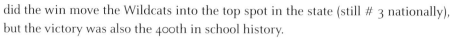

Saint Ignatius tailback Peter Fitzpatrick races through a huge hole opened by his offensive line against Euclid on Sept. 2, 1989. (Saint Ignatius High School Yearbook)

did the win move the Wildcats into the top spot in the state (still # 3 nationally), but the victory was also the 400th in school history.

The Wildcats closed out the regular season with three more impressive victories and qualified for the Division I playoffs for the second consecutive season as they ran their win streak to 25.

Saint Ignatius opened its 1989 Division I playoff run on Saturday, November 4, with a game against Western Reserve High of Warren, Ohio, at 8-0 the only undefeated team in the division besides the Wildcats. Saint Ignatius would enjoy a 9-0 lead after one quarter, but this would be no blowout. Western Reserve cut the lead to 9-7 at the half and the score remained that way until the Wildcats added the clinching points in the fourth quarter to come away with a hard-fought 16-7 win.

That victory, which moved the Wildcats into second place in the national polls, also set up a rematch with the Euclid Panthers, the fifth meeting in three years between the two teams—a game that was destined to become a classic and one of the greatest games in Ohio high school football history.

More than 11,000 fans overflowed Baldwin-Wallace College's Finnie Stadium on November 11 for this regional final contest. A safety and a 67-yard touchdown return by Robert Smith on the Wildcats' ensuing free kick staked Euclid to a 9-0 lead just five minutes into the game. The Wildcats came back to make it 9-7 after one quarter and took a 13-9 lead in the second; but a Euclid touchdown just before the intermission gave the Panthers a 16-13 lead at halftime.

On their first possession of the third quarter, the Wildcats regained the lead, 19-16, on a 15-yard Joe Pickens touchdown aerial. The Euclid defense would then step up to put the Wildcats into a huge hole as they intercepted a pair of Pickens aerials, both picks resulting in Euclid touchdowns.

With just 10:01 left to play following Euclid's latest touchdown, the Wildcats trailed by 30 to 19; they

Saint Ignatius head coach Chuck Kyle reviews strategy with his offense during the Ohio Division I state championship game with Moeller on Nov. 26, 1989. (Rev. James F. Flood)

◄ *Saint Ignatius quarterback Joe Pickens rifles another pass down field for some of the 311 yards he gained through the air against Moeller in the 1989 Ohio Division I state championship game, Nov. 26, 1989. (Mark Zaremba)*

▼ *This reception by Saint Ignatius wide receiver Mark Ruddy was good for a touchdown, his second TD reception against Moeller in the 1989 Ohio Division I state championship game. (Rev. James F. Flood)*

needed two scores to get back in the game, and they needed to get one of them quickly. The Wildcats got exactly what they needed when Tim Kennedy fielded the ensuing kickoff at his own 15-yard line and followed a line of blockers down the right side of the field all the way to the end zone for an 85-yard touchdown. A try for a two-point conversion failed, but the Wildcats had cut their deficit to a more manageable five points at 30-25.

Now fired up, the Saint Ignatius defense forced the Panthers to punt on their next possession, regaining the ball at the Wildcats' 36-yard line. Facing third and 17, quarterback Joe Pickens went to the air, lofting the ball down the middle of the field in the direction of wide receiver John Jaeckin. The ball sailed through the hands of Euclid's Robert Smith, bounced off the shoulder pads of another Euclid defender—and fell into the hands of the Wildcats' John Jaeckin who was lying on his back some 30 yards down field. In Saint Ignatius football lore, this is now known as the "Immaculate Reception".

Nine plays later, the Wildcats' Peter Fitzpatrick scored the touchdown that put Saint Ignatius back in the lead. Again the two-point conversion failed, but with 1:47 left in the game, the Wildcats were back on top, 31-30.

Following the kickoff, the Euclid Panthers were on the move and had crossed midfield when the Wildcats' Pat Friend ended their dream of an upset with an interception that secured the Wildcats' 31-30 victory. The Euclid Panthers had lost only four games in 1988 and 1989—all four had been at the hands of the Saint Ignatius Wildcats.

Not only did the Wildcats' victory advance them to a Division I semifinal game, but on Tuesday, November 14, when the new *USA Today* Super 25 poll came out, the Wildcats had advanced to the # 1 spot in the country. When asked by reporters about that, Wildcats head coach Chuck Kyle said, "It's quite an honor, but I'd rather have that two weeks from now."

In their Division I semifinal game, the Wildcats would be taking on a team whose name and accomplishments were legendary throughout both Ohio and the nation as a whole. The Tigers of Massillon Washington High School entered their contest with the Wildcats with a record of 10-2. The two teams had never met in a game before, but had scrimmaged earlier in the year. Of that scrimmage Chuck Kyle noted, "We played them in our first scrimmage and

▼ *The whole city of Cleveland was proud of its only national champion in 25 years. (Karl Ertle)*

Cleveland St. Ignatius (13-0)
Last week: 1. Won 2nd consecutive Division I title and 29th consecutive game 34-28 against Cincinnati Moeller before 28,000 at Columbus. Joe Pickens was 12-for-22 passing for 311 yards, three TDs. Mark Ruddy caught four passes for 144 yards, two TDs.

▲ *The* USA Today *final Super 25 told the whole country who the best high school football team of 1989 was.*

they really hammered us. They don't respect us and we have something to prove to them."

The game was played on Saturday, November 18, at the Akron Rubber Bowl before one of the largest crowds to witness an Ohio high school football playoff game, just under 25,000. The Wildcats struck early and led 13-0 just two seconds into the second quarter; but Massillon dominated play during the second quarter and tallied just before the intermission to make it a 13-7 game at the half. Saint Ignatius came out after the halftime break and took control of the game, scoring 22 points and pushing its lead to 35-7 before the Tigers were again able to dent the scoreboard. When the final whistle sounded, the Wildcats' convincing 42-21 victory allowed them to advance to the state championship game for the second consecutive season.

If the Massillon Tigers represented a team of legendary stature from an earlier era, then the Wildcats' opponent in the Division I state championship game was a legendary team of more recent vintage. The Crusaders of Archbishop Moeller High School entered the title game with a record of 11-2. This was Moeller's ninth trip to the Division I championship game, looking for its eighth title. The game was played on Sunday afternoon, November 26, at the stadium at Ohio State University. The official attendance was 17,667, but it seemed as if twice that many were actually there.

The game was a battle of "aerial warfare" that set a record that still stands for most yards passing, 658, in a Division I championship game. In a back and forth first half the Wildcats took only a minute and a half to jump to a 7-0 lead, appropriately enough on an 80-yard Pickens to Mark Ruddy pass play. Moeller then tied the score on a 63-yard pass before the Wildcats regained the lead, 14-7, all within the first quarter. A pair of second quarter TDs gave Moeller a 21-14 lead at the half.

The second half belonged to Saint Ignatius. The Wildcats scored a touchdown in the third quarter to tie the score at 21-21, and then added a pair of six-pointers in the fourth to take a 34-21 lead with 2:24 left in the game. Meanwhile, the Saint Ignatius defense held Moeller to minus-1 yard rushing and 132 yards through the air in the final two quarters. The Crusaders scored a late touchdown with a little more than a minute left in the game to close to within 34-28, but their onside kick try was recovered by the Wildcats, who then ran out the clock.

For the second straight season, the Saint Ignatius Wildcats had gone undefeated, 13-0, in winning the Division I state championship. And also for the second straight season, they had overcome a halftime deficit in the championship game to gain the title. Postseason honors were aplenty for the Wildcats, beginning with being named the nation's # 1 team by *USA Today*. Head coach Chuck Kyle was named *USA Today*'s "Coach of the Year", while quarterback Joe Pickens earned All-America honors.

The Saint Ignatius Wildcats entered the 1990 campaign on a 29-game win streak. As the season progressed, it looked as if the Wildcats might never lose again as they again completed the regular season a perfect 10-0 while outscoring the opposition by an average of 32-7 and allowing only one team to score more than eight points. The Wildcats' win streak had now reached 39, the longest streak in Northeastern Ohio history and the second longest ever in Ohio. The Wildcats had now gone three consecutive seasons without a loss, as well as being named Division I's top team in the final AP poll for those same three seasons.

The Wildcats' first playoff opponent was the Falcons of Austintown Fitch High School, 8-2. It took only 24 seconds for the Wildcats to learn that this was going to be a real dogfight when they fell behind 6-0. The game went back and forth and at the half Fitch held a surprising 20-14 lead. Saint Ignatius regained the advantage, 21-20, on its first possession of the second half, but the Falcons immediately answered with a touchdown of their own to retake the lead, 26-21. Fitch added another touchdown later in the third quarter to increase its advantage to 33-21 as the game proceeded into its final 12 minutes. The Wildcats scored a touchdown late in the fourth quarter to cut the Fitch lead to 33-28, and then regained possession of the ball with 2:27 left to play for one last try to move ahead. However, the Fitch defense stopped them cold and for once the Wildcats were unable to come up with a miracle finish.

Having lost just one game in the last three seasons, the Wildcats were again looking for good things to happen in 1991, including a longer run in the playoffs.

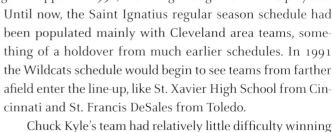

Until now, the Saint Ignatius regular season schedule had been populated mainly with Cleveland area teams, something of a holdover from much earlier schedules. In 1991 the Wildcats schedule would begin to see teams from farther afield enter the line-up, like St. Xavier High School from Cincinnati and St. Francis DeSales from Toledo.

Chuck Kyle's team had relatively little difficulty winning its first six games that year, including a 20-17 victory over the Cleveland area's then top-ranked team from Lake Catholic. The Wildcats then hit a couple of bumps in the road. Cleveland's Villa Angela-St. Joe's, 1-5, stunned the Wildcats by handing them an 8-0 shutout defeat, in part the result of Wildcats starting quarterback Kevin Mayer getting sidelined with a sprained ankle in the first quarter. Sophomore quarterback Scott Mutryn started the next game against arch rival St. Ed's, but the lack of a seasoned quarterback again cost the team and they fell by a 14-10 count.

With their record now at 6-2, the Wildcats' postseason really started with their next game because another loss would probably knock them out of the running

▲ *Saint Ignatius placekicker Fernando Paez boots home the winning point against Massillon in a 1991 Ohio Division I semifinal game. (Jim Cahill)*

After catching a pass from halfback Eric Haddad, Saint Ignatius running back Mike Sako races into the end zone with what proved to be the winning touchdown in the Wildcats' come-from-behind victory over Centerville in the 1991 Ohio Division I state championship game. (Jim Cahill)

for a playoff spot. With Kevin Mayer now healthy and back behind center, the Cats handed Cincinnati St. Xavier a 39-10 thumping and Toledo's St. Francis DeSales a 12-7 defeat. Those two victories secured for the Wildcats a Division I playoff spot.

The Wildcats breezed through their first two playoff games, handing the Lakewood Rangers a 34-0 loss and holding off a stubborn team of Berea High Braves, 21-7. This set up a semifinal showdown with the Massillon Washington Tigers, the second time in three seasons that these two teams had met in a Division I semifinal game. Both teams entered the game with identical 10-2 records, Massillon having finished eighth in the final AP poll and the Wildcats 11th.

The game was played on Saturday night, November 23, a windy and rainy night at Akron's Rubber Bowl, but that did not stop more than 20,000 high school football fans from filling the Bowl's seats. After a scoreless first quarter, Massillon pushed across a touchdown late in the second to take a 7-0 lead into the halftime break.

On the receiving end of the second half kickoff, the Wildcats began play at their 48-yard line and promptly marched 52 yards in 10 plays to tie the game at 7-7. Following this, a pair of fumbles by Massillon deep in the Saint Ignatius end of the field cost the Tigers prime scoring opportunities, but with just 4:36 left in the game the Tigers scored a touchdown to take a 13-7 lead, the PAT try hitting the right upright and bouncing away.

Following the ensuing kickoff, the Wildcats began play at their own 46-yard line knowing that it was now or never. Nine plays later, the Wildcats' Jack Mulloy went the final two yards for the game-tying touchdown and Fernando Paez booted the extra point that gave the Wildcats the lead with 1:23 left on the game clock. Massillon was unable to move the ball on its final possession, the Wildcats coming away with a dramatic 14-13 victory.

Being part of
History of Ignatius
Football is fun!

Morgan

▸ *This little cartoon, drawn by 1936 Saint Ignatius alumnus James "Spook" Morgan, says it all about how it feels to play football at Saint Ignatius High School.*

The 1991 Ohio Division I state championship game would find Saint Ignatius squaring off with the Elks of Centerville High School, 12-1. It was a cold, overcast December 1 when the two teams met at Canton's Fawcett Stadium in the final game of the season. Within the game's first seven minutes, a pair of Wildcat turnovers set up a pair of Centerville touchdowns that gave the Elks an early 14-0 lead. Saint Ignatius got onto the scoreboard via a safety, then quickly added a touchdown following Centerville's free kick to whittle the Elks' lead to 14-9 with just 19 seconds left in the first quarter. The Elks held off the Wildcats for the balance of the half, scoring the only touchdown of the second quarter to push their lead to 21-9 at the half.

In the third quarter, a 72-yard reception and run by the Wildcats' Dean Lamirand cut the Centerville lead to 21-16. At 7:10 of the fourth quarter, the Wildcats dipped into their bag of tricks and came out with a halfback pass, Eric Haddad to Mike Sako, 38 yards for a touchdown. Haddad then caught a pass for the two-point conversion that gave the Wildcats a 24-21 lead. Neither team scored over the final seven minutes of the game.

For the third time in as many championship games, the Saint Ignatius Wildcats had overcome a halftime deficit to bring home the Division I state championship. The Wildcats' second half comebacks in the Division I championship game were beginning to take on legendary proportions.

The Wildcats had lost a total of three games during the last two seasons; it would be another five years before they would suffer their next three defeats.

The Saint Ignatius Wildcats had ended the 1991 season riding a six-game winning streak, which they continued at the start of the '92 campaign. Victories over Akron Buchtel, 21-10, and Sandusky High, 31-15, opened the season—and then the

Wildcats' defense really went to work. Showing off one of the best defensive units in school history, the Wildcats cruised through the remaining eight games of their regular season schedule, winning five by shutout and outscoring the opposition 260-22.

Once again finishing the season atop the AP's Division I poll, the Wildcats began their 1992 playoff run against the Euclid Panthers on Saturday night, November 14. Before Euclid had run five plays on offense, the Wildcats had jumped to a 17-0 lead in the first quarter. The Panthers rallied and a pair of touchdowns early in the third quarter pulled Euclid even with the Wildcats at 20-20. Saint Ignatius regained the lead, 26-20, but Euclid came right back to take a 27-26 advantage. Finally, with just 3:19 left in the game, junior halfback Eric Haddad scored from two yards out, giving the Wildcats a 32-27 lead that they held for the last three minutes of the game.

▾ *Placekicker Nick Paez's PAT in the third overtime gave Saint Ignatius an exciting 35-34 victory over arch rival St. Ed in the 1993 national high school football "Game of the Year" on Oct. 23, 1993. (Jim Cahill)*

All the Way to #1

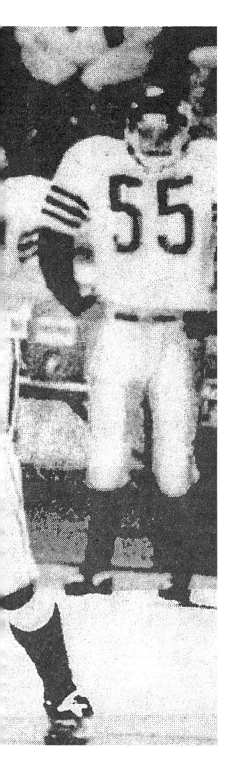

The Wildcats' next two playoff games were not quite as dramatic as they defeated Mentor, 38-13, and Austintown Fitch, 31-7.

The Division I state championship game at Fawcett Stadium was what some called a "dream match up". The Wildcats would be taking on Cincinnati's St. Xavier High School. Both teams represented Jesuit schools, both had identical 13-0 records, and both were also nationally ranked, the Wildcats as high as # 7 and the Bombers at # 24.

The Wildcats took a 10-7 lead after the first quarter, but St. Xavier came back to hold a 14-10 advantage at the half. Early in the third quarter, the Wildcats closed out a short 44-yard drive to regain the lead, 17-14. With the Wildcats' defense shutting down the Bombers throughout the second half, Saint Ignatius added an insurance touchdown midway through the fourth quarter and went on to win the game 24-14.

For the fourth time in as many Ohio Division I state championship games, the Saint Ignatius Wildcats had overcome a halftime deficit to win the 1992 state title game. The legend of the Wildcats' second half adjustments continued to grow.

Once a school has won a championship in any sport, there is always pressure on that team to bring home another title the following season. That pressure comes not only from the players themselves, but from the high expectations of loyal fans and alumni. That would be the case for the Saint Ignatius Wildcats' football team in 1993, but to accomplish that the Wildcats would have to do something done only once before in Ohio Division I football—win a third consecutive Division I state championship.

As if all of that did not add up to "great expectations", there was another factor to consider. In every conceivable 1993 preseason poll—be it local, state wide, or national in scope—the Saint Ignatius Wildcats were ranked # 1. If ever a team had a target on its back, it was the '93 Wildcats. With all of the intense publicity that went along with this, it would be the greatest challenge for the Wildcats to stay focused on the job at hand—winning the current week's game.

It would be up to Chuck Kyle and his coaching staff to make sure the team remained focused on what needed to be done. Led by four preseason All-America picks in quarterback Scott Mutryn, tailback Eric Haddad, offensive tackle Eric Gohlstin, and offensive tackle/defensive end Mike Buzin, all of them three-year varsity veterans, the Wildcats had the personnel capable of getting the job done.

◄ *Wide receiver Darin Kershner eludes a Euclid tackler after making a reception during the Wildcats' 42-7 playoff victory over the Panthers on Nov. 20, 1993. (Jim Cahill)*

▲ *Saint Ignatius tailback Eric Haddad turns the corner en route to a 79-yard punt return touchdown against Walsh Jesuit in a 1993 Ohio Division I semifinal game, won by the Wildcats 34-0. (Jim Cahill)*

▲ *Saint Ignatius All-America quarterback Scott Mutryn finds the seam and goes 14 yards for a touchdown against Moeller in the 1993 Ohio Division I state championship game. (Jim Cahill)*

If there were any doubts as to how the Wildcats would react to all of this, those doubts were eliminated in the very first game on Friday night, September 3. Playing Akron's Buchtel High School, themselves a two-time state champion, the Wildcats took a 7-0 lead in the first quarter and then exploded for 26 more points in the second en route to a 39-6 victory.

Over the next six weeks it was more of the same as the Wildcats rolled over team after team, pushing their record to 7-0 by outscoring the opposition 208-23. Then came Week Eight.

The biggest rivalry in Northeastern Ohio is that between Saint Ignatius located on Cleveland's near west side and the St. Edward High School Eagles, about five miles further west in Lakewood. If both teams entered this game without a victory between them they would still sell out the stadium. That was definitely not the case in 1993. The Wildcats were undefeated at 7-0, while the Eagles were 5-1; both teams needed a victory in this game to solidify a playoff spot.

The game was played on Saturday night, October 23, at Lakewood Stadium, a stadium built to hold about 7,500 people. But on this night there were an estimated 14,000 on hand, the overflow crowd standing 10-deep behind the fence that surrounded the gridiron. Those fans were expecting a great game—what they got was one for the ages.

The first quarter ended in a scoreless deadlock as defense dominated the early going. The Eagles broke on top 7-0 late in the second quarter, but just seconds before the intermission, the Wildcats tied the score at 7-7. Saint Ignatius scored the only touchdown of the third quarter and added another early in the fourth period to take a 21-7 lead with 8:21 left in the game.

Just when all those in attendance were ready to concede this edition of the "Holy War" to the Wildcats, the Eagles struck back. Taking the ensuing kickoff, St. Ed marched right down the field. Taking almost five minutes off the clock, they found the end zone to cut the Saint Ignatius lead to 21-14. Having no other choice, the Eagles put their chances on an onside kick—and recovered the ball at the Saint Ignatius 49-yard line. With just 25 seconds left to play, St. Ed quarterback Bob Adams hit WR Kevin Knestrick with a 35-yard touchdown pass, the PAT tying the score at 21-21.

A short 25 seconds later the game ended still tied at 21-21, sending the contest into overtime. It was the first overtime game that the Wildcats had ever played.

In the overtime period both, teams would have a chance to score from the 20-yard line. Neither team did, sending the game into a second OT—and the crowd into bedlam. Saint Ignatius had the ball first in the second extra period and scored a touchdown, the PAT giving them a 28-21 lead. When St. Ed got its chance with the ball, they too scored a touchdown and converted the PAT, leaving the score tied at 28-28 and sending the game into a third overtime period.

Alternating possessions to start each OT, it was now St. Ed's turn to go on offense first. On first down quarterback Bob Adams lofted a pass down the sideline to WR Ryan Ezzie, who made the catch and never broke stride as he raced into the end zone. To their great dismay, however, the Eagles' try for the extra point sailed wide left. The Eagles had again taken the lead, 34-28, but the missed extra point gave the Wildcats an opening if they could also score a touchdown.

When the Wildcats had their chance on offense in the third OT, it took them five plays, but a 15-yard pass from quarterback Scott Mutryn to WR Keith Laschinger finally netted the six-pointer. With the score now tied, 34-34, Wildcats placekicker Nick Paez calmly added the PAT that gave Saint Ignatius a 35-34 victory in what has been regarded by many as the greatest high school football game in Cleveland history. Later that year, this game would be named the national high school football "Game of the Year."

After that most dramatic game, the Wildcats' final two games of the regular season seemed almost anticlimactic as they defeated both Padua Franciscan High School, 42-13, and Holy Name, 48-26, to finish the season undefeated for the fifth time in the last six years.

As dominant as the Wildcats had been in blowing through their regular schedule, they were even more so in the playoffs. First the Strongsville Mustangs were

▲ *This time, Saint Ignatius quarterback Scott Mutryn finds himself on the receiving end of a pass, a play that resulted in a touchdown during the 1993 season. (Saint Ignatius School Paper)*

▸ *Huddled around the 1993 Division I state championship trophy and head coach Chuck Kyle are three of the four Wildcats selected as All-Americans that season: QB Scott Mutryn, (14), defensive lineman Mike Buzin (76), and tailback Eric Haddad (16). (Jim Cahill)*

"They (the opposition) think that they can throw our name and tradition out the door. There's no way around it, fellas, we are tradtion!"
-- Coach Kyle

IF EVER A GAME WAS PLAYED FOR THE NATIONAL CHAMPIONSHIP, THIS WAS IT.

sent packing by a 35-0 score, followed by a 42-7 thumping of the Euclid Panthers. The Division I semifinal game was played in a rain soaked and muddy Fawcett Stadium in Canton, but that did not seem to bother the Wildcats as they handed Walsh Jesuit a 34-0 defeat.

Just one more game to go. Just one more victory to let everyone know that the Saint Ignatius Wildcats really were what everyone had been telling them since before the season had begun—the best team in the land. The only team standing in their way was Division I's # 2 team, the Crusaders of Moeller High School, the most successful team thus far during Ohio's playoff era. This was the second time that these two teams had met for the state championship, Saint Ignatius winning that first meeting by 34-28 back in 1989. A victory by the Wildcats in this game would tie Moeller's record of three consecutive Division I championships.

There had not been a game played for the high school football national championship since 1939. Saint Ignatius had been ranked # 1 since day one; Moeller entered this game as the country's sixth best team. If ever a game was played for the national championship, this was it.

Just the week before, the Wildcats had played their semifinal game at Canton's Fawcett Stadium on a muddy field in a monsoon. On Saturday afternoon, December 11, the Division I state championship game would be played at Massillon's Tiger Stadium, but the weather had changed and now the playing conditions included a bitterly cold 18 degrees, a stiff "breeze" that made the wind chill considerably colder, and a snowfall that varied from light to heavy throughout the contest.

The Wildcats were on the receiving end of the opening kickoff and began play at their own 20-yard line. It took the Cats just five plays to go the length of the field, Scott Mutryn hooking up with diminutive WR Darin Kershner on a 27-yard touchdown pass. The extra point gave the Wildcats a 7-0 lead just two minutes into the game.

The Crusaders came right back with a field goal on their first possession and added another early in the second quarter to make it a 7-6 game.

It was at this point that the Wildcats took control of the game. Marching 73 yards behind the running and pass catching of tailback Eric Haddad, the Wildcats again went right down the field, the touchdown coming on a 27-yard screen pass to Haddad. Following a poor punt by the Crusaders, the Wildcats were soon back in business at the Moeller 42-yard line. Five plays later quarterback Scott Mutryn, finding no open receivers, scored on a 14-yard scramble. The points after both touchdowns were good and at the half the Wildcats had built a comfortable 21-6 lead.

For the first time in their five state championship games, the Wildcats entered the second half with a lead, a lead that they would protect and add to. Moeller was

1. CLEVELAND ST. IGNATIUS
2. RIALTO (CALIF.) EISENHOWER
3. DECATUR (GA.) SOUTHWEST DEKALB
4. SARASOTA (FLA.) RIVERVIEW
5. CONVERSE (TEXAS) JUDSON
6. HARRISBURG (PA.)
7. MONTGOMERY (ALA.) LEE
8. CINCINNATI PRINCETON
9. LA PUENTE (CALIF.) BISHOP AMAT
10. MIDDLETOWN (N.J.) SOUTH

FINAL RANKINGS

1 CLEVELAND ST. IGNATIUS (14-0)
Last week: 1. Season recap: Won second national championship and fifth Division I state title in six years. Eric Haddad set school season records with 1,904 yards rushing and 33 TDs and career record with 51 TDs. Scott Mutryn was 113-for-208 passing for 1,637 yards and 22 TDs.

2 RIALTO (CALIF.) EISENHOWER (14-0)
Last week: 2. Season recap: Won first Southern Section Division title as QB Glenn Thompkins set school season total offense record with 2,636 yards. Marlon Farlow scored record 19 TDs.

3 PITTSBURGH NORTH HILLS (15-0)
Last week: 3. Season recap: Won first Class AAAA state title as Eric Kasperowicz set school career passing records with 5,550 yards, 57 TDs. One-year records: 81 catches for 1,536 yards by Kenny Bollens and 23 TDs by freshman running back Lavar Arrington.

4 DUNWOODY (GA.) (15-0)
Last week: 4. Season recap: Won first Class AAAA state title, 21-7 against Snellville South Gwinnett before 15,000. Larry Mann and Grasa Miller combined for seven sacks and Rod Perrymond ran 25 times for 225 yards and one TD.

5 MIAMI SOUTHRIDGE (15-0)
Last week: 6. Season recap: Won second Class 5A state title, 69-36, against Bradenton Manatee. Set 19 championship-game records, including 69 points and 99-yard kickoff return TD by Darren Davis. His brother Troy, scored on a 97-yard kickoff return and Don McKnight blocked a punt returning it 32 yards for a TD.

6 BRADENTON (FLA.) SOUTHEAST (15-0)
Last week: 5. Season recap: Overcame 17-7 deficit to win first Class 4A state title, 20-17, vs. Panama City Bay. Rich Robich made 14 tackles, Carl Hines had three of team's 13 tackles for loss and Reggie Davis had two interceptions. Paul Maechtle was named Florida coach of the year.

7 CONCORD (CALIF.) DE LA SALLE (13-0)
Last week: 7. Season recap: Set state record with 665 points while winning North Coast Section Class 3A title for ninth time in 12 years. Defensive and special teams combined for 17 TDs, with Robert Portis scoring six times on kick returns.

8 FRESNO (CALIF.) CLOVIS WEST (14-0)
Last week: 8. Season recap: Won second consecutive Central Section Class 4A title with section-record 647 points, including record 44 TD (rushing and passing) by McKay Christiansen. Aaron Johnson set national record with 86 PAT.

9 DURHAM (N.C.) NORTHERN DURHAM (15-0)
Last week: 9. Season recap: Won first Class 4A state title with school-record 15 victories. Stelan Cameron had school-record 63 catches for 1,418 yards, 22 TDs. Junior QB Jason Peace was 107-for-178 passing for 2,040 yards, 29 TDs.

10 ALLENTOWN (PA.) CENTRAL CATHOLIC (14-0)
Last week: 10. Season recap: Won first Class AAA state title with school-record 484 points, 3,691 yards rushing. Jose Delgado scored school season record 29 TDs and Tim Cransey had career-record 52 TD passes.

on the receiving end of the second half kickoff, but an interception soon gave the ball back to the Wildcats at the Moeller 22. The Wildcats tried for the knockout punch, but the Moeller defense stood tall and halted the Wildcats at the six-yard line. Placekicker Nick Paez then added to the Wildcats' total with a 22-yard field goal that pushed the Saint Ignatius lead to 24-6.

Moeller went three and out on its next possession, the Wildcats regaining the ball at their 48-yard line following the Crusaders' punt. On first down, Eric Haddad took the handoff from Scott Mutryn and raced downfield on a spectacular 52-yard touchdown run, the extra point making it a 31-6 game and all but ending Moeller's hopes for another state title. Moeller finally found the end zone late in the third quarter and both teams traded TDs in the final frame.

By a score of 38-20 the Saint Ignatius Wildcats had won their third consecutive Ohio Division I state championship, fifth in the last six seasons. The victory also finalized the Wildcats' claim to the national championship as they accomplished the almost unbelievable feat of holding the nation's top spot from wire to wire. It was the Wildcats' second national title in five seasons and they were the first unanimous choice in eight years as the nation's top high school football team.

Over the previous two and a half seasons, the Wildcats had put together another great win streak, one that was currently at 34 games and counting. Even more than in previous seasons, however, in 1994 the Wildcats would really have their hands full in extending that streak. The reason—the Wildcats' success had finally caught up to them as far as their schedule was concerned. As teams across the country that have enjoyed similar success have also found out, no longer were any of the local teams, either Cleveland area or even Northeastern Ohio, willing to schedule the powerful Wildcats—unless, of course, they felt that they had a better-than-even chance of defeating Saint Ignatius. In 1994 only two schools from the Wildcats' home county of Cuyahoga were willing to take on Saint Ignatius in football: the Strongsville Mustangs and arch rival St. Ed. The other teams making up the balance of the Wildcats 1994 regular season schedule now stretched from Toledo in the west to Youngstown in the east and Cincinnati in the south, plus one team from Erie, Pa. Scheduling difficulty is a problem that the Wildcats have had to deal with ever since. And one that has only become worse over the years.

◄ *The 1993* USA Today *Super 25 preseason and final rankings—the team at the top never changed throughout the entire season.*

Despite playing these far flung opponents, the Wildcats got off to a good start in '94. Akron Buchtel was defeated, 38-14, and Strongsville went down, 47-16. Then came games against a pair of Toledo teams. Former state champion St. Francis DeSales gave the Wildcats a battle before succumbing, 28-17, while St. John's Jesuit was no problem, 38-6. The Wildcats were now ranked 4th in the *USA Today* Super 25 and # 1 in Ohio.

The Wildcats then traveled to the other side of the state to take on the Spartans of Boardman High School, just outside Youngstown. After grabbing a 7-0 lead at 2:04 of the first quarter, the Wildcats added a second touchdown about four minutes later to take a 14-0 lead early in the second quarter. Boardman scored on a field goal later in the second quarter to make the score 14-3 at the half. The Spartans then exploded for a pair of touchdowns and 15 points to take an 18-14 lead after three quarters. Neither team scored in the fourth quarter, the Spartans pulling the upset that halted the Wildcats' win streak at 38.

Shaking off the effects of their stunning defeat, the following Saturday the Wildcats exploded for 27 points in the first quarter as they handed visiting Erie Central a 47-0 shellacking. That victory propelled the Wildcats to a five-game win streak to close out the regular season, a streak that included victories over Canton McKinley 19-9, St. Ed 24-10, and Moeller, 41-7.

Over the last several seasons, Saint Ignatius had seemed to get even stronger as the team entered the "second season", i.e., the Division I playoffs, and 1994 was no different. The Wildcats opened the playoffs by blasting Shaker Heights, 38-12, then had rematches with two teams they had played earlier in the year. Strongsville was again trounced, this time by 40-10. Meeting Canton McKinley in a semifinal game at the Akron Rubber Bowl, the Wildcats had little trouble defeating the Bulldogs this time around, coming away with a 41-19 triumph.

Saint Ignatius defensive lineman John Krafcik sacks the Brunswick High quarterback during the 1995 Ohio Division I state championship game. (Jim Cahill)

In the 1994 Division I state championship game played at Massillon's Tiger Stadium, the Wildcats would be facing a relatively unheralded team from Westerville South High School in the Columbus area. Westerville, also named the Wildcats, was in the playoffs for the very first time and had upset three state-ranked schools to advance to the championship game.

In a game that was dominated by defense, Westerville took the opening kickoff and marched to the Saint Ignatius 27-yard line before they were forced to give up the ball on downs. After Saint Ignatius went three and out, Westerville again went on offense, this time driving to the Saint Ignatius 10-yard line before again giving up the ball on downs. Saint Ignatius was having some initial problems with Westerville's veer offense, but it only took those two drives for the Saint Ignatius Wildcats to figure it out. For the balance of the game Westerville South did not make a single first down.

Meanwhile, the Saint Ignatius offense went to work. The Cleveland Wildcats scored single touchdowns in both the second and third quarters and added field goals in both the third and fourth quarters to come away with a record fourth consecutive Ohio Division I state championship, 20-3.

In the final 1994 national polls, the Wildcats finished as high as # 12.

For the 1995 season, head coach Chuck Kyle had 11 returning starters, the most thus far in his 13 years at the helm of the Wildcats. Five of those returnees were in their third year with the varsity, so the Wildcats would have the benefit of plenty of experience. Despite all of those veteran players, the 1995 Saint Ignatius Wildcats would not be the most prolific scoring team, averaging a modest 23 points per game during the regular season. However, the Wildcats traditionally strong defense would make those points hold up.

The Wildcats were ranked # 1 in the first AP Ohio Division I poll of the season, while the National Prep Poll put the Wildcats at # 1 in its preseason poll and *USA Today* had the Wildcats fifth in the country.

The Wildcats' '95 schedule was almost identical to that of 1994, with only two changes: Euclid High School replaced Akron Buchtel to open the season and Harrisburg (Pa.) High School replaced Toledo Whitmer to finish the campaign.

In the season opener against Euclid, defense dominated the first half, with the Wildcats getting the game's first points just 43 seconds before the intermission to take a 6-0 lead. The second half was all Wildcats as they found their offense and continued with strong defensive play to cruise to a 27-0 victory. The following week, Strongsville played a stubborn game, especially on defense, but the Wildcats managed to come away with a 19-7 win. Traveling west to Toledo for their third game, the Wildcats steadily built a 17-3 lead against St. Francis DeSales High School during the first two quarters, adding a second half field goal for a 20-3 final.

Back at Lakewood Stadium for their fourth game, the Wildcats faced off against St. John's Jesuit, also 3-0, visiting from Toledo. The Titans stunned the Wildcats with a touchdown just 51 seconds into the game and added another several minutes later to take a 14-0 lead at 4:44 of the first quarter. It took the Wildcats just a minute and a half to get back into the game with a touchdown of their own. They added a second TD just a minute into the second quarter, but a missed PAT left the Wildcats trailing by a point, 14-13. After forcing a St. John's punt, the

Wildcats marched in for another touchdown; this time they missed on a two-point conversion, but had finally taken the lead at 19-14.

The first half was quickly winding down, but not the game's action. Following the Wildcats' ensuing kickoff the Titans quickly swept down the field, scoring a touchdown and a two-point conversion to take a 22-19 lead into the halftime break.

The Wildcats were on the receiving end of the second half kickoff and Drew Haddad's 61-yard return gave Saint Ignatius a first down at the St. John's 15-yard line. Four plays later, the Wildcats were again in the end zone and this time they added the PAT to regain the lead, 26-22, just a minute into the second half. There would be no more scoring during the third quarter in this back and forth game, but early in the fourth period the Titans again found the end zone to take a 29-26 lead. It would take the Wildcats less than two minutes to answer that touchdown with one of their own as they regained the lead 33-29 with 7:38 left to play.

A wild game deserved a wild finish and this one had it. With just 10 seconds remaining on the game clock, St. John's appeared to have scored a touchdown on a 25-yard pass play, but a motion penalty against the Titans nullified the score. On the last play of the game, Wildcats' linebacker Chris Hovan sacked the Titans quarterback to preserve a 33-29 victory for Saint Ignatius.

Over the next several weeks, the Wildcats tough season continued, but somehow they found a way to prevail. In Week Five, they built a 10-0 lead midway through the second quarter and then hung on to defeat Boardman, 10-6. The next two games against Erie Central and Canton McKinley were also nail biters, but the Cats won both by identical 13-0 scores. The Wildcats found a little added scoring punch during their last three regular season games when they defeated St. Ed 27-10, Moeller 24-12, and Harrisburg (Pa.) High School by a 47-21 count.

As the Wildcats began post-season play they were # 1 in the final AP Ohio Division I poll, having now been that poll champion six times in the last eight years. In the national rankings, the Wildcats were still # 1 in the National Prep Poll and had moved up to # 2 in *USA Today*'s Super 25.

▲ *Saint Ignatius' two-time All-Ohio tight end Dan O'Leary goes for extra yards after a catch against the Strongsville Mustangs in this 1995 Ohio Division I playoff game. (Saint Ignatius School Paper)*

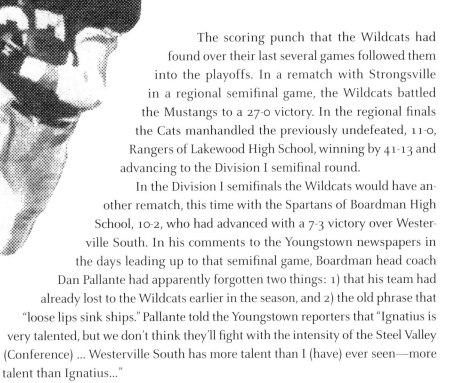

The scoring punch that the Wildcats had found over their last several games followed them into the playoffs. In a rematch with Strongsville in a regional semifinal game, the Wildcats battled the Mustangs to a 27-0 victory. In the regional finals the Cats manhandled the previously undefeated, 11-0, Rangers of Lakewood High School, winning by 41-13 and advancing to the Division I semifinal round.

In the Division I semifinals the Wildcats would have another rematch, this time with the Spartans of Boardman High School, 10-2, who had advanced with a 7-3 victory over Westerville South. In his comments to the Youngstown newspapers in the days leading up to that semifinal game, Boardman head coach Dan Pallante had apparently forgotten two things: 1) that his team had already lost to the Wildcats earlier in the season, and 2) the old phrase that "loose lips sink ships." Pallante told the Youngstown reporters that "Ignatius is very talented, but we don't think they'll fight with the intensity of the Steel Valley (Conference) ... Westerville South has more talent than I (have) ever seen—more talent than Ignatius..."

Saint Ignatius tailback Matt Bunsey sprints for a big gain against the Brunswick Blue Devils in the 1995 Ohio Division I state championship game. (Saint Ignatius School Paper)

One of the trainers at Saint Ignatius got hold of these comments, enlarged them, and posted them in the team's locker room for the players to look at every day at practice. When game day came around, the Boardman coach probably wished that he had been more discreet in his comments as the Wildcats crushed the Spartans, 41-6.

The Wildcats had now advanced to the Division I state championship game for the fifth consecutive season. Like the semifinal game, the 1995 Division I state championship game also had an interesting and unusual background. The Wildcats were supposed to play 13-0 Colerain High School from Cincinnati, which had advanced to its first title game by destroying the Blue Devils of Brunswick High, 49-7. However, after that game it was discovered that Colerain had played the entire season with an ineligible player; the Cardinals thus had to forfeit all of their games, including the semifinal victory over Brunswick. It was the first time that an Ohio football playoff game had ever been forfeited. The Ohio High School Athletic Association gave Saint Ignatius the option of accepting the state championship trophy outright or playing Brunswick, now 13-0, for the championship. The Wildcats chose to play Brunswick—Game On!

The 1995 Division I state championship game was played at Massillon's Tiger Stadium on Saturday evening, December 2. A scoreless first quarter was followed by a wild second period in which the Wildcats took a 6-0 lead just 43 seconds into the quarter, but a Brunswick rally left the Wildcats trailing at the half, 15-13.

Five In A Row, Baby!!

Wildcats Bring The State Title Home Again!!

The Saint Ignatius Wildcats trailing at the half in an Ohio Division I state championship game—seems like we have been here before. And like before, the Wildcats made the necessary adjustments during the intermission. Exploding for 21 points in the third quarter, the Wildcats jumped to a 34-15 lead and finished the game with a 41-21 victory.

For an unprecedented fifth consecutive season, the Saint Ignatius Wildcats had taken home the Ohio Division I championship trophy, an accomplishment still unequalled by any other school in any division. They had won seven state titles in the last eight years, tying with Moeller and Newark Catholic for the most playoff state championships. The Wildcats had now won an incredible 20 consecutive playoff games, with an overall postseason record of 28-1

In 1995 the Wildcats finished # 1 in every national poll except *USA Today*, where they finished second to Pennsylvania's Berwick High School. It was the Wildcats second national title in the last three seasons, their third since 1989.

The Wildcats closed out the balance of the 20th century with a caliber of play that only enhanced their title as "The Team of the Decade" as awarded by *Student Sports* magazine.

Unlike the 1995 season, in 1996 Wildcats' head coach Chuck Kyle would have to replace the vast majority of his starters, 16 in all, with only a few weeks in which to get everyone ready for another grueling season. In one of the rainiest seasons anyone could recall, the Wildcats sloshed thru the '96 campaign to a record of 7-2, dropping games to Lake Catholic, 21-12, and arch rival St. Ed, 12-9 in overtime.

Despite the two losses, the Wildcats again qualified for the postseason and, without a tenth game on their schedule, they had an extra week in which to prepare for the postseason. Instead of rain, however, it was heavy snow that greeted the teams when the Wildcats defeated Euclid, 23-2, in the first round of the playoffs and then came back the following week in another snowstorm to hand the Hudson High Explorers a 53-12 thrashing. In a Division I semifinal game, the Wildcats next took on the Bulldogs of Canton McKinley. Saint Ignatius had previously defeated the Bulldogs by 47-19 back in Week Seven; this game would be much closer, but the outcome the same, as the Wildcats prevailed, 31-24.

Playing in the Division I state championship game for an unprecedented sixth straight season, the Wildcats would be facing the Spartans of Lima Senior High School, 12-1, playing in their first championship game. The Wildcats took a 16-3 lead early in the second quarter, but Lima came back to lead 17-16 at the half. Five seconds into the fourth quarter, the Spartans had pushed their lead to 31-16 when the Wildcats began their comeback. Following Lima's latest touchdown, it took the Wildcats a little more than a minute to cut the Spartans' lead to 31-23. However, Lima would add another touchdown a few minutes later and hold on for a 38-30 win. For the first time in six years, there was a new Ohio Division I state champion.

The next two seasons would see the Wildcats continue their success of the 90s, with the added bonus of a great two-year rivalry with not one, but two national championship caliber teams.

After the Wildcats opened their 1997 season with a 36-6 won over Buchtel, Week Two brought on the game that was dubbed "The Clash of the Titans." In 1995 Saint Ignatius and Pennsylvania's Berwick High School had shared the national championship. Now, just two years later these same two teams, again ranked at the top of the national polls, were facing off against each other. With Berwick's Bulldogs riding a 41-game win streak, ranked as high as fourth in the country, and playing the game in Berwick, the Bulldogs were made a slight favorite over the Wildcats, who were ranked as high as tenth in the polls. So much for the predictions and the home field advantage; the Wildcats jumped out to a 20-0 halftime lead and went back to Cleveland with a 37-6 victory.

After winning their next four games the Wildcats faced another huge showdown, this time with another nationally ranked team of Bulldogs, those from Canton's McKinley High School. Saint Ignatius was ranked # 1 in Ohio and as high as # 4 in the country. McKinley was # 2 in Ohio and # 1 in the *USA Today* Super 25. It was an incredible game, one of several games in which the Wildcats were involved during the 1990s that were labeled as either the "Game of the Decade" or "Game of the Century". The Wildcats trailed throughout and were able to cut the McKinley lead to 35-32 with just 57 seconds to play, but could get no closer.

Saint Ignatius won its next three games to qualify for the Division I playoffs with a 9-1 record. They got by their first two playoff opponents with a 30-21 win over Strongsville and a 9-0 shutout of Shaker Heights. This set up a Division I semifinal rematch—another "Game of the Decade"—with Canton McKinley, the Bulldogs now ranked # 1 in both Ohio and the nation. The Wildcats were # 2 in Ohio and # 8 in the country. Another Ohio Division I playoff game that came as close as it could to being for the national championship.

The Wildcats jumped out to a surprising 16-0 lead late in the first half, but allowed the Bulldogs to get a score late in the second quarter to make it a 16-6 game at the intermission. The Wildcats added a third quarter field goal and led 19-6 with

THE YEARS 1992-1996 REPRESENT THE "GOLDEN ERA" OF BERWICK BULLDOGS FOOTBALL: 72-2-0, 4 STATE CHAMPIONSHIPS, 2 NATIONAL CHAMPIONSHIPS.

7:23 left in the game, but McKinley came back to cut the lead to 19-14 three minutes later. When the Wildcats failed to run out the clock during the final minutes of the fourth quarter, the Bulldogs stunned Saint Ignatius by scoring a miraculous TD with just 13 seconds left in the game to pull out a truly stunning 20-19 victory.

Canton McKinley went on to win both the Ohio and national championships in 1997, the Bulldogs' second national title, the first coming back in 1934.

It would be more "Battling with the Bulldogs" for Saint Ignatius in 1998. After another opening victory over Buchtel, 42-13, the Wildcats again boarded the buses for Berwick, Pennsylvania. This time, with the Wildcats ranked # 4 in the country and Berwick not ranked in the Top 25, Saint Ignatius was the heavy favorite. It was an exciting game, played over the last quarter and a half without a game clock (the officials on the field keeping the time, the scoreboard clock had been knocked out of commission by a placekick). It was a close game all the way, but for the second time in their last three outings going back to the semifinal loss to McKinley the previous year, the Wildcats lost in the final minute, 30-28, as the result of a Berwick field goal.

Five weeks later, the Wildcats avenged their losses of the previous season to Canton McKinley by knocking off the defending national champion, 31-21.

The Wildcats would end the regular season with a record of 8-2 and again qualify for the playoffs. After playoff victories over Shaker Heights, 45-20, and Strongsville, 43-21, the Wildcats again met Canton McKinley in a Division I semifinal game. It was another tremendous Ignatius-McKinley gridiron battle. On the final play of the game, with the Wildcats down 31-24 and the ball at their own 46-yard line, Wildcats QB Tom Arth arched a "Hail Mary" pass downfield to WR Peter Koch. Koch made the catch, but was bounced out of bounds a mere six inches from the end zone with the clock showing 00:00.

For the 1999 season, Chuck Kyle had just four returning starters around whom to build another Wildcats team. The Cats struggled a bit in the early going, defeating Midpark High, 20-12, but losing to Boardman, 26-21. They then ran off six consecutive victories before dropping a wild affair to Cincinnati St. Xavier, 50-33. After winning their final regular season game, the Wildcats qualified for the playoffs for the 12th consecutive year (a run that would eventually reach a state record 23 in a row), this time with a record of 8-2.

In 1999 the Ohio playoffs had been expanded to five games by increasing the number of regional qualifiers from four to eight teams. The Wildcats marched steadily through the playoffs, defeating Euclid 28-14, Shaker Heights 29-14, Solon 29-24, and Pickerington 48-8, to reach the Division I finals for the seventh time during the decade. In the Division I state championship game, the Wildcats would have to face Wayne High School of Huber Heights without starting quarterback Bryan Panteck, who was injured in the game with Pickerington. Starting his very first varsity game, in the biggest game of the season, would be sophomore quarterback Nate Szep. The whole team stepped up to support Szep, and after trailing early, 7-0, the Wildcats came back to win the game by a score of 24-10.

The Saint Ignatius victory gave the Wildcats their sixth Division I championship of the '90s, a state record eighth state playoff championship overall.

Over the last 12 years of the 20th century, the Saint Ignatius Wildcats, the "Team of the Decade of the '90s" (plus a couple years) put together a run of success seldom equaled by any school in the country, playing a roster of teams that became increasingly more difficult and often included teams of national championship caliber. The Wildcats qualified for Ohio's Division I playoffs, considered by many to be the toughest in the country, all 12 of those seasons, advancing to the semifinals or finals 11 times. For the eight-year period 1988 thru 1995, the Wildcats' success was unparalleled: a near perfect 104 wins against just four defeats; three national championships; seven state championships, including an astonishing five in a row.

Like Moeller a few years before them, and Massillon Washington in the middle of the century, the Saint Ignatius Wildcats of head coach Chuck Kyle gave off an aura of legendary invincibility few teams can claim—or equal.

———————

It has been previously related that the Saint Ignatius Wildcats played some incredible games in the late 1990s with a couple of Bulldogs teams, those representing both Berwick High School and Canton McKinley. Those two teams have pretty impressive histories of their own.

The city of Berwick is located in the eastern part of Pennsylvania, about 150 miles northwest of Philadelphia. The high school fielded its first football team in 1888, losing the only game that it played. No more football is known to have been played at the school until a single game in 1900, which was also lost. It was not until 1907 that Berwick High played a somewhat regular football schedule, which was temporarily discontinued for four years, 1915-1918, due to World War I.

From 1920 until 1970, the Bulldogs enjoyed on and off gridiron success, but with the arrival of George Curry to coach the team in 1971, Berwick's real football success began.

George Curry was born in 1944 and grew up outside Wilkes-Barre, Pa., in the suburb of Larksville. Curry played virtually every position on the football team during his four years at Larksville High School and was named a second team All-State linebacker his senior year. He also played on the school's basketball and baseball teams.

Graduating in 1962, he went to Temple University on a full football scholarship, playing nose guard and linebacker. Upon graduation he opted out of a possible dental career to take up coaching and, in the fall of 1967, he became the head coach at little Lake-Lehman High School. Coaching four years at Lake-Lehman, Curry led the

The 1983 national champion Berwick Bulldogs. (Berwick High School Yearbook)

team to a 23-10-1 record. This success earned him an opportunity to coach at Berwick High School in 1971, where he was to remain for the next 35 years.

After starting with three modestly successful seasons at Berwick, Curry's teams then went 16-16-0 from 1974 to 1976. The Bulldogs rebounded nicely in 1977, posting a record of 12-1-0 and winning what was then known as the Eastern Conference Class A playoff championship for only the second time, the first since 1960. (At that time there were no state championship playoffs in Pennsylvania.)

In the four years beginning with 1981, the Bulldogs enjoyed a period of success theretofore unknown at the school. That year Berwick posted its first undefeated-untied season in 40 years, going 13-0-0 as the Bulldogs swept through their 11-game regular season schedule and then won the Eastern Conference A championship with playoff victories over Lakeland High School, 25-11, and Coughlin High, 40-0. In 1982 the Bulldogs finished 11-1-0 after losing to Coughlin, 31-6, in the first round of the Eastern Conference A playoffs, but that only made the 1983 season all the more special.

After posting a couple of shutout victories to open their '83 slate, the Bulldogs first team defense gave up its first points of the season to Hazelton High, a first half field goal. Fourth quarter Hazelton touchdowns against the Berwick reserves made the 28-17 game look closer at than it really was.

Four more shutouts followed. On Friday night, October 21, against the Shikellamy High School Braves, the Bulldogs built up a 16-0 lead after three quarters, but in the final stanza the Braves came roaring back. Scoring a touchdown and a two-point conversion, the Braves then added a second touchdown to shrink Berwick's lead to 16-14. When the Braves again attempted a two-point conversion, Bulldogs nose guard Scott Ratamess saved the day by sacking the Shikellamy quarterback to preserve Berwick's 16-14 victory.

After that scare Berwick then breezed through their remaining five games, including Eastern Conference A playoff victories over Wyoming Valley West, 27-0, and North Pocono, 41-0. In a season in which the Bulldogs had shut out 11 of 13 foes in posting a perfect 13-0-0 record, they had outscored their opponents 465-31. Their outstanding showing had also earned for the Bulldogs sole possession of the national championship for 1983.

In 1984 the Bulldogs posted their fourth consecutive undefeated regular season, but lost in the semifinals of the Eastern Conference A playoffs by dropping a 14-3 decision to Valley View High School. Over the next three seasons, the Bulldogs' success continued as they qualified for the Eastern Conference A playoffs each year.

Pennsylvania had its first playoffs to decide state champions in 1988, with the high schools divided into four classifications. Berwick was placed in Class AAA for the next-to-largest schools. Putting together their best season to date, the Bulldogs sailed through their regular schedule unscathed to enter the post season at 11-0-0. In the Eastern Conference A playoffs, now a preliminary to the state playoffs, the Bulldogs defeated North Pocono, 27-0, and Pottsville, 42-14. In the Class AAA Eastern State Final game, in essence the AAA semifinals, Berwick defeated Middletown, 14-12. In the AAA state finals, Berwick was a heavy underdog to the favorite Aliquippa High School, but on game day the cream rose to the top and the Bulldogs emerged with a 13-0 victory in the first-ever Pennsylvania Class AAA state championship game.

Completing their season with a perfect 15-0-0 record, the Bulldogs finished third in the *USA Today* Super 25 national rankings.

In 1989 the Bulldogs again had an outstanding season as they pushed their win streak to 29. The playoffs were much tougher for Berwick this time around and, after winning a couple of close games to reach the AAA state championship game for the second year in a row, the Bulldogs came up just a bit short in dropping the title game to Perry High School, 20-8.

Both 1990 and 1991 would be playoff, but not championship, seasons for Berwick. However, those seasons would set the stage for what would become the greatest era of Berwick High School football.

Led by quarterback Ron Powlus, who would later that year be named the national high school football "Player of the Year", the 1992 Bulldogs roared through their first six games by an average score of 40-6. On October 16, Hazelton High came to town for a game at the Bulldogs' Crispin Field and almost upset the dog house. Berwick took a 7-0 lead in the first quarter on a 42-yard touchdown aerial by Powlus. Hazelton finally got on the scoreboard with a third quarter touchdown, but the Bulldogs' Bill Hetler blocked the PAT try to preserve a 7-6 lead. Early in the fourth quarter, Powlus broke free for a 61-yard touchdown scamper that sealed Berwick's 14-6 victory.

After that close call, the aroused Bulldogs easily dispatched their remaining four regular season foes. The Bulldogs seemed to play even tougher in the post season as they shut out both Shamokin, 49-0, and North Pocono, 35-0, to win the Eastern Conference title and advance to the Class AAA semifinal, known as the Eastern State championship game.

Whenever a team advances to the final four, it can expect a tough game. And Berwick got just that when it faced off against Manheim Central, but a big 21-point second quarter propelled the Bulldogs to a 29-6 victory.

In the Class AAA championship game for the first time since 1988, Berwick took the field against the Cougars of Blackhawk High School. The Cougars took the opening kickoff and marched right down the field for a touchdown and an early 6-0 lead—it marked the first time all season that Berwick had trailed in a game. The rest of the game, however, was all Bulldogs as they overcame 15 penalties and outscored Blackhawk 33-0 over the balance of the game for a 33-6 victory.

The team's second Class AAA playoff championship and 15-0-0 record also earned for the Bulldogs their second national championship from *USA Today*.

▾ *The 1992 Berwick Bulldogs football team, champions of both Pennsylvania Class AAA and the* USA Today *Super 25 national rankings. (Berwick High School Yearbook)*

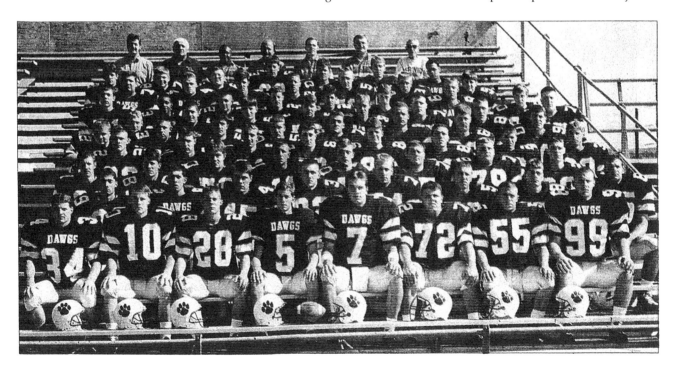

*The 1995 Berwick Bulldogs,
Pennsylvania's Class AAA
champions and USA Today's
Super 25 national titlists.
(Berwick High School Yearbook)*

Berwick extended its win streak to 28 in 1993 before dropping the Class AAA semifinal game to Allentown Central Catholic by a 13-8 score. The Bulldogs were right back at it the following season and, despite a single early season loss, Berwick again qualified for the playoffs. The first two rounds went relatively smoothly as Berwick defeated Honesdale, 49-0, and North Pocono, 36-7. In the Class AAA quarterfinal game against Allentown Central Catholic, the Bulldogs had another real battle with the Vikings, but this time the Bulldogs were able to come away with a 29-18 win. Manheim Central gave Berwick an even tougher fight the following week in the AAA semifinal game, but the Bulldogs again prevailed in a wild, high-scoring affair, 37-30.

The 1994 Class AAA state championship game against Sharon High School was somewhat less dramatic as the Bulldogs captured their second state title in three years, 27-7. Closing out the season with a 10-game winning streak and a final record of 14-1-0, the Bulldogs finished as high as 15th in the final 1994 national polls.

The Berwick win streak would continue into the 1995 season. The streak, however, very nearly came to an end in Week Two against Glen Mills. Berwick insured its 21-14 victory by recovering a Glen Mills fumble deep in the Bulldog' own end of the field with a little over two minutes to play. The rest of the season was not as intense, with the Bulldogs averaging slightly less than 40 points per game as they easily completed the regular season 11-0-0, extending their win streak to 21.

It was more of the same when the Bulldogs opened the postseason by easily defeating Valley View High School, 49-13, and North Schuykill, 31-3. In the Eastern State Class AAA semifinal game, things were decidedly different. Playing Manheim Central, the Bulldogs fell behind 17-0 at the half and had allowed the Barons to march up and down the field to the tune of more than 200 yards of offense. After one of head coach George Curry's better halftime exhortations, the Bulldogs came out and played a completely different game over the final two quarters. Berwick outscored Manheim, 18-0, over those last two periods, but the Bulldogs still needed an interception by defensive back Bryan Smith with just 40 seconds remaining to preserve their amazing 18-17 comeback victory.

After that heart pounding win, the Class AAA state championship game was almost anticlimactic as Berwick pounded Sharon High School for the second straight year, this time winning by 43-6. That victory allowed the Bulldogs to extend their win streak to 25 while winning a second consecutive state title, their third in four seasons. *USA Today* named the Bulldogs their national champion for 1995, Berwick's second national championship in four years and third overall.

The 1996 campaign would provide another clean sweep for the Bulldogs as they rolled through the regular season, posting 10 consecutive victories. The team's winning ways continued into the postseason and this time there would be no need for any last minute heroics as the Bulldogs swept their five playoff games by an average score of 32-5, defeating Blackhawk in the Class AAA state championship game, 34-13. The Bulldogs again finished high in the final national rankings, topping out at # 4.

Berwick would win another Pennsylvania Class AAA championship in 1997, but not without a couple of slips along the way. The Bulldogs opened the season by defeating Woodson High School (Washington, D.C.) by a 41-0 score, ironically enough it was Berwick's 41st consecutive win. Then came the upset defeat at the hands of Saint Ignatius that ended the streak. The Bulldogs would lose a second game during the season, but then swept through the playoffs to win their fourth consecutive Class AAA state championship. In 1998 Berwick finished 12-1-0; no state title that year, but they still managed to finish as high as # 12 in the national rankings.

The other team of Bulldogs with whom the Saint Ignatius Wildcats had some intense games during the 1990s was the "Pups" who came from McKinley High School in Canton, Ohio. Like fellow Stark County residents, the Tigers of Massillon Washington High School, the McKinley Bulldogs had one of the most successful football teams of the 20th century. Their overall record of 679-273-37, .705, places the Bulldogs among the top half-dozen teams of the 20th century as far as total victories. McKinley's 10 state championships and pair of national titles only enhance the Bulldogs' reputation as one of the nation's best.

McKinley's rivalry with nearby Massillon Washington is legendary. While the Bulldogs earned those 10 state championships from 1900-1999, they might have had almost double that number had it not been for Massillon, which nine times handed the Bulldogs their lone defeat of a season. McKinley returned the "favor" by eight times putting an end to an otherwise perfect Massillon season.

McKinley's rivalry with Saint Ignatius covered 13 games over the latter part of the 20th century. Their first meeting came in 1981, when the Wildcats, who would

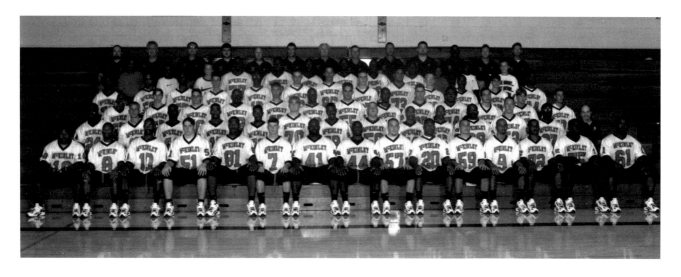

▲ *The 1997 national champion Bulldogs from Canton McKinley High School. (Photo compliments of AD Greg Malone)*

finish 5-5 that season, gave the soon-to-be state champion Bulldogs their toughest game of the season but still lost to McKinley, 14-7. McKinley also defeated Saint Ignatius the following year, 25-14.

The series between the Bulldogs and the Wildcats became an annual event beginning in 1994 and often was not limited to just one game per season. However, the most intense games, as previously noted, came during the 1997 and 1998 seasons.

In 1997 McKinley held off a late charge by the Wildcats in Week Seven to pull out a dramatic 35-32 victory. In the Division I semifinal game that year, the Bulldogs were all but dead and buried, but rallied in the game's final minutes to pull out a stunning 20-19 victory. McKinley then defeated Moeller, 31-16, the following week to complete a perfect 14-0 season and bring home both the Ohio and national championships. That year the Bulldogs played before more than 185,000 people, better than 13,200 per game.

In 1998 the Bulldogs saw their chance for a second consecutive perfect season get side tracked when they dropped a 31-21 decision to Saint Ignatius in Week Seven. The Bulldogs came back in the Division I semifinal game to avenge that defeat and send the Wildcats home for the season after a 31-24 McKinley victory. As they had done the year before, McKinley then defeated a Cincinnati team, this time St. Xavier, by a score of 33-10 to win its 10th state championship.

The Wildcats of Cleveland Saint Ignatius, Berwick High School's Bulldogs, and the Bulldogs of Canton McKinley High School—a trio of Midwest powers who dominated high school football at the state and national level during the 1990's.

## CHAPTER 12

THE GREATEST WIN STREAK EVER

De La Salle High School
Concord, California

D e La Salle High School, like Cincinnati Moeller and Saint Ignatius an all boys Catholic school, opened in 1965 in Concord, California. At that time Concord, located about 30 miles northwest of San Francisco, was still experiencing something of a boom that saw the population jump from about 6,000 to more than 36,000 in about 15 years—on its way to a present day figure of more than 120,000 souls. A new Catholic girls school, Carondelet, opened at the same time across the street from De La Salle.

De La Salle, run by the Christian Brothers, began with just 115 students. Despite being the only Catholic high school in Contra Costa County to accept boys, with another not slated to open for at least 10 years, De La Salle had a hard time attracting students. So hard, in fact, that the Christian Brothers hierarchy was seriously considering closing the school. As is true at most high schools, athletics were important to the students at De La Salle, but not so much to the brothers running the school. In the early days the school, competing in what was then the Catholic Athletic League, fielded teams for baseball, basketball, golf, tennis, cross country and soccer—but not football.

In visiting local Catholic grade schools, Bro. Norman Cook, De La Salle's first principal, quickly discovered that a major obstacle to attracting incoming freshmen (and the interest of their parents) was the school's lack of a football team. Something had to be done, but what and how with the school already operating in the red?

In 1970 at a school fund-raiser, Bro. Norman met Ed Hall, a San Francisco police officer who was interested in starting a football team at De La Salle. Hall said that he would get some fellow officers to volunteer as coaches and raise all of the necessary funds himself. Bro. Norman knew that having a football team would be a key ingredient in getting the school to a better place, both financially and as regarded the student population. He immediately went to work trying to convince the Christian Brothers District Council of the need for a football team at the school. Bro. Norman's efforts proved successful and De La Salle was granted permission to establish a football program, with Ed Hall as its first head coach.

▲ *Patrick Walsh of the*
De La Salle Spartans is the
center of congratulatory
teammates after scoring a
touchdown against Pittsburg
High in 1991. The Spartans
would end up losing that
game, 35-27, their last
defeat during the 20th
century. (All photos in this
chapter are from the De La
Salle Spartan Yearbook.)

The 1971 season saw De La Salle, nicknamed the Spartans, field a junior varsity team that enjoyed some success with a final record of 6-2. Unfortunately, that success did not carry over to the first varsity season the following year and the Spartans finished 1-5, getting shut out three times. Despite Hall's enthusiasm and tireless effort, the team continued to lose, posting a record of 17-37-6 in its first seven seasons. The losing and frustration finally caught up with Hall and he resigned after the 1978 campaign. As Neil Hayes wrote in his book about the De La Salle football team entitled "When the Game Stands Tall", "Hall's resignation stunned the administration, but many of his players saw it coming. He hadn't been as intense in 1978. By the end of the season the man whose boundless energy established the program looked old and tired."

The De La Salle principal at that time, Bro. Michael Meister, decided that in hiring Ed Hall's successor he wanted a teacher first and a football coach second. So this is what the search committee considered as it evaluated all of the applicants for the position. In the end, Bro. Michael hired a young man who had just one year's experience as a high school assistant coach and a desire to teach religious studies. His name was Robert Ladouceur.

Bob Ladouceur was born in 1954 in Detroit, Michigan. He was in the second grade when his father moved the family to San Ramon, California. Bob attended San Ramon High School, but did not play football until his junior and senior years. He was a halfback on offense and also played in the defensive backfield where he earned second team all-league honors as a junior. At this time, the San Ramon football team was using the triple-option offense as devised by University of Texas head coach Darryl Royal. In his senior season, Ladouceur gained 620 yards and averaged more than 10 yards per carry, earning him all-conference honors as well as being named the team's MVP.

Upon graduation in 1972, Ladouceur attended the University of Utah on a full football scholarship; but, becoming disenchanted with football at the school, he left after just one year. Bob then enrolled at San Jose State University, but was not really thinking about playing football. The San Jose head coach was Darryl Rogers, a college teammate of Ladouceur's high school coach, Fred Houston. Through Houston's encouragement, and some timely words to his friend Darryl Rogers, Bob Ladouceur joined the San Jose team in 1974. Ladouceur played on the team through the 1976 season, but saw limited action due to several injuries.

Graduating from San Jose State in 1976 with a degree in criminal justice, Bob began working as a juvenile probation officer. Becoming disillusioned with that job, he started looking around for something else. Interested in theology, he enrolled at nearby St. Mary's College and for four semesters took the courses leading to a degree in religious studies. At this time a friend of Ladouceur's asked him to assist with the Monte Vista High School jayvee football team. The next year Bob was the varsity backfield coach—and finally realized what he wanted to do with his life.

In September of 1978, Bob Ladouceur saw the notice in a local newspaper that Ed Hall had resigned as the De La Salle coach. He applied for the job, stressing his religious studies background at the several interviews that he had, almost never touching on football. Bro. Michael was known to do things "outside the box" so it did not surprise some when he chose Bob Ladouceur as his new football coach. However, as Neil Hayes notes in his book,

> *"Hiring Ladouceur wasn't a popular decision. Several coaches with higher pro-files had applied for the job, and controversy swirled around the announce-ment. Even Hall was less than thrilled with the decision. He had written a letter to Brother Michael recommending that assistant coach Bill Mott be named his successor.*

> *"'The shit hit the fan afterwards,' Brother Michael said. 'The phone calls I got— 'Have you lost your mind?' 'Are you crazy?' 'You don't have a clue about football.' Nobody thought I had made a good choice because Bob was unknown.'"*

Bob Ladouceur was taking over a team that had never had a winning sea-son, its best mark being 4-4-1 in 1974. When he held his first meeting as head coach for prospective players, Bob opened the meeting by writing two things on the chalk board. The first was "5-4", his goal for the coming 1979 season. The second was "Beat Moreau"—Moreau Catholic was De La Salle's archrival and a team that the Spartans had yet to defeat. He had already grabbed the team's attention.

To help fulfill these goals, Ladouceur introduced the triple-option veer of-fense that he had experienced in high school, virtually copying page for page the playbook used at San Ramon High School by Coach Fred Houston. The veer provided the Spartans with a running attack that featured technique over brute force and was more suited to the physically smaller Spartans players. In addition, as one article later noted about Coach Ladouceur, "He also inaugurated off season weight-training workouts three mornings a week. He said that they were option-al. No one believed him."

Still playing mostly Catholic Athletic League teams in 1979, the Spartans ex-ceeded Ladouceur's first season goal by finishing with a 6-3 record, but they failed to defeat Moreau, dropping a 26-24 decision. It was the last time that Moreau ever beat a De La Salle football team.

In 1980 the Spartans were even better, winning eight of the 10 games that they played. The following year they again lost only twice in nine games, dropping close contests to College Park High School, 19-17, and Salesian, 21-17.

▲ *De La Salle quarterback Mike Bastianelli eludes a Logan High defender during the 1992 3A Section playoffs.*

▲ *De La Salle head coach Bob Ladouceur had the best winning percentage of the 20th century in high school football, .942.*

De La Salle had closed out the 1981 season with four consecutive victories. When the Spartans opened the 1982 campaign with three more victories, it marked the first time that the team had ever won as many as seven games in a row. And they kept on winning. After what proved to be their toughest game of the season in Week Five, a 9-6 victory in a defensive struggle against Benicia High, the Spartans rolled through their last five games by an average score of 47-8. This was a stunning turnaround for the Spartans; as recently as 1978 they had barely scored 50 points for the entire season.

Finishing the 1982 regular season a perfect 10-0, including four shutouts (and allowing only one touchdown on three other occasions), for the first time in their history the De La Salle Spartans had qualified for the North Coast Section (NCS) playoffs. A word of explanation here. California did not have playoffs to determine an overall state champion until 2006. Before that year, with the schools divided by student population into four classes (A-2A-3A-4A), the postseason playoffs only determined sectional champions; state champions, though unofficial at this time, were determined by a poll, normally the one taken by *Cal-Hi Sports*.

In their first ever North Coast Section playoff game, the Spartans struggled a bit, but managed to defeat the team from Campolindo High School, 17-6. This game made the NCS finals seem almost anticlimactic as the Spartans demolished Arroyo High, 49-0. Not only had De La Salle won its first NCS championship, but the Spartans had also managed to finish second in the final Class 2A poll.

Reaching the playoffs, finishing high in the state poll—this was all new and heady stuff for De La Salle football. It would quickly become the norm.

With their win streak now at 16, the Spartans opened the 1983 campaign with a 7-7 tie with San Ramon Valley High School, then ran off four more victories to extend their undefeated streak to 21. In Week Six, however, De La Salle came up against another tough team from Salesian High School, which this time put an end to the Spartans' streak by handing De La Salle a 24-13 defeat. The Spartans closed out the season with four more victories to again qualify for the postseason, but in their opening round NCS Class 2A playoff game they were sent packing by Miramonte High, 13-7.

Finishing the '83 season with a record of 8-2-1, the Spartans were looking to regain their perfect season form of 1982 again in 1984. After opening the season with a pair of relatively easy victories, the Spartans took on Skyline High School in Week Three. Throwing a curve or two at De LaSalle, Skyline used a little trickery in the form of a fake field goal and a fake PAT kick to hold off the Spartans in the second half and pull out a 22-21 victory.

Using a stifling defense and an overpowering offense, hallmarks of De La Salle football over the balance of the century, the Spartans won their next six games to finish the '84 regular season with an 8-1 record and advance to the NCS 2A playoffs. As good as they were during the regular season, the Spartans were even better in the postseason. Averaging 45 points per game while allowing an average of 13, De La Salle won all three of its playoff games to win another NCS sectional championship and finish the season with a record of 11-1.

From 1981 to 1984, the Spartans had lost five games, not a bad record for four seasons. Over the remainder of the 20th century, another 15-plus seasons, the De La Salle Spartans would lose only four more games.

FROM 1981 TO 1984, THE SPARTANS HAD LOST FIVE GAMES, NOT A BAD RECORD FOR FOUR SEASONS. OVER THE REMAINDER OF THE 20TH CENTURY, ANOTHER 15-PLUS SEASONS, THE DE LA SALLE SPARTANS WOULD LOSE ONLY FOUR MORE GAMES.

Coach Ladouceur's Spartans had missed their goal of an undefeated season in 1984 by just a single point, but that would not be the case in 1985 or 1986. In 1985 the Spartans took no chances that they would suffer another one-point defeat as they won every game by an average of just under 36 points per game, regular season and playoffs alike. The Spartans' NCS 2A playoff championship propelled them to a # 1 ranking in the *Cal-Hi Sports* 3A state poll, the Spartans' first # 1 ranking. (From 1985 thru 1995, De La Salle would play in one NCS class playoff, but be ranked in the poll for the next highest class.) Establishing another first for the team, De La Salle finished the '85 season ranked 25th in the final *USA Today* Super 25 poll, De La Salle's first finish among the national elite.

It was more of the same in 1986. The season began with a couple of close calls, a 32-28 victory over Bellarmine High of San Jose to open the season and a 27-20 victory over Antioch High in Week Three. After that, the offense found its stride as De La Salle won the last six games of the regular season by a combined 323-87. The lopsided victories continued into the NCS 3A playoffs, De La Salle having moved up a class. The Spartans crushed Eureka High School in the first round 56-7. The next couple of playoff games were not as one-sided, but the Spartans still managed to win another NCS championship with victories over Clayton Valley, 24-6, and Monte Vista, 24-7. Despite running their victory string to 33 in a row and finishing second in California's Class 4A final rankings, the Spartans failed to finish in any of the final national polls.

The victories kept piling up for De La Salle in 1987. A De La Salle touchdown with just under three minutes remaining gave the Spartans a 29-23 win in Week Two over St. Francis High School of Mountain View, a perennial state power and the # 6 team in Northern California. The team from Kennedy High in Richmond almost ended the Spartans' winning ways in Week Eight, but they held on for a 24-

▲ *Spartans running back Atari Cullen (21) follows his blockers during De La Salle's big game with Mater Dei in 1998.*

21 victory. In the NCS 3A playoffs De La Salle gained a 32-6 victory over Rancho Cotate and then handled Ygnacio Valley, 34-7. The Spartans' winning streak had now reached 44, then the longest active streak in the country.

Those two playoff victories set up a NCS 3A title game re-match with Monte Vista. The two teams were ranked # 1 and # 2 as the season got underway, and not much had changed since then. De La Salle quarterback Brad Heyde and Monte Vista linebacker Jim Coleman had grown up playing football together on the same street—in Toledo, Ohio. That was just one of several connections between the two schools, including that Bob Ladouceur had started his high school coaching career at Monte Vista and his brother Tom was now an assistant coach there.

After a scoreless first half, De La Salle took a 7-0 lead in the third quarter, but late in the same period Monte Vista scored a touchdown of its own, but missed the extra point. With about eight minutes left in the fourth quarter and facing a fourth and seven, the Mustangs turned a fake punt into a 40-yard touchdown. The Mustangs then ran another trick play going for the two-pointer, a halfback pass to quarterback Stewart Hansen gaining the two points and a 14-7 lead. A late drive by the Spartans ended in a touchdown that made the score 14-13 with a little more than a minute to play. Ladouceur sent in the placekicking team, then called a time out and sent in the offense in an effort to win the game with a two-point conversion. In one of the most controversial calls in NCS history, the officials ruled that the De La Salle ball carrier had stepped out of bounds before the ball had crossed the plane of the goal. To make matters a little worse, when later viewing the game films, Bob Ladouceur noticed that there were only 10 Spartans on the field for that crucial play.

Monte Vista had stopped De La Salle's streak with a 14-13 victory, the Spartans finishing third in the final 1987 Class 4A poll.

The 1988 campaign would find De La Salle playing in its second new conference since the break-up of the Catholic Athletic League a few years earlier. First the Spartans had been placed in the Golden Bay Athletic League, a move that among other things required De La Salle to travel further than any other team in the league. At the same time, the Spartans were moved up from Class 2A to Class 3A for the NCS playoffs in the hope that the bigger schools would prove to be more of a challenge for them. In 1988 De La Salle was again switched to a new league, this time to the Bay Valley Athletic League, considered to be the best, i.e., toughest, league in Northern California and featuring teams such as Pittsburg, Antioch, El Cerrito, and Pinole Valley high schools.

Despite the move to the new conference, for the third time in four seasons the Spartans had a perfect campaign in 1988—so much for throwing them to the wolves. Only the Pirates of Pittsburg High School, losing to De La Salle by 28-21, and Pinole Valley High, which dropped a 28-25 decision to the Spartans, proved to

▸ *De La Salle's Nicholas Barbero (12) sprints for yardage against Northgate High during the 1998 season.*

be troublesome. The NCS 3A playoffs were even less of a challenge for De La Salle than the regular season games. In the first round the Spartans defeated Eureka High by 41-6, then knocked off Montgomery High School in the second round, 35-13. The finals against Granada High proved to be an even easier encounter for the Spartans as they shut out the Loggers, 42-0, to win the Class 3A North Section championship. The Spartans finished second in the Class 4A poll and for the first time since 1985 they also finished in the national rankings, this time at # 10.

De La Salle had not lost two games in the same regular season since 1981. That is, not until 1989. The Spartans opened that campaign with a 35-14 win over San Ramon Valley and it looked to be the start of another De La Salle romp through the schedule. However, in Week Two St. Francis High held the Spartans to just 16 points in posting a thrilling 18-16 victory. The Spartans rebounded the following week to defeat Napa High, 41-28.

Week Four brought the El Cerrito Gauchos to the De La Salle schedule. Desperate situations call for desperate solutions and, for El Cerrito head coach Frank Milo, trying to defeat De La Salle was close to being just that. Switching from their normal I-formation to a wing-T in the second half of the game, the Gauchos were able to produce just enough offense to defeat the Spartans, 14-13.

Having split their first four games, it seemed to some as if the Spartans had finally come back to earth, that the switch to the new conference was having the desired effect on the Spartans—but such was not to be the case. Regrouping after the loss to El Cerrito, De La Salle went on to win the last six games of the regular season and qualify for the NCS playoffs for the eighth consecutive time. As they seemed to have done so many times in the past, the Spartans again saved their best for last. They easily defeated all three playoff opponents, running up 118 points to just 16 allowed to capture another NCS 3A playoff crown. Even with two defeats the Spartans managed to finish eighth in the final 1989 Class 4A *Cal-Hi* state rankings.

For the fifth time in the last nine seasons, the De La Salle Spartans posted a perfect season in 1990, finishing 13-0. Their defense was not as dominant as some in the past, the 1990 "D" posting only one shutout; however, except for a 31-28 decision over Antioch High, the final outcome of the other games was never in doubt. This included the NCS 3A playoffs, where De La Salle defeated Cardinal Newman, 42-14, Foothill High School, 31-6, and Piner High by a 49-24 count to win another NCS championship. The Spartans finished fourth in the final 4A *Cal-Hi* state poll, and 24th in the final National Prep Poll.

The Spartans opened the 1991 season with a 54-0 victory over San Ramon Valley High. The next three games were much more competitive, but the Spartans came away with victories in all of them, including a 28-16 win over Pittsburg. Three more blowouts followed before the Spartans were again tested, first by Antioch, which De La Salle defeated, 21-3, and then Ygnacio Valley, which finally succumbed to the Spartans, 13-9. A 51-18 thrashing of Pinole Valley closed out the regular season and extended the Spartans' win streak to 32 in a row.

In the NCS 3A playoffs, the Spartans opened with their highest point total in five years, defeating Montgomery High School, 61-14. Washington High then fell to the Spartans by 33-7, setting up a rematch with Pittsburg for the 3A title.

De La Salle had been the nation's fourth ranked team when the Spartans defeated Pittsburg earlier in the season; despite that, the Pirates felt that they could beat Bob Ladouceur's team. Almost at the last minute, just a couple of days before the NCS title game, the Pittsburg coaching staff came up with a plan that they felt would give the Pirates an edge. Like Skyline and El Cerrito in previous years, the Pirates decided to change their offense in the second half in an effort to nullify De La Salle's halftime adjustments, feeling that De La Salle could not plan to defend something it had never seen before.

The first half of the game ended in a 21-21 tie. When the second half began with Pittsburg on offense, instead of its usual split-back offensive formation, the Pirates unveiled their new attack. The two running backs who were normally behind the quarterback repositioned themselves as receivers, leaving no one in the backfield but the quarterback, or at most one running-back directly behind the quarterback. As hoped, and planned, the change worked as the Pirates promptly marched down the field 82 yards to take a 28-21 lead midway through the third quarter. Early in the fourth quarter, De La Salle scored a touchdown, but the PAT try sailed wide, leaving Pittsburg with a 28-27 lead with 9:35 left in the game.

The score remained that way until, with just 2:15 left on the game clock, Pittsburg's Percy McGee intercepted a De La Salle pass deep in the Pirates' end of the field and returned it 79 yards for a touchdown. The PAT gave the Pirates a 35-27 lead—and, as it turned out, the game.

De La Salle's latest win streak had ended after 34 in a row. The Spartans had finished the season sixth in the *Cal-Hi Sports* final 4A poll, but the defeat had cost them their national ranking for 1991.

▾ *De La Salle defensive lineman Joseph Miklos chases down the Clayton Valley quarterback on this play during the 1998 season.*

NCS 1998 Football Championship

▲ *The De La Salle Spartans celebrate after winning the 1998 Class 4A North Coast Section championship.*

In his first three years as the head coach at De La Salle High School, Bob Ladouceur's Spartans had enjoyed their first three winning seasons ever, posting a good 21-7 won-lost record. Compared to the team's record in the pre-Ladouceur years, the Spartans may have thought that "it doesn't get any better than this." But it did. From 1982 thru 1991 the Spartans played like few other teams have ever played and put together four perfect seasons and 115 victories, and one tie, in 123 games. Again, the Spartans and their faithful no doubt felt that "it doesn't get any better than this," and their opponents were certainly hoping that it would not. Both were wrong, to the delight of some and the great dismay of many more.

Following their upset loss to Pittsburg in the 1991 NCS 3A finals, the Spartans came back in '92 and played like a team on a mission, and woe to those who got in their way. Scoring at a pace previously unseen at De La Salle, the Spartans roared through their schedule, regular season and playoffs, scoring a then school record 629 points. They never scored fewer than 34 points in any one game and the Spartans average margin of victory was 39.4 points; their closest game was the season opener against Merced High School, which De La Salle won 34-14. In Week Five the Spartans had their rematch with Pittsburg, and won by a score of 44-7 over a good Pirates team.

How good was that Pirates team? They made it all the way back to the NCS 3A finals for the second consecutive season—and for the second consecutive season they were playing De La Salle for the championship. Showing that the score of the earlier game was no fluke, the Spartans handed the Pirates a 41-6 thrashing—no second half surprises for the Spartans this time. De La Salle finished the season 13-0, atop the *Cal-Hi* Class 4A rankings and as high as third in the national polls.

As unbelievable as it may sound, the Spartans were even better in 1993, when they set the school's all-time scoring record of 665 points while increasing its winning margin to 42 points per game. Once again, however, the Pirates of Pittsburg High threatened to derail a De La Salle win streak when the two teams met at Pirate Stadium before more than 6,500 fans in Week Six. De La Salle held a 20-13 lead late in the fourth quarter when the Pirates ripped off a lightning quick 66-yard scoring drive in just five plays. With both teams completely exhausted from the intense battle, the Pittsburg coaches did not want to play for a tie and a possible overtime. The Pirates successfully scored the two-point conversion to take a 21-20 lead with just under a minute left in the game.

Another Pittsburg upset victory seemed all but certain, but this De La Salle team was not to be denied. The ensuing kickoff was returned to the Spartans 38-yard line. A 16-yard pass completion put the ball at the Pittsburg 46-yard line with just 23 seconds left to play.

Realistically, the Spartans were simply hoping to move the ball into field goal range for a shot at a game winning three-pointer. It did not work out that way. Quarterback Mike Bastianelli again dropped back to pass on the next play. With his primary target covered, Bastianelli looked for someone else and found tight end Nick Geldermann over the middle at the Pirates' 35-yard line. Geldermann made the catch, immediately eluded one tackler, and then broke a tackle at the 10-yard line before running into the end zone with 11 seconds left on the clock. The Spartans had gone on top, 26-21, and that would be the final score.

The Spartans again finished 13-0 in 1993, this time defeating Pinole Valley in the NCS 3A championship, 46-14. Surprisingly, the Spartans only finished second in the final *Cal-Hi* 4A poll that season, and as high as fourth in the national rankings.

In 1994 the De La Salle Spartans would enjoy a truly landmark season. The lopsided scores continued unabated as the Spartans easily went through their schedule, a 35-21 victory over Antioch High School being the only game in which an opponent lost by fewer than 29 points. Finishing with a 13-0 record and a third consecutive NCS 3A championship, the Spartans were back on top in the final *Cal-Hi* 4A poll. And for the first time in school history, the Spartans had a new piece

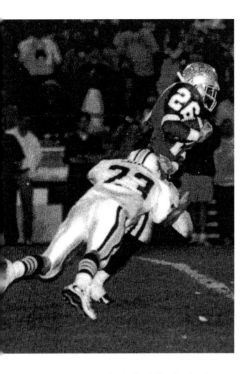

▲ *De La Salle defensive back Jonathan Tucker (26) comes away with an interception during the Spartans 1999 season.*

of hardware to add to their trophy case—both the National Sports News Service (NSNS) and the National Prep Poll (NPP) had named the De La Salle Spartans as the nation's # 1 team.

The seasons of 1995, 1996, and 1997 would see the Spartans continue to roll through their schedule, with each season having its similarities and differences. For example, in each of those seasons the Spartans would go undefeated (13-0 in '95, 12-0 in both '96 and '97), win the NCS championship (3A in 1995, 4A the other two seasons), finish first in the final *Cal-Hi* 4A poll each season, and finish as high as second in the national rankings each season.

In 1995 De La Salle defeated James Logan High 41-8 in Week Eight. It was the fourth time that the two teams had met and De La Salle had won every meeting by virtually the same margin. However, the real significance to this game was that it was De La Salle's 48th consecutive victory, and as such it set a new record for California high school football.

In 1996 the Spartans set a couple of team records on defense and several others on offense. For instance, the Spartans won seven games by shutout that season and held the opposition to just 53 total points—both new team records. When De La Salle defeated Clayton Valley by 75-0 it set a new mark for points scored and greatest margin of victory.

A 55-7 victory over Pittsburg in the eighth game of the 1997 season tied a record that some thought would never be equaled. From 1968-1975, Hudson High School of Hudson, Mich., went 72 consecutive football games without a tie or a defeat. De La Salle's victory over Pittsburg equaled that mark. The following week, the Spartans defeated College Park High, 56-0, to set a new undefeated mark—and each succeeding victory just added to the record.

The 1998 season opened as had every season since 1990, with a couple of lopsided De La Salle victories, 48-13 over Nevada Union-Grass Valley High School and a 48-20 defeat of Bakersfield High. The Spartans had now extended their winning streak to 78. Getting to number 79 would be the greatest challenge a Bob Ladouceur team had yet faced. On September 27, 1998, in front of more than 21,000 people—about 17,000 more than they usually attracted—the De La Salle Spartans would take on the team considered to be the best in California during the 1990s, the Monarchs of Mater Dei High School.

Mater Dei High School is located in Santa Ana, California, near Los Angeles. While De La Salle was dominating the Northern Section playoffs during the 1990s, Mater Dei was doing the same thing in the Southern Section with three championships, more than any other Southern Section school. From 1991-1997, the Monarchs had posted a record of 85-8-1 against a schedule that was on average a bit more stringent than that of De La Salle's predominantly league schedule. Mater Dei had also been named national champion in both 1994 and 1996 by *USA Today*.

For a few years now, there had been rumblings that De La Salle's schedule was too weak, even though the Spartans had changed leagues twice and had been moved up to the big school Class 4A. Despite these changes, there were those who felt that the Spartans still needed to take on even stronger opponents. In an attempt to arrange games that would have enhanced the De La Salle schedule, some talks had taken place as far back as 1992 (with Cleveland's Saint Ignatius High School, for instance), but nothing ever came of them. A match with Mater Dei was one of those games that was being pushed—the best of Northern California versus the best of Southern California. Finally arranged, this game with Mater Dei in 1998 would be the first of a four-game series between the Spartans and the Monarchs. For those in the Spartans camp who wanted this game, perhaps they had forgotten that you should be careful what you wish for—De La Salle was considered to be the underdog in this game.

The game was played at Edison International Field in Anaheim, the Spartans going on the road south for this first meeting. Mater Dei kicked off to open the game and Monarchs' head coach Bruce Rollinson tried to catch the Spartans napping with an onside kick. De La Salle was not fooled, recovering the ball at its own 34-yard line. The Spartans promptly marched 66 yards in 10 plays for the game's first touchdown and an early 7-0 lead. Later in the quarter, the Monarchs recovered a De La Salle fumble at the Spartans' 10-yard line. Quarterback Matt Grootegood scoring on a keeper on the very next play.

With the score tied at 7-7, the Monarchs again tried an onside kick and again the Spartans foiled the effort by recovering the ball at their own 38-yard line. This time it took De La Salle only five plays to again find the end zone and regain the lead, 14-7. Later in the quarter following a Mater Dei punt, the Spartans marched 72 yards for a third touchdown and a 21-7 halftime advantage.

After the halftime break, the Monarchs came roaring back and on a pair of touchdown passes tied the score at 21-21. De La Salle added its fourth touchdown of the game to regain the lead early in the fourth quarter, then held off a late Mater Dei threat by recovering a Monarchs fumble with 1:32 remaining in the game. The 28-21 victory was the biggest thus far in De La Salle Spartans football history.

There may have been some carry over the following week from the intensity of this game as the Spartans had to really battle to get by a

▾ *Spartans quarterback
Brian Callahan (15) has
plenty of protection as
he scans the field for
an open receiver during
the 1999 season.*

stubborn team from St. Francis High School, 21-0. After that it was clear sailing for De La Salle all the way to the team's seventh consecutive NCS championship as the Spartans won their last seven games by an average of 53-9, including a 55-13 win over Castor Valley High in the Class 4A championship.

De La Salle finished first in the final *Cal-Hi Sports* Class 4A poll and in all three of the major national polls to garner its second national title.

The 1999 season was one that many Californians, and high school football fans across the country, looked forward to as it would feature the long-awaited rematch between De La Salle and Mater Dei. Now that the Monarchs had seen the Spartans up close and personal, another close battle was anticipated. Both teams were nationally ranked in the preseason polls, but some of the gleam was taken off the rematch when the Monarchs lost their season opener to Clovis West High School, 24-17.

Be that as it may, the game went on as scheduled, but it was not the down-to-the-last-minute nail biter that had been anticipated. De La Salle took a 7-0 lead after the first quarter and was ahead 21-0 at the half. The Spartans added another 21 points in the second half and again kept the Monarchs out of the end zone. De La Salle's one-sided 42-0 victory, its second consecutive win over the team that many felt was the best in California, helped to alleviate much of the criticism of the Spartans and their supposedly weak schedule.

▲ This diving attempt for an interception by De La Salle's Demetrius Williams (21) was successful in this game during the 1999 season.

As they had done the year before, the Spartans followed their game with Mater Dei with one against St. Francis High. This year there would be no lingering after affects from the Mater Dei game as the Spartans handed St. Francis a convincing 35-7 defeat. The Spartans easily rolled through the rest of their schedule. Two weeks after the St. Francis game, Ygnacio Valley hit De La Salle for 32 points, but the Spartans more than doubled that with 71 of their own.

Finishing the regular season at 10-0, De La Salle defeated Castro Valley, 55-21, in its opening 4A playoff game, then won its eighth consecutive NCS title with a 38-14 victory over San Leandro High. For the sixth consecutive season, and the seventh time in the last eight years, the Spartans were named the # 1 team in *Cal-Hi's* 1999 Class 4A poll. For the second consecutive season, they were also named national champion as well.

WHEN BOB LADOUCEUR TOOK OVER THE DE LA SALLE FOOTBALL TEAM THE SPARTANS WERE THE LOCAL DOORMAT. TWENTY-ONE YEARS LATER, THE SPARTANS WERE USING THE REST OF THE STATE AS THEIR DOORMAT.

From 1982-1999, De La Salle finished in the final national Top 25 more than any other team, just ahead of Cleveland Saint Ignatius and Valdosta.

De La Salle's victory over Castro Valley allowed the team to close out the 20th century with its 100th consecutive victory, the longest winning streak of the century.

When Bob Ladouceur took over the De La Salle football team the Spartans were the local doormat. Twenty-one years later, the Spartans were using the rest of the state as their doormat; Coach Lad's record from 1978-1999 was 236-14-1, .942. Ladouceur introduced a new philosophy and system at De La Salle, one that could be summed up in three words: discipline, precision, and execution. As Neil Hayes noted in his book about the Spartans, "Ladouceur's program is based on the belief that if you do everything precisely right, if you make a commitment to your coaches and teammates and sweat through all of the grueling hours of workouts, and bond with your teammates and play for them and not for yourself, winning just happens. It's a byproduct. But in the end the byproduct isn't as important as paying attention to the details."

## CHAPTER 13

SO, WHO WAS THE BEST?

The teams and coaches portrayed in this book represent the very best that American high school football has to offer, not only during the 20th century, but throughout its long history. However, there will always be the question, probably a competitive American thing, that people want answered: "Who was the best team?" We have presented more than a dozen possible choices. You no doubt will have your favorite for that title. We will now give ours.

One can argue that either a playoff system or a poll system is the more accurate or better way to determine a national high school football champion, or even a state champion for that matter. Both systems have their plusses and minuses. In a playoff situation a team has to prove itself on the gridiron in a game supposedly against the other "best team" in the country. But how are those final two best teams to be determined, since obviously there cannot be a nationwide playoff to eliminate all but those last two teams? As we have seen in the preceding pages there actually have been games that are recognized as having determined a national champion. The last of those playoff games took place in the late 1930s. However, because of state athletic association rules against playing games after state playoffs have been completed, there will never be another high school national championship game.

In a poll scenario, one bad game—one bad quarter—even one bad play—and the otherwise faultless performance of an entire season can seem to be for naught. The polls are seemingly relentless in not allowing a team with a loss to be named # 1, although the historical record shows that at least a half-dozen teams with a blemish on their record (even one team with two losses) have been named national champion, not to mention numerous teams with ties on their final ledger.

And then there is the question of the criteria used by each poll to select its top team, because no two polls are alike. Do we use a human poll or a computerized one (but are they not somewhat the same because a human must program the computer)? What criteria should be given more weight than others, or are they all to be used equally? Quality of competition is a huge factor, but how is that to be determined? Or do we combine the criteria of several polls to make one composite poll? Today there are composite listings that combine the results of several polls, which is another way to determine a "true" national champion. That may or may not be the best system, but it was not a system that was available during the 20th century.

Be that as it may, it is irrelevant what *type of* system for determining a national champion was in use at any particular time during the past—because we must go by the system that *was* in use. In other words, it really does not matter *how* a team was named national champion, the only thing that matters is that Team X or Team Y *was* named the champion and is recognized as such for that year.

Another item of confusion that has cropped up during this study has been the question of what does the term "team" refer to? As was mentioned in the Preface, the term "team" can either refer to the players representing a school for one single season, or it can refer to the collection of players representing a school over an extended period of time. While our study here has described the latter, we can still answer the question of the former, i.e., "Which was the best high school football team for a single season?"

Through the years the names of several teams have cropped up as being the single best team ever, or in our case, during the 20th century. While this discussion usually takes place on the local or state level, there are still those teams whose accomplishments and reputation are of such magnitude that word of them reaches the national audience. One such team was the 1919 squad from Harrisburg (Pa.) Tech. Coached by Paul Smith, Harrisburg finished the season a perfect 12-0-0 to claim the Pennsylvania championship and a national championship for the second consecutive year. The 1919 Maroons outscored their opponents by an incredible 701-0, averaging just over 58 points per game.

Another team often mentioned when the best of all-time is discussed is the 1940 Tigers of Massillon Washington High School. The last Massillon team coached by Paul Brown, these Tigers brought Massillon its fourth national championship and sixth Ohio title within a span of just six seasons.

Also in the mix for the single best team is the Valdosta High School Wildcats team of 1971 coached by Wright Bazemore. Seemingly saving his best for the final year of a long and distinguished coaching career, Bazemore's Wildcats finished 13-0-0 to claim their second national title in three seasons and their third overall. These Wildcats won the state championship game that year by a whopping 62-12.

However, the one team that stands out above all the others has held that distinction for almost the entire 20th century—the 1914 edition of the Crimson Tide of Everett High School in Everett, Mass. Coached by Cleo O'Donnell, the Crimson Tide compiled a final mark of 13-0-0, including a 62-0 victory over previously undefeated Stamford (Conn.) High School in a game for the national championship.

That year Everett outscored its opponents by 600-0. The 1915 edition of the *Spalding's Official Football Guide*, in reviewing the 1914 interscholastic football season, said of the Everett team that "the eleven was recognized as the greatest contingent of schoolboys ever developed in the long history of the gridiron sport in New England... Everett High's style of play comprised a frequent use of the forward pass and a running attack that was propelled by a swift quartet of backs, reinforced by a line that was able to tear open holes through an opposing front that was more like a finished varsity [i.e. college] eleven than that of a schoolboy team."

But you do not have to take our word that Everett High School produced the nation's single best team. In February of 1960, *Sport Magazine* listed the greatest high school football teams of all-time—and at the top of that list was the Crimson Tide of Everett High School. Again, in August of 1982, almost 70 years after they played, none other than *Sports Illustrated* published its choice for the best team ever—and again the one representing Everett High School in the fall of 1914 got the nod.

While Everett High School is the choice for the single-season best team, our question here is a bit broader: What high school had the best football program over an extended period of time during the 20th century? Like the various polls, there are many criteria that can be used to make this determination. For our purposes we will stick to four.

The first criterion deals with a team's total number of victories during the 20th century. However, simply using the raw number of wins would be unfair because there is a great variance in the total number of games played during the century by the teams in our study, ranging from a low of 312 for De La Salle to a high of 992 for Everett (Mass.) High School. While a team with a very long history that includes an inordinate number of victories certainly deserves to be recognized, to somewhat even out the playing field for this category a team's winning percentage would appear to be the more appropriate gauge.

The Wildcats of Valdosta High School, who started playing football in 1913, own the most victories of any high school football team during the 20th century with 774 (see Appendix III). While Valdosta's 20th century win percentage of .821 is still very good, two younger programs in the study have slightly better winning percentages. Moeller High School (1960) has won 346 games out of only 412 played for a percentage of .842, and De La Salle (1972) has won 253 games out of just 312 played to give the Spartans a percentage of .824. Also in the mix is Massillon's Washington High School (1891) with a second best total of 719 victories and a winning percentage of .761 for games played throughout the 20th century.

Quality of competition is another factor that was used in determining the best program (see Appendix V). This factor is a little more difficult to quantify, but we have come up with a solution that is a viable one (see Appendix II). From

1900-1999, there were 130 national championships awarded. Of that number, 27 of those championships were won by Ohio schools, which is almost double the next best total of 14 for Illinois and 13 championships for Texas and for California. Ohio's teams have also proven to be more consistent champions by virtue of the fact that teams from the Buckeye State have won national championships in every decade of the 20th century from 1910 thru the 1990s. No other state has won national titles on so consistent a basis.

Perhaps the most important factor to be considered is the quality of a team's victories. Specifically, how many championships, both state and national, was a team able to claim by its victories. As regards state championships won, there is a clear difference between the top three teams in our study and all of the rest. Massillon Washington and Miami Senior high schools have each won 24 state championships during the 20th century and Valdosta has 23 such titles. The next highest totals belong to the two Everett high schools, with Everett (Mass.) High School winning 16 state titles and Everett (Wash.) High School capturing 14.

As for national championships, Massillon Washington High School stands above all the rest with nine titles—with Valdosta (6), Oak Park (5), Miami Senior (5) and Moeller (5) in a close-knit bunch right behind.

There is one other criterion that was used in determining the best high school football program of the 20th century. That had to do with the time frame in which these various teams were at their championship peak. In other words, once a team made it to the top, how long was it able to stay there. Anyone who has followed high school sports, and in particular high school football, knows that in the vast majority of cases a team is not able to sustain a truly championship run at any level—be it local, state or national—for more than a year or two. It is a simple factor of the great turnover in "personnel", i.e., students, at the high school level. At best, a coach may have the excellent players upon which to build a championship team for only a year or two; on a rare occasion one or two outstanding players make it to the varsity for three years. To maintain a long term champion at the high school level takes a steady supply of good-to-outstanding players combined with an outstanding head coach and a coaching staff that knows how to get the best out of even mediocre players.

The teams portrayed in this book are of the highest caliber, at the very top of the high school game; however even these, the best of the best, were not always able to stay at the top for very long. Some schools, like Coral Gables and Reagan high schools, enjoyed short but very successful championship eras; Coral Gables winning four national championships in five seasons while Reagan captured three titles in only a four year span. Miami Senior won three national championships over a six year period during the early 1960s, after having had two championships during back-to-back seasons in 1942-1943. An impressive record, but the intervening 17 years between national titles works against this being considered an extended championship "era" for the Stingarees.

Cleveland's Saint Ignatius High School enjoyed one of the relatively longer runs of national success from 1988-1995. During that time, the Wildcats won three national championships and seven Ohio Division I titles. In addition to their three national titles the Wildcats finished as high as second place in the national Top 25 four more times during those seasons, the best total finish of any team in the country for that time period.

De La Salle High School also had an eight year run of outstanding success, one that extended from 1992 thru the end of the century in 1999. The Spartans won three national titles during those years; but, due to the fact that California had no declared state champions until 2007, the Spartans were never credited with even one state championship. Incredibly, during those eight seasons De La Salle never finished below # 4 in the national polls, the best showing by any school in the country to close out the century.

Archbishop Moeller High School's championship record places the Crusaders among the truly elite of high school football. For the 11-year period from 1975 to 1985, Moeller football was the standard by which all other teams were measured. During those 11 years, the Crusaders finished among the national Top 20 every season, a record that has never been equaled. That run included five national championships in the span of just seven seasons, as well as seven state championships.

The Valdosta High School Wildcats are unique among high school football teams in that they enjoyed not one, but two, championship eras during the 20th century. The first, under head coach Wright Bazemore, spanned the ten years from 1962-1971. During that time, the Wildcats won three national championships, finished no lower than eighth in the country on four other occasions and brought home eight state championships. The Wildcats' second championship era took place under head coach Nick Hyder and lasted from 1978-1992. Those 15 years produced three more national championships for the Wildcats, saw them finish among the national Top 20 four more times, and brought home seven additional state titles (see Appendix VI).

Championship eras of eight to 15 years at the high school level are truly impressive, but there is one school whose championship years exceeded even that. That school is Massillon's Washington High School, or as most people know it, simply "Massillon." For the 31-year period from 1935 thru 1965, Massillon put up some unbelievably remarkable championship numbers in winning 20 state titles and nine national championships, numbers that turned a small town Ohio football team into a legendary national institution. Just as everyone knew who Knute Rockne was during the 1920s, few sports enthusiasts did not recognize the name

"Massillon" when it was mentioned and—like Knute Rockne—it is still a highly recognized name.

Within that 31-year span, the greatest championship run in the history of football at any level, there is an even more impressive 20-year period from 1935-1954 when the Tigers brought home a total of seven national championships and an equally incredible 15 state titles. Over the remaining 11 years of its championship run, Massillon won two additional national titles, finished seventh or better three other times, and brought home five more state championships. The Tigers compiled an equally impressive won-lost record of 274-27-11, for a winning percentage of .896, during their 31-year championship era.

Further evidence underpinning Massillon's prominence can be discerned by understanding the quality of its coaching (see Appendix VI). During the Tigers' championship era Paul Brown, Chuck Mather, and Leo Strang combined for nine national and 15 state championships, while the team's other head coaches at this time contributed another five state titles. No other school can boast such a line-up of championship coaches.

There they are, the factors upon which is based our choice for the greatest high school football team of the 20th century: victories and winning percentage, quality of competition, national and state championships won (and their combined total), length of each team's championship era. Valdosta High is correct in stating that with 774 victories it is the winningest high school football team of the 20th century. De La Salle can be justifiably proud of its unprecedented win streak of 100 consecutive victories to close out the last years of the 20th century.

However, championships are what it is all about, the ultimate goal that all teams strive for and by which they are remembered. When all of the above factors are combined and taken into consideration only one team can emerge on top, the team that owns the most national championships spread out over the longest continuous championship era of the 20th century—the Tigers of Massillon Washington High School.

CHAPTER SUMMARY

The following is a list of the schools portrayed in each chapter, along with their featured years.

CHAPTER 1—THE FIRST GREAT TEAM
Oak Park High School (Oak Park, Il)—1910-1920
Fostoria High School (Fostoria, OH)—1912

CHAPTER 2—COAST TO COAST
Everett High School (Everett, MA)—1911-1915
Everett High School (Everett, WA)—1911-1920
Harrisburg Tech (Harrisburg, PA)—1916-1920

CHAPTER 3—GLASS CITY CHAMPIONS
Scott High School (Toledo, OH)—1913-1923
Waite High School (Toledo, OH)—1922-1932

CHAPTER 4—PB AND THE TIGERS
Washington High School (Massillon, OH)—1933-1940

CHAPTER 5—THE TIGERS—PART II
Washington High School (Massillon, OH)—1948-1965

CHAPTER 6—WRIGHT BAZEMORE'S VALDOSTA WILDCATS
Valdosta High School (Valdosta, GA)—1941-1971

CHAPTER 7—THE STINGAREES
Miami Senior High School (Miami, FL)—1931-1965

CHAPTER 8—TWO GREAT TEAMS, FIVE CHAMPIONSHIP SEASONS
Coral Gables High School (Miami, FL)—1951-1969
John H. Reagan Early College High School
(Austin , TX)—1966-1970

CHAPTER 9—THE MOELLER MYSTIQUE
Archbishop Moeller High School (Cincinnati, OH)—1963-1982

CHAPTER 10—VALDOSTA—THE NICK HYDER YEARS
Valdosta High School (Valdosta, GA)—1971-1995

CHAPTER 11—THE TEAM OF THE '90s AND TWO BULLDOGS
Saint Ignatius High School (Cleveland, OH)—1983-1999
Berwick High School (Berwick, PA)—1983-1995
McKinley High School (Canton, OH)—1997-1998

CHAPTER 12—THE GREATEST WIN STREAK EVER
De La Salle High School (Concord, CA)—1978-1999

CHAPTER 13—SO, WHO WAS THE BEST?
Summary and Final Conclusions

20TH CENTURY NATIONAL CHAMPIONS OF HIGH SCHOOL FOOTBALL

Compilators: Tim Hudak & Pflug, LLC

YEAR		WINNING TEAM	CITY / STATE	SCORE	LOSING TEAM	CITY / STATE	SELECTOR
1900	S	Moline	Moline, IL				Lyons
1901	Not Known						
1902	G	Hyde Park Chicago	Chicago, IL	105-0	Brooklyn Boys High	Brooklyn, NY	Lyons; Hudak
1903	G	North Division	Chicago, IL	76-0	Brooklyn Boys High	Brooklyn, NY	Lyons; Hudak
1904	G	Central	Detroit, MI	6-5	Central	Toledo, OH	NSNS; Hudak
1905	Not Known						
1906	G	Seattle HS	Seattle, WA	11-5	North Division	Chicago, IL	Lyons; Hudak
1907	Not Known						
1908	G	Englewood	Chicago, IL	11-4	Butte HS	Butte, MT	Lyons; Hudak
1909	S	Englewood	Chicago, IL				Lyons; Hudak
1910	G	Oak Park	Oak Park, IL	6-3	Washington HS	Portland, OR	NSNS
1911	G	Oak Park	Oak Park, IL	17-0	St Johns Prep	Danvers, MA	NSNS
1912	G	Oak Park	Oak Park, IL	32-14	Everett	Everett, MA	NSNS
	G	Fostoria	Fostoria, OH	74-0	Central	Buffalo, NY	NSNS
1913	G	Oak Park	Oak Park, IL	32-7	Scott	Toledo, OH	NSNS
1914	G	Everett	Everett, MA	62-0	Stamford HS	Stamford, CT	NSNS
1915	S	Everett	Everett, MA	0-0	Central	Detroit, MI	NSNS
	S	Central	Detroit, MI	0-0	Everett	Everett, MA	NSNS
1916	S	San Diego	San Diego, CA				NSNS
	G	Scott	Toledo, OH	13-0	Haverhill	Haverhill, MA	NSNS; Lyons; Hudak
1917	Not Known						
1918	S	Tech	Harrisburg, PA				NSNS
1919	G	Tech	Harrisburg, PA	56-0	Portland	Portland, ME	NSNS
	S	Everett	Everett, WA	7-7	Scott	Toledo, OH	Hudak
	S	Scott	Toledo, OH	7-7	Everett	Everett, WA	Hudak
1920	G	Oak Park	Oak Park, IL	19-6	Steele	Dayton, OH	NSNS
	G	Everett	Everett, WA	16-7	East Tech	Cleveland, OH	NSNS
1921	S	Duval	Jacksonville, FL				NSNS
1922	G	Scott	Toledo, OH	32-0	Corvalis	Corvalis, OR	NSNS
1923	G	Scott	Toledo, OH	24-20	Washington HS	Cedar Rapids, IA	NSNS
	G	Shaw	E. Cleveland, OH	26-0	Salem HS	Salem, MA	NSNS
1924	S	Washington HS	Cedar Rapids, IA				Lyons
	G	Waite	Toledo, OH	46-0	Everett	Everett, MA	NSNS
1925	G	Pine Bluff	Pine Bluff, AR	61-0	Stivers	Dayton, OH	NSNS
1926	G	Tuscaloosa	Tuscaloosa, AL	42-0	Senn	Chicago, IL	NSNS
1927	G	Waco	Waco, TX	44-12	Cathedral Latin	Cleveland, OH	NSNS
1928	S	Medford	Medford, OR				NSNS
1929	G	Tuscaloosa	Tuscaloosa, AL	42-0	University City High	St. Louis, MO	NSNS
1930	S	Union	Phoenix, AZ				NSNS
1931	S	Ashland HS	Ashland, KY				NSNS
1932	S	New Rochelle	New Rochelle, NY				NSNS

KEY

National Champions Selected 98
National Championship Games Played. . . . 32
National Champions. 130
Championship Game Played. . . . . G
Selected Champion . . . . S

NSNS: National Sports News Service
USA: USA Today
NPP: National Prep Poll
Hudak: Tim Hudak
Lyons: Simon Lyons

LSA: Louisana Sports Association
Fox: Fox Fab 50
Bianco: Tony Bianco
ISS: Imperial Sports Syndicate
NHSFRB: National High School Football Record Book

20TH CENTURY NATIONAL CHAMPIONS OF HIGH SCHOOL FOOTBALL

Compilators: Tim Hudak & Pflug, LLC

YEAR		WINNING TEAM	CITY / STATE	SCORE	LOSING TEAM	CITY / STATE	SELECTOR
1932	G	Waite	Toledo, OH	13-7	Miami HS	Miami, FL	NSNS
1933	G	Capital Hill	Oklahoma City, OK	55-12	Harrison Tech	Chicago, IL	NSNS
1934	S	McKinley	Canton, OH				NSNS
1935	S	Washington HS	Massillon, OH				NSNS
1936	S	Washington HS	Massillon, OH				NSNS
1937	S	Austin	Chicago, IL				NSNS
	G	Evansville Memorial	Evansville, IN	21-0	McKeesport HS	McKeesport, PA	Lyons; Hudak
1938	G	Dupont Manual	Louisville, KY	28-20	New Britain	New Britain, CT	NSNS; LSA
1939	G	Pine Bluff	Pine Bluff, AR	26-0	Baton Rouge HS	Baton Rouge, LA	NSNS; LSA
	S	Washington HS	Massillon, OH				NSNS
No National Championship games played after 1939							
1940	S	Washington HS	Massillon, OH				NSNS
1941	S	Leo	Chicago, IL				NSNS
1942	S	Miami HS	Miami , FL				NSNS
1943	S	Miami HS	Miami , FL				NSNS
1944		No Award Made					
1945		No Award Made					
1946	S	Central	Little Rock, AR				NSNS
1947	S	Roosevelt	E. Chicago, IN				NSNS
	S	Classical	Lynn, MA				NSNS
1948	S	Waco	Waco, TX				NSNS
1949	S	Wichita Falls	Wichitaw, TX				NSNS
1950	S	Washington HS	Massillon, OH				NSNS
1951	S	Weymouth	Weymouth, MA				NSNS
1952	S	Washington HS	Massillon, OH				NSNS
1953	S	Washington HS	Massillon, OH				NSNS
1954	S	Vallejo	Vallejo, CA				NSNS
1955	S	San Diego	San Diego, CA				NSNS
1956	S	Abilene	Abilene, TX				NSNS
1957	S	Central	Little Rock, AR				NSNS
	S	Downey	Downey, CA				NSNS
1958	S	Wichita Falls	Wichita Falls, TX				NSNS
	S	Oak Ridge	Oak Ridge, TN				NSNS
1959	S	Washington HS	Massillon, OH				NSNS
1960	S	Miami HS	Miami, FL				Hudak
1961	S	Washington HS	Massillon, OH				NSNS
1962	S	Valdosta	Valdosta, GA				NSNS
	S	Miami HS	Miami, FL				ISS
	S	St. Ignatius	San Francisco, CA				ISS
1963	S	St. Rita	Chicago, IL				NSNS
1964	S	Coral Gables	Coral Gables, FL				NSNS
1965	S	Miami HS	Miami, FL				NSNS
1966	S	El Rancho	Pico Rivera, CA				NSNS
1967	S	Reagan	Austin, TX				NSNS
	S	Coral Gables	Coral Gables, FL				NSNS
1968	S	Reagan	Austin, TX				NSNS
	S	Coral Gables	Coral Gables, FL				NSNS
1969	S	Valdosta	Valdosta, GA				NSNS
	S	Coral Gables	Coral Gables, FL				NSNS

YEAR		WINNING TEAM	CITY / STATE	SCORE	LOSING TEAM	CITY / STATE	SELECTOR
1970	S	Reagan	Austin, TX				NSNS
1971	S	Valdosta	Valdosta, GA				NSNS
1972	S	Bristol	Bristol, TN				NSNS
1973	S	Baylor	Chatanooga, TN				NSNS
1974	S	Thomasville	Thomasville, GA				NSNS
1975	S	Loyola	Los Angeles, CA				NSNS; Lyons
1976	S	Moeller	Cincinnati, OH				NSNS
	S	Warner Robins	Warner Robins, GA				NSNS; Lyons
1977	S	Moeller	Cincinnati, OH				NSNS
1978	S	Annandale	Annandale, VA				NSNS
	S	Stratford	Houston, TX				Lyons
1979	S	Moeller	Cincinnati, OH				NSNS
1980	S	Moeller	Cincinnati, OH				NSNS
1981	S	Warner Robins	Warner Robins, GA				NSNS
1982	S	Moeller	Cincinnati, OH				NSNS; USA
1983	S	Berwick	Berwick, PA				NSNS; USA
1984	S	Valdosta	Valdosta, GA				NSNS; USA
1985	S	E. St. Louis	St. Louis, IL				NSNS; USA
1986	S	Valdosta	Valdosta, GA				NSNS; USA
1987	S	Fontana	Fontana, CA				NPP
	S	Penn Hills	Pittsburg, PA				USA
	S	Plano	Plano, TX				NSNS
1988	S	Pine Forrest	Penasocola, FL				NSNS; USA
	S	Vigor	Prichard, AL				NPP
1989	S	Saint Ignatius	Cleveland, OH				USA
	S	Permian	Odessa, TX				NSNS; NPP
1990	S	Aldine	Houston, TX				NPP
	S	Eisenhower	Lawton, OK				USA
	S	Rushton	Rushton, LA				NSNS
1991	S	Ben Davis	Indianapolis, IN				NSNS; NPP
	S	La Grange	La Grange, GA				USA
1992	S	Valdosta	Valdosta, GA				NSNS; NPP
	S	Berwick	Berwick, PA				USA
1993	S	Saint Ignatius	Cleveland, OH				NSNS; NPP; USA
1994	S	De La Salle	Concord, CA				NSNS; NPP
	S	Mater Dei	Santa Ana, CA				USA
1995	S	Berwick	Berwick, PA				USA
	S	Saint Ignatius	Cleveland, OH				NSNS; NPP
1996	S	Hampton	Hampton, VA				NSNS; NPP
	S	Mater Dei	Santa Ana, CA				USA
1997	S	McKinley	Canton, OH				USA
	S	Hampton	Hampton, VA				NSNS; NPP
1998	S	De La Salle	Concord, CA				NSNS; NPP; USA
	S	West Monroe	West Monroe, LA				Bianco
1999	S	De La Salle	Concord, CA				NSNS
	S	Lee	Midland, TX				USA
	S	Evangel Christian	Shreveport, LA				Fox; Bianco; NPP

KEY

National Champions Selected 98	NSNS: National Sports News Service	LSA: Louisana Sports Association
National Championship Games Played. . . . 32	USA: USA Today	Fox: Fox Fab 50
National Champions. 130	NPP: National Prep Poll	Bianco: Tony Bianco
Championship Game Played. . . . . G	Hudak: Tim Hudak	ISS: Imperial Sports Syndicate
Selected Champion . . . . S	Lyons: Simon Lyons	NHSFRB: National High School Football Record Book

CHAMPIONS SORTED BY RANKING

Compilators: Tim Hudak & Pflug, LLC

CHAPTER	RANK	TEAM	CITY / STATE	CATEGORY 1		CATEGORY 2		CATEGORY 3					CATEGORY 4			TEAM TOTAL %
				NC	% OF NC	SC	% OF SC	W	L	T	TOT	% OF W	WIN %	% OF W %		
4,5	1st	Washington	Massillon, OH	9	15.3%	24	14.0%	719	214	35	968	8.6%	76.08%	6.4%		44.3%
6,10	2nd	Valdosta	Valdosta, GA	6	10.2%	23	13.4%	774	156	33	963	9.3%	82.09%	7.0%		39.8%
7	3rd	Miami HS	Miami, FL	5	8.5%	24	14.0%	522	238	28	788	6.3%	68.02%	5.8%		34.4%
2	4th	Everett	Everett, MA	2	3.4%	16	9.3%	580	339	73	992	6.9%	62.15%	5.3%		24.9%
9	5th	Moeller	Cincinnatti, OH	5	8.5%	7	4.1%	346	64	2	412	4.1%	84.22%	7.1%		23.8%
2	6th	Everett	Everett, WA	2	3.4%	14	8.1%	521	249	31	801	6.2%	66.98%	5.7%		23.4%
4	7th	McKinley	Canton, OH	2	3.4%	10	5.8%	679	273	37	989	8.1%	70.53%	6.0%		23.3%
1	8th	Oak Park	Chicago, IL	5	8.5%	4	2.3%	555	278	33	866	6.6%	65.99%	5.6%		23.0%
11	9th	Berwick	Berwick, PA	3	5.1%	6	3.5%	646	272	43	961	7.7%	69.46%	5.9%		22.2%
11	10th	Saint Ignatius	Cleveland, OH	3	5.1%	8	4.7%	531	250	32	813	6.4%	67.28%	5.7%		21.8%
8	11th	Coral Gables	Coral Gables, FL	4	6.8%	6	3.5%	345	142	11	498	4.1%	70.38%	6.0%		20.4%
1	12th	Fostoria	Fostoria, OH	1	1.7%	10	5.8%	607	343	39	989	7.3%	63.35%	5.4%		20.1%
3	13th	Scott	Toledo, OH	4	6.8%	5	2.9%	395	382	43	820	4.7%	50.79%	4.3%		18.7%
8	14th	Austin Reagan	Austin, TX	3	5.1%	3	1.7%	291	95	11	397	3.5%	74.69%	6.3%		16.6%
3	15th	Waite	Toledo, OH	2	3.4%	4	2.3%	454	345	48	847	5.4%	56.43%	4.8%		15.9%
12	16th	De La Salle	Concord, CA	3	5.1%	0	0.0%	253	51	8	312	3.0%	82.37%	7.0%		15.1%
2	17th	Harrisburg Tech*	Harrisburg, PA	2	3.4%	7	4.1%	128	51	12	191	1.5%	70.16%	5.9%		14.9%
SUMMARY				61	100.0%	179	100.0%	8346	3742	519	12607	100.0%	1180.97%	100.0%		400.0%

Harrisburg Tech open 1906-1926

KEY

NC	National Championships	W	Games Won	TOT	Total Games Played
SC	State Championships	L	Games Lost	W%	Win Pct.
		T	Games Tied		

RANKING CATEGORIES

There are four Categories of recognition against which all teams must measure their achievements. They are as follows:

Category 1. National Championships Won (NC)

The highest prized category of all is National Championships. There were 130 NC's awarded during the 20th century to 75 teams, 48 of which won but 1 National Championship, and 16 more winning but 2. Also, the teams in this book collectively won 61 national championships, 46.9 % of all 130 national championships won during the 20th century.

RANK		TEAM	CITY / STATE	NC	% OF NC	YEAR OF FIRST SEASON
1st		Washington	Massillon, OH	9	15.3%	1891
2nd		Valdosta	Valdosta, GA	6	10.2%	1913
3rd	tie	Oak Park	Chicago, IL	5	8.5%	1891
3rd	tie	Miami HS	Miami, FL	5	8.5%	1911
3rd	tie	Moeller	Cincinnatti, OH	5	8.5%	1963

Category 2. State Championships Won (SC)

There were 179 SC's won by the 17 teams in this book. It becomes clear that SC's are roughly one third as revered as NC's. [179 ÷ 3 = 60]. Another way to look at it is a state championship is for but one state, whereas a national championship covers all 50 states (since 1959).

RANK		TEAM	CITY / STATE	SC	% OF SC	YEAR OF FIRST SEASON
1st	tie	Washington	Massillon, OH	24	14.0%	1891
1st	tie	Miami HS	Miami, FL	24	14.0%	1911
2nd		Valdosta	Valdosta, GA	23	13.4%	1913
3rd		Everett	Everett, MA	16	8.1%	1894

Category 3. Total Games Won (TOT)

Though highly prized, the number of games won does not indicate a team's ability to win national or even state championships. Teams starting football later during the 20th century are at a distinct disadvantage in this category.

RANK	TEAM	CITY / STATE	WINS	YEAR OF FIRST SEASON
1st	Valdosta	Valdosta, GA	774	1913
2nd	Washington	Massillon, OH	719	1891
3rd	McKinley	Canton, OH	679	1894
4th	Berwick	Berwick, PA	646	1888

Category 4. Win Percentage (Win %)

Like Total Games Won, a high Win % is a distinct measure of excellent performance over the 20th century. Since some teams commenced playing football later in the century than others, Win % is an indicator of a team's success.

RANK	TEAM	CITY / STATE	WIN %	YEAR OF FIRST SEASON
1st	Moeller	Cincinnatti, OH	84.2%	1963
2nd	De La Salle	Concord, CA	82.4%	1972
3rd	Valdosta	Valdosta, GA	82.1%	1913
4th	Washington	Massillon, OH	76.1%	1891

FINAL TEAM RANKINGS

RANK	TEAM	CITY / STATE	NC	SC	WIN %	WINS
1st	Washington	Massillon, OH	9	24	76.1%	719
2nd	Valdosta	Valdosta, GA	6	23	82.1%	774
3rd	Miami HS	Miami, FL	5	24	68.0%	522
4th	Everett	Everett, MA	2	16	62.1%	580

NATIONAL CHAMPIONSHIPS WON BY TEAM

TEAMS	STATES	CITY	NC YEARS	NC'S WON	TOTAL %	TEAM %
Washington	OH	Massillon	1935, 36, 39, 40, 50, 52, 53, 59, 61	9	6.9%	6.9%
Valdosta	GA	Valdosta	1962, 69, 71, 84, 86, 92	6	4.6%	4.6%
Miami Senior	FL	Miami	1942, 43, 60, 62, 65	5		3.8%
Moeller	OH	Cincinnati	1976, 77, 79, 80, 82	5	11.5%	3.8%
Oak Park	IL	Oak Park	1910, 11, 12, 13, 20	5		3.8%
Scott	OH	Toledo	1916, 19, 22, 23	4	6.2%	3.1%
Coral Gables	FL	Coral Gables	1964, 67, 68, 69	4		3.1%
Saint Ignatius	OH	Cleveland	1989, 93, 95	3		2.3%
Reagan	TX	Austin	1967, 68, 70	3	9.2%	2.3%
De La Salle	CA	Concord	1994, 98, 99	3		2.3%
Berwick	PA	Berwick	1983, 92, 95	3		2.3%
McKinley	OH	Canton	1934, 97	2		1.5%
Waite	OH	Toledo	1924, 32	2		1.5%
Waco	TX	Waco	1927, 48	2		1.5%
Wichita Falls	TX	Wichita	1949, 58	2		1.5%
San Diego	CA	San Diego	1916, 55	2		1.5%
Mater Dei	CA	Santa Ana	1994, 96	2		1.5%
Englewood	IL	Chicago	1908, 09	2		1.5%
Warner Robins	GA	Warner Robins	1976, 81	2		1.5%
Tech	PA	Harrisburg	1918, 19	2	24.6%	1.5%
Everett	MA	Everett	1914, 15	2		1.5%
Pine Bluff	AR	Pine Bluff	1925, 39	2		1.5%
Central	AR	Little Rock	1946, 57	2		1.5%
Tuscaloosa	AL	Tuscaloosa	1926, 29	2		1.5%
Hampton	VA	Hampton	1996, 97	2		1.5%
Everett	WA	Everett	1919, 20	2		1.5%
Central	MI	Detroit	1904, 15	2		1.5%
Shaw	OH	E. Cleveland	1923	1		0.8%
Fostoria	OH	Fostoria	1912	1		0.8%
Permian	TX	Odessa	1989	1		0.8%
Abilene	TX	Abilene	1956	1		0.8%
Stafford	TX	Houston	1978	1		0.8%
Plano	TX	Plano	1987	1	36.9%	0.8%
Aldine	TX	Houston	1990	1		0.8%
Lee	TX	Midland	1999	1		0.8%
Vallejo	CA	Vallejo	1954	1		0.8%
Downey	CA	Downey	1957	1		0.8%
El Rancho	CA	Pico Rivera	1966	1		0.8%

NATIONAL CHAMPIONSHIPS WON BY TEAM

TEAMS	STATES	CITY	NC YEARS	NC'S WON	TOTAL %	TEAM %
Loyola	CA	Los Angeles	1975	1		0.8%
Fontana	CA	Fontana	1987	1		0.8%
St. Ignatius	CA	San Francisco	1962	1		0.8%
Moline	IL	Moline	1900	1		0.8%
Hyde Park	IL	Chicago	1902	1		0.8%
North Division	IL	Chicago	1903	1		0.8%
Austin	IL	Chicago	1937	1		0.8%
Leo	IL	Chicago	1940	1		0.8%
St. Rita	IL	Chicago	1963	1		0.8%
E. St. Louis	IL	St. Louis	1985	1		0.8%
Thomasville	GA	Thomasville	1974	1		0.8%
La Grange	GA	La Grange	1991	1		0.8%
Duval	FL	Jacksonville	1921	1		0.8%
Pine Forrest	FL	Pensacola	1988	1		0.8%
Penn Hills	PA	Pittsburgh	1987	1		0.8%
Classical	MA	Lynn	1847	1		0.8%
Weymouth	MA	Weymouth	1951	1		0.8%
Evans Memorial	IN	Evansville	1937	1		0.8%
Roosevelt	IN	E. Chicago	1947	1	36.9%	0.8%
Ben Davis	IN	Indianapolis	1991	1		0.8%
Vigor	AL	Prichard	1988	1		0.8%
Medford	OR	Medford	1928	1		0.8%
Annandale	VA	Annandale	1978	1		0.8%
Rushton	LA	Rushton	1990	1		0.8%
West Monroe	LA	West Monroe	1998	1		0.8%
Evangel Christian	LA	Shreveport	1999	1		0.8%
Seattle H.S.	WA	Seattle	1906	1		0.8%
Ashland	KY	Ashland	1931	1		0.8%
Dupont Manual	KY	louisville	1938	1		0.8%
Capitol Hill	OK	Oklahoma City	1933	1		0.8%
Eisenhower	OK	Lawton	1990	1		0.8%
Oak Ridge	TN	Oak Ridge	1958	1		0.8%
Bristol	TN	Bristol	1972	1		0.8%
Baylor	TN	Chattanooga	1973	1		0.8%
Washington HS	IA	Cedar Rapids	1924	1		0.8%
Union	AZ	Phoenix	1930	1		0.8%
New Rochelle	NY	New Rochelle	1932	1		0.8%
TOTAL NATIONAL CHAMPIONSHIPS				**130**	**100.0%**	

Note: There were 75 National Championship Teams in the 20th Century.

NATIONAL CHAMPIONSHIPS WON BY STATE

#1 OHIO

# TEAMS	CHAMPION(S)	CITY	NATIONAL CHAMPIONSHIP YEARS	# NC'S	% of TOTAL NC'S
1	Washington	Massillon	1935, 36, 39, 40, 50, 52, 53, 59, 61	9	
2	Moeller	Cincinnati	1976, 77, 79, 80, 82	5	
3	Scott	Toledo	1916, 19, 22, 23	4	
4	Saint Ignatius	Cleveland	1989, 93, 95	3	
5	Waite	Toledo	1924, 32	2	
6	McKinley	Canton	1934, 97	2	
7	Shaw	E. Cleveland	1923	1	
8	Fostoria	Fostoria	1912	1	
TOTALS				**27**	**20.8%**

#2 ILLINOIS

# TEAMS	CHAMPION(S)	CITY	NATIONAL CHAMPIONSHIP YEARS	# NC'S	% of TOTAL NC'S
1	Oak Park	Oak Park	1910, 11, 12, 13, 20	5	
2	Englewood	Chicago	1908, 09	2	
3	Hyde Park	Chicago	1902	1	
4	North Division	Chicago	1903	1	
5	Austin	Chicago	1937	1	
6	Leo	Chicago	1941	1	
7	St. Rita	Chicago	1963	1	
8	East St. Louis	East St. Louis	1985	1	
9	Moline	Moline	1900	1	
TOTALS				**14**	**10.8%**

#3 TEXAS

# TEAMS	CHAMPION(S)	CITY	NATIONAL CHAMPIONSHIP YEARS	# NC'S	% of TOTAL NC'S
1	Reagan	Austin	1967, 68, 70	3	
2	Waco	Waco	1927, 48	2	
3	Wichita Falls	Wichita Falls	1949, 58	2	
4	Permian	Odessa	1989	1	
5	Abilene	Abilene	1956	1	
6	Stratford	Houston	1978	1	
7	Plano	Plano	1987	1	
8	Aldine	Houston	1990	1	
9	Lee	Midland	1999	1	
TOTALS				**13**	**10.0%**

NATIONAL CHAMPIONSHIPS WON BY STATE

#4 CALIFORNIA

# TEAMS	CHAMPION(S)	CITY	NATIONAL CHAMPIONSHIP YEARS	# NC'S	% of TOTAL NC'S
1	De La Salle	Concord	1994, 98, 99	3	
2	San Diego	San Diego	1916, 55	2	
3	Mater Dei	Santa Ana	1994, 96	2	
4	Vallejo	Vallejo	1954	1	
5	Downey	Downey	1957	1	
6	St Ignatius	San Francisco	1962	1	
7	El Rancho	Pico Rivera	1966	1	
8	Loyola	Los Angeles	1975	1	
9	Fontana	Fontana	1987	1	
TOTALS				13	10.0%

#5 FLORIDA

# TEAMS	CHAMPION(S)	CITY	NATIONAL CHAMPIONSHIP YEARS	# NC'S	% of TOTAL NC'S
1	Miami HS	Miami	1942, 43, 60, 62, 65	5	
2	Coral Gables	Coral Gables	1964, 67, 68, 69	4	
3	Duval	Jacksonville	1921	1	
4	Pine Forrest	Pensacola	1988	1	
TOTALS				11	8.5%

#6 GEORGIA

# TEAMS	CHAMPION(S)	CITY	NATIONAL CHAMPIONSHIP YEARS	# NC'S	% of TOTAL NC'S
1	Valdosta	Valdosta	1962, 69, 71, 84, 86, 92	6	
2	Warner Robins	Warner Robins	1976, 81	2	
3	Thomasville	Thomasville	1974	1	
4	La Grange	La Grange	1991	1	
TOTALS				10	7.7%

#7 PENNSYLVANIA

# TEAMS	CHAMPION(S)	CITY	NATIONAL CHAMPIONSHIP YEARS	# NC'S	% of TOTAL NC'S
1	Berwick	Berwick	1983, 92, 95	3	
2	Tech	Harrisburg	1918, 19	2	
3	Penn Hills	Pittsburg	1987	1	
TOTALS				6	4.6%

#8 MASSACHUSETTS

# TEAMS	CHAMPION(S)	CITY	NATIONAL CHAMPIONSHIP YEARS	# NC'S	% of TOTAL NC'S
1	Everett	Everett	1914, 15	2	
2	Classical	Lynn	1947	1	
3	Weymouth	Weymouth	1951	1	
TOTALS				4	3.1%

NATIONAL CHAMPIONSHIPS WON BY STATE

#8 ARKANSAS

# TEAMS	CHAMPION(S)	CITY	NATIONAL CHAMPIONSHIP YEARS	# NC'S	% of TOTAL NC'S
1	Pine Bluff	Pine Bluff	1925, 39	2	
2	Central	Little Rock	1946, 57	2	
TOTALS				4	3.1%

#9 INDIANA

# TEAMS	CHAMPION(S)	CITY	NATIONAL CHAMPIONSHIP YEARS	# NC'S	% of TOTAL NC'S
1	Evans Memorial	Evansville	1937	1	
2	Roosevelt	E. Chicago	1947	1	
3	Ben Davis	Indianapolis	1991	1	
TOTALS				3	2.3%

#9 VIRGINIA

# TEAMS	CHAMPION(S)	CITY	NATIONAL CHAMPIONSHIP YEARS	# NC'S	% of TOTAL NC'S
1	Hampton	Hampton	1996, 97	2	
2	Annandale	Annandale	1978	1	
TOTALS				3	2.3%

#9 ALABAMA

# TEAMS	CHAMPION(S)	CITY	NATIONAL CHAMPIONSHIP YEARS	# NC'S	% of TOTAL NC'S
1	Tuscaloosa	Tuscaloosa	1926, 29	2	
2	Vigor	Prichard	1988	1	
TOTALS				3	2.3%

#9 LOUISIANA

# TEAMS	CHAMPION(S)	CITY	NATIONAL CHAMPIONSHIP YEARS	# NC'S	% of TOTAL NC'S
1	Rushton	Rushton	1990	1	
2	West Monroe	West Monroe	1998	1	
3	Evangel Christian	Shreveport	1999	1	
TOTALS				3	2.3%

#9 WASHINGTON

# TEAMS	CHAMPION(S)	CITY	NATIONAL CHAMPIONSHIP YEARS	# NC'S	% of TOTAL NC'S
1	Everett	Everett	1919, 20	2	
2	Seattle HS	Seattle	1906	1	
TOTALS				3	2.3%

NATIONAL CHAMPIONSHIPS WON BY STATE

#9 TENNESSEE

# TEAMS	CHAMPION(S)	CITY	NATIONAL CHAMPIONSHIP YEARS	# NC'S	% of TOTAL NC'S
1	Oak Ridge	Oak Ridge	1958	1	
2	Bristol	Bristol	1972	1	
3	Baylor	Chattanooga	1973	1	
TOTALS				3	2.3%

#10 MICHIGAN

# TEAMS	CHAMPION(S)	CITY	NATIONAL CHAMPIONSHIP YEARS	# NC'S	% of TOTAL NC'S
1	Central	Detroit	1904, 15	2	
TOTALS				2	1.5%

#10 KENTUCKY

# TEAMS	CHAMPION(S)	CITY	NATIONAL CHAMPIONSHIP YEARS	# NC'S	% of TOTAL NC'S
1	Ashland HS	Ashland	1931	1	
2	Dupont Manual	Louisville	1938	1	
TOTALS				2	1.5%

#10 OKLAHOMA

# TEAMS	CHAMPION(S)	CITY	NATIONAL CHAMPIONSHIP YEARS	# NC'S	% of TOTAL NC'S
1	Capitol Hill	Oklahoma City	1933	1	
2	Eisenhower	Lawton	1990	1	
TOTALS				2	1.5%

#11 OREGON

# TEAMS	CHAMPION(S)	CITY	NATIONAL CHAMPIONSHIP YEARS	# NC'S	% of TOTAL NC'S
1	Medford	Medford	1928	1	
TOTALS				1	0.8%

#11 IOWA

# TEAMS	CHAMPION(S)	CITY	NATIONAL CHAMPIONSHIP YEARS	# NC'S	% of TOTAL NC'S
1	Washington HS	Cedar Rapids	1924	1	
TOTALS				1	0.8%

#11 ARIZONA

# TEAMS	CHAMPION(S)	CITY	NATIONAL CHAMPIONSHIP YEARS	# NC'S	% of TOTAL NC'S
1	Union	Phoenix	1930	1	
TOTALS				1	0.8%

#11 NEW YORK

# TEAMS	CHAMPION(S)	CITY	NATIONAL CHAMPIONSHIP YEARS	# NC'S	% of TOTAL NC'S
1	New Rochelle	New Rochelle	1932	1	
TOTALS				1	0.8%

TOTAL NATIONAL CHAMPIONSHIPS		130	100%

COMPARING MASSILLON AND VALDOSTA
The Two Best Records

MASSILLON TIGERS

YEAR	COACH	W	L	T	%	SC	NC	YEAR
1909	Ralph "Hap" Fugate	9	0	1		1	0	1909
1916	John Snavely	10	0	0		1	0	1916
1922	Dave Stewart	10	0	0		1	0	1922
1935	Paul Brown	10	0	0		1	1	1935
1936	Paul Brown	10	0	0		1	1	1936
1937	Paul Brown	8	1	1		1	0	1937
1938	Paul Brown	10	0	0		1	0	1938
1939	Paul Brown	10	0	0		1	1	1939
1940	Paul Brown	10	0	0		1	1	1940
1941	William "Bud" Houghton	9	0	1		1	0	1941
1943	Elwood "Kam" Kammer	10	0	0		1	0	1943
1948	Chuck Mather	9	1	0		1	0	1948
1949	Chuck Mather	9	1	0		1	0	1949
1950	Chuck Mather	10	0	0		1	1	1950
1951	Chuck Mather	9	1	0		1	0	1951
1952	Chuck Mather	10	0	0		1	1	1952
1953	Chuck Mather	10	0	0		1	1	1953
1954	Tom Harp	9	1	0		1	0	1954
1959	Leo Strang	10	0	0		1	1	1959
1960	Leo Strang	10	1	0		1	0	1960
1961	Leo Strang	11	0	0		1	1	1961
1964	Eark Bruce	10	0	0		1	0	1964
1965	Eark Bruce	10	0	0		1	0	1965
1970	Bob Commings	10	0	0		1	0	1970
TOTALS		**233**	**6**	**3**	**96.3%**	**24**	**9**	

NATIONAL CHAMPIONSHIPS MASSILLON COACHES

YEAR	COACH	W	L	T	%	NC	YEAR
1935	Paul Brown	10	0	0		1	1935
1936	Paul Brown	10	0	0		1	1936
1939	Paul Brown	10	0	0		1	1939
1940	Paul Brown	10	0	0		1	1940
1950	Chuck Mather	10	0	0		1	1950
1952	Chuck Mather	10	0	0		1	1952
1953	Chuck Mather	10	0	0		1	1953
1959	Leo Strang	10	0	0		1	1959
1961	Leo Strang	11	0	0		1	1961
TOTALS		**91**	**0**	**0**	**100%**	**9**	

SC AND NC CHAMPIONSHIPS

COACH	SC	NC
Paul Brown	6	4
Chuck Mather	6	3
Leo Strang	3	2
Earl Bruce	2	
Ralph "Hap" Fugate	1	
John Snavely	1	
Dave Stewart	1	
William "Bud" Houghton	1	
Elwood "Kam" Kammer	1	
Tom Harp	1	
Bob Commings	1	
TOTAL	**24**	**9**
Years between 1st & Last Championships	62	27
Avg. # of yrs between championships	2.6	3.0

All the Way to #1

COMPARING MASSILLON AND VALDOSTA
The Two Best Records

VALDOSTA WILDCATS

YEAR	COACH	W	L	T	%	SC	NC	YEAR
1940	Bobby Hooks	12	0	0		1	0	1940
1947	Wright Bazemore	12	0	0		1	0	1947
1951	Wright Bazemore	9	3	0		1	0	1951
1952	Wright Bazemore	14	0	0		1	1	1952
1953	Wright Bazemore	13	0	1		1	1	1953
1956	Wright Bazemore	13	0	0		1	0	1956
1957	Wright Bazemore	13	0	0		1	0	1957
1960	Wright Bazemore	12	0	0		1	1	1960
1961	Wright Bazemore	12	0	0		1	1	1961
1962	Wright Bazemore	12	0	0		1	0	1962
1965	Wright Bazemore	11	1	0		1	0	1965
1966	Wright Bazemore	13	0	0		1	0	1966
1968	Wright Bazemore	13	0	0		1	0	1968
1969	Wright Bazemore	12	0	1		1	1	1969
1971	Wright Bazemore	13	0	0		1	0	1971
1978	Nick Hyder	14	0	1		1	1	1978
1982	Nick Hyder	15	0	0		1	1	1982
1984	Nick Hyder	15	0	0		1	0	1984
1986	Nick Hyder	15	0	0		1	1	1986
1989	Nick Hyder	14	1	0		1	0	1989
1990	Nick Hyder	13	0	1		1	1	1990
1992	Nick Hyder	14	0	0		1	0	1992
1998	Mike O'Brien	14	1	0		1	0	1998
TOTALS		**298**	**6**	**4**	**97.4%**	**23**	**6**	

NATIONAL CHAMPIONSHIPS MASSILLON COACHES

YEAR	COACH	W	L	T	%	NC	YEAR
1962	Wright Bazemore	12	0	0		1	1962
1969	Wright Bazemore	12	0	1		1	1969
1971	Wright Bazemore	13	0	0		1	1971
1984	Nick Hyder	15	0	0		1	1984
1986	Nick Hyder	15	0	0		1	1986
1992	Nick Hyder	14	0	0		1	1992
TOTALS		**81**	**0**	**1**	**99.4%**	**6**	

SC AND NC CHAMPIONSHIPS

COACH	SC	NC
Wright Bazemore	14	3
Nick Hyder	7	3
Bobby Hooks	1	
Mike O'Brien	1	
TOTAL	**23**	**6**
Years between 1st & Last Championships	59	31
Avg. # of yrs between championships	2.57	5.2

KEY

NC	National Championships	W	Games Won	%	Win Pct.
SC	State Championships	L	Games Lost		
		T	Games Tied		

CHAMPIONSHIP COACHES OF THE 20TH CENTURY

Compilators: Tim Hudak & Pflug, LLC

COACH	TEAM	HIGH SCHOOL LEVEL				COLLEGE LEVEL			
		SC YEARS	SC	NC YEARS	NC	TEAM	NC YEARS	NC	
Paul Brown	Massillon	*1930, 35, 36, 37, 38, 39, 40	7	1935, 36, 39, 40	4	Ohio State	1942	1	
W. Bazemore	Valdosta	1947, 51, 52, 53, 56, 57, 60, 61, 62, 65, 66, 68, 69, 71	14	1962, 69, 71	3				
Bob Zuppke	Oak Park	Unknown dates	4	1910, 11, 12, 20	4	Illinois	1914, 19, 23, 27	4	
Chuck Kyle	Saint Ignatius	1988, 89, 91, 92, 93, 94, 95, 99	8	1989, 93, 95	3				
Nick Hyder	Valdosta	1978, 82, 84, 86, 89, 90, 92	7	1984, 86, 92	3				
Nick Kotys	Coral Gables	1963, 64, 67, 68	4	1964, 67, 68, 69	4				
Chuck Mather	Massillon	1948, 49, 50, 51, 52, 53	6	1950, 52, 53	3				
Gerry Faust	Moeller	1975, 76, 77, 79, 80	5	1976, 77, 79, 80	4				
Bob Ladouceur	De La Salle	No SC's in CA during 20th cen.	0	1994, 98, 99	3				
Bear Bryant						Alabama	1961, 64, 65, 66, 73, 75, 77, 78, 79	9	
Tom Osborne						Nebraska	1980, 81, 82, 83, 93, 94, 95, 97	8	
Woody Hayes						Ohio State	1954, 57, 61, 68, 69, 73, 74, 75	8	
Fielding Yost						Michigan	1901, 02, 03, 04, 18, 23, 25, 26	8	
Barry Switzer						Oklahoma	1973, 74, 75, 78, 80, 85, 86	7	
Bud Wilkinson						Oklahoma	1949, 50, 53, 55, 56, 57	6	
Knute Rockne						Notre Dame	1919, 20, 24, 27, 29, 30	6	
Curley Lambeau									
George Halas									
V. Lombardi									
Chuck Noll									

* 1930 State Championship won at Severn Prep in Maryland.

KEY

NC   National Championship
SC   State Championship

TOT PRO. NC   Total Professional Championships
TOT NC   Total National Championships
TOT C   Total Championships (HS+Coll.+Pro)

CHAMPIONSHIP COACHES OF THE 20TH CENTURY

		PROFESSIONAL LEVEL								TOTALS	
TEAM	NC YEARS								TOT PRO. NC	TOT NC	TOT C
Cleveland	1946, 47, 48, 49, 50, 54, 55	AAFC	4	NFL	3				7	12	19
										3	17
										8	12
										3	11
										3	10
										4	8
										3	9
										4	9
										3	3
										9	9
										8	8
										8	8
										8	8
										7	7
										6	6
										6	6
Green Bay	1929, 30, 31, 36, 39, 44			NFL	6				6	6	6
Chicago	1921, 33, 40, 41, 46, 63			NFL	6				6	6	6
Green Bay	1961, 62, 65, 66, 67			NFL	3	SB	2		5	5	5
Pittsburg	1974, 75, 78, 79					SB	4		4	4	4

Paul Brown is the only coach ever to win national championships (12) at the high school (4), college (1), and professional (7) levels [all during the 21 years between 1935-1955].

Paul Brown coached Massillon to 6 SC & 4 NC in the 6 years between 1935-1940, as well as the Cleveland Browns to 10 consecutive national championship games between 1946-55, winning 7.

Bibliography

BOOKS

Baker, James. *A Century of Glory and Tradition.... Canton McKinley and Massillon Washington Football.* North Olmsted, Ohio. 1995

Beerman, Dick. *We Are the "Big Moe".* 2010

Boardman, Arnold. *112 Years of Crimson Tide Football: Everett High School, 1893-2004.* Privately Published 2004

Brichford, Maynard. *Bob Zuppke, The Life and Football Legacy of the Illinois Coach.* McFarland& Company, Inc., Publishers, Jefferson, North Carolina. 2009

Brown, Paul, with Jack Clary. *PB, The Paul Brown Story.* Atheneum, New York. 1979

Bynum, Mike, ed. *The Best of Texas High School Football.* Canada Hockey LLC, Birmingham, Ala. 2006

Camp, Walter, ed. *Spalding's Official Foot Ball Guide*

Cantor, George. *Paul Brown, The Man Who Invented Modern Football.* Triumph Books, Chicago. 2008

Dressman, Denny. *Gerry Faust, Notre Dame's Man in Motion.* A.S. Barnes & Company, Inc. 1981

Grange, Harold E. *"Red". Zuppke of Illinois.* A.L. Glasser, Inc., Chicago. 1937

Hayes, Neil. *When the Game Stands Tall.* Frog, Ltd., Berkeley, California. 2003

Hudak, Timothy L. *The Charity Game, The Story of Cleveland's Thanksgiving Day High School Football Classic.* Sports Heritage Specialty Publications, Cleveland, Ohio.2002

Hudak, Timothy L. *Wildcats! A History of St. Ignatius High School Football. Vol. I-III.* Sports Heritage Specialty Publications, Cleveland, Ohio. 2008

Krizay, Kane. *Cheers and Tears, 25 Years of the Ohio High School Football Championships.* KMK Publishing Co., Medina, Ohio. 1997

Nelson, Jon. *Georgia High School Football: Peach State Pigskin History.* The History Press, Charleston, S.C. 2011

White, Jr., John E. *The Massillon Tigers Story, The First Hundred Years.* Classic Press, Prescott, Arizona. 1994

NEWSPAPERS

Atlanta Journal-Constitution

Austin American-Statesman

Bangor Daily News—Bangor, Me.

Boston Evening Transcript

Boston Globe

Boston Post

The Bryan Times

Cincinnati Enquirer

Cincinnati Post

Cleveland *Plain Dealer*

Cleveland Press

Chicago Tribune

Dosta Outlook—Valdosta (Ga.)High School Newspaper

Everett (Wash.) *Daily Herald*

Fostoria Daily Review

Harrisburg *Evening News*

Harrisburg *Sunday Patriot-News*

Kingsport Times News—Kingsport, Tenn.

Kodak—Everett (Wash.) High School Newspaper

Los Angeles Times

Massillon *Evening Independent*

Massillon *Independent*

Miami Herald

Miami News

Reagan Radar—John H. Reagan Early College High School Newspaper

Times Enterprise—Thomasville, Ga.

Toledo Blade

Toledo News-Bee

Toledo Times

Trapeze—Oak Park and River Forest High School Newspaper

Valdosta Daily Times

Westhaven Register—Westhaven, Conn.

Bibliography

YEARBOOKS

The Annual—Washington High School, Cedar Rapids, Iowa

Chintimini—Corvallis High School, Corvallis, Oregon

Cavaleon—Coral Gables High School, Coral Gables, Florida

De La Salle Spartan Yearbook

Ignatian—Saint Ignatius High School, Cleveland, Ohio

Massillonian—Washington High School, Massillon, Ohio

Miahi—Miami Senior High School, Miami, Florida

NESIKA—Everett High School, Everett, Washington

Sandspur—Valdosta High School, Valdosta, Georgia

Scottonian—Scott High School, Toledo, Ohio

SPUR—John H. Reagan Early College High School, Austin, Texas

Tabula—Oak Park and River Forest High School

Tatler—Harrisburg Tech, Harrisburg, Pennsylvania

Warrior—Waite High School, Toledo, Ohio

OTHER SOURCES

Georgia High School Football Historians Association Website

High School Football Database (www.hsfdatbase.com)

Lowndes County (Ga.) Historical Society Museum Archives

Massillon Football Booster Club Museum and Archives

National High School Football Record Book, Doug Huff, ed.

National Sports News Service, *Newsletter*, Vol. 1, No. 5 (Football) June 1981

The Life and Legend of Enoch Bagshaw—Podcast by David Dilgard, Northwest
    History Dept., Everett Public Library, Everett, Washington

The Pulse—School magazine of Washington High School, Cedar Rapids, Iowa

Valdosta High School Media Guide

Valdosta Scene Magazine

About the Authors

Timothy Hudak is a graduate of the University of Hawaii, where he earned a Bachelor's Degree in History. He has been studying the history of football at the high school and collegiate levels for more than 25 years. This is Mr. Hudak's eighth book about high school football. In addition, he has written almost four dozen articles and book reviews on high school and college athletics and occasionally teaches a course about the history of college football at local community colleges. Mr. Hudak and his wife, Patti Graziano, live in Cleveland, Ohio.

John R. Pflug, Jr. is a graduate of Brown University where he majored in political science. John's father Bob was both a high school player in Ohio and a high school football coach in Pennsylvania, both of which earned Bob Pflug high school Hall of Fame recognition. This generated in John an abiding interest in the sport of football. He has spent the last 15 years researching the history of high school football, in particular the high school football national champions of the 20th century. Mr. Pflug and his wife, Carol, reside at "Headquarters", the family farm in Browns Cove, Albemarle County, Virginia.

TILTON   SMITH   THOMAS   SCHIMKE   GRANT   McCARTHY   BOERNER   HISE   EDWARDS   PFLUG   FLETCHER   MI
(Sub-Guard)   (Sub-Guard)   (Sub-End)   (Sub-End)   Q.B.   T.   H.B.   C.   C.   R.G. (captain)   E.